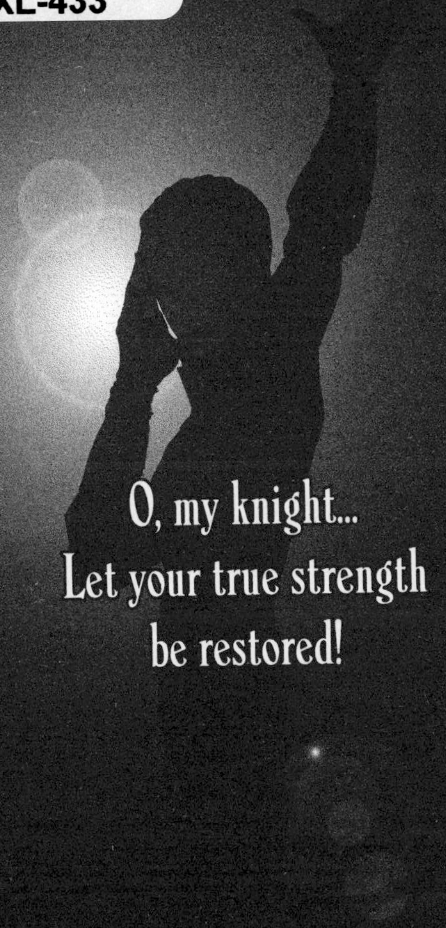

O, my knight...
Let your true strength
be restored!

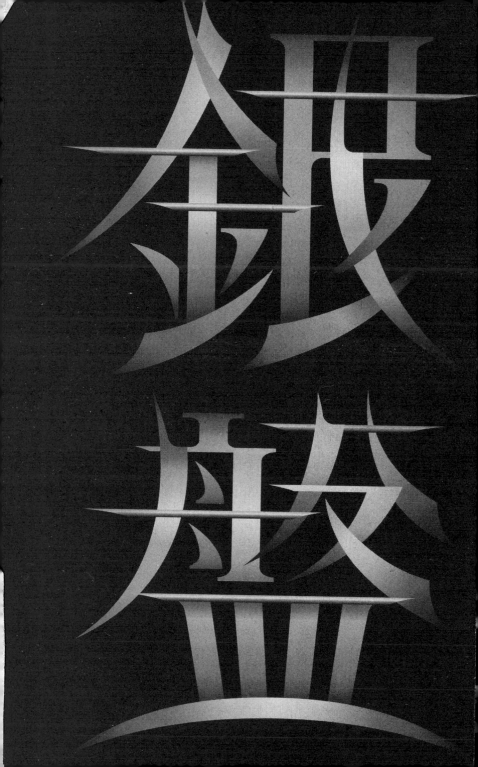

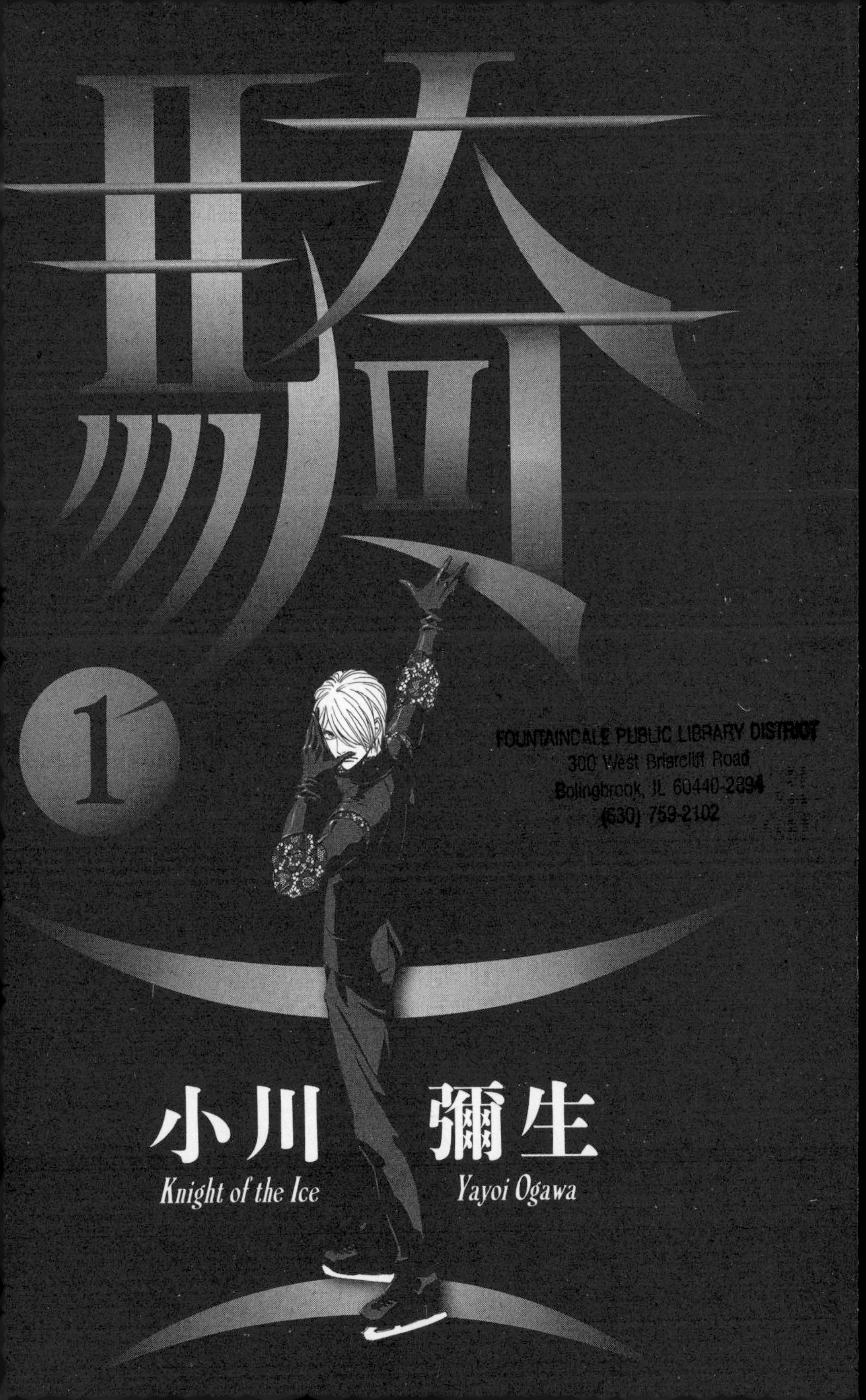
騎
1
小川 彌生
Knight of the Ice
Yayoi Ogawa

Contents

Spell 1
The First Casting

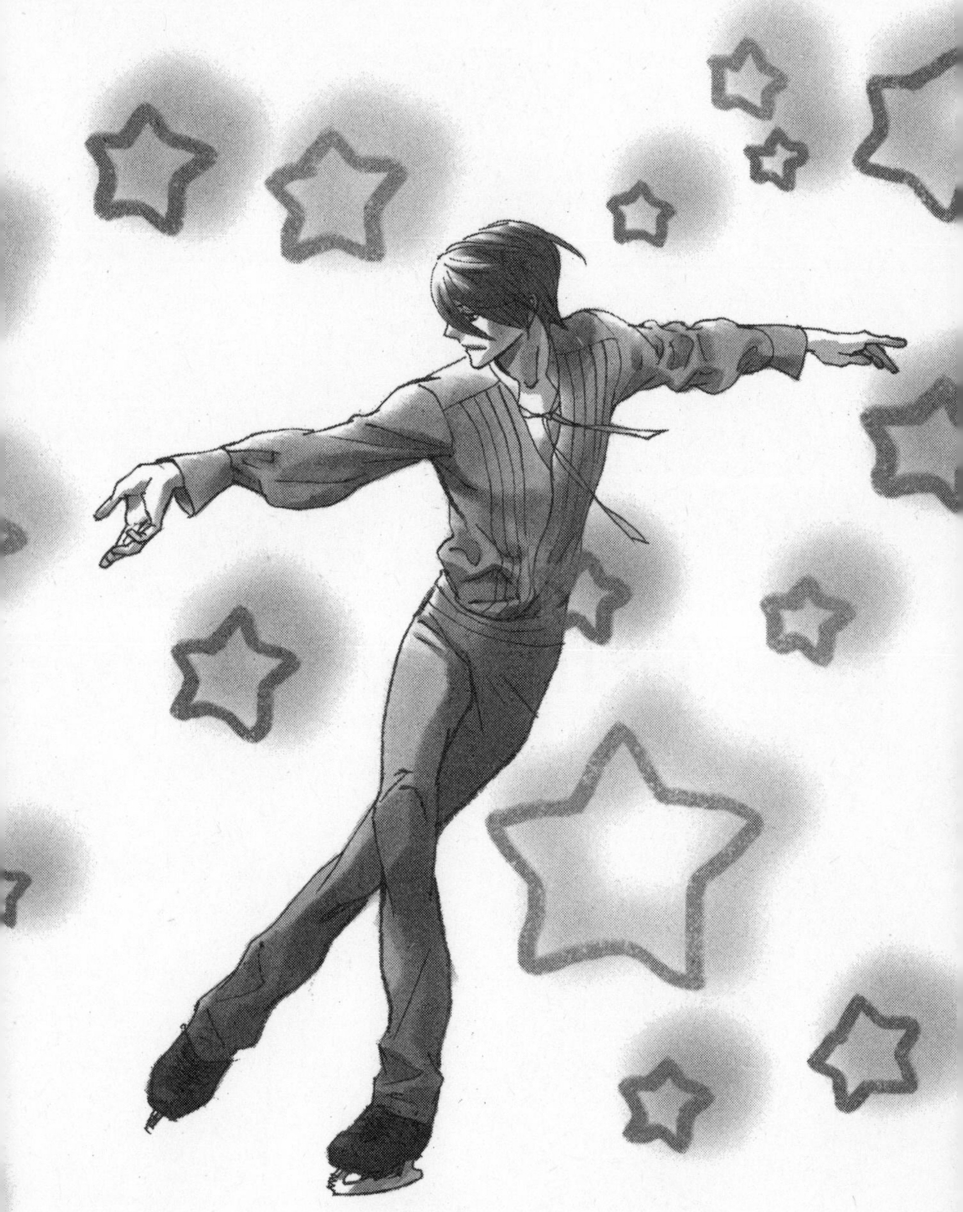

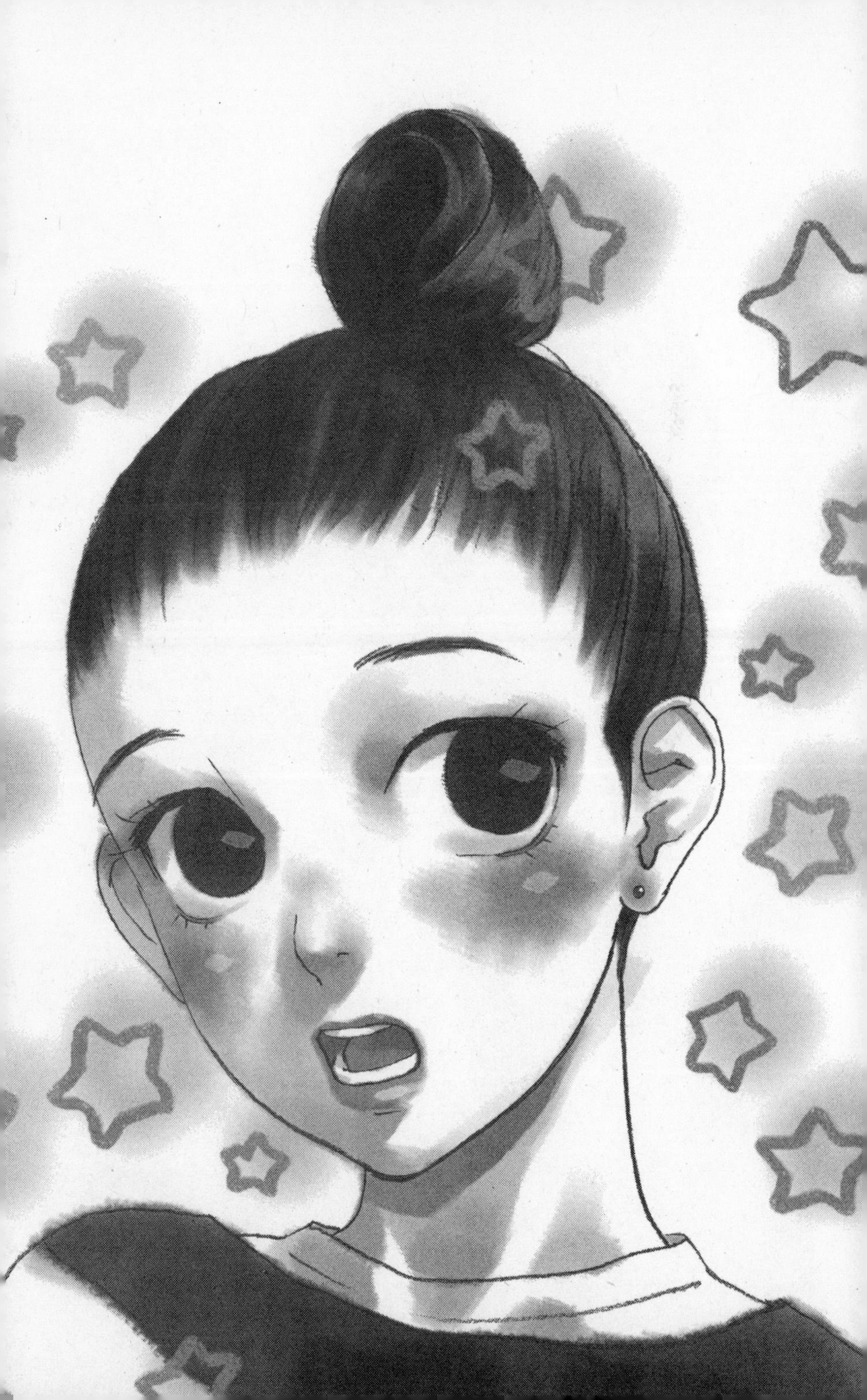

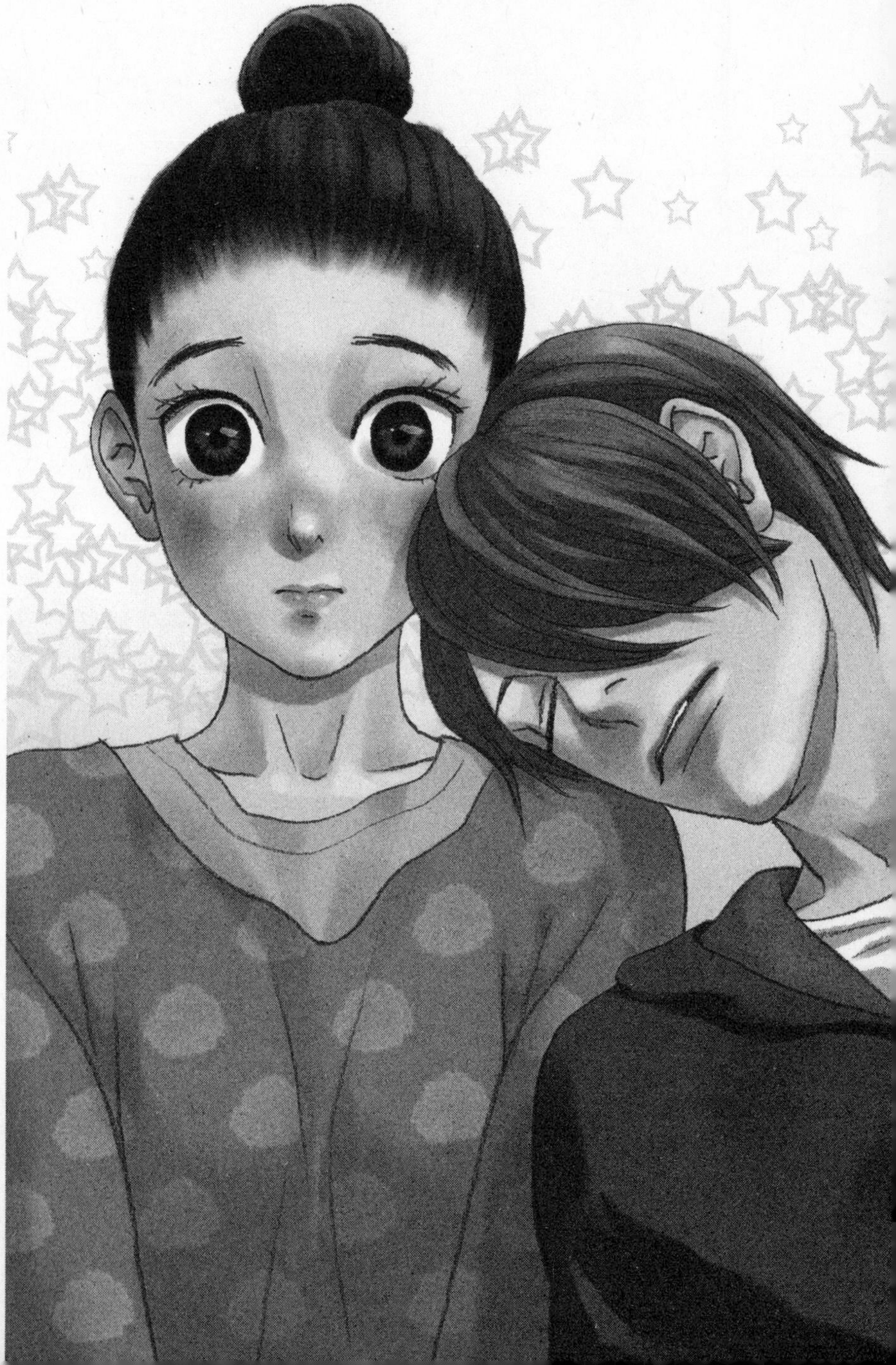

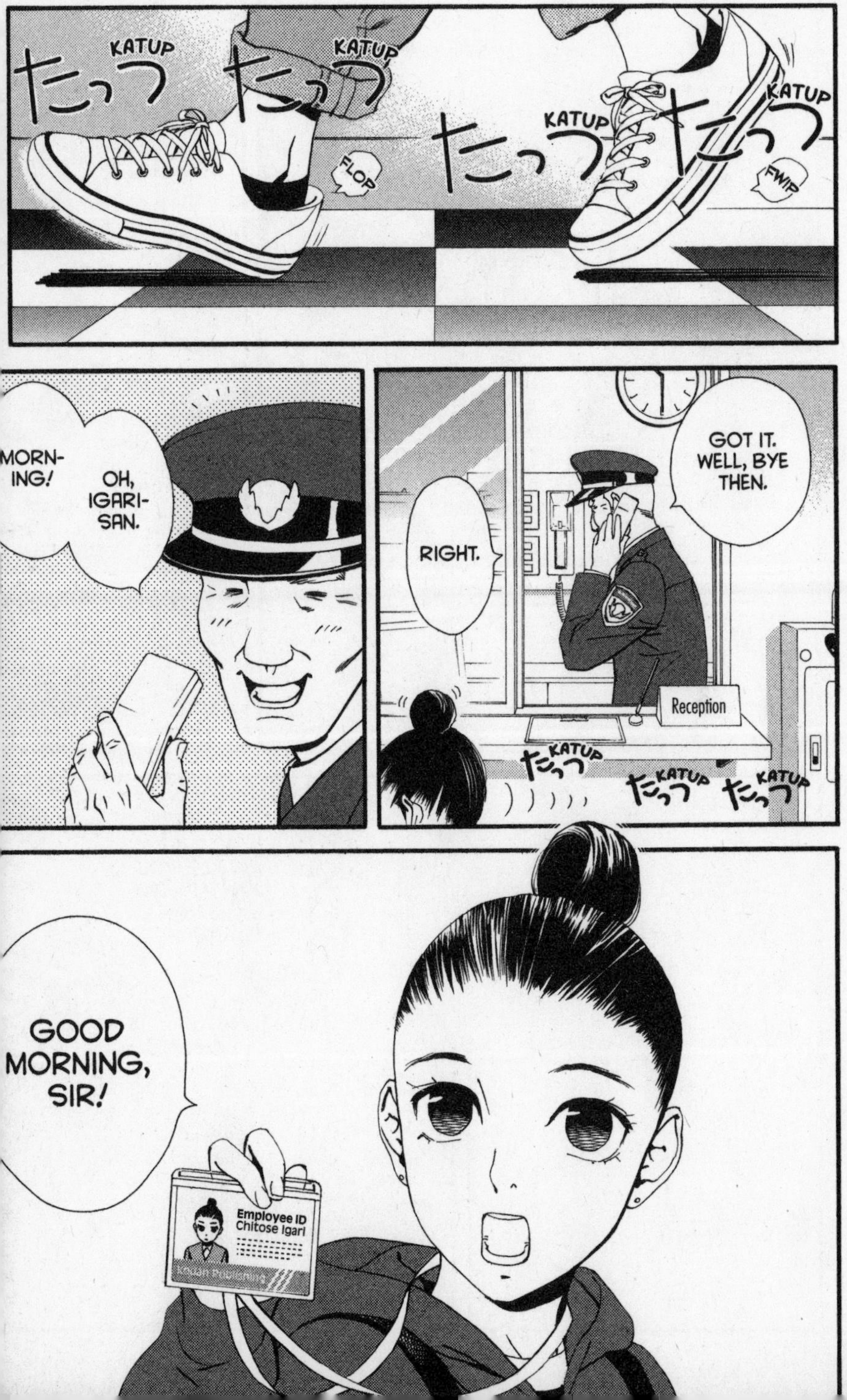
KATUP
KATUP
FWIP
KATUP
KATUP
FLOP
GOT IT. WELL, BYE THEN.
RIGHT.
Reception
KATUP
KATUP
KATUP
OH, IGARI-SAN.
MORNING!
GOOD MORNING, SIR!
Employee ID
Chitose Igari

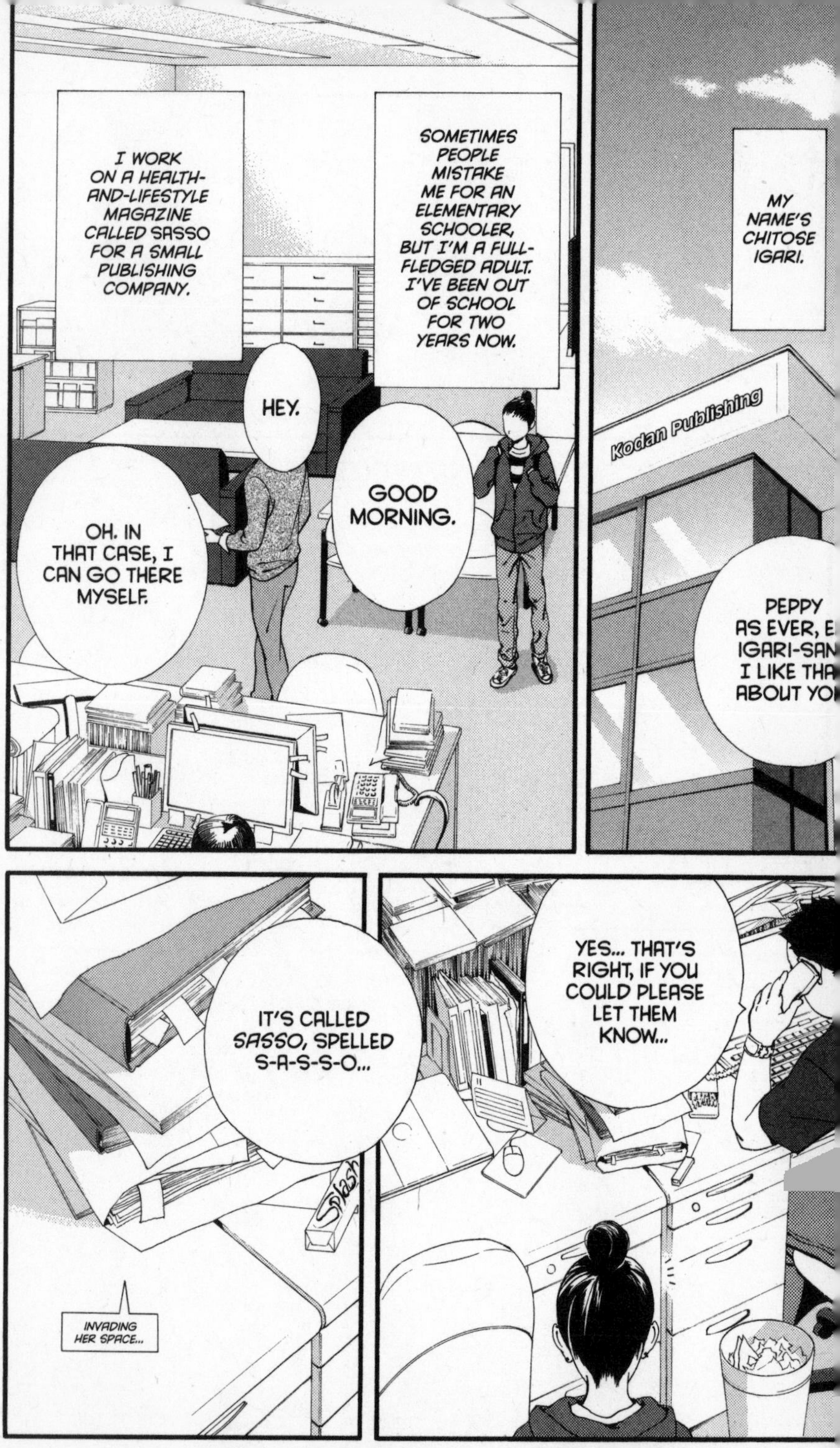
MY NAME'S CHITOSE IGARI.
Kodan Publishing
PEPPY AS EVER, E
IGARI-SAN
I LIKE THA
ABOUT YO
SOMETIMES PEOPLE MISTAKE ME FOR AN ELEMENTARY SCHOOLER, BUT I'M A FULL-FLEDGED ADULT. I'VE BEEN OUT OF SCHOOL FOR TWO YEARS NOW.
I WORK ON A HEALTH-AND-LIFESTYLE MAGAZINE CALLED SASSO FOR A SMALL PUBLISHING COMPANY.
GOOD MORNING.
HEY.
OH. IN THAT CASE, I CAN GO THERE MYSELF.
YES... THAT'S RIGHT, IF YOU COULD PLEASE LET THEM KNOW...
IT'S CALLED SASSO, SPELLED S-A-S-S-O...
Splash
INVADING HER SPACE...

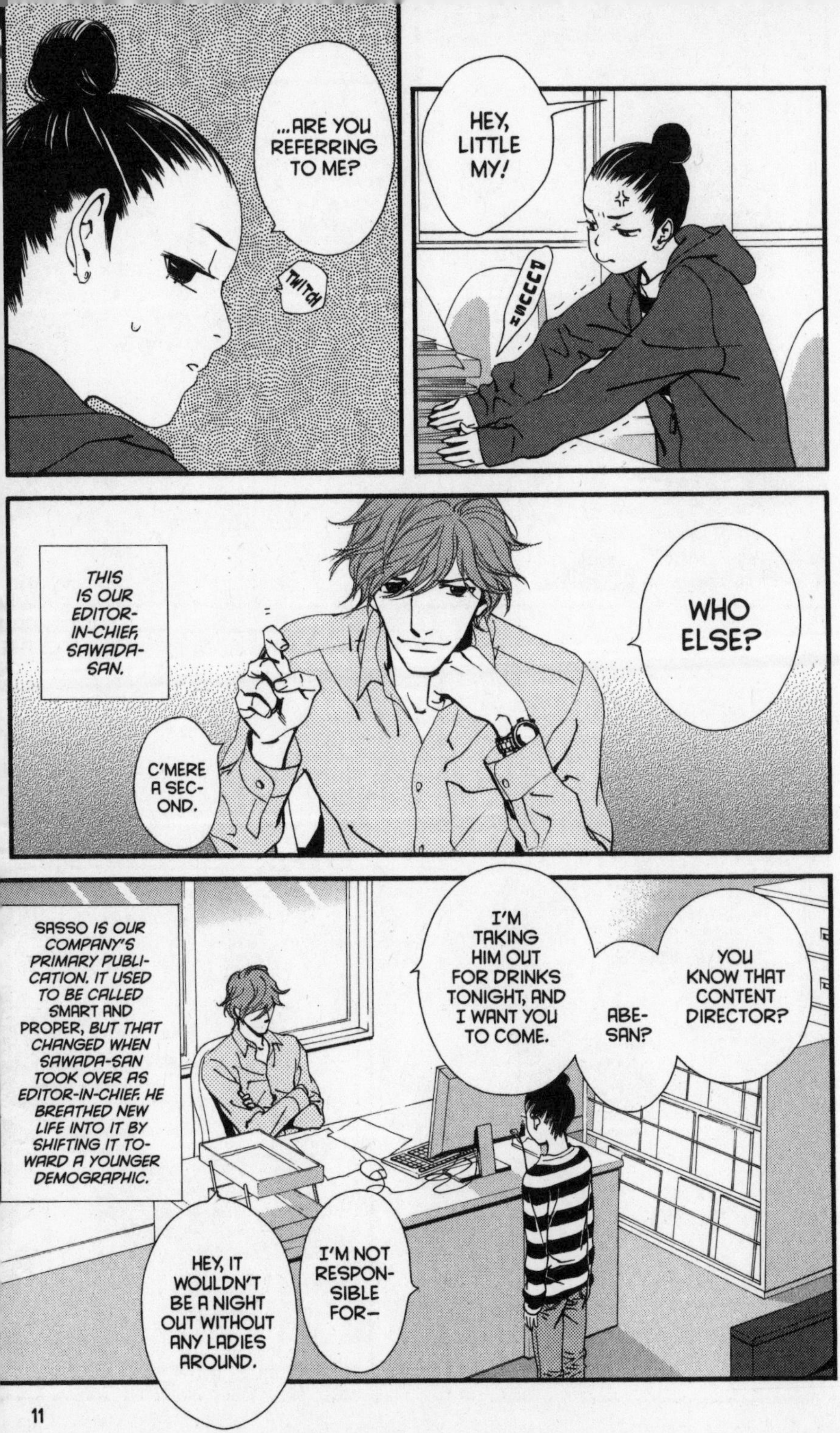
HEY, LITTLE MY!
SCUUU!
...ARE YOU REFERRING TO ME?
TWITCH
WHO ELSE?
THIS IS OUR EDITOR-IN-CHIEF, SAWADA-SAN.
C'MERE A SEC-OND.
YOU KNOW THAT CONTENT DIRECTOR?
ABE-SAN?
I'M TAKING HIM OUT FOR DRINKS TONIGHT, AND I WANT YOU TO COME.
SASSO IS OUR COMPANY'S PRIMARY PUBLI-CATION. IT USED TO BE CALLED SMART AND PROPER, BUT THAT CHANGED WHEN SAWADA-SAN TOOK OVER AS EDITOR-IN-CHIEF. HE BREATHED NEW LIFE INTO IT BY SHIFTING IT TO-WARD A YOUNGER DEMOGRAPHIC.
I'M NOT RESPON-SIBLE FOR—
HEY, IT WOULDN'T BE A NIGHT OUT WITHOUT ANY LADIES AROUND.

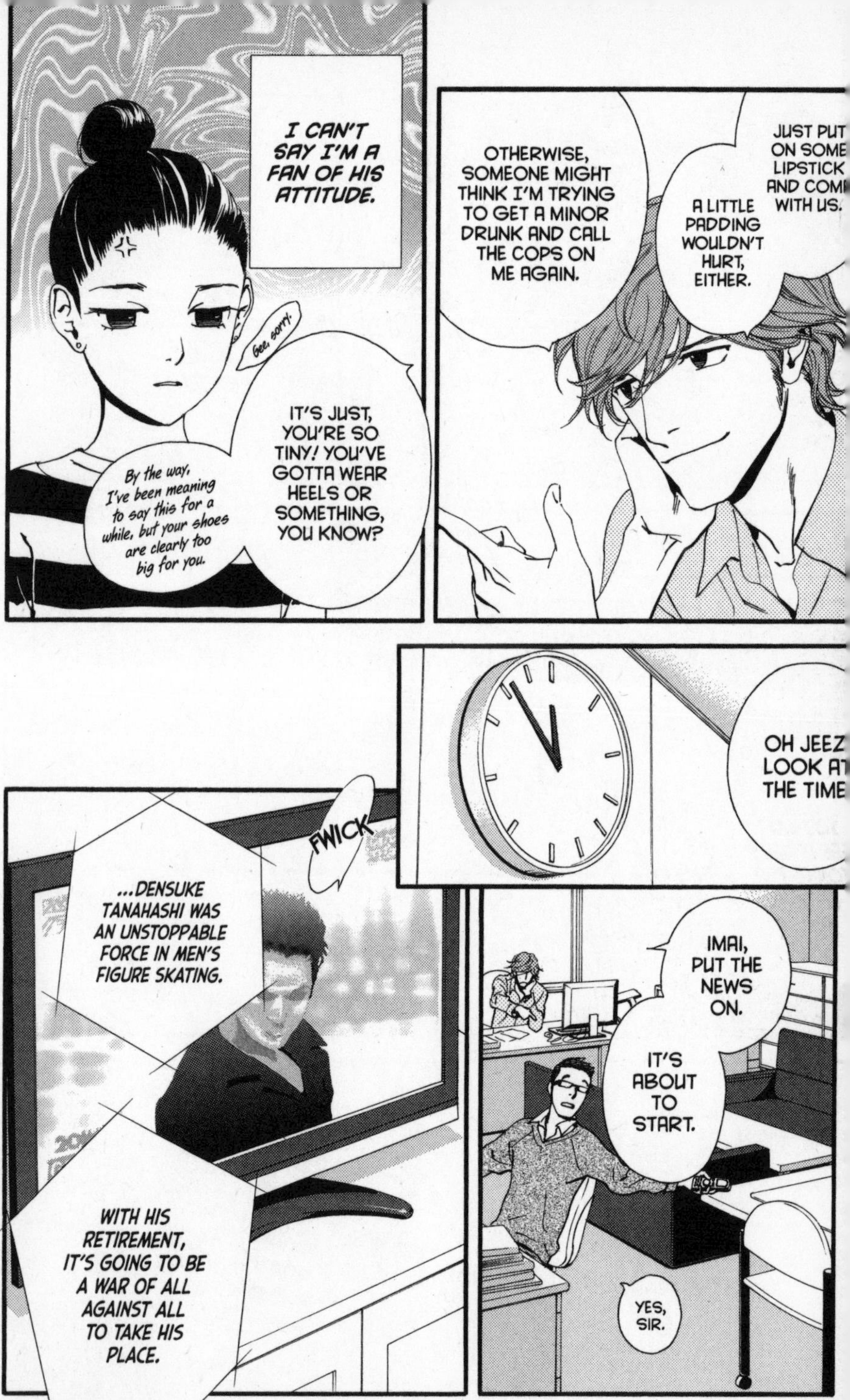
JUST PUT ON SOME LIPSTICK AND COM WITH US.
A LITTLE PADDING WOULDN'T HURT, EITHER.
OTHERWISE, SOMEONE MIGHT THINK I'M TRYING TO GET A MINOR DRUNK AND CALL THE COPS ON ME AGAIN.
I CAN'T SAY I'M A FAN OF HIS ATTITUDE.
Gee, sorry.
IT'S JUST, YOU'RE SO TINY! YOU'VE GOTTA WEAR HEELS OR SOMETHING, YOU KNOW?
By the way, I've been meaning to say this for a while, but your shoes are clearly too big for you.
OH JEEZ LOOK AT THE TIME
IMAI, PUT THE NEWS ON.
IT'S ABOUT TO START.
YES, SIR.
FWICK
...DENSUKE TANAHASHI WAS AN UNSTOPPABLE FORCE IN MEN'S FIGURE SKATING.
WITH HIS RETIREMENT, IT'S GOING TO BE A WAR OF ALL AGAINST ALL TO TAKE HIS PLACE.

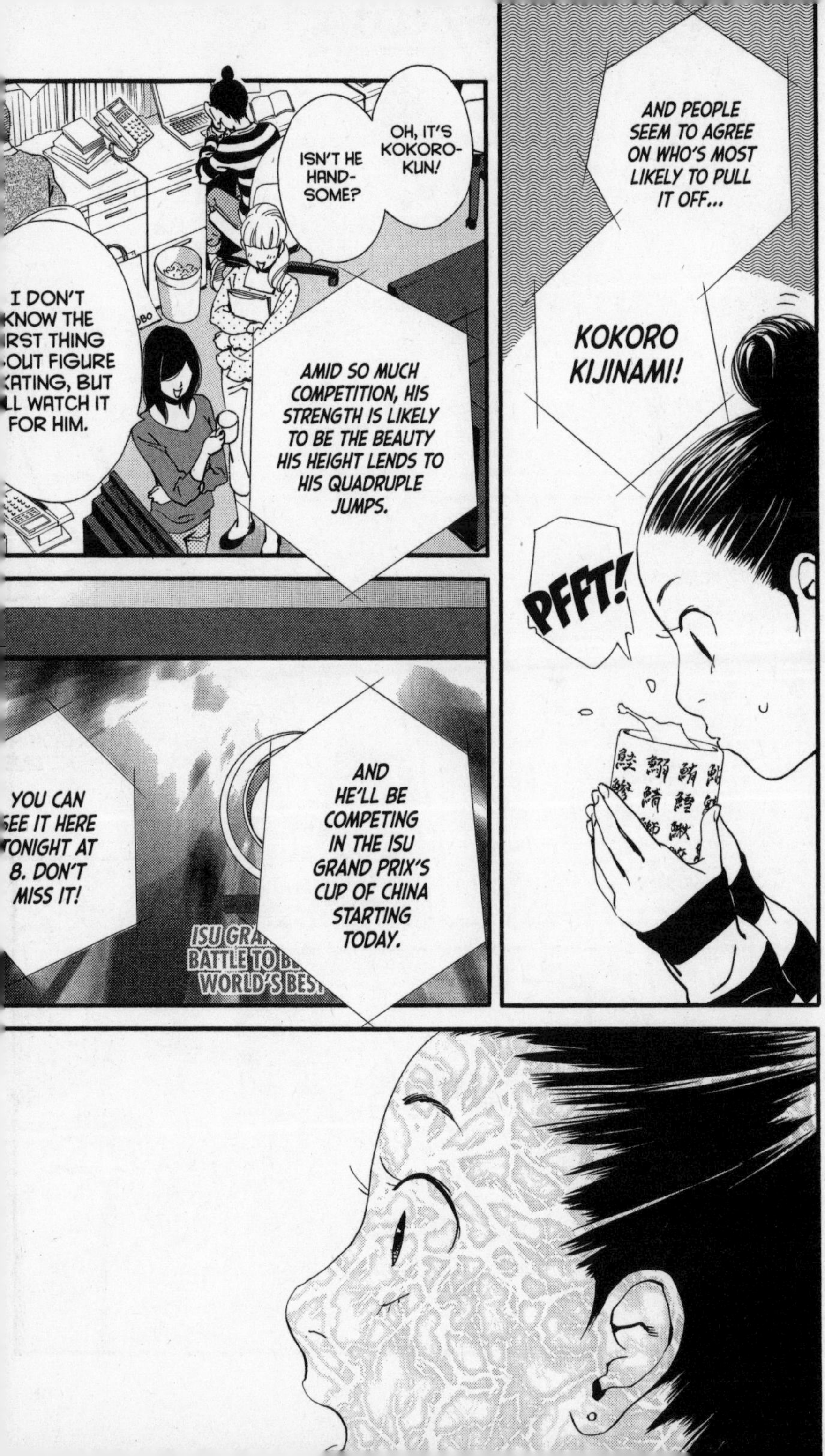
AND PEOPLE SEEM TO AGREE ON WHO'S MOST LIKELY TO PULL IT OFF...
KOKORO KIJINAMI!
PFFT!
OH, IT'S KOKORO-KUN!
ISN'T HE HAND-SOME?
AMID SO MUCH COMPETITION, HIS STRENGTH IS LIKELY TO BE THE BEAUTY HIS HEIGHT LENDS TO HIS QUADRUPLE JUMPS.
I DON'T KNOW THE IRST THING OUT FIGURE ATING, BUT LL WATCH IT FOR HIM.
AND HE'LL BE COMPETING IN THE ISU GRAND PRIX'S CUP OF CHINA STARTING TODAY.
YOU CAN EE IT HERE TONIGHT AT 8. DON'T MISS IT!
ISU GRA
BATTLE TO BE
WORLD'S BEST

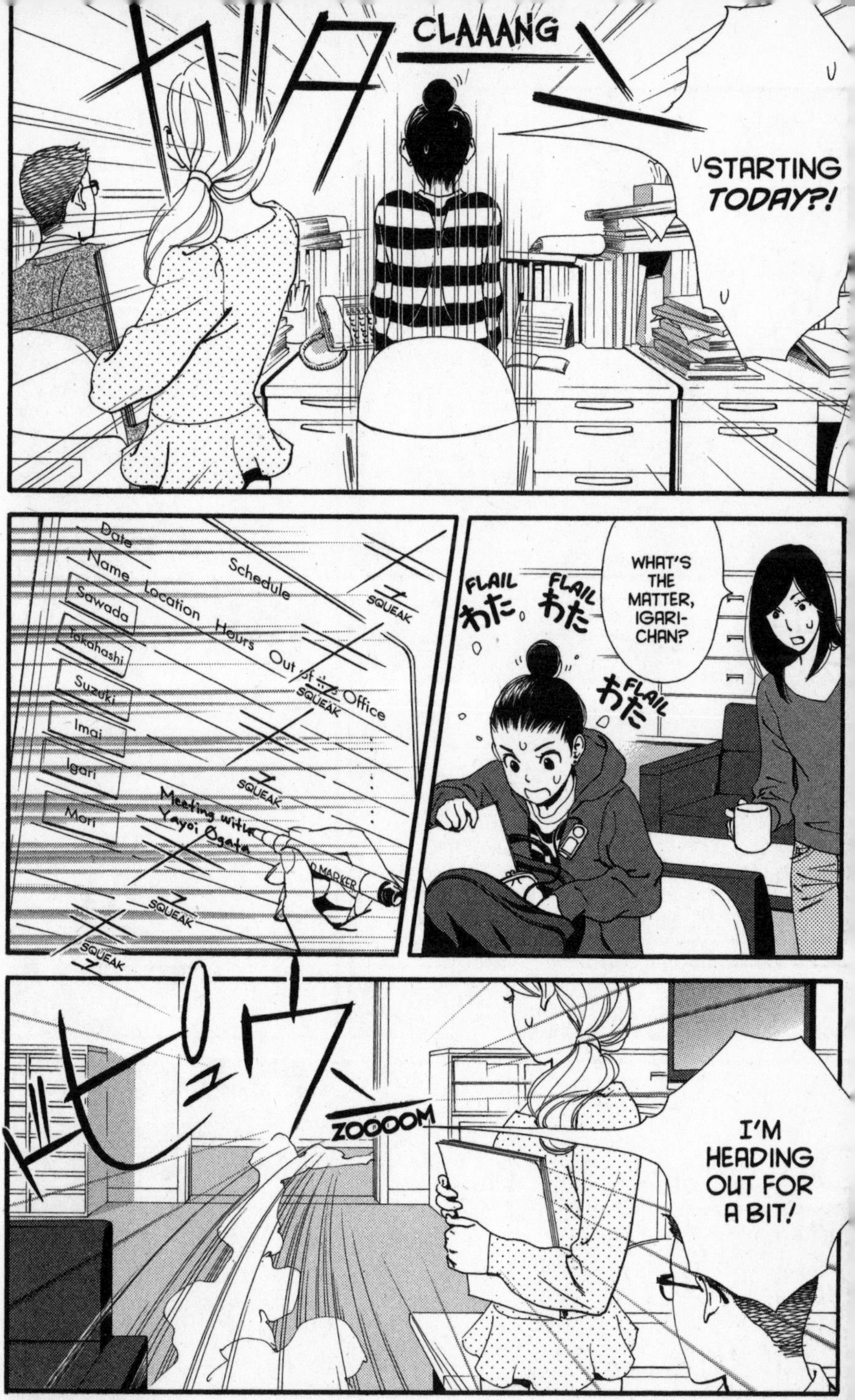
CLAAANG
STARTING TODAY?!
WHAT'S THE MATTER, IGARI-CHAN?
FLAIL わた
FLAIL わた
FLAIL わた
Date
Name
Location
Hours
Schedule
Out of Office
Sawada
Takahashi
Suzuki
Imai
Igari
Mori
Meeting with Yayoi Ogata
SQUEAK
SQUEAK
SQUEAK
SQUEAK
SQUEAK
SQUEAK
MARKER
ZOOOOM
I'M HEADING OUT FOR A BIT!

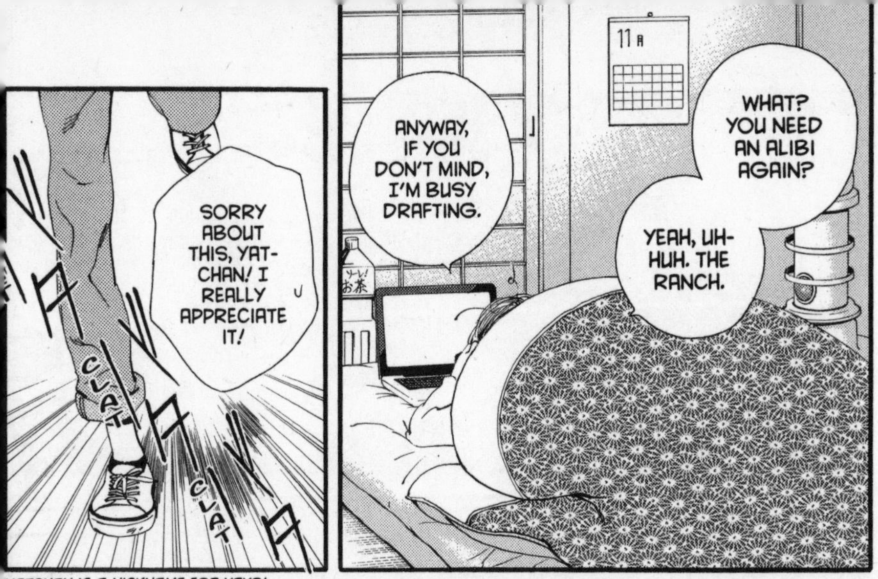
WHAT? YOU NEED AN ALIBI AGAIN?
YEAH, UH-HUH. THE RANCH.
ANYWAY, IF YOU DON'T MIND, I'M BUSY DRAFTING.
SORRY ABOUT THIS, YAT-CHAN! I REALLY APPRECIATE IT!
CLAT
CLAT

YATCHAN IS A NICKNAME FOR YAYOI.

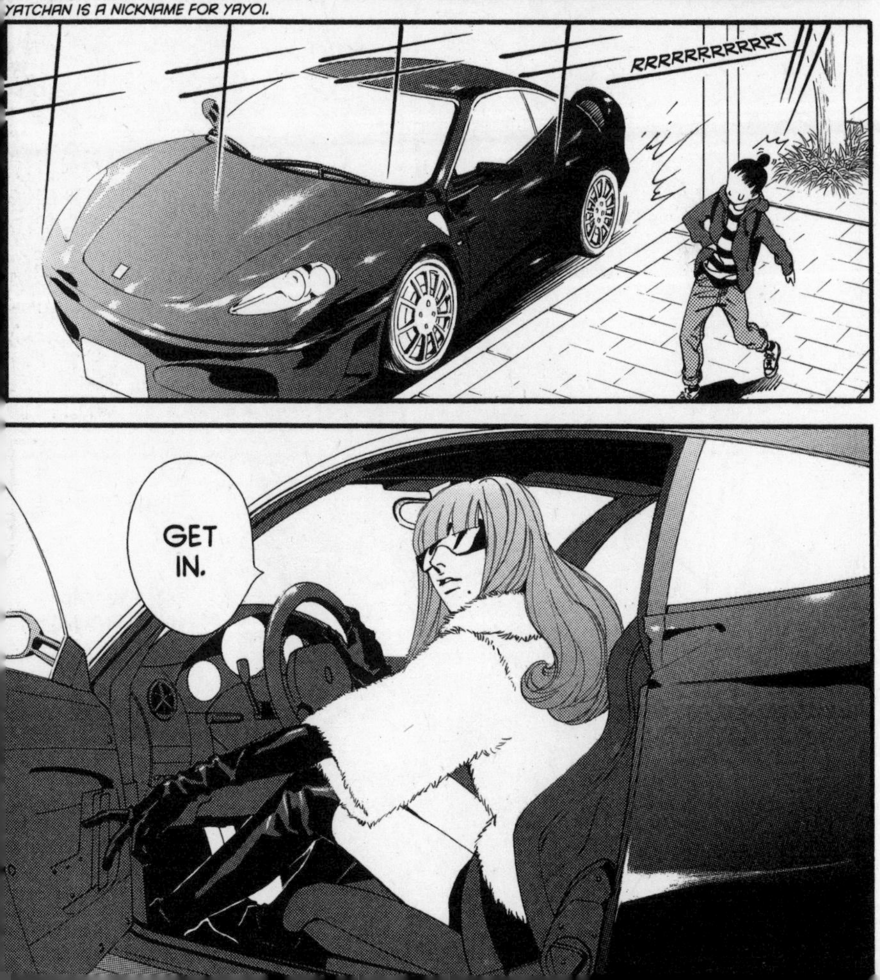
RRRRRRRRRRT
GET IN.

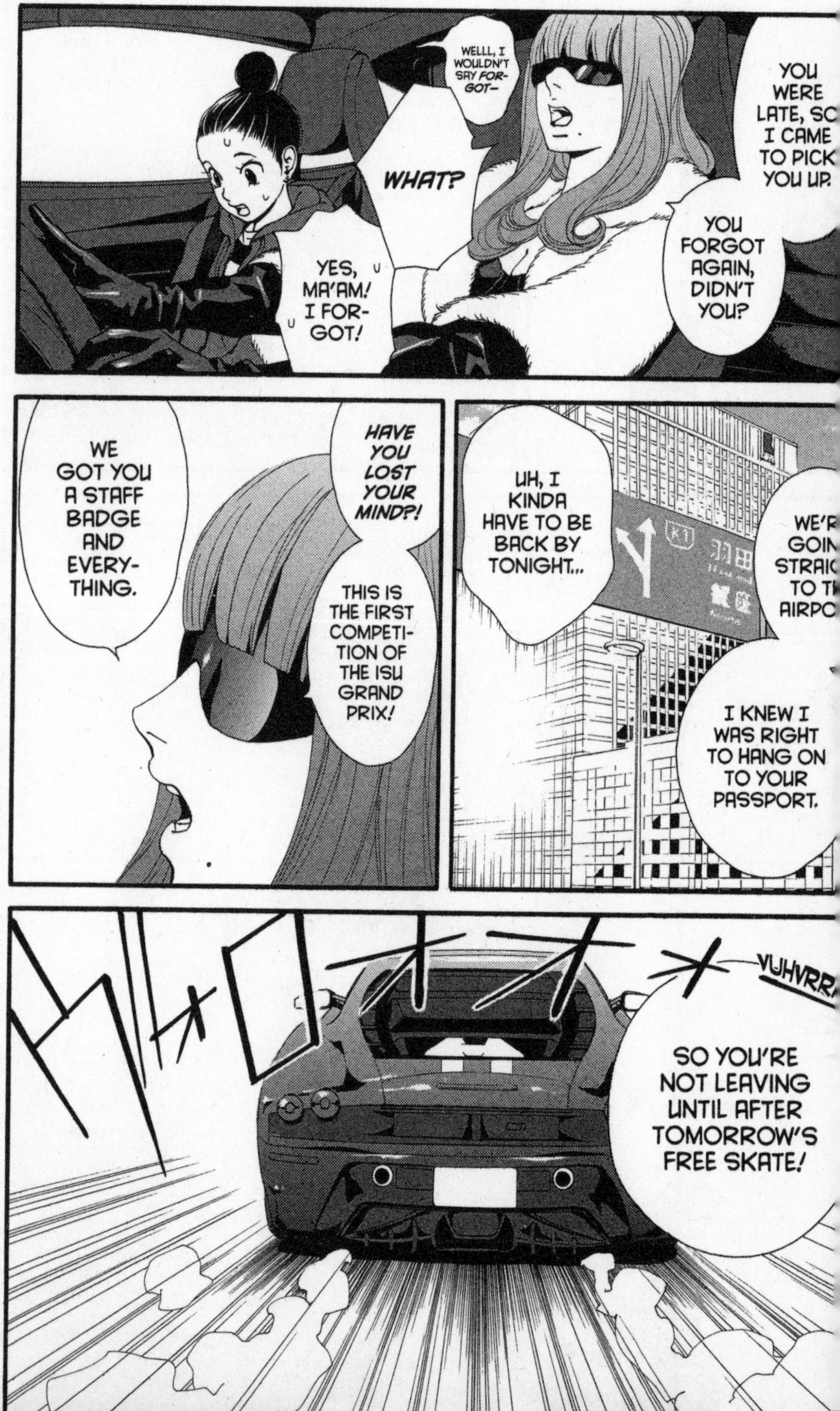

YOU WERE LATE, S I CAME TO PICK YOU UP.
YOU FORGOT AGAIN, DIDN'T YOU?
WELLL, I WOULDN'T SAY FOR-GOT—
WHAT?
YES, MA'AM! I FOR-GOT!
WE'R GOI STRAI TO T AIRPO
UH, I KINDA HAVE TO BE BACK BY TONIGHT...
I KNEW I WAS RIGHT TO HANG ON TO YOUR PASSPORT.
HAVE YOU LOST YOUR MIND?!
THIS IS THE FIRST COMPETI-TION OF THE ISU GRAND PRIX!
WE GOT YOU A STAFF BADGE AND EVERY-THING.
VUHVRR
SO YOU'RE NOT LEAVING UNTIL AFTER TOMORROW'S FREE SKATE!

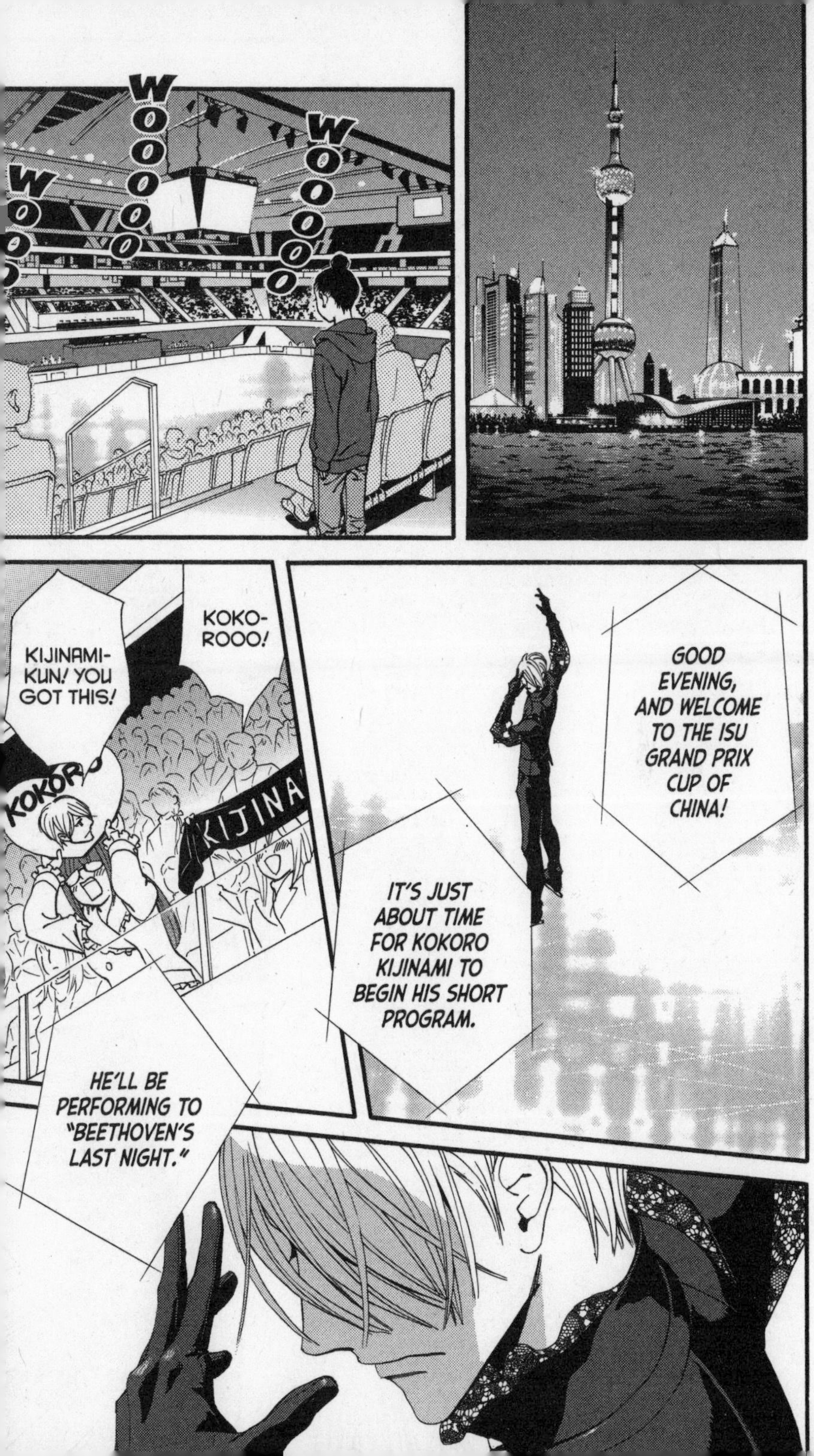
WOOOOOOO
WOOOOOOO
WOOOO
GOOD EVENING, AND WELCOME TO THE ISU GRAND PRIX CUP OF CHINA!
IT'S JUST ABOUT TIME FOR KOKORO KIJINAMI TO BEGIN HIS SHORT PROGRAM.
KOKO-ROOO!
KIJINAMI-KUN! YOU GOT THIS!
KOKORO
KIJINA
HE'LL BE PERFORMING TO "BEETHOVEN'S LAST NIGHT."

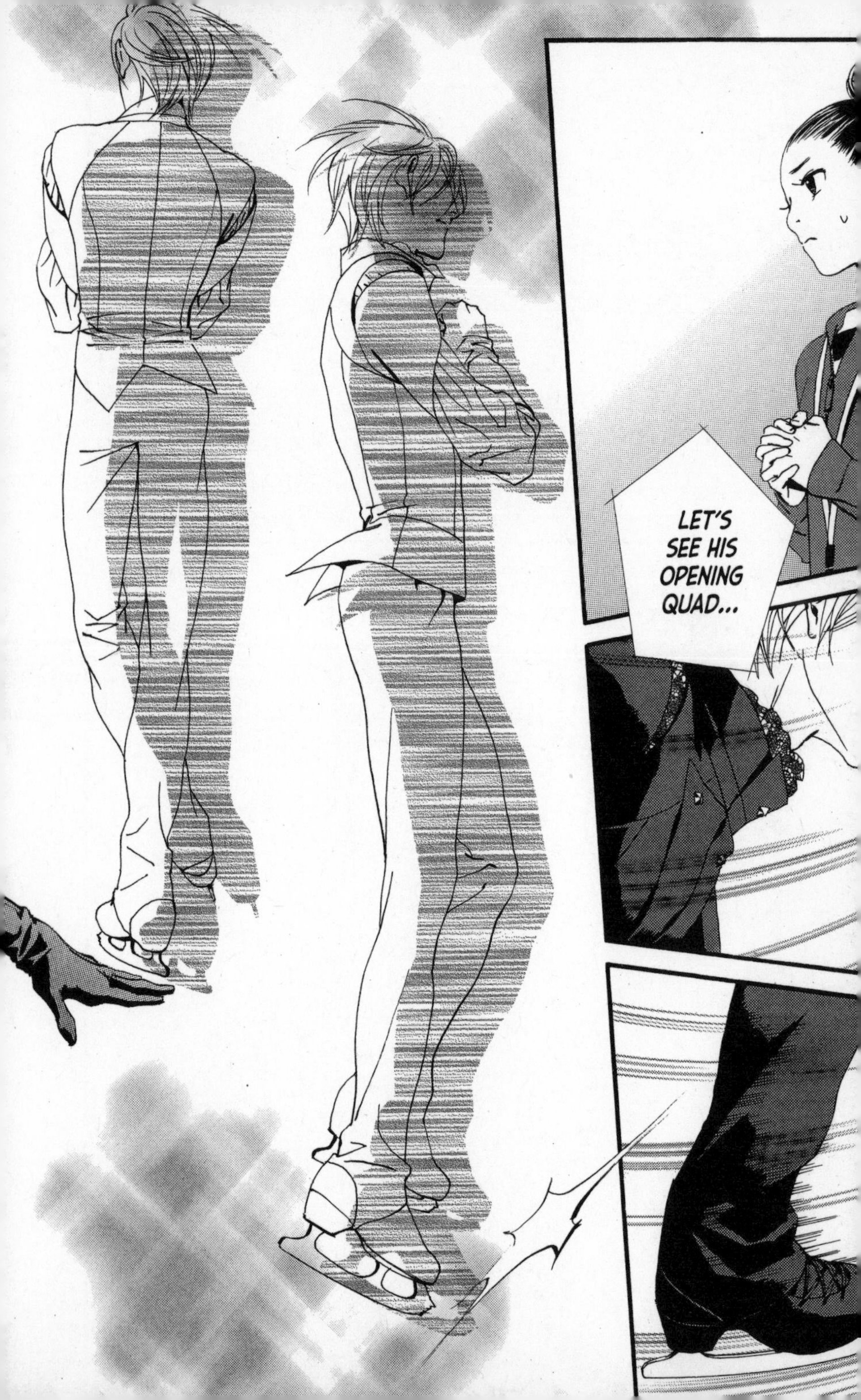
LET'S SEE HIS OPENING QUAD...

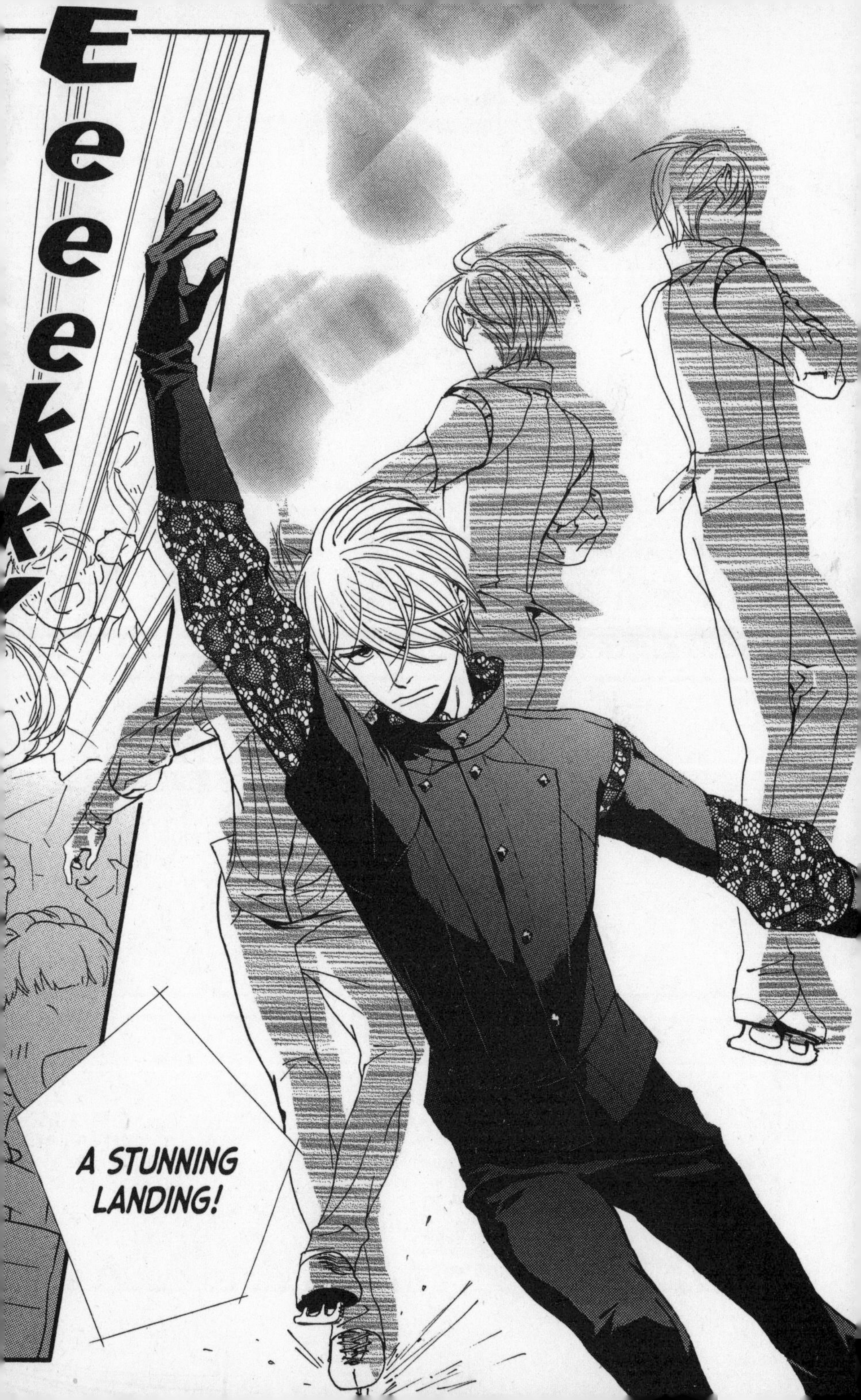
Eeeekk
A STUNNING LANDING!

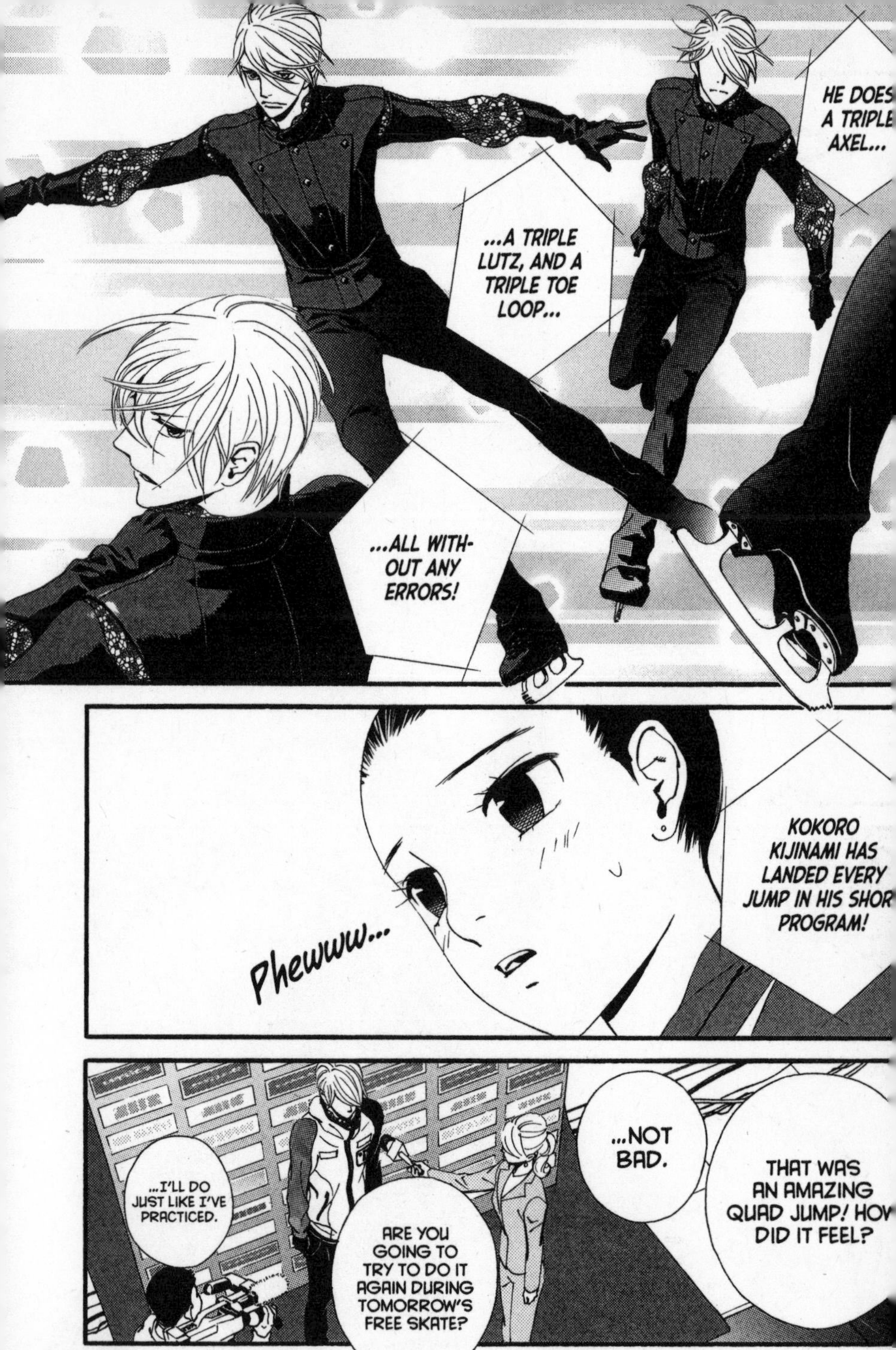
HE DOES A TRIPLE AXEL...
...A TRIPLE LUTZ, AND A TRIPLE TOE LOOP...
...ALL WITH-OUT ANY ERRORS!
KOKORO KIJINAMI HAS LANDED EVERY JUMP IN HIS SHOR PROGRAM!
Phewww...
THAT WAS AN AMAZING QUAD JUMP! HOW DID IT FEEL?
...NOT BAD.
ARE YOU GOING TO TRY TO DO IT AGAIN DURING TOMORROW'S FREE SKATE?
...I'LL DO JUST LIKE I'VE PRACTICED.

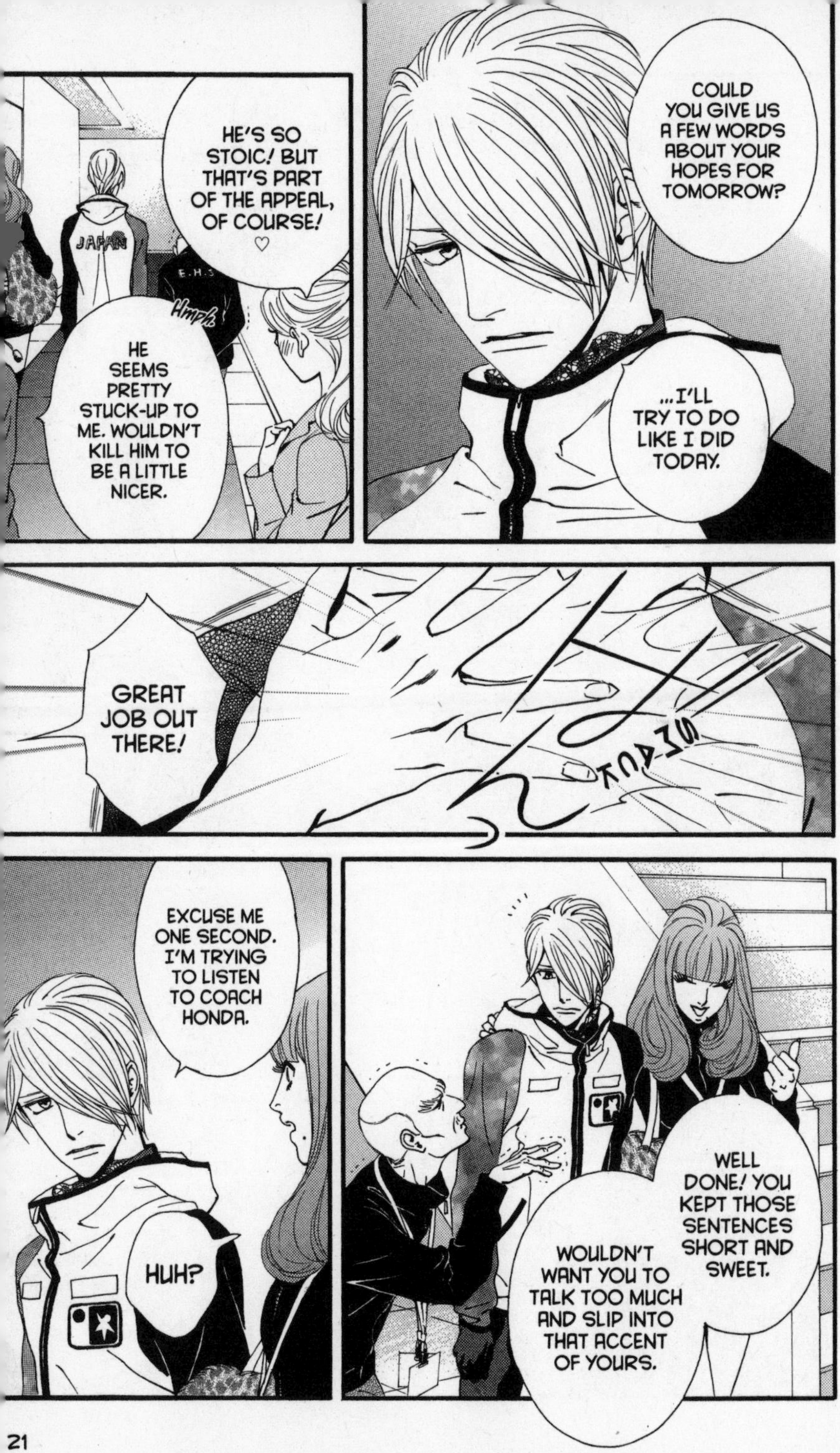
COULD YOU GIVE US A FEW WORDS ABOUT YOUR HOPES FOR TOMORROW?
...I'LL TRY TO DO LIKE I DID TODAY.
HE'S SO STOIC! BUT THAT'S PART OF THE APPEAL, OF COURSE! ♡
Hmph.
HE SEEMS PRETTY STUCK-UP TO ME. WOULDN'T KILL HIM TO BE A LITTLE NICER.
GREAT JOB OUT THERE!
WELL DONE! YOU KEPT THOSE SENTENCES SHORT AND SWEET.
WOULDN'T WANT YOU TO TALK TOO MUCH AND SLIP INTO THAT ACCENT OF YOURS.
EXCUSE ME ONE SECOND. I'M TRYING TO LISTEN TO COACH HONDA.
HUH?

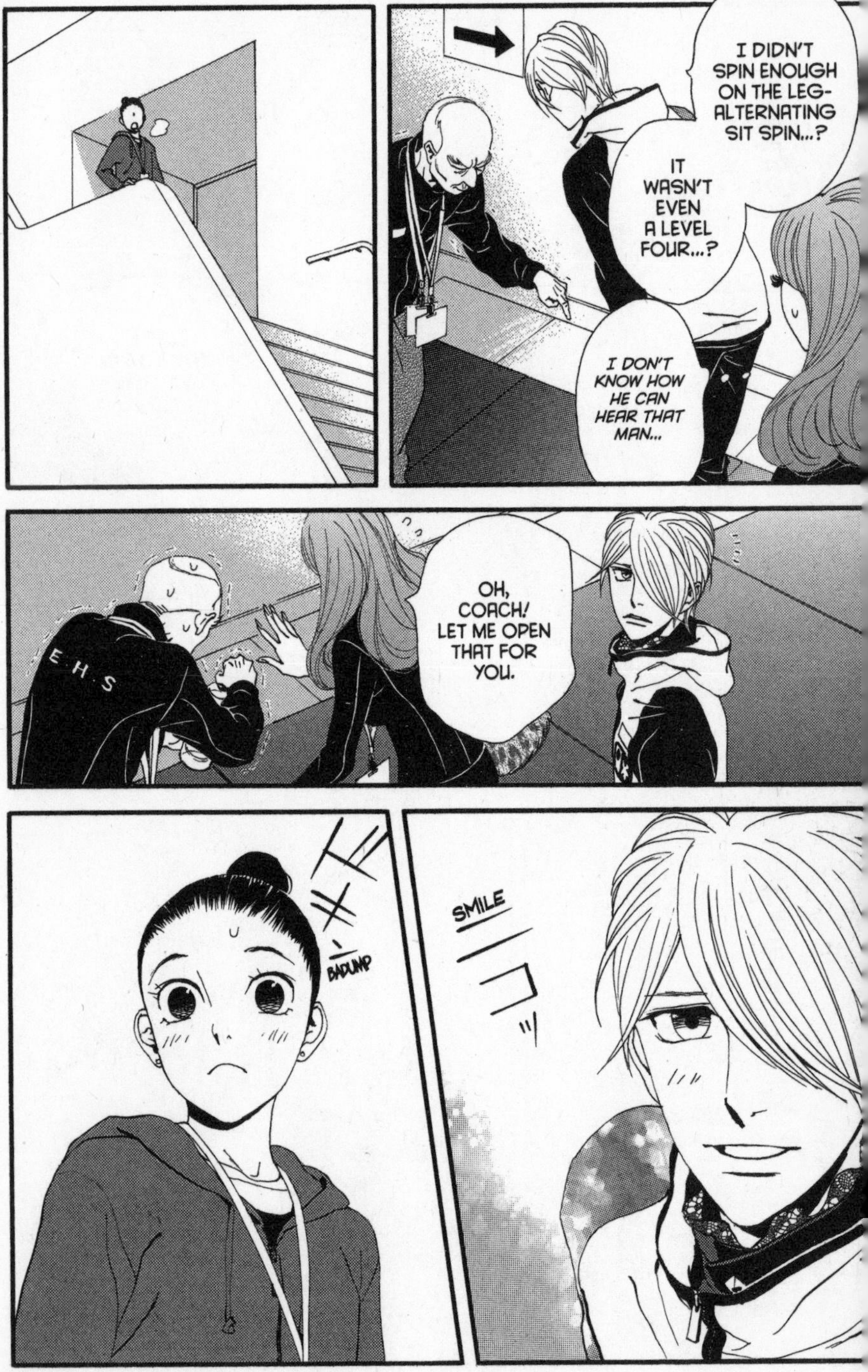
I DIDN'T SPIN ENOUGH ON THE LEG-ALTERNATING SIT SPIN...?
IT WASN'T EVEN A LEVEL FOUR...?
I DON'T KNOW HOW HE CAN HEAR THAT MAN...
E.H.S
OH, COACH! LET ME OPEN THAT FOR YOU.
SMILE
BADUMP

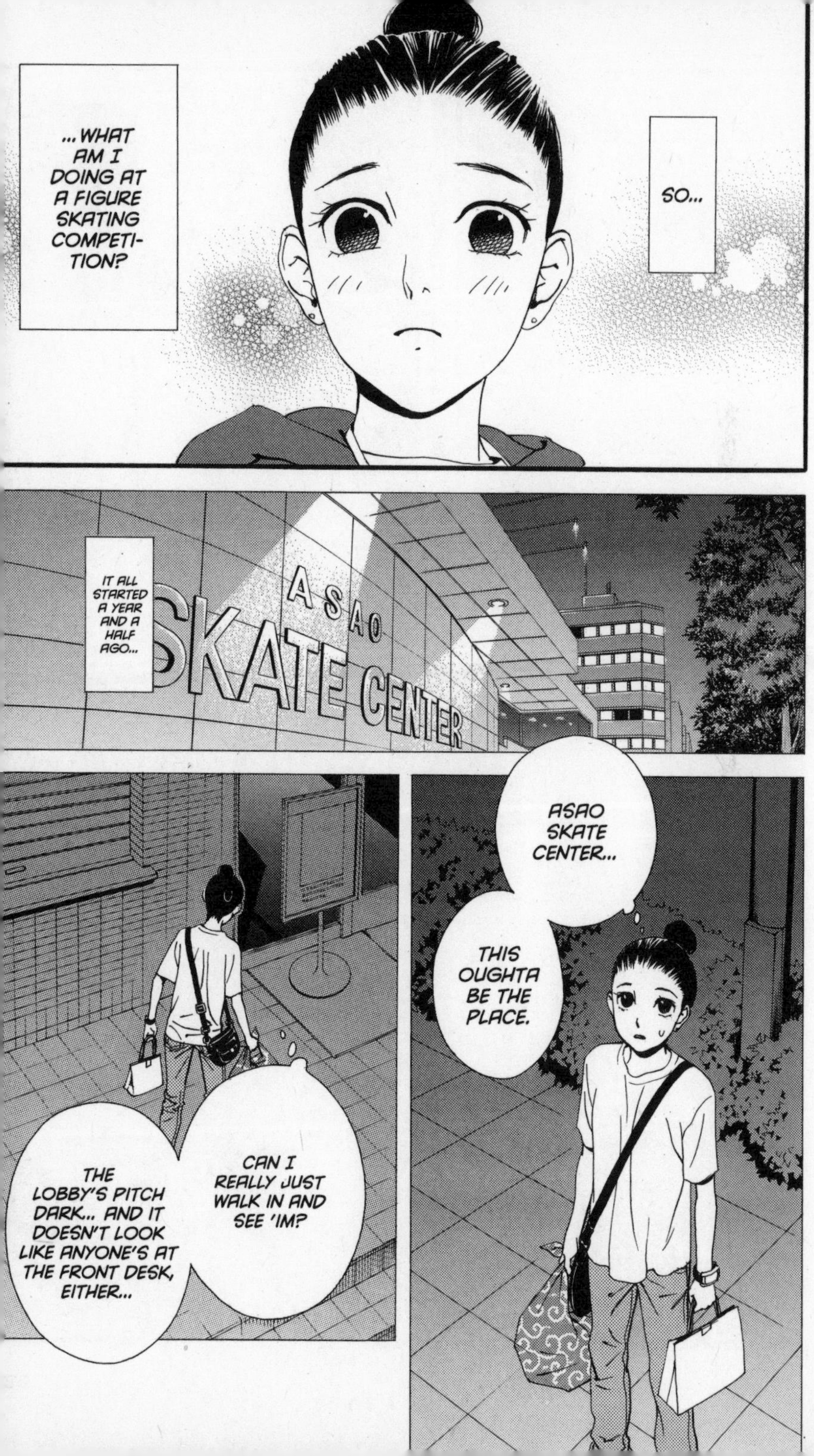
SO...
...WHAT AM I DOING AT A FIGURE SKATING COMPETITION?
IT ALL STARTED A YEAR AND A HALF AGO...
ASAO SKATE CENTER
ASAO SKATE CENTER...
THIS OUGHTA BE THE PLACE.
CAN I REALLY JUST WALK IN AND SEE 'IM?
THE LOBBY'S PITCH DARK... AND IT DOESN'T LOOK LIKE ANYONE'S AT THE FRONT DESK, EITHER...

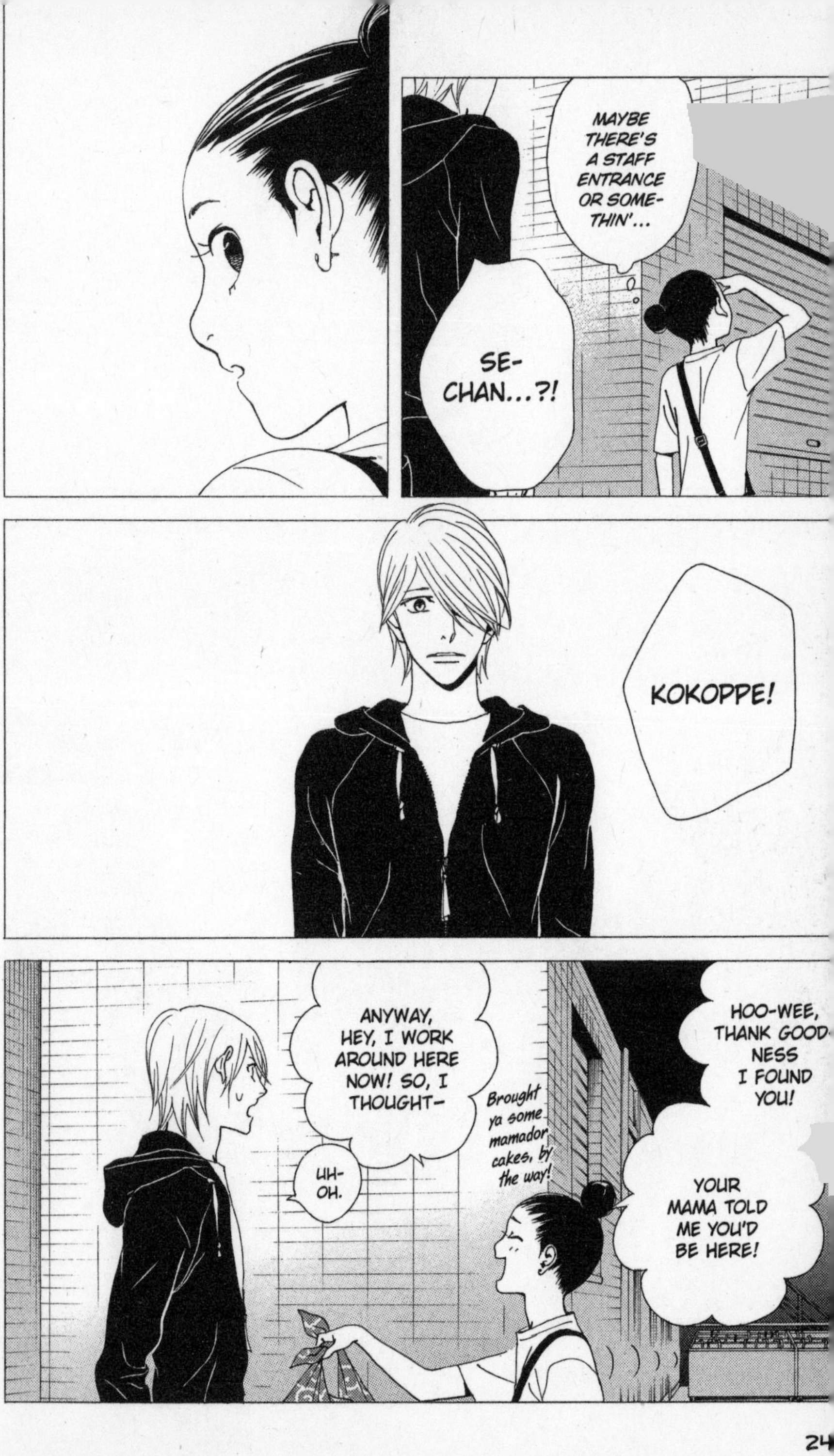
MAYBE THERE'S A STAFF ENTRANCE OR SOME- THIN'...
SE- CHAN...?!
KOKOPPE!
HOO-WEE, THANK GOOD NESS I FOUND YOU!
YOUR MAMA TOLD ME YOU'D BE HERE!
Brought ya some mamador cakes, by the way!
ANYWAY, HEY, I WORK AROUND HERE NOW! SO, I THOUGHT-
UH- OH.

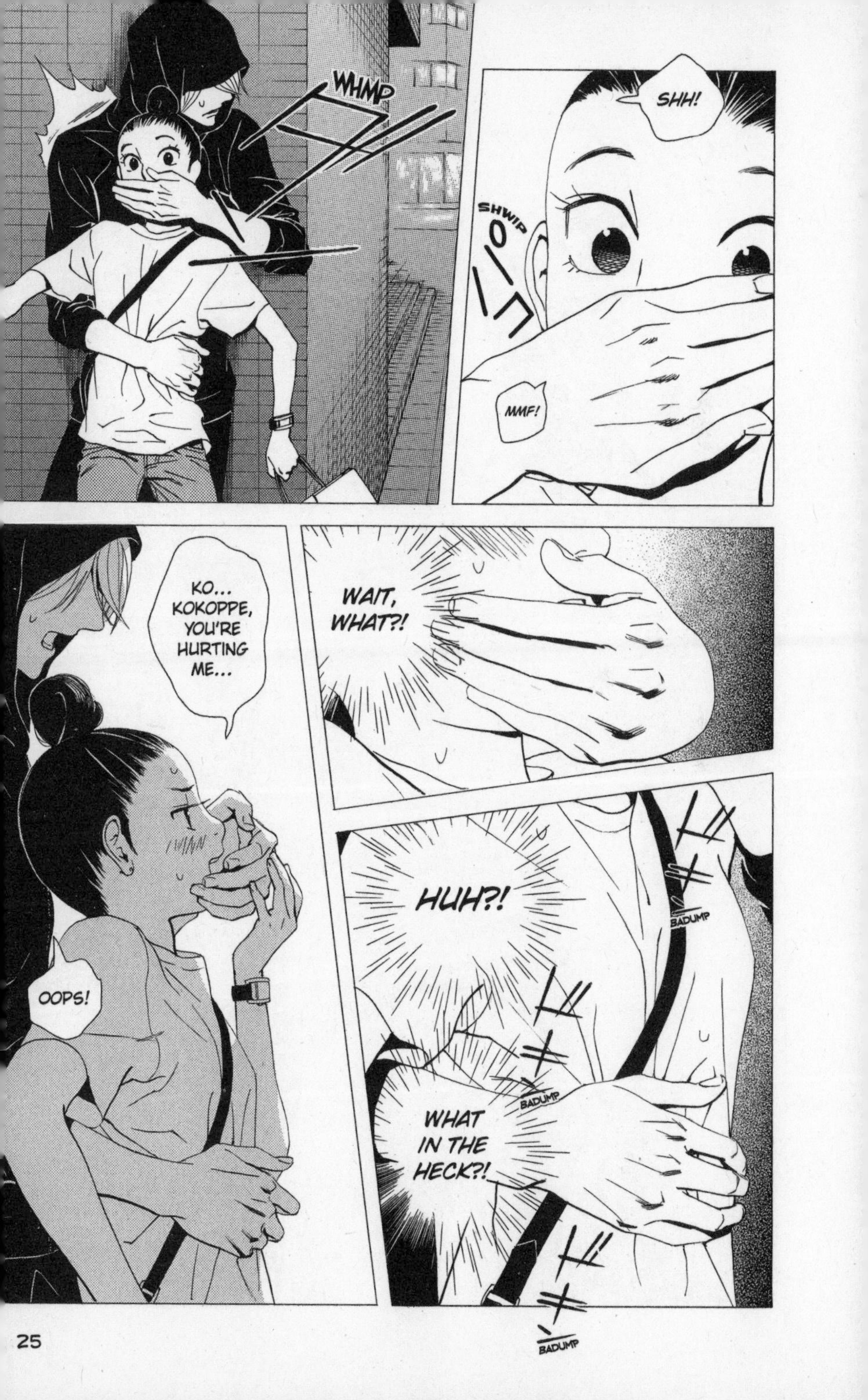
SHH!
SHWIP
MMF!
WHMP
WAIT, WHAT?!
HUH?!
BADUMP
WHAT IN THE HECK?!
BADUMP
BADUMP
KO... KOKOPPE, YOU'RE HURTING ME...
OOPS!

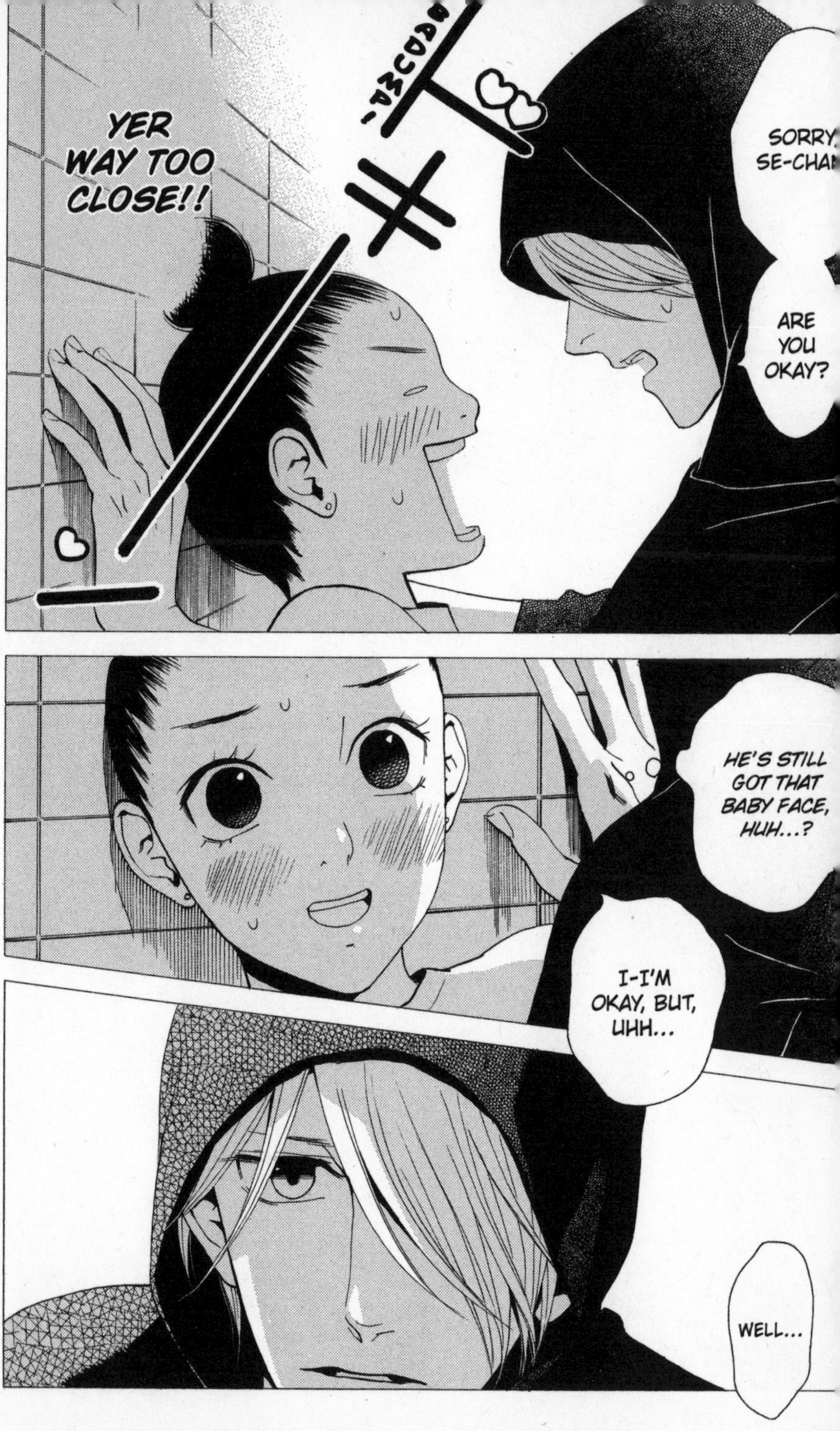
SORRY, SE-CHA
ARE YOU OKAY?
BADUMP-
YER WAY TOO CLOSE!!
HE'S STILL GOT THAT BABY FACE, HUH...?
I-I'M OKAY, BUT, UHH...
WELL...

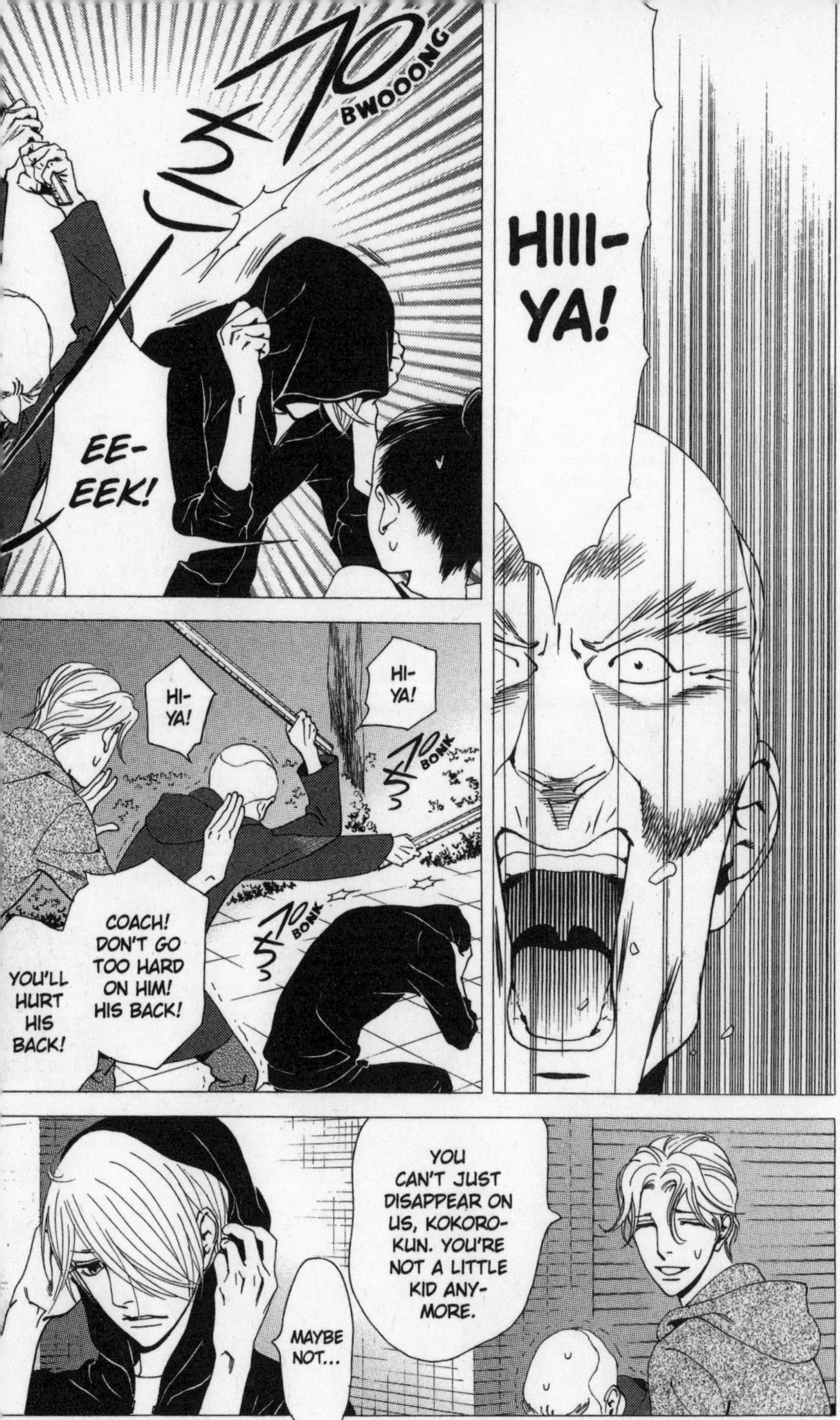
HIII-YA!
BWOOONG
EE-EEK!
HI-YA!
BONK
HI-YA!
BONK
COACH! DON'T GO TOO HARD ON HIM! HIS BACK!
YOU'LL HURT HIS BACK!
YOU CAN'T JUST DISAPPEAR ON US, KOKORO-KUN. YOU'RE NOT A LITTLE KID ANY-MORE.
MAYBE NOT...

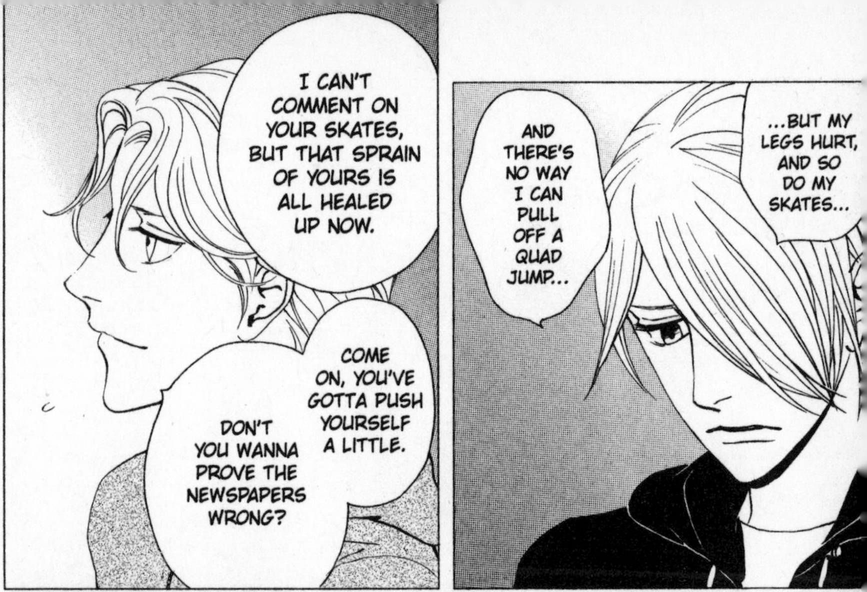
...BUT MY LEGS HURT, AND SO DO MY SKATES...
AND THERE'S NO WAY I CAN PULL OFF A QUAD JUMP...
I CAN'T COMMENT ON YOUR SKATES, BUT THAT SPRAIN OF YOURS IS ALL HEALED UP NOW.
COME ON, YOU'VE GOTTA PUSH YOURSELF A LITTLE.
DON'T YOU WANNA PROVE THE NEWSPAPERS WRONG?

Dominic here doesn't mince words with guys.

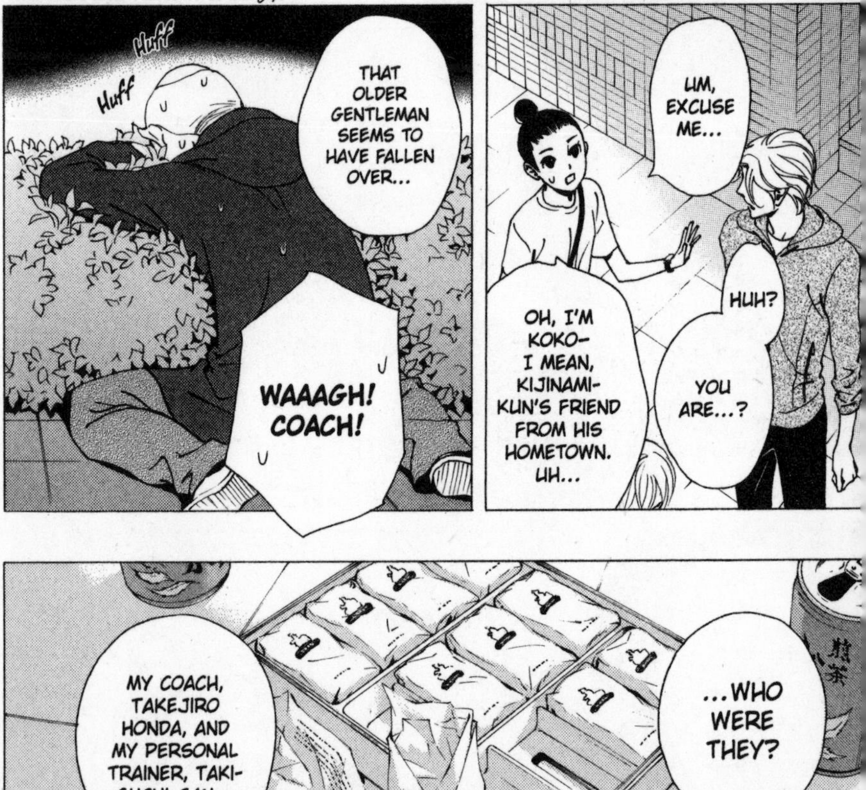
UM, EXCUSE ME...
HUH?
YOU ARE...?
OH, I'M KOKO- I MEAN, KIJINAMI-KUN'S FRIEND FROM HIS HOMETOWN. UH...
Huff
Huff
THAT OLDER GENTLEMAN SEEMS TO HAVE FALLEN OVER...
WAAAGH! COACH!
...WHO WERE THEY?
MY COACH, TAKEJIRO HONDA, AND MY PERSONAL TRAINER, TAKI-GUCHI-SAN...

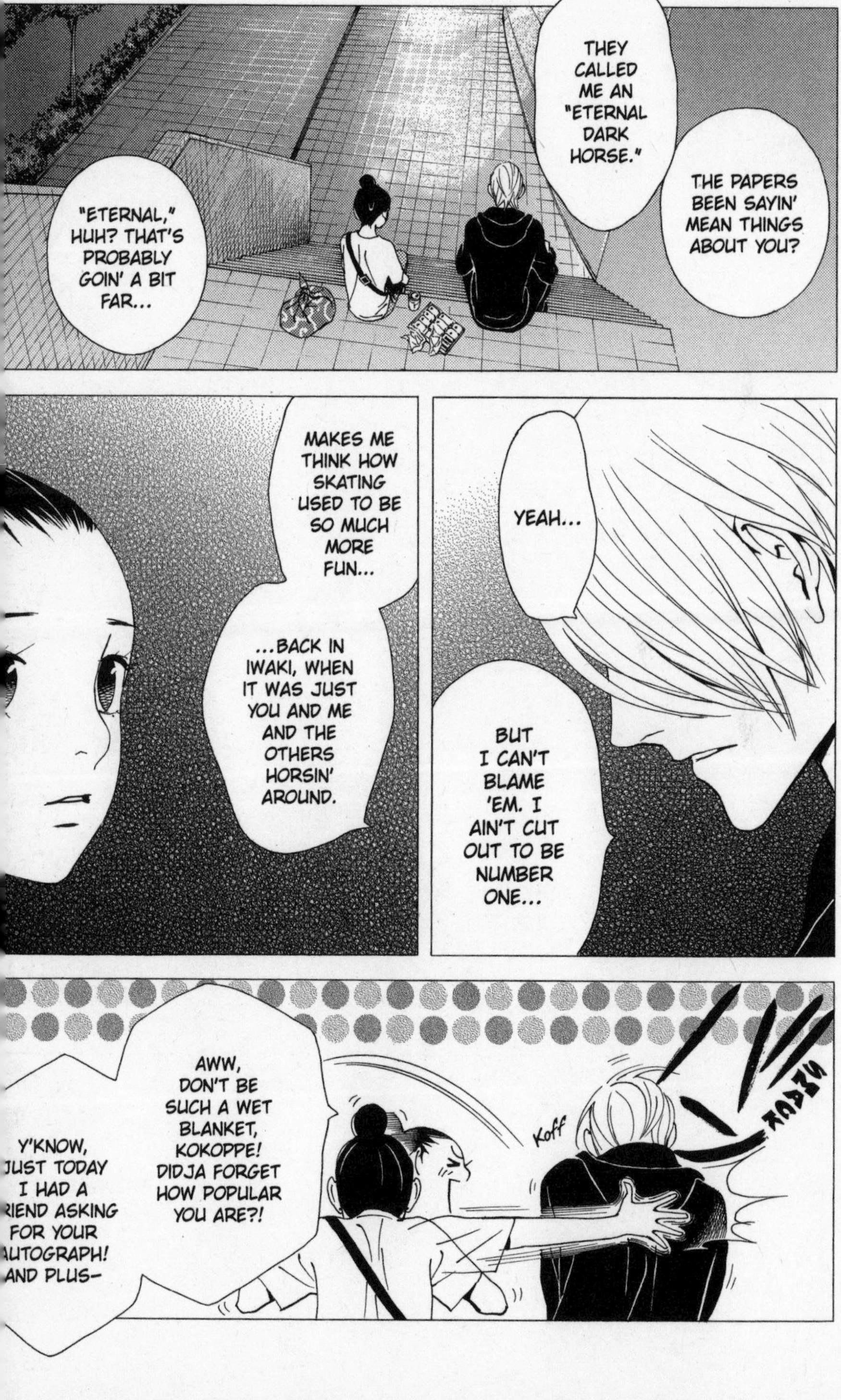
THE PAPERS BEEN SAYIN' MEAN THINGS ABOUT YOU?
THEY CALLED ME AN "ETERNAL DARK HORSE."
"ETERNAL," HUH? THAT'S PROBABLY GOIN' A BIT FAR...
YEAH...
BUT I CAN'T BLAME 'EM. I AIN'T CUT OUT TO BE NUMBER ONE...
MAKES ME THINK HOW SKATING USED TO BE SO MUCH MORE FUN...
...BACK IN IWAKI, WHEN IT WAS JUST YOU AND ME AND THE OTHERS HORSIN' AROUND.
SMACK
Koff
AWW, DON'T BE SUCH A WET BLANKET, KOKOPPE! DIDJA FORGET HOW POPULAR YOU ARE?!
Y'KNOW, JUST TODAY I HAD A RIEND ASKING FOR YOUR UTOGRAPH! AND PLUS–

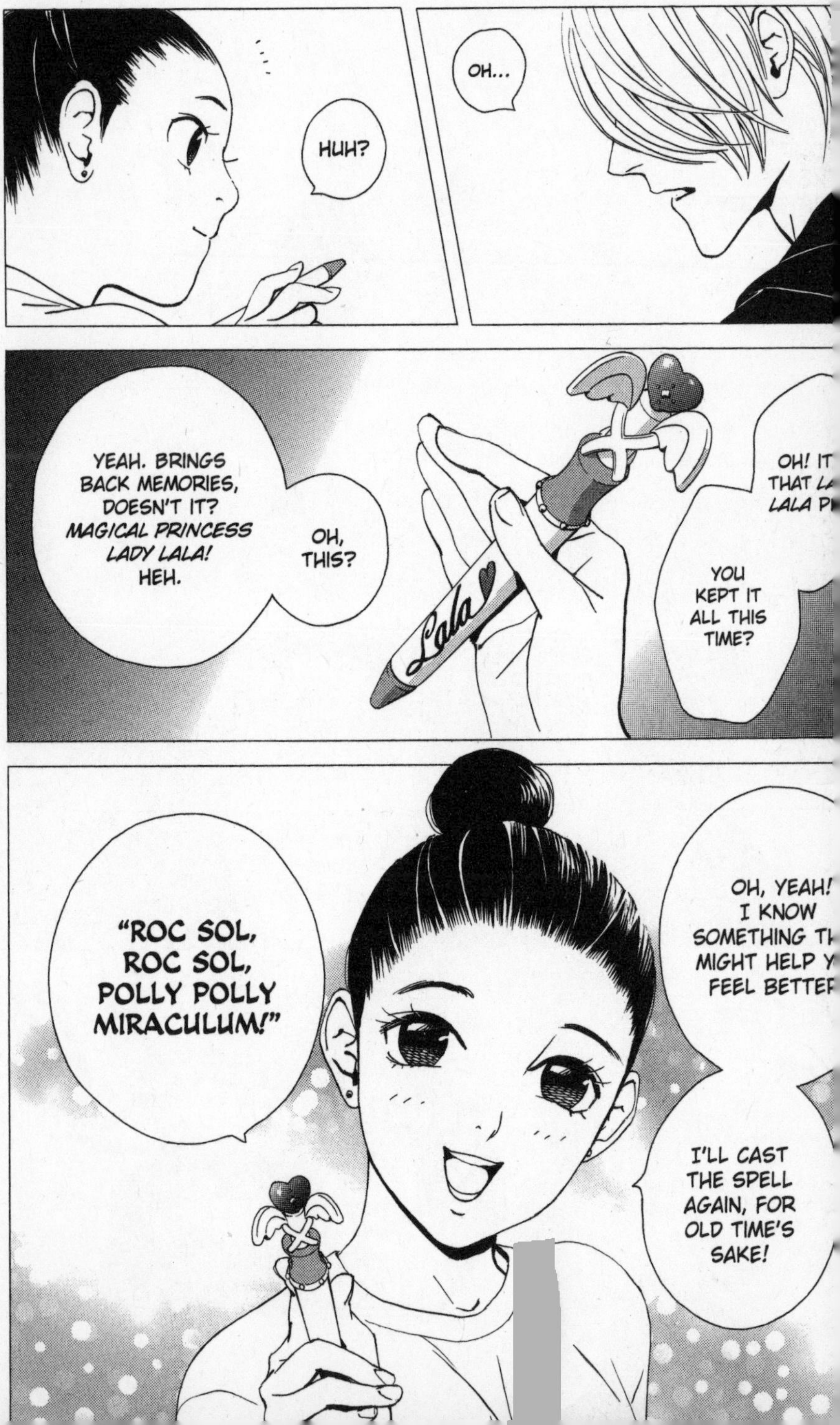
OH...
HUH?
OH! IT THAT LA LALA P
YOU KEPT IT ALL THIS TIME?
OH, THIS?
YEAH. BRINGS BACK MEMORIES, DOESN'T IT? *MAGICAL PRINCESS LADY LALA!* HEH.
Lala
OH, YEAH! I KNOW SOMETHING TH MIGHT HELP Y FEEL BETTER
I'LL CAST THE SPELL AGAIN, FOR OLD TIME'S SAKE!
"ROC SOL, ROC SOL, POLLY POLLY MIRACULUM!"

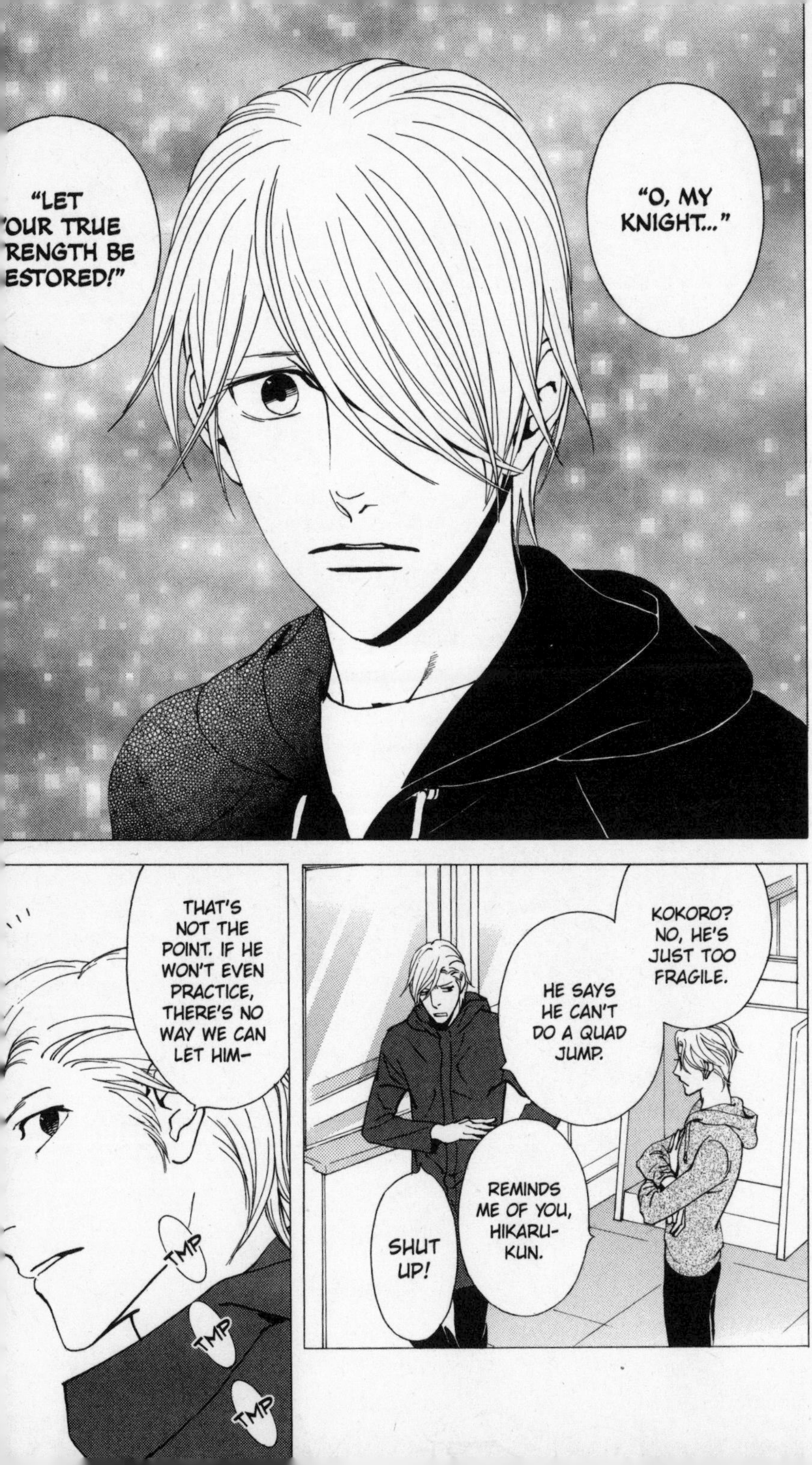
"O, MY KNIGHT..."
"LET 'OUR TRUE RENGTH BE ESTORED!"
KOKORO? NO, HE'S JUST TOO FRAGILE.
HE SAYS HE CAN'T DO A QUAD JUMP.
REMINDS ME OF YOU, HIKARU-KUN.
SHUT UP!
THAT'S NOT THE POINT. IF HE WON'T EVEN PRACTICE, THERE'S NO WAY WE CAN LET HIM-
TMP
TMP
TMP

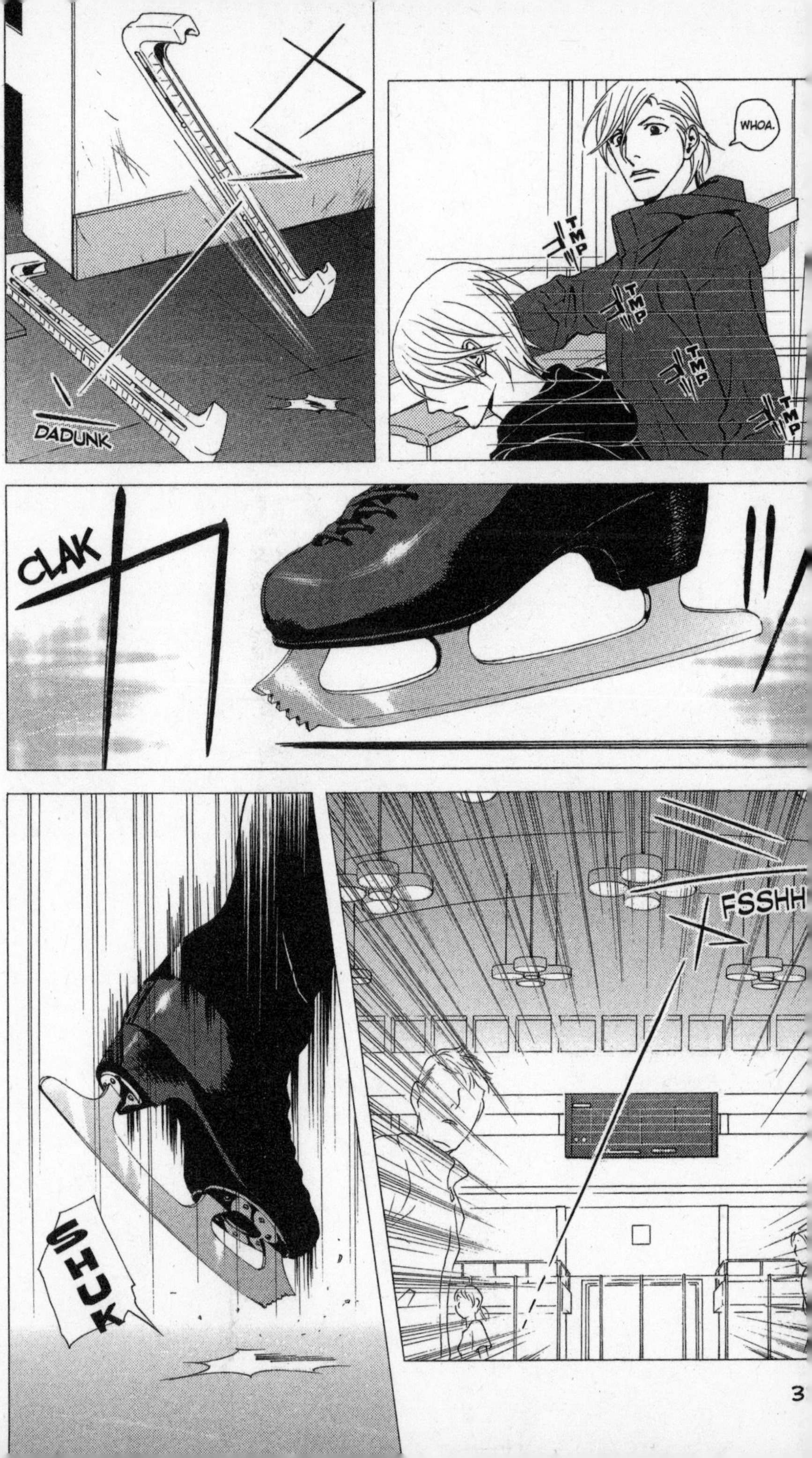
WHOA.
TMP
TMP
TMP
TMP
DADUNK
CLAK
FSSHH
SHUK

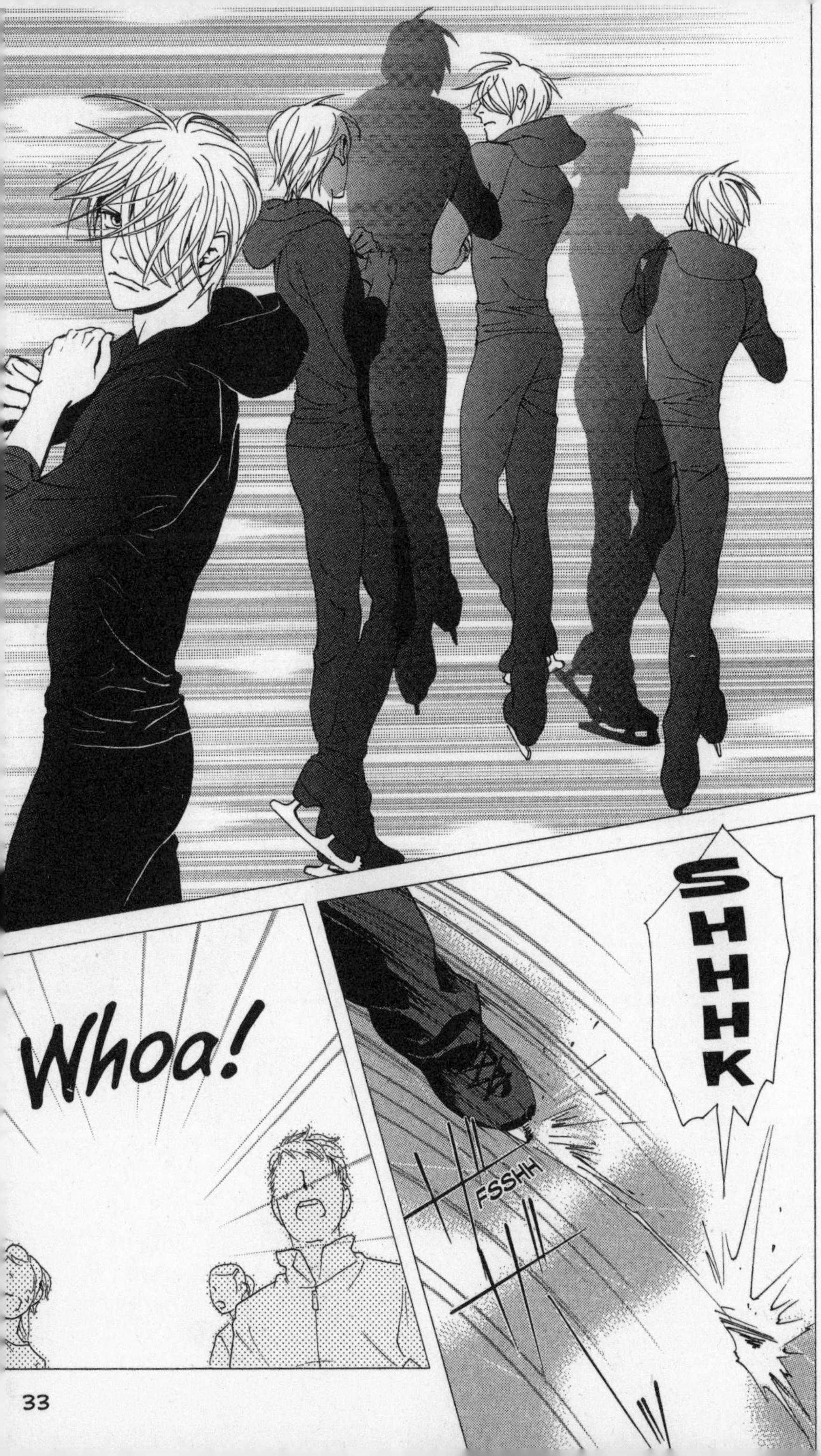
SHHHK
FSSHH
Whoa!

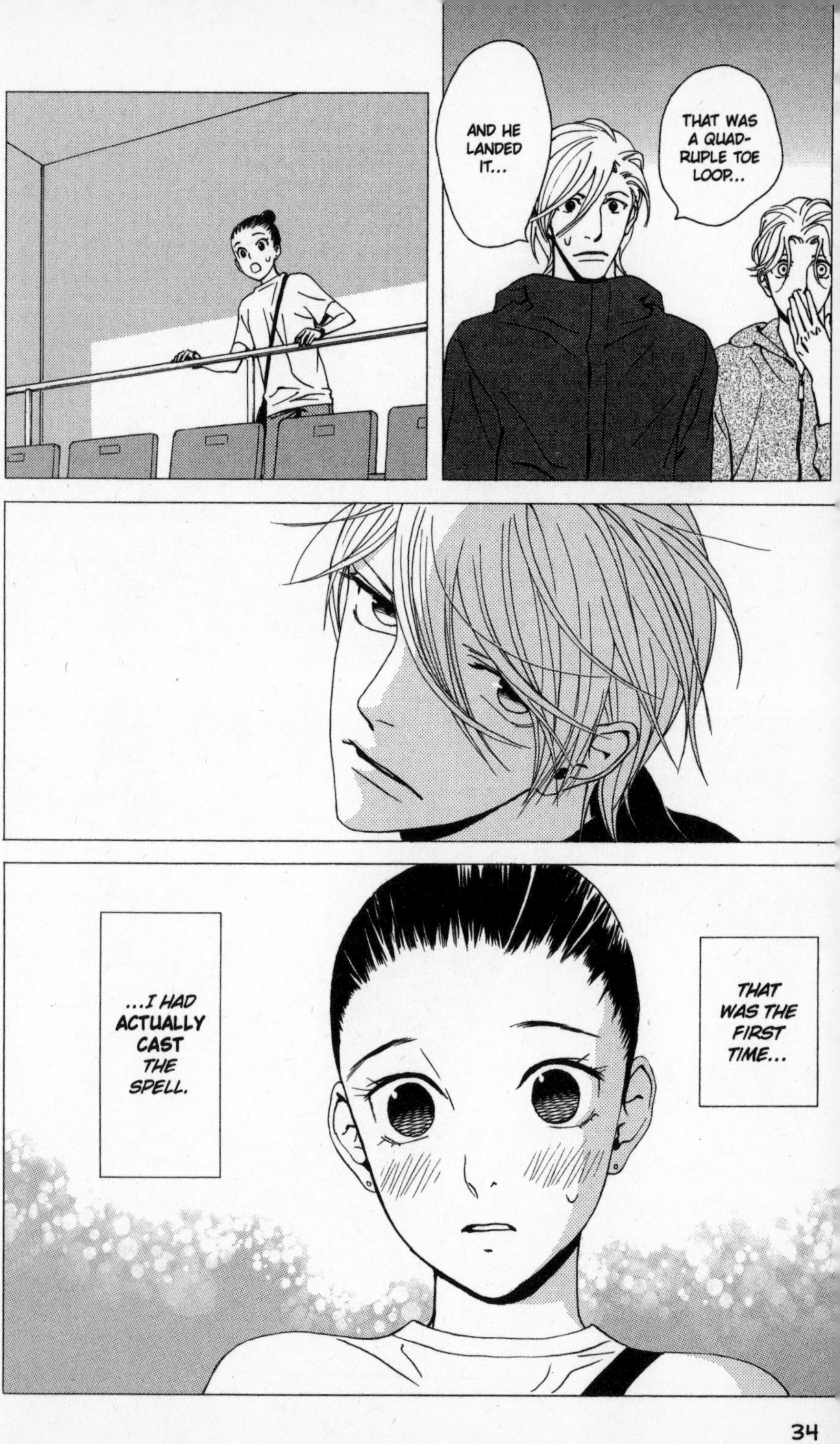
THAT WAS A QUAD-RUPLE TOE LOOP...
AND HE LANDED IT...
THAT WAS THE FIRST TIME...
...I HAD ACTUALLY CAST THE SPELL.

Spell 2
Bedroom Secrets

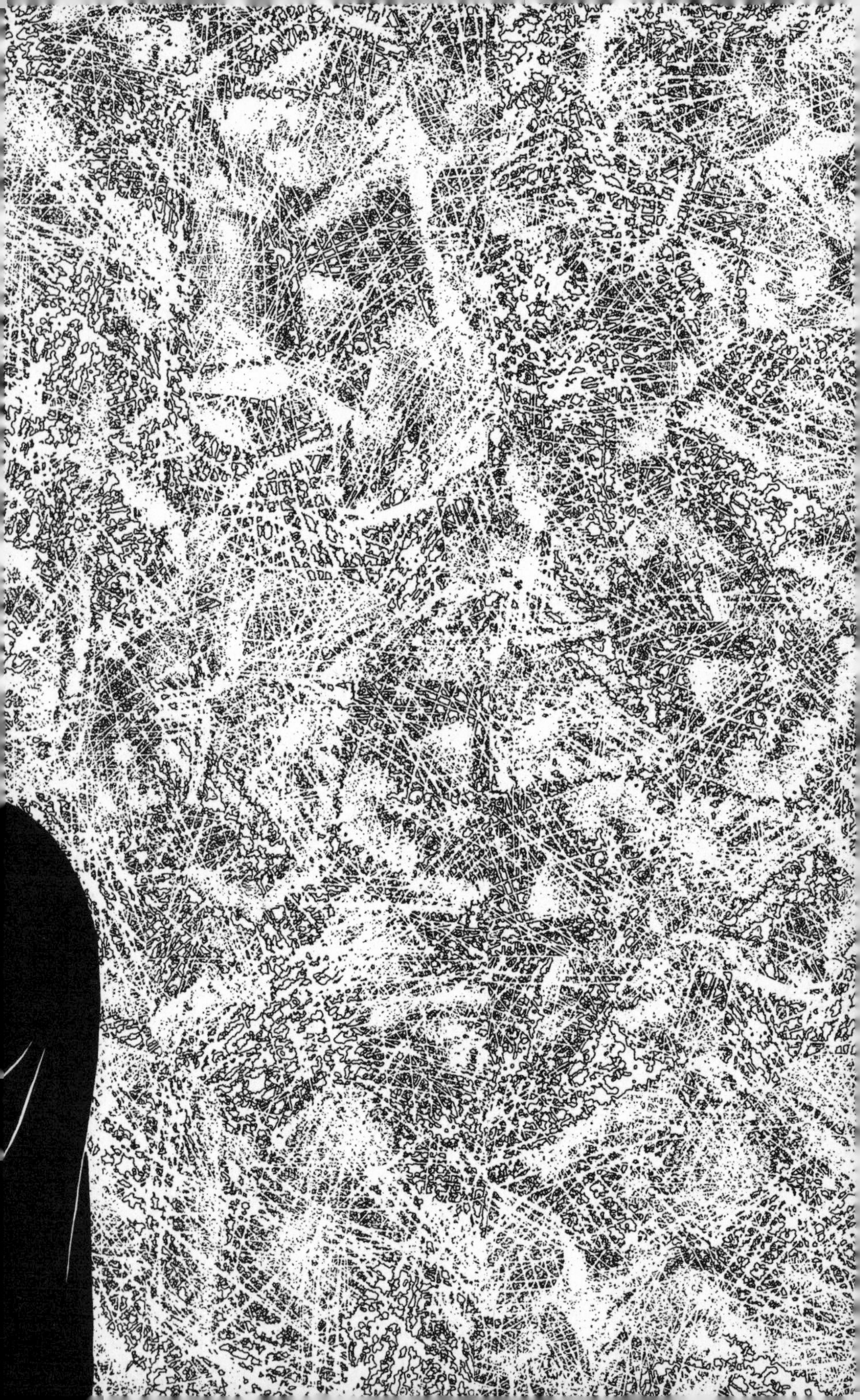

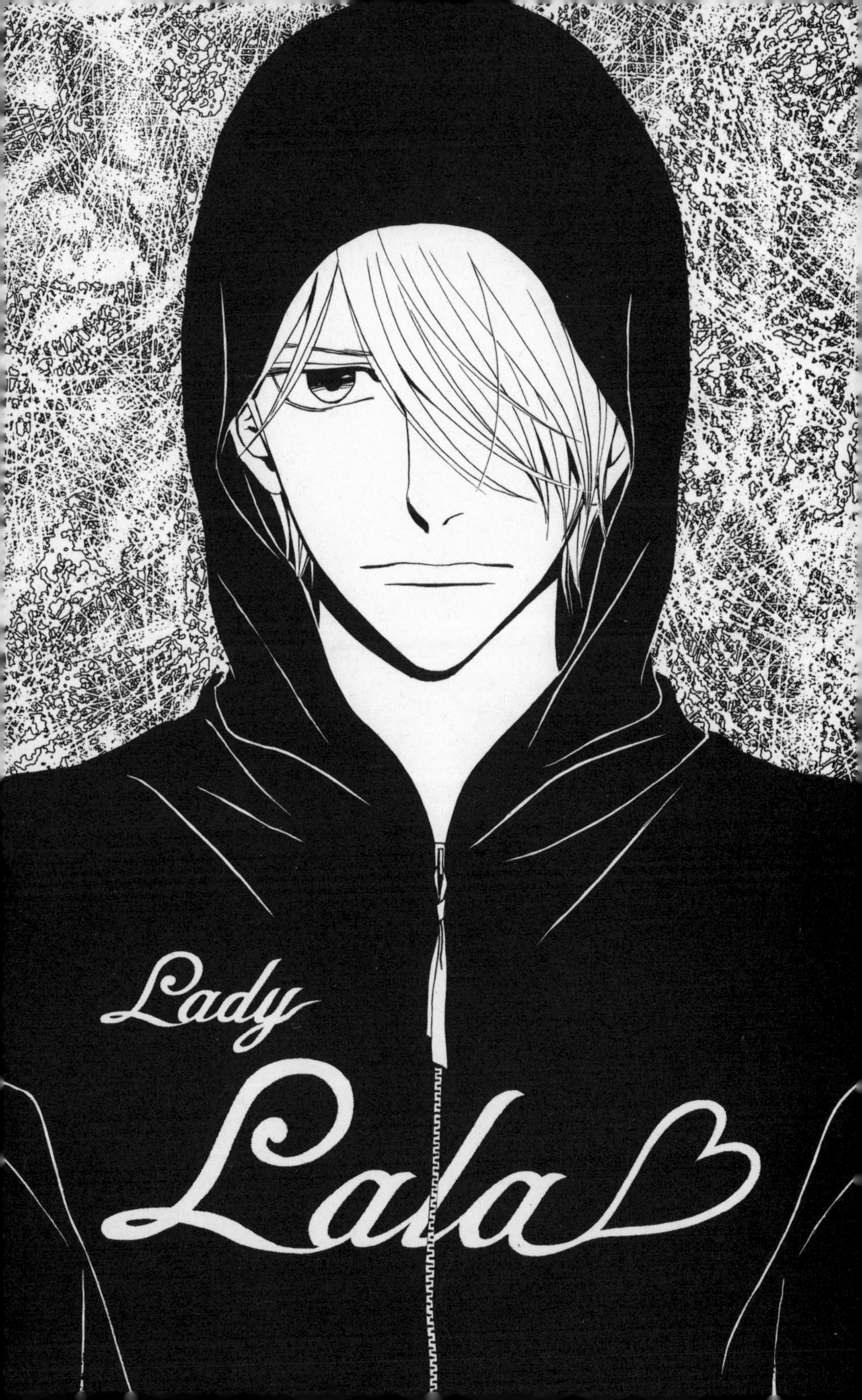
Lady
Lala

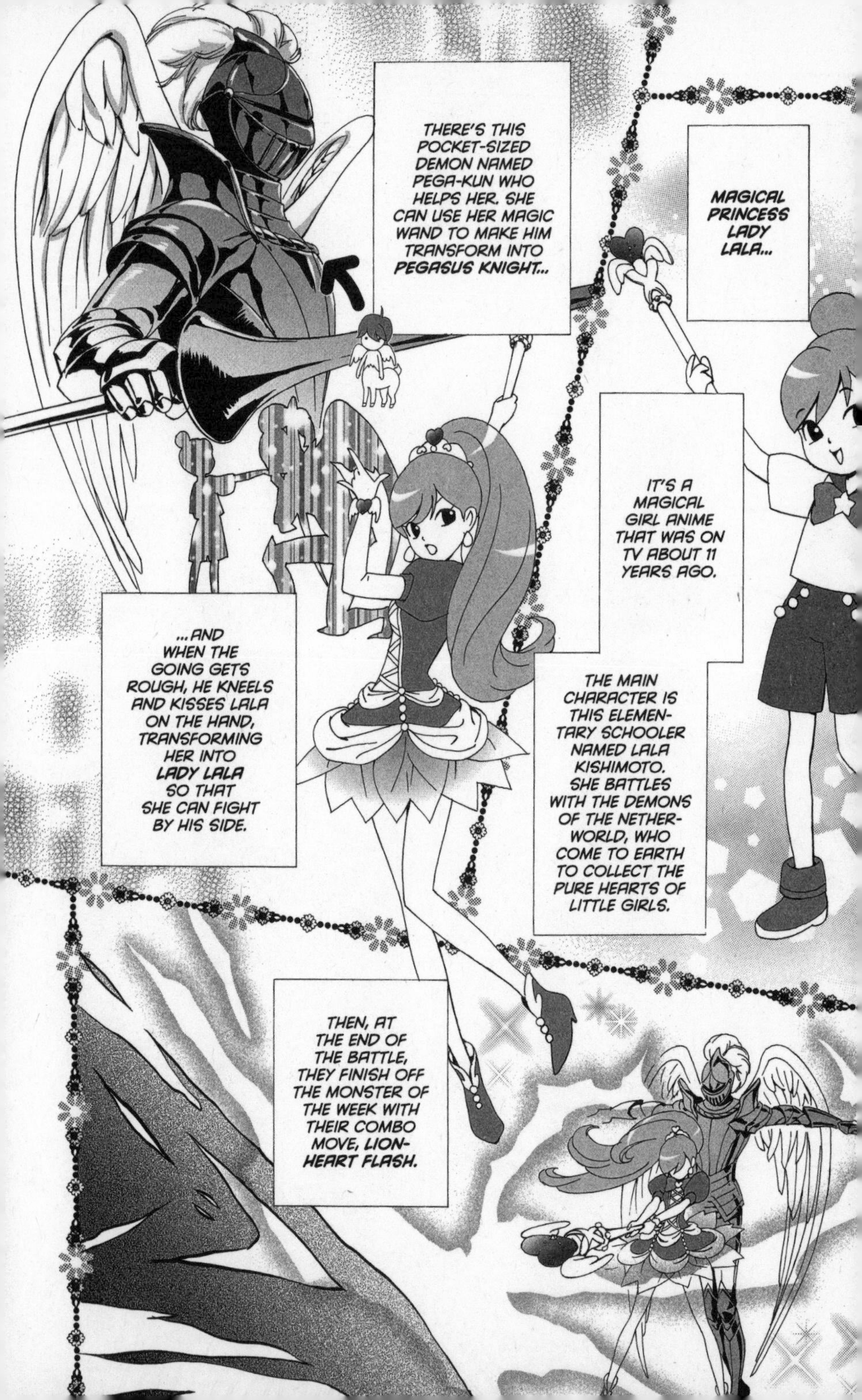
MAGICAL PRINCESS LADY LALA...
IT'S A MAGICAL GIRL ANIME THAT WAS ON TV ABOUT 11 YEARS AGO.
THE MAIN CHARACTER IS THIS ELEMENTARY SCHOOLER NAMED LALA KISHIMOTO. SHE BATTLES WITH THE DEMONS OF THE NETHERWORLD, WHO COME TO EARTH TO COLLECT THE PURE HEARTS OF LITTLE GIRLS.
THERE'S THIS POCKET-SIZED DEMON NAMED PEGA-KUN WHO HELPS HER. SHE CAN USE HER MAGIC WAND TO MAKE HIM TRANSFORM INTO PEGASUS KNIGHT...
...AND WHEN THE GOING GETS ROUGH, HE KNEELS AND KISSES LALA ON THE HAND, TRANSFORMING HER INTO LADY LALA SO THAT SHE CAN FIGHT BY HIS SIDE.
THEN, AT THE END OF THE BATTLE, THEY FINISH OFF THE MONSTER OF THE WEEK WITH THEIR COMBO MOVE, LIONHEART FLASH.

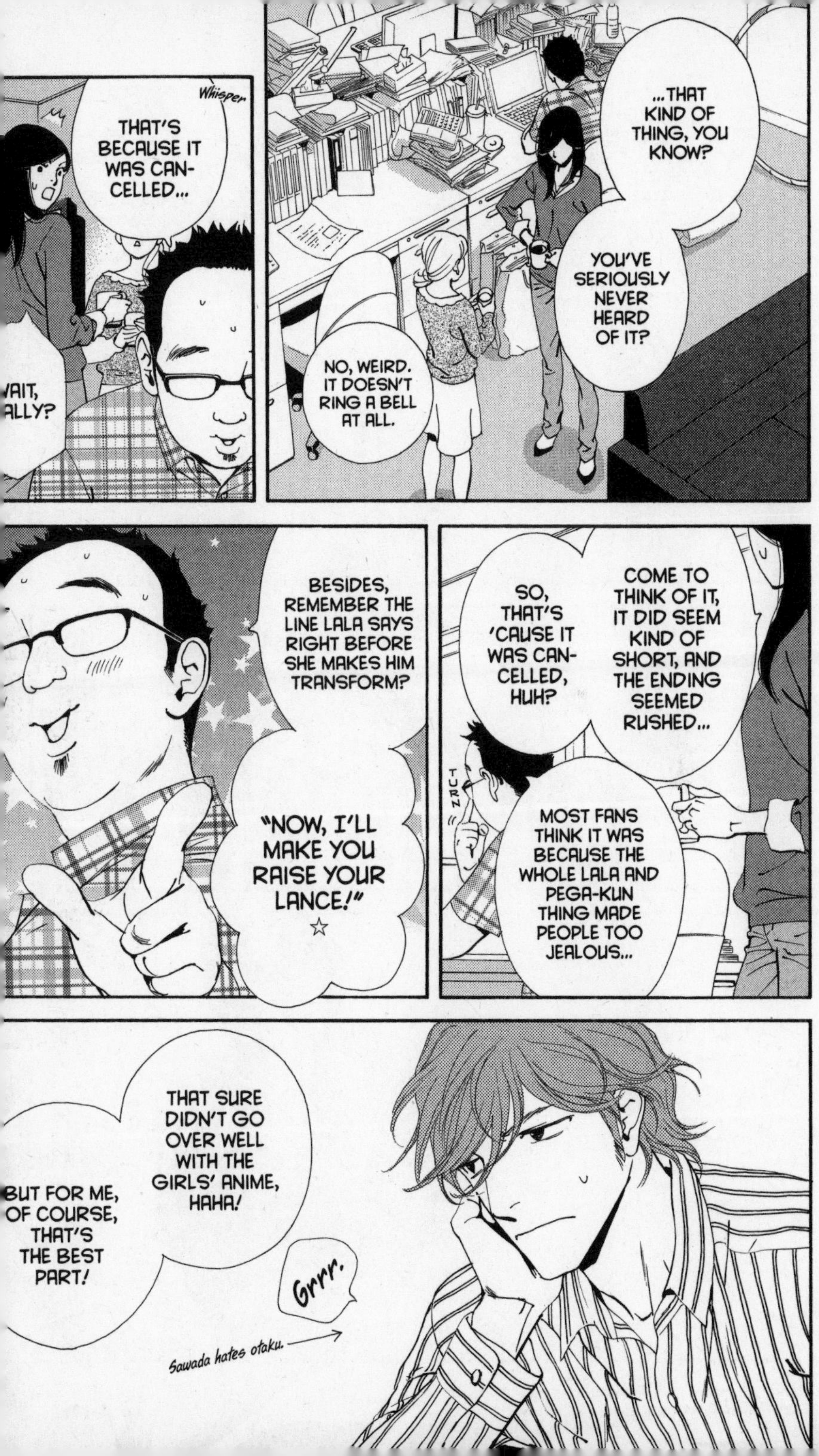
...THAT KIND OF THING, YOU KNOW?
YOU'VE SERIOUSLY NEVER HEARD OF IT?
NO, WEIRD. IT DOESN'T RING A BELL AT ALL.
Whisper
THAT'S BECAUSE IT WAS CANCELLED...
AIT, ALLY?
COME TO THINK OF IT, IT DID SEEM KIND OF SHORT, AND THE ENDING SEEMED RUSHED...
SO, THAT'S 'CAUSE IT WAS CANCELLED, HUH?
TURN
MOST FANS THINK IT WAS BECAUSE THE WHOLE LALA AND PEGA-KUN THING MADE PEOPLE TOO JEALOUS...
BESIDES, REMEMBER THE LINE LALA SAYS RIGHT BEFORE SHE MAKES HIM TRANSFORM?
"NOW, I'LL MAKE YOU RAISE YOUR LANCE!" ☆
THAT SURE DIDN'T GO OVER WELL WITH THE GIRLS' ANIME, HAHA!
BUT FOR ME, OF COURSE, THAT'S THE BEST PART!
Grrr.
Sawada hates otaku.

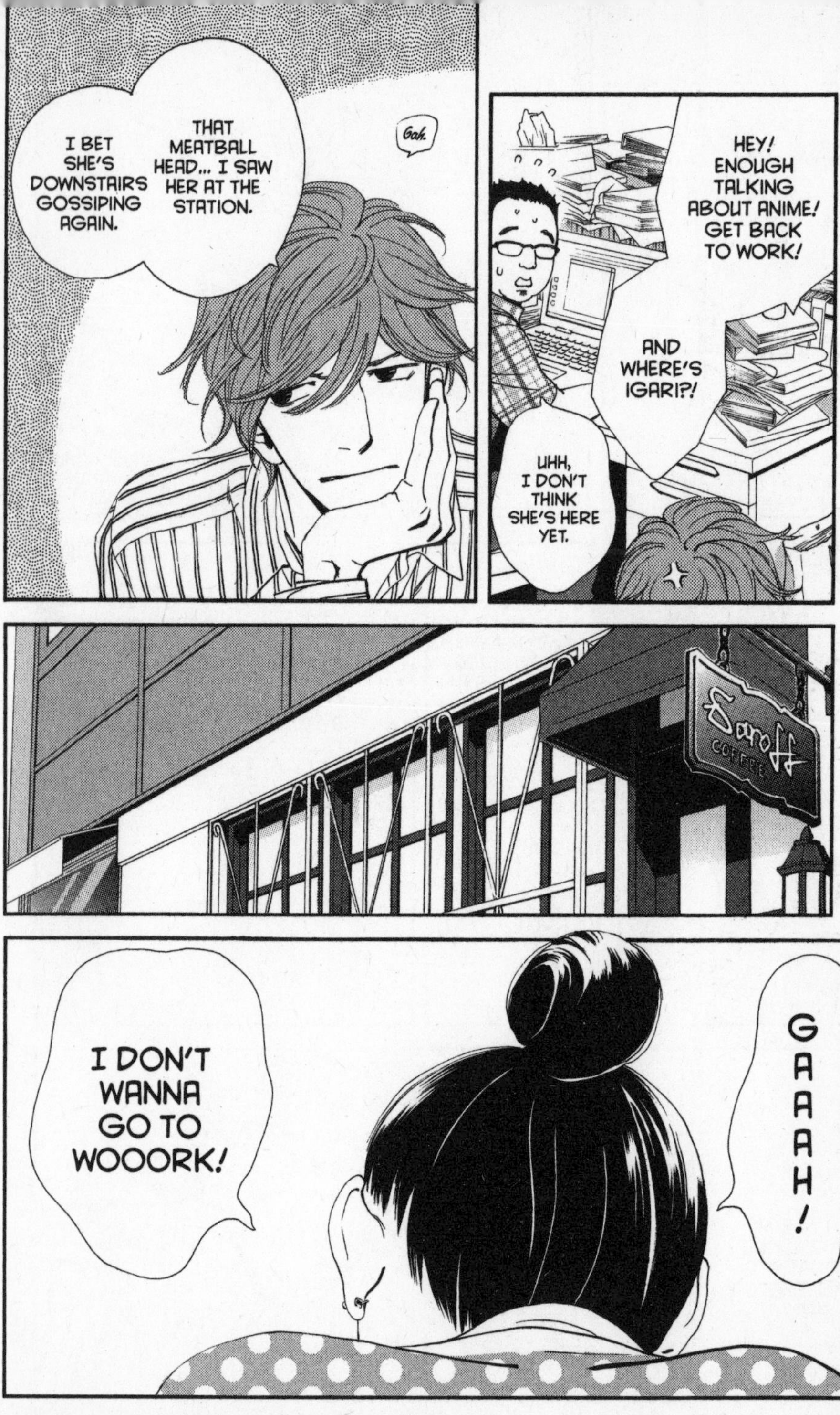
HEY! ENOUGH TALKING ABOUT ANIME! GET BACK TO WORK!
AND WHERE'S IGARI?!
UHH, I DON'T THINK SHE'S HERE YET.
Gah.
THAT MEATBALL HEAD... I SAW HER AT THE STATION.
I BET SHE'S DOWNSTAIRS GOSSIPING AGAIN.
GAAAH!
I DON'T WANNA GO TO WOOORK!

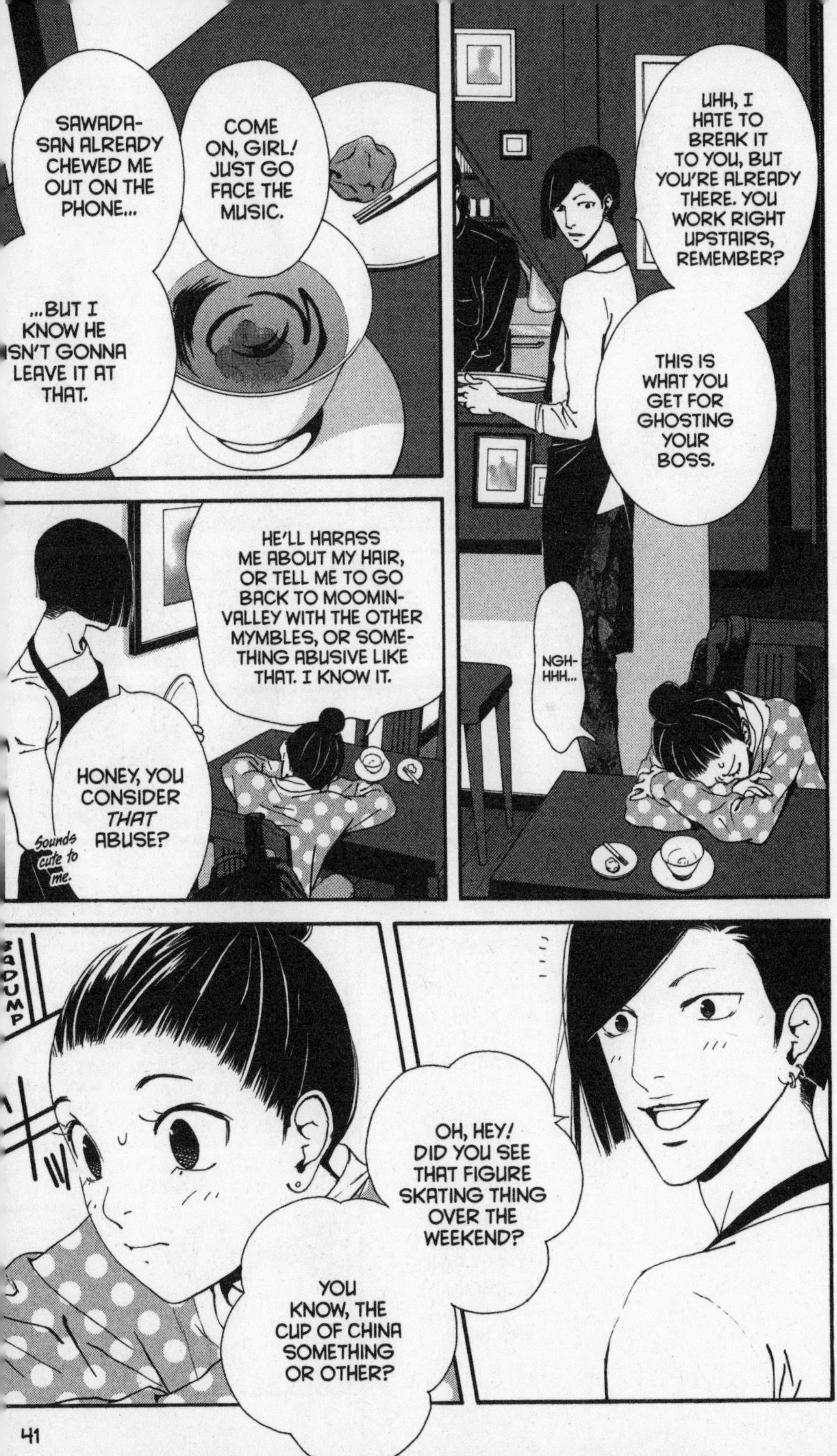
UHH, I HATE TO BREAK IT TO YOU, BUT YOU'RE ALREADY THERE. YOU WORK RIGHT UPSTAIRS, REMEMBER?
THIS IS WHAT YOU GET FOR GHOSTING YOUR BOSS.
NGH-HHH...
COME ON, GIRL! JUST GO FACE THE MUSIC.
SAWADA-SAN ALREADY CHEWED ME OUT ON THE PHONE...
...BUT I KNOW HE ISN'T GONNA LEAVE IT AT THAT.
HE'LL HARASS ME ABOUT MY HAIR, OR TELL ME TO GO BACK TO MOOMIN-VALLEY WITH THE OTHER MYMBLES, OR SOME-THING ABUSIVE LIKE THAT. I KNOW IT.
HONEY, YOU CONSIDER *THAT* ABUSE?
Sounds cute to me.
OH, HEY! DID YOU SEE THAT FIGURE SKATING THING OVER THE WEEKEND?
YOU KNOW, THE CUP OF CHINA SOMETHING OR OTHER?
BADUMP

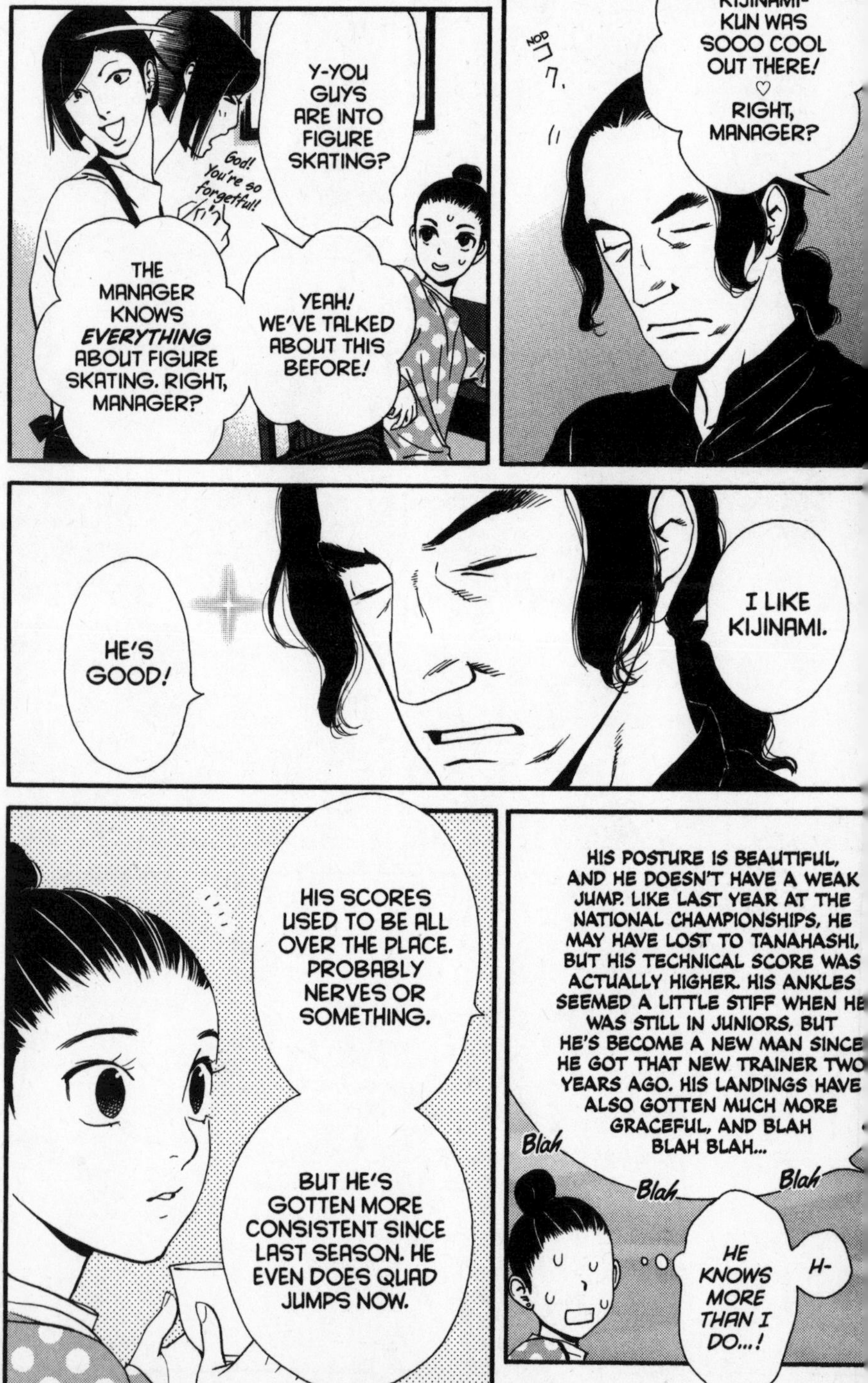
KIJINAMI-KUN WAS SOOO COOL OUT THERE! ♡ RIGHT, MANAGER?
NOD
Y-YOU GUYS ARE INTO FIGURE SKATING?
YEAH! WE'VE TALKED ABOUT THIS BEFORE!
God! You're so forgetful!
THE MANAGER KNOWS *EVERYTHING* ABOUT FIGURE SKATING. RIGHT, MANAGER?
I LIKE KIJINAMI.
HE'S GOOD!
HIS POSTURE IS BEAUTIFUL, AND HE DOESN'T HAVE A WEAK JUMP. LIKE LAST YEAR AT THE NATIONAL CHAMPIONSHIPS, HE MAY HAVE LOST TO TANAHASHI, BUT HIS TECHNICAL SCORE WAS ACTUALLY HIGHER. HIS ANKLES SEEMED A LITTLE STIFF WHEN HE WAS STILL IN JUNIORS, BUT HE'S BECOME A NEW MAN SINCE HE GOT THAT NEW TRAINER TWO YEARS AGO. HIS LANDINGS HAVE ALSO GOTTEN MUCH MORE GRACEFUL, AND BLAH BLAH BLAH...
Blah
Blah
Blah
H-
HE KNOWS MORE THAN I DO...!
HIS SCORES USED TO BE ALL OVER THE PLACE. PROBABLY NERVES OR SOMETHING.
BUT HE'S GOTTEN MORE CONSISTENT SINCE LAST SEASON. HE EVEN DOES QUAD JUMPS NOW.

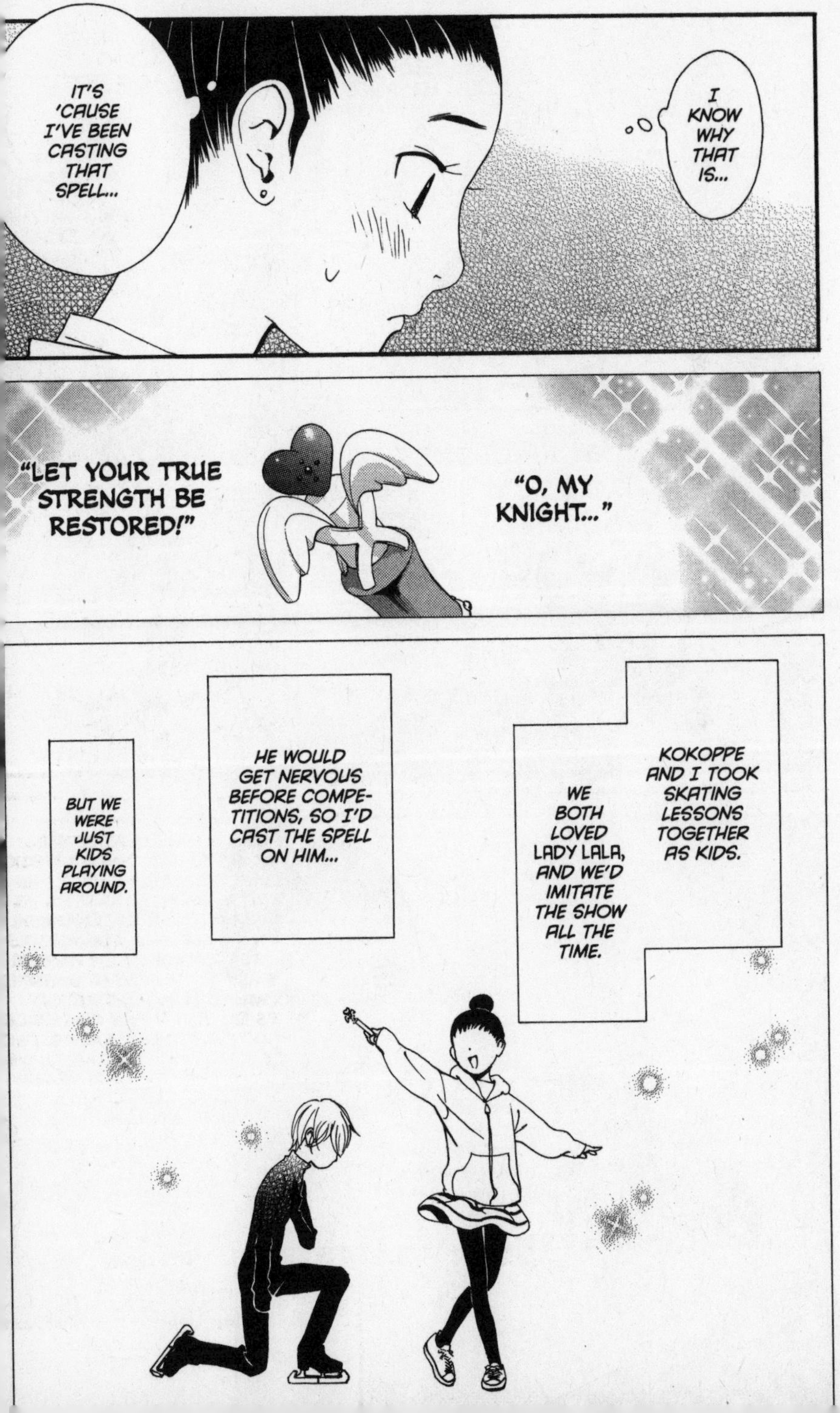
I KNOW WHY THAT IS...
IT'S 'CAUSE I'VE BEEN CASTING THAT SPELL...
"O, MY KNIGHT..."
"LET YOUR TRUE STRENGTH BE RESTORED!"
KOKOPPE AND I TOOK SKATING LESSONS TOGETHER AS KIDS.
WE BOTH LOVED LADY LALA, AND WE'D IMITATE THE SHOW ALL THE TIME.
HE WOULD GET NERVOUS BEFORE COMPE-TITIONS, SO I'D CAST THE SPELL ON HIM...
BUT WE WERE JUST KIDS PLAYING AROUND.

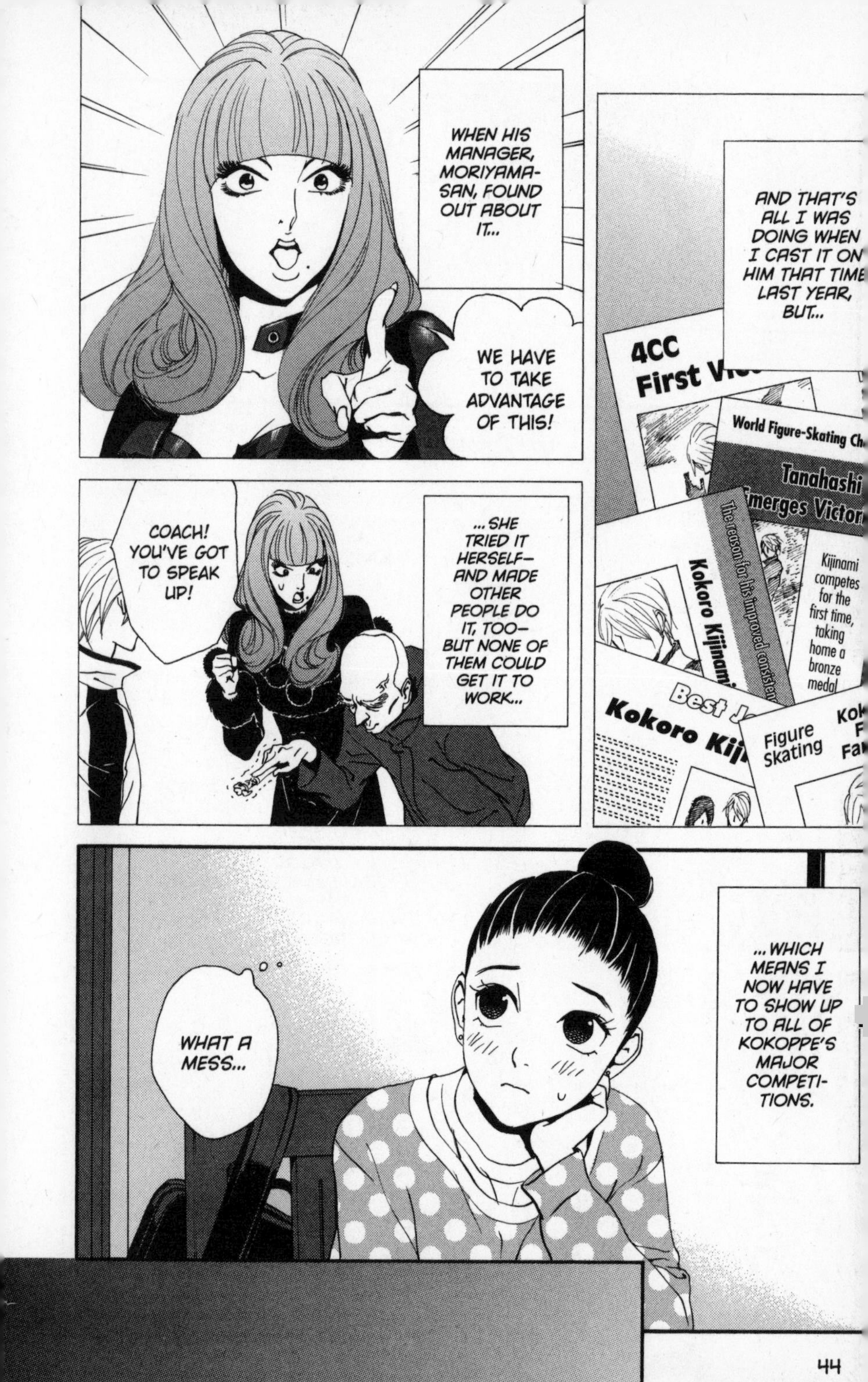
AND THAT'S ALL I WAS DOING WHEN I CAST IT ON HIM THAT TIME LAST YEAR, BUT...
4CC
Tanahashi
Kijinami competes for the first time, taking home a bronze medal
Figure Skating
WHEN HIS MANAGER, MORIYAMA-SAN, FOUND OUT ABOUT IT...
WE HAVE TO TAKE ADVANTAGE OF THIS!
...SHE TRIED IT HERSELF—AND MADE OTHER PEOPLE DO IT, TOO—BUT NONE OF THEM COULD GET IT TO WORK...
COACH! YOU'VE GOT TO SPEAK UP!
...WHICH MEANS I NOW HAVE TO SHOW UP TO ALL OF KOKOPPE'S MAJOR COMPETITIONS.
WHAT A MESS...

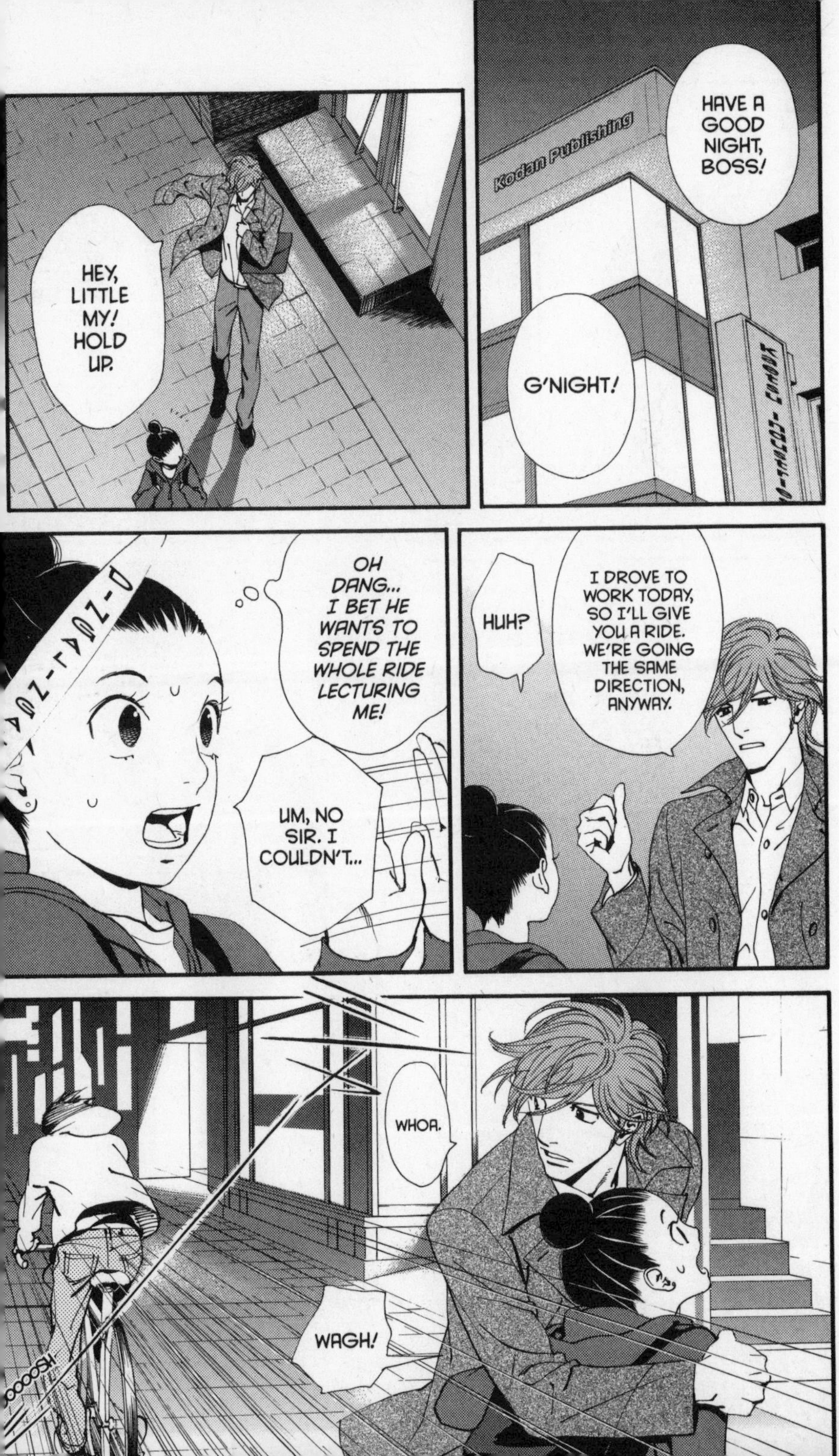
Kodan Publishing
HAVE A GOOD NIGHT, BOSS!
G'NIGHT!
HEY, LITTLE MY! HOLD UP.
I DROVE TO WORK TODAY, SO I'LL GIVE YOU A RIDE. WE'RE GOING THE SAME DIRECTION, ANYWAY.
HUH?
OH DANG... I BET HE WANTS TO SPEND THE WHOLE RIDE LECTURING ME!
UM, NO SIR. I COULDN'T...
WHOA.
WAGH!

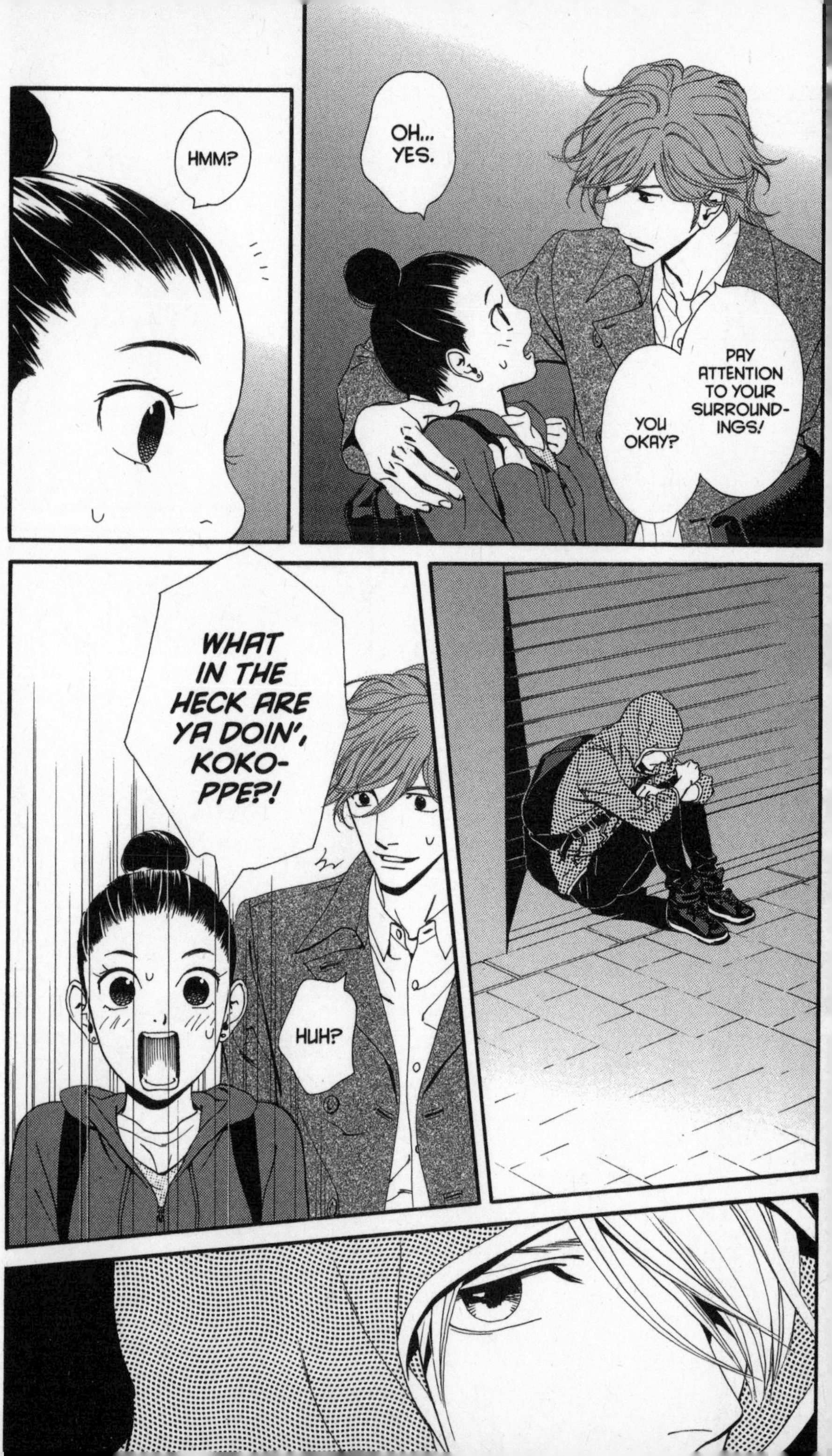
PAY ATTENTION TO YOUR SURROUND-INGS!
YOU OKAY?
OH... YES.
HMM?
WHAT IN THE HECK ARE YA DOIN', KOKO-PPE?!
HUH?

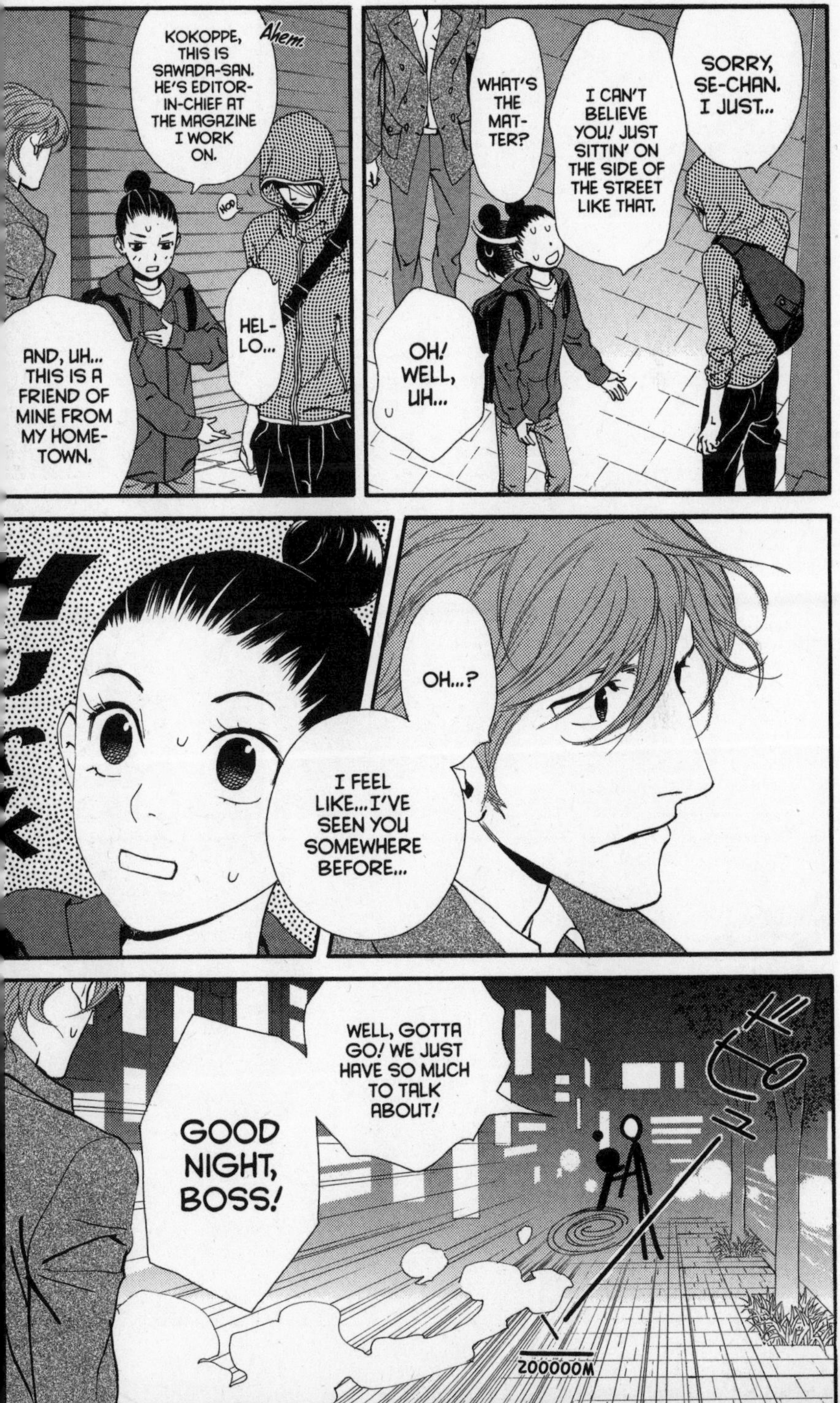
SORRY, SE-CHAN. I JUST...
I CAN'T BELIEVE YOU! JUST SITTIN' ON THE SIDE OF THE STREET LIKE THAT.
WHAT'S THE MAT-TER?
OH! WELL, UH...
Ahem.
KOKOPPE, THIS IS SAWADA-SAN. HE'S EDITOR-IN-CHIEF AT THE MAGAZINE I WORK ON.
NOD
HEL-LO...
AND, UH... THIS IS A FRIEND OF MINE FROM MY HOME-TOWN.
OH...?
I FEEL LIKE...I'VE SEEN YOU SOMEWHERE BEFORE...
WELL, GOTTA GO! WE JUST HAVE SO MUCH TO TALK ABOUT!
GOOD NIGHT, BOSS!
ZOOOOOM

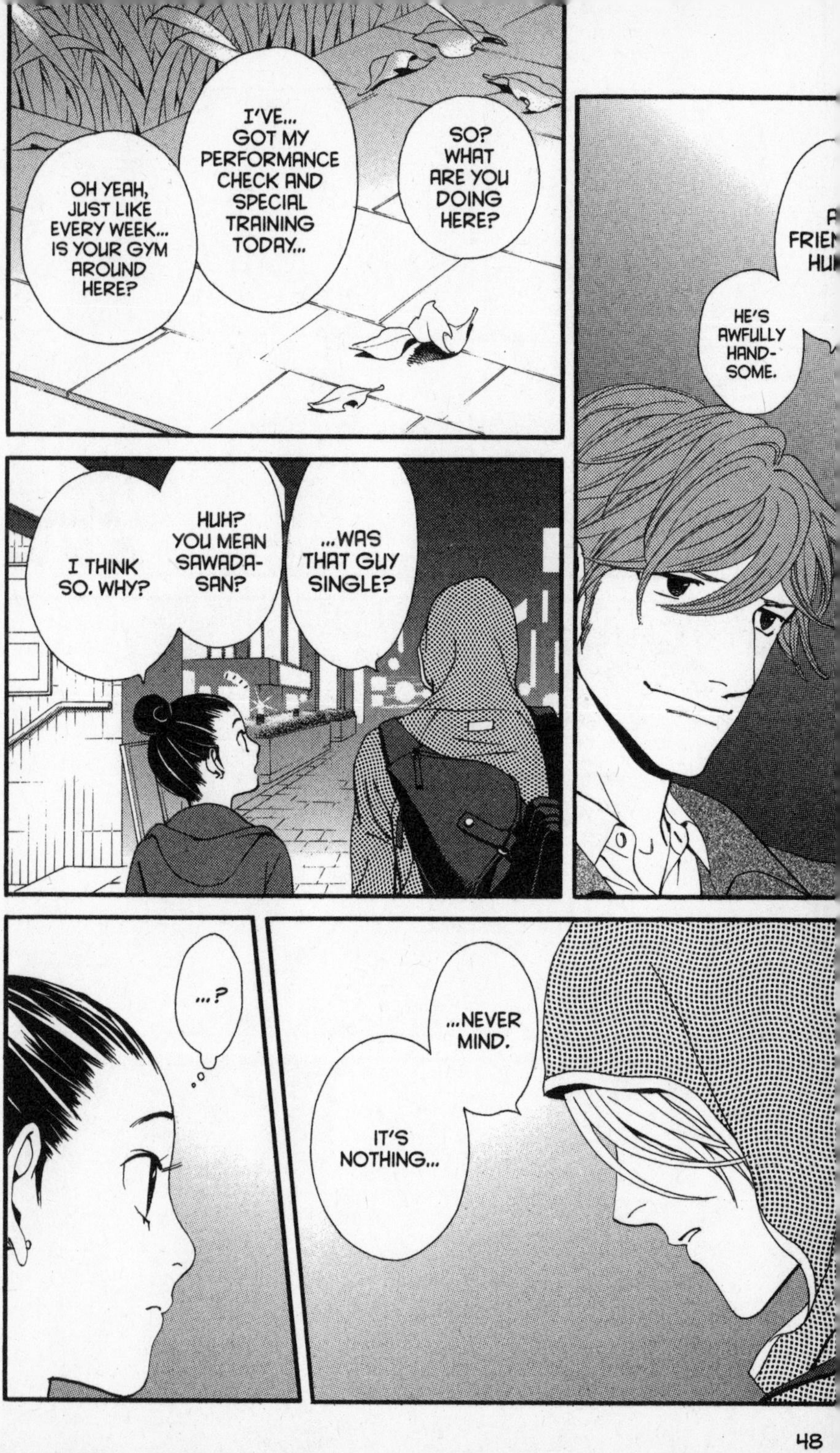
HE'S AWFULLY HAND-SOME.
SO? WHAT ARE YOU DOING HERE?
I'VE... GOT MY PERFORMANCE CHECK AND SPECIAL TRAINING TODAY...
OH YEAH, JUST LIKE EVERY WEEK... IS YOUR GYM AROUND HERE?
...WAS THAT GUY SINGLE?
HUH? YOU MEAN SAWADA-SAN?
I THINK SO. WHY?
...NEVER MIND.
IT'S NOTHING...
...?

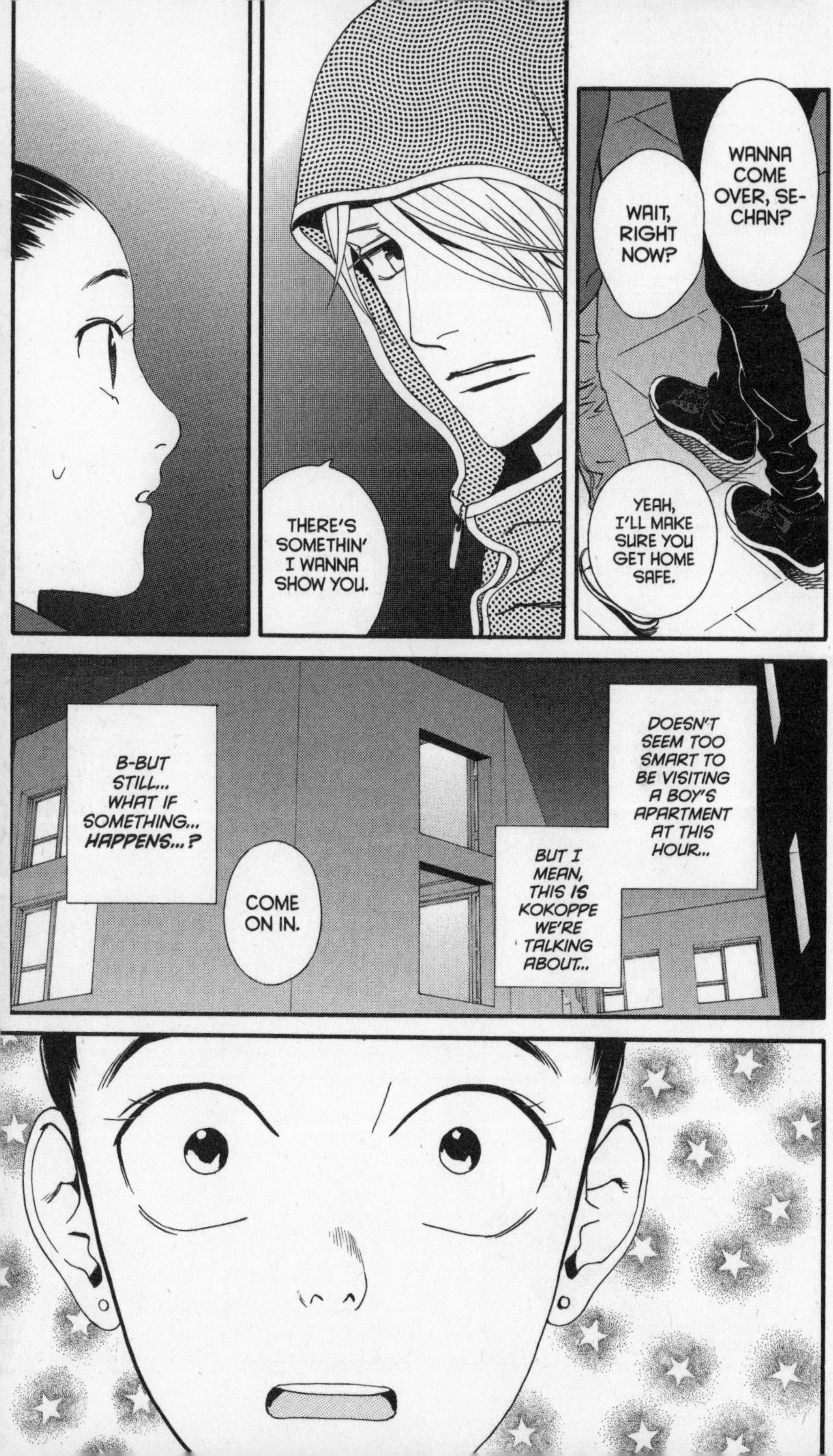
WANNA COME OVER, SE-CHAN?
WAIT, RIGHT NOW?
YEAH, I'LL MAKE SURE YOU GET HOME SAFE.
THERE'S SOMETHIN' I WANNA SHOW YOU.
DOESN'T SEEM TOO SMART TO BE VISITING A BOY'S APARTMENT AT THIS HOUR...
BUT I MEAN, THIS *IS* KOKOPPE WE'RE TALKING ABOUT...
COME ON IN.
B-BUT STILL... WHAT IF SOMETHING... *HAPPENS...?*

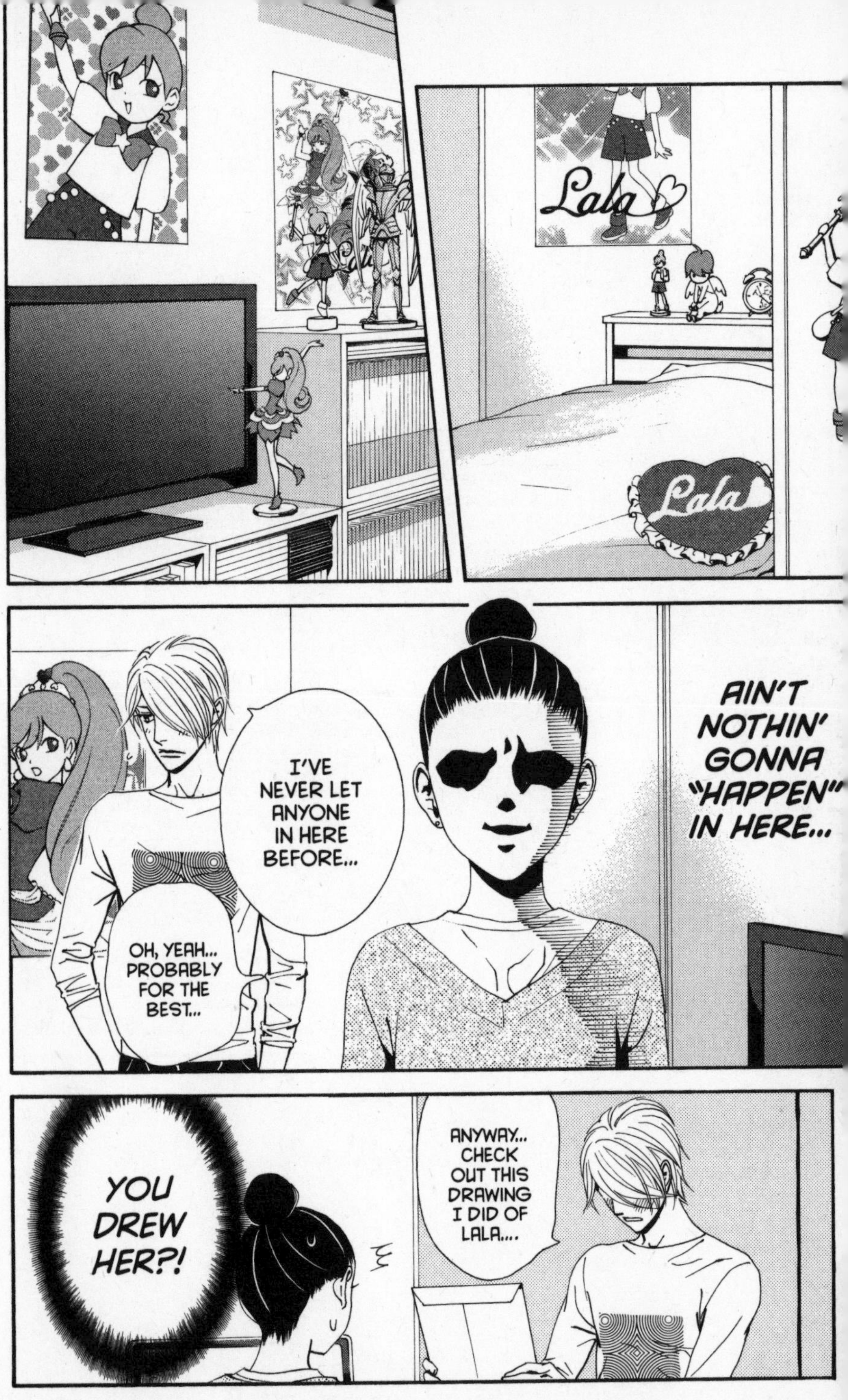
Lala
Lala
AIN'T NOTHIN' GONNA "HAPPEN" IN HERE...
I'VE NEVER LET ANYONE IN HERE BEFORE...
OH, YEAH... PROBABLY FOR THE BEST...
ANYWAY... CHECK OUT THIS DRAWING I DID OF LALA....
YOU DREW HER?!

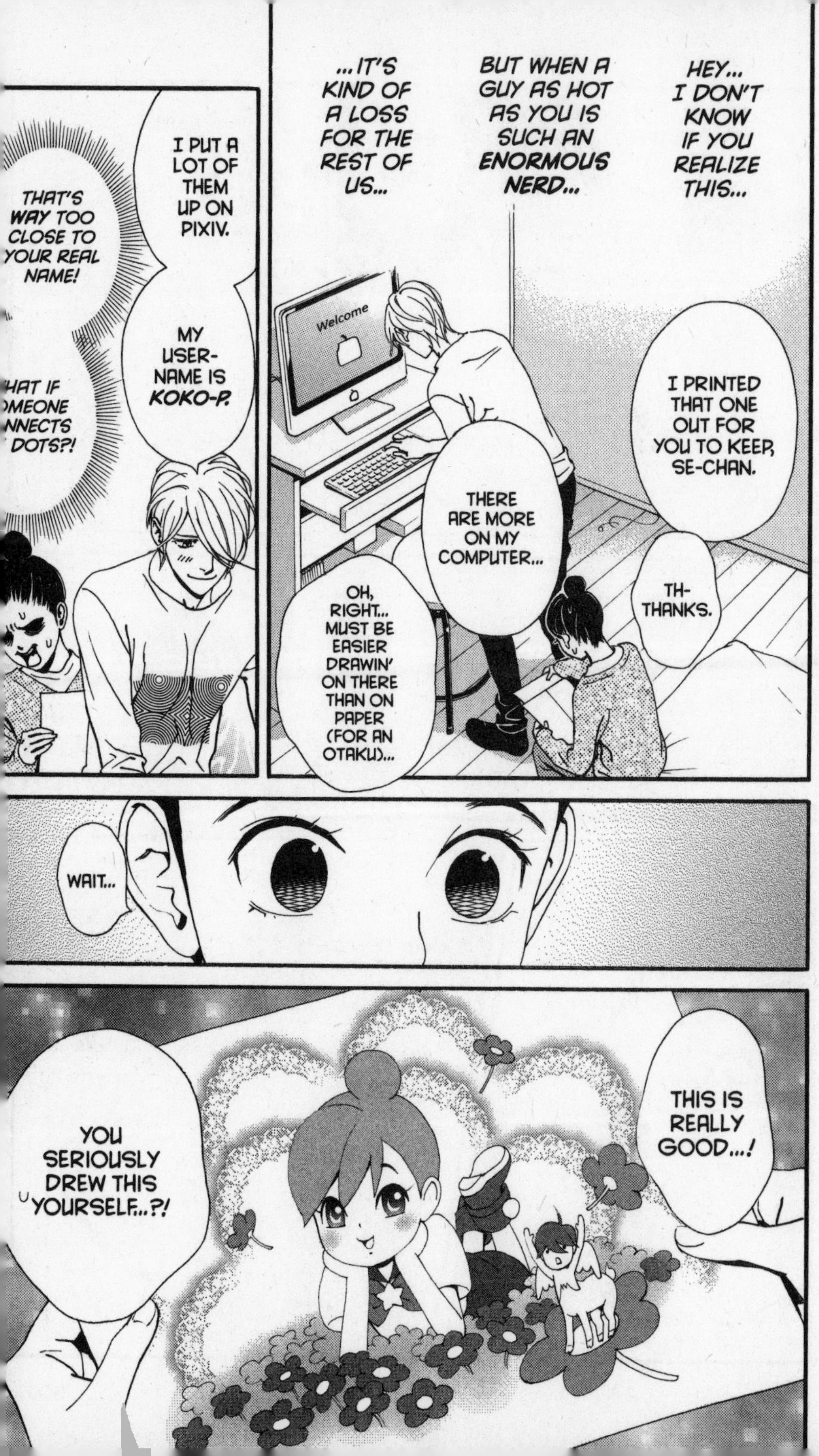
HEY... I DON'T KNOW IF YOU REALIZE THIS...
BUT WHEN A GUY AS HOT AS YOU IS SUCH AN ENORMOUS NERD...
...IT'S KIND OF A LOSS FOR THE REST OF US...
Welcome
I PRINTED THAT ONE OUT FOR YOU TO KEEP, SE-CHAN.
TH-THANKS.
THERE ARE MORE ON MY COMPUTER...
OH, RIGHT... MUST BE EASIER DRAWIN' ON THERE THAN ON PAPER (FOR AN OTAKU)...
I PUT A LOT OF THEM UP ON PIXIV.
MY USER-NAME IS KOKO-P.
THAT'S WAY TOO CLOSE TO YOUR REAL NAME!
HAT IF OMEONE NNECTS DOTS?!
WAIT...
THIS IS REALLY GOOD...!
YOU SERIOUSLY DREW THIS YOURSELF...?!

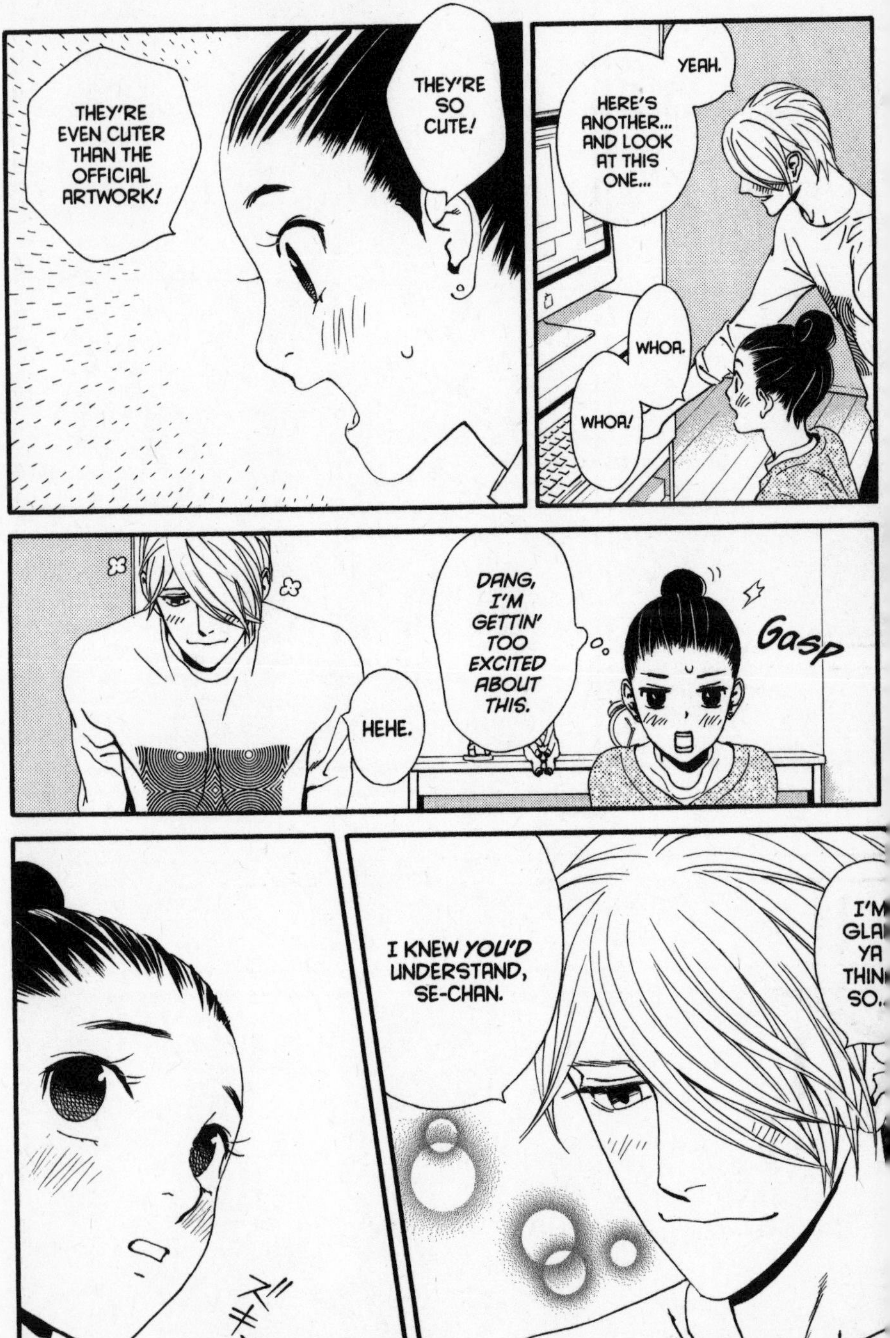
YEAH.
HERE'S ANOTHER... AND LOOK AT THIS ONE...
WHOA.
WHOA!
THEY'RE SO CUTE!
THEY'RE EVEN CUTER THAN THE OFFICIAL ARTWORK!
Gasp
DANG, I'M GETTIN' TOO EXCITED ABOUT THIS.
HEHE.
I'M GLA YA THIN SO..
I KNEW *YOU'D* UNDERSTAND, SE-CHAN.
PANG

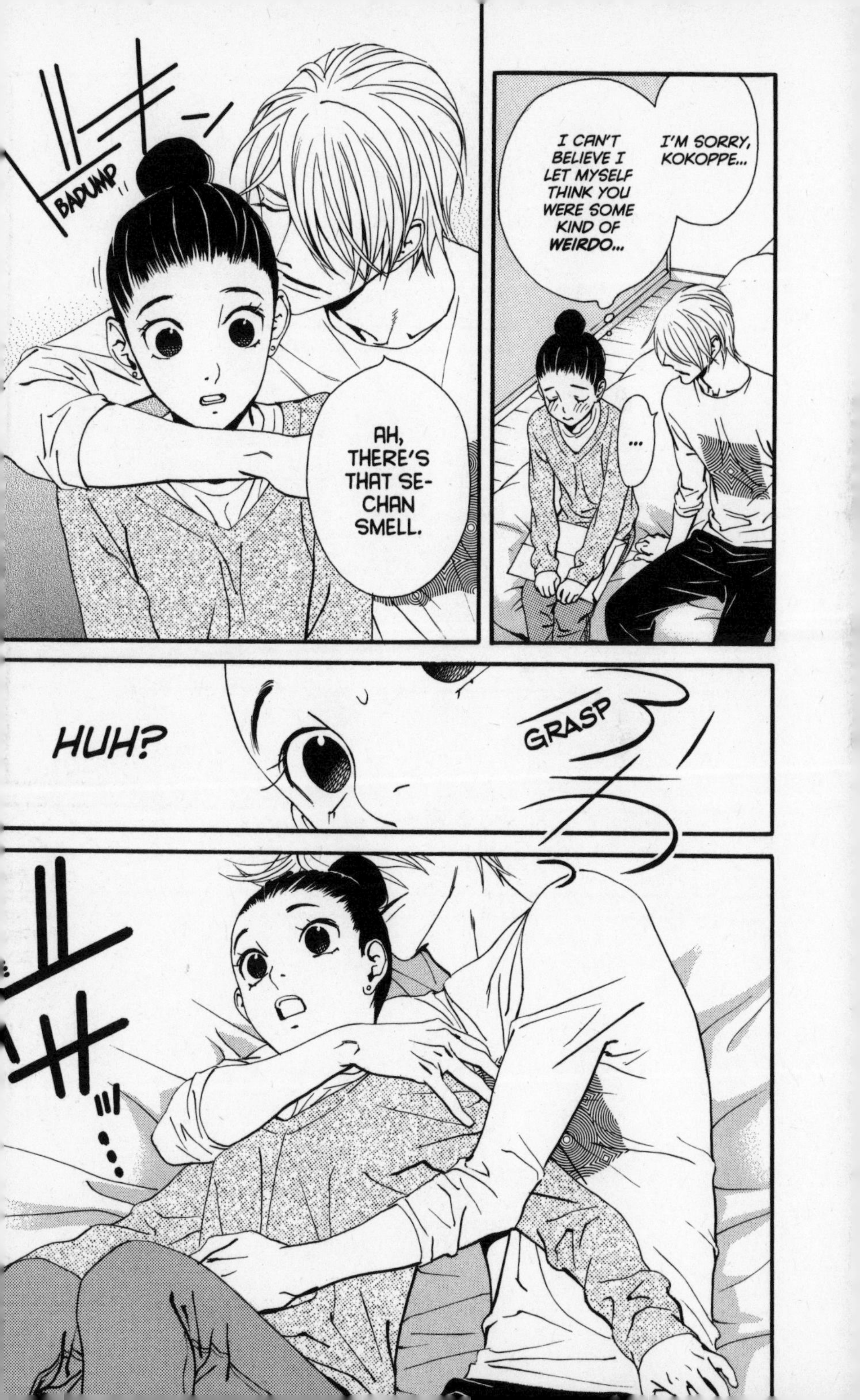
I'M SORRY, KOKOPPE...
I CAN'T BELIEVE I LET MYSELF THINK YOU WERE SOME KIND OF WEIRDO...
...
BADUMP
AH, THERE'S THAT SE-CHAN SMELL.
GRASP
HUH?

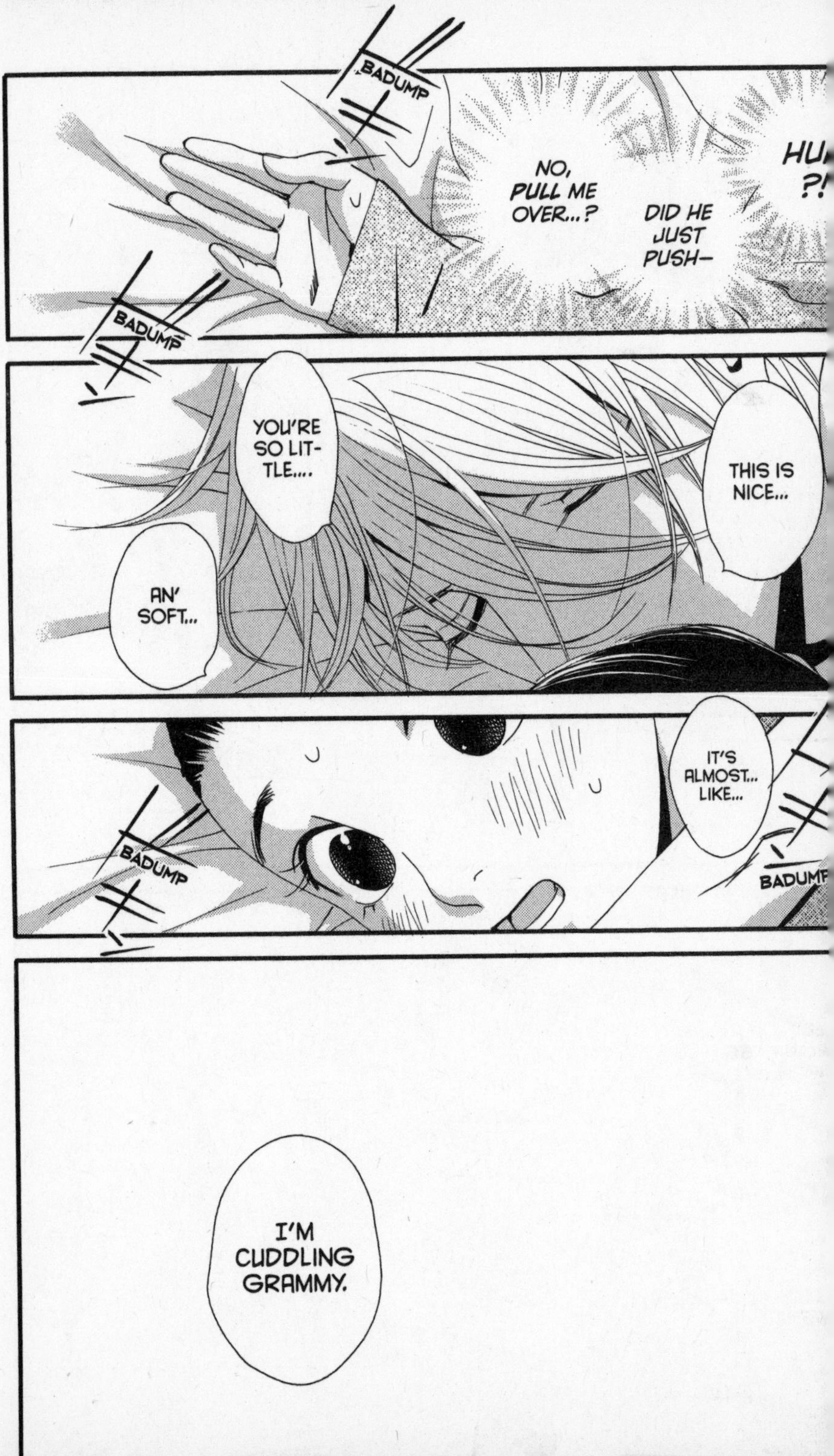
HU ?!
DID HE JUST PUSH—
NO, PULL ME OVER...?
BADUMP
BADUMP
THIS IS NICE...
YOU'RE SO LIT-TLE....
AN' SOFT...
IT'S ALMOST... LIKE...
BADUMP
BADUMP
I'M CUDDLING GRAMMY.

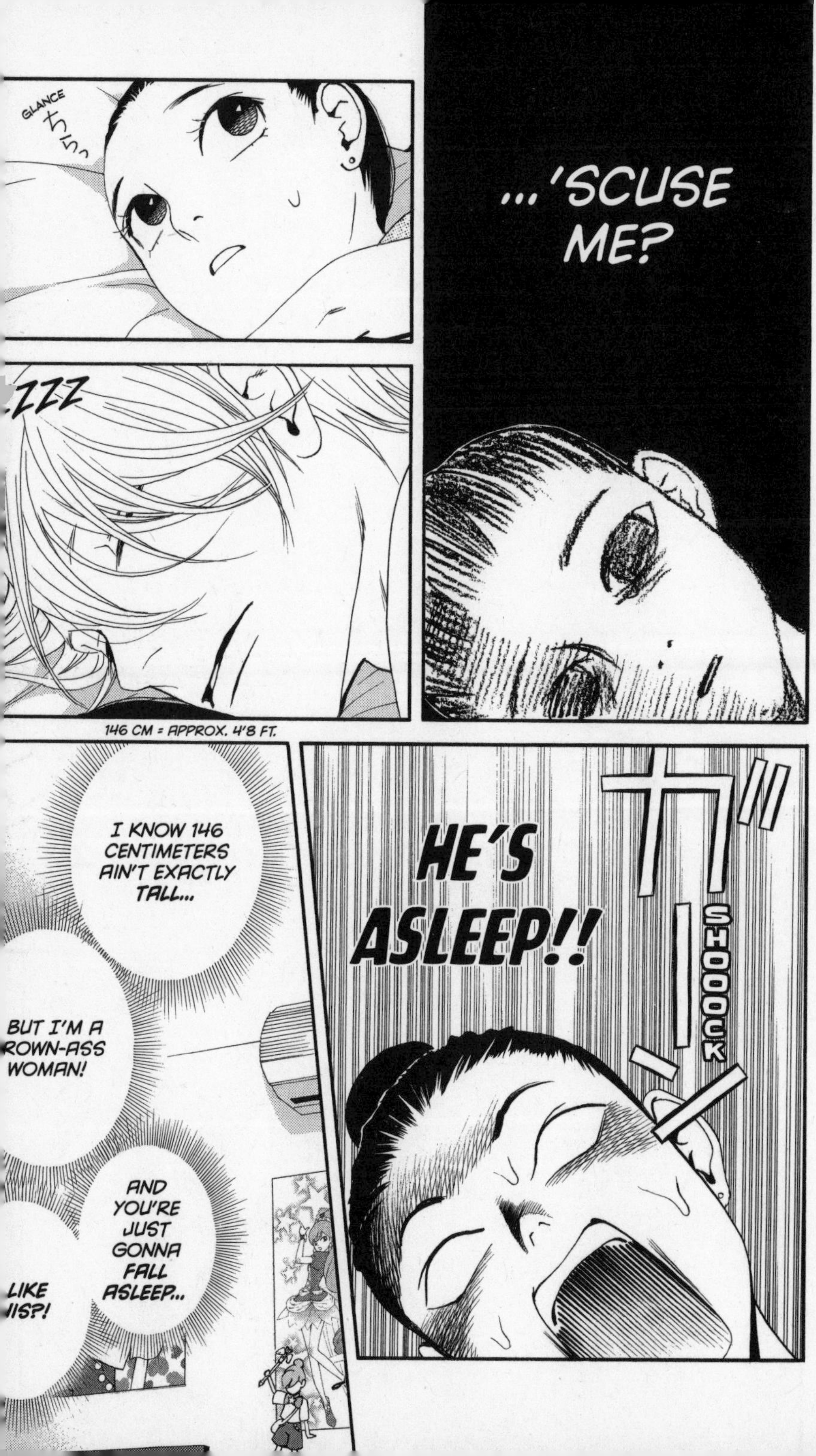
...'SCUSE ME?
GLANCE
ZZZ
146 CM = APPROX. 4'8 FT.
HE'S ASLEEP!!
SHOOOCK
I KNOW 146 CENTIMETERS AIN'T EXACTLY TALL...
BUT I'M A ROWN-ASS WOMAN!
AND YOU'RE JUST GONNA FALL ASLEEP...
LIKE IIS?!

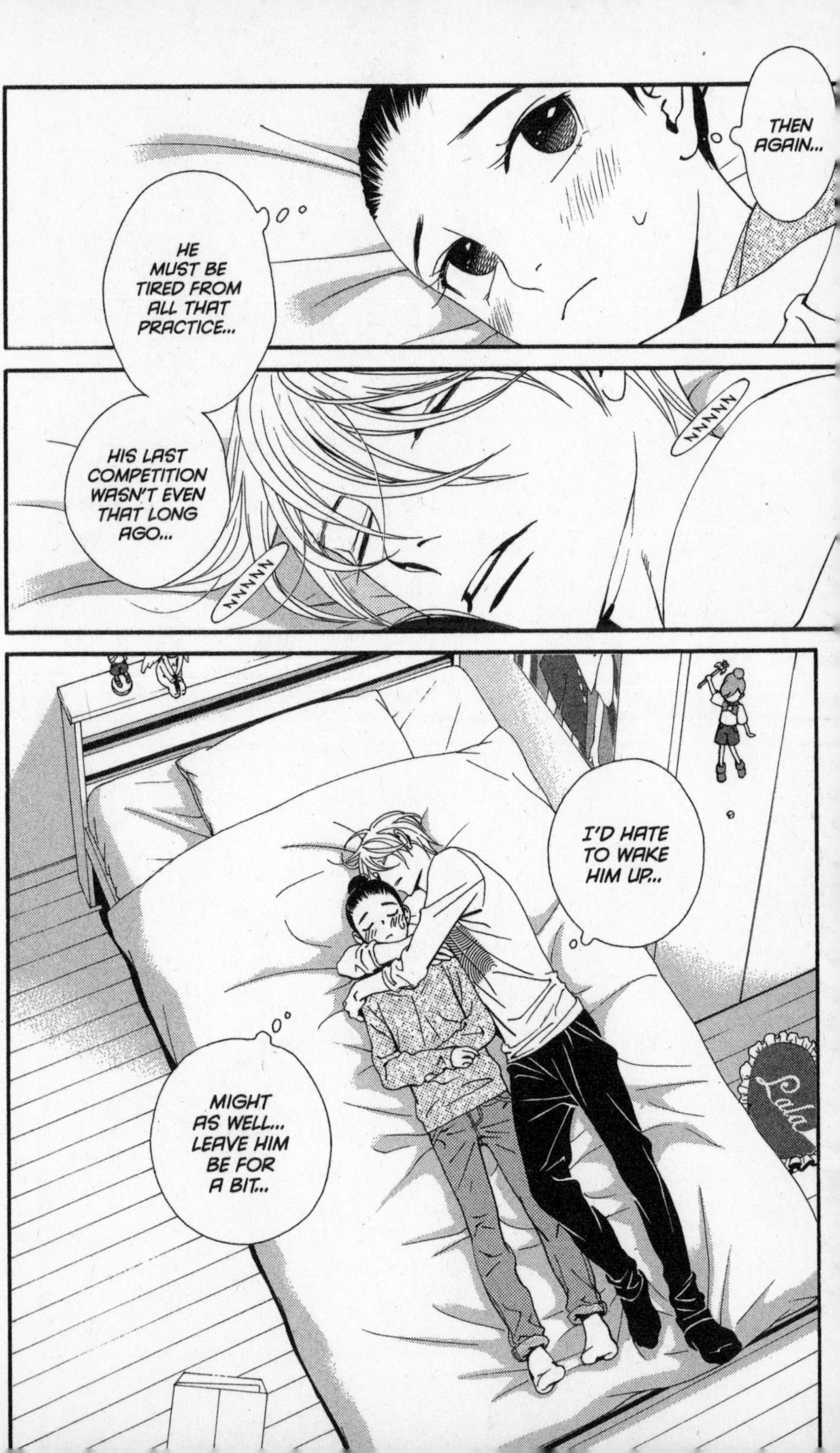
THEN AGAIN...
HE MUST BE TIRED FROM ALL THAT PRACTICE...
NNNNN
HIS LAST COMPETITION WASN'T EVEN THAT LONG AGO...
NNNNN
I'D HATE TO WAKE HIM UP...
MIGHT AS WELL... LEAVE HIM BE FOR A BIT...
Lala

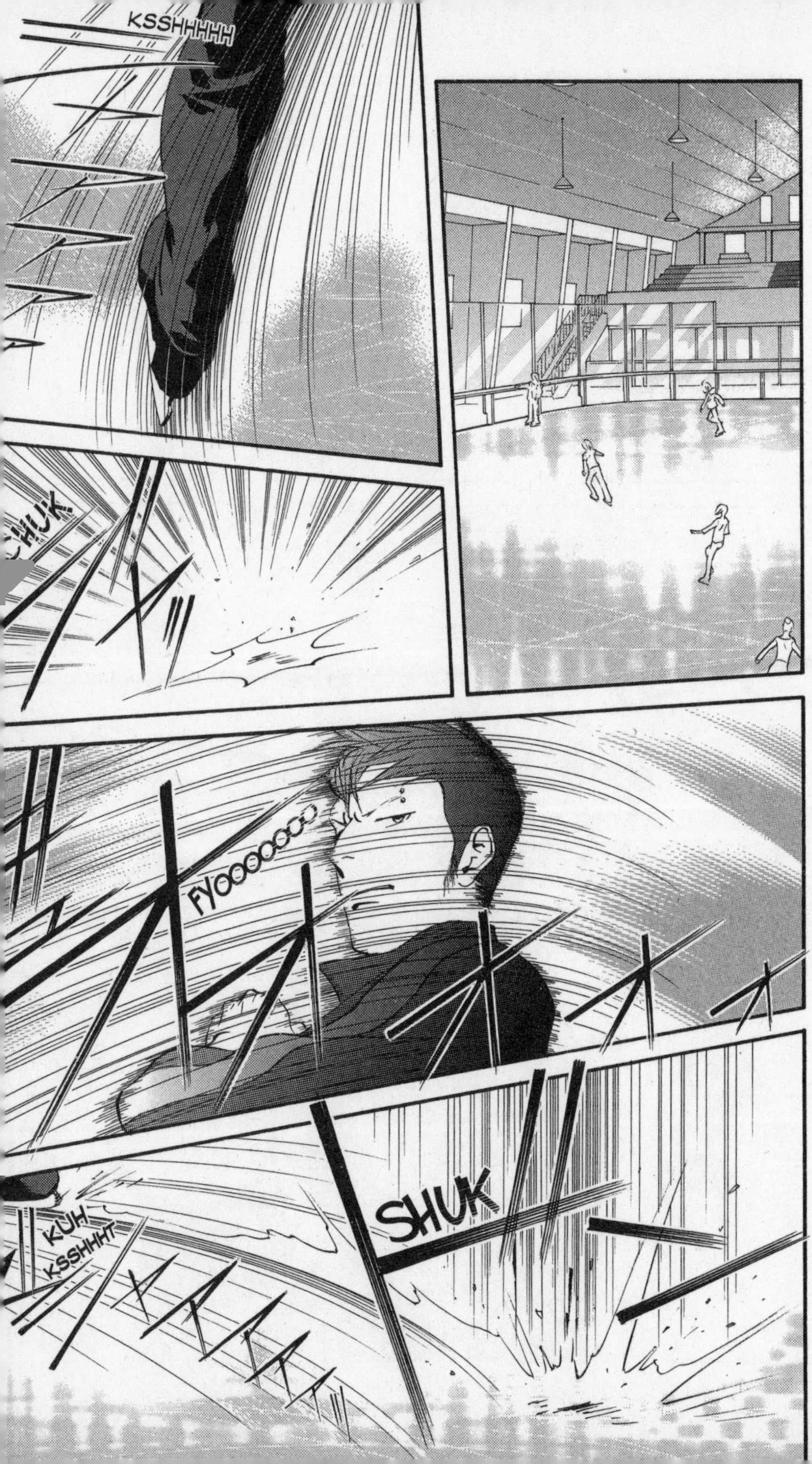
KSSHHHHH
CHUK
FYOOOOOOO
SHUK
KUH KSSHHHT

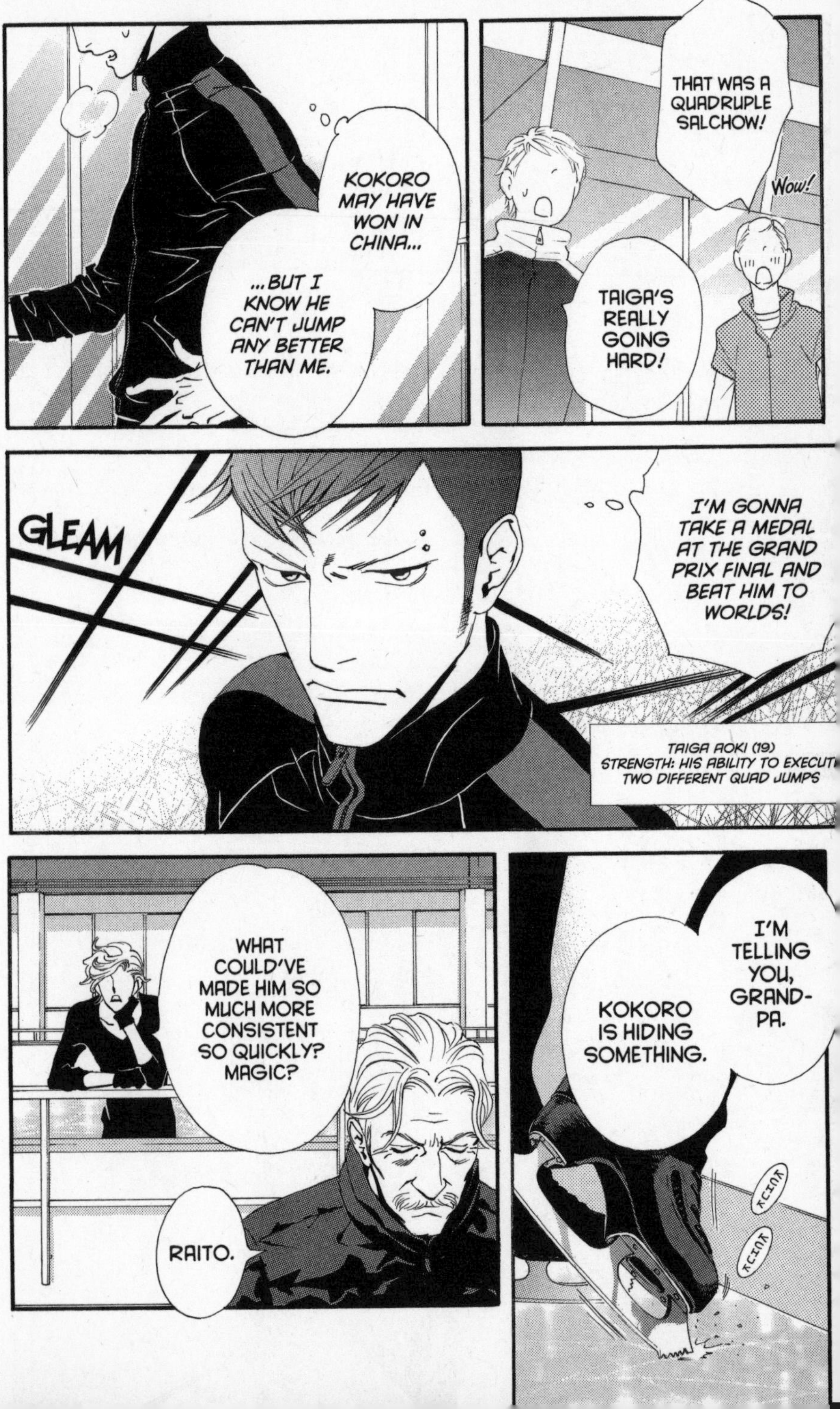
THAT WAS A QUADRUPLE SALCHOW!
Wow!
TAIGA'S REALLY GOING HARD!
KOKORO MAY HAVE WON IN CHINA...
...BUT I KNOW HE CAN'T JUMP ANY BETTER THAN ME.
I'M GONNA TAKE A MEDAL AT THE GRAND PRIX FINAL AND BEAT HIM TO WORLDS!
GLEAM
TAIGA AOKI (19)
STRENGTH: HIS ABILITY TO EXECUT
TWO DIFFERENT QUAD JUMPS
I'M TELLING YOU, GRAND-PA.
KOKORO IS HIDING SOMETHING.
WHAT COULD'VE MADE HIM SO MUCH MORE CONSISTENT SO QUICKLY? MAGIC?
RAITO.

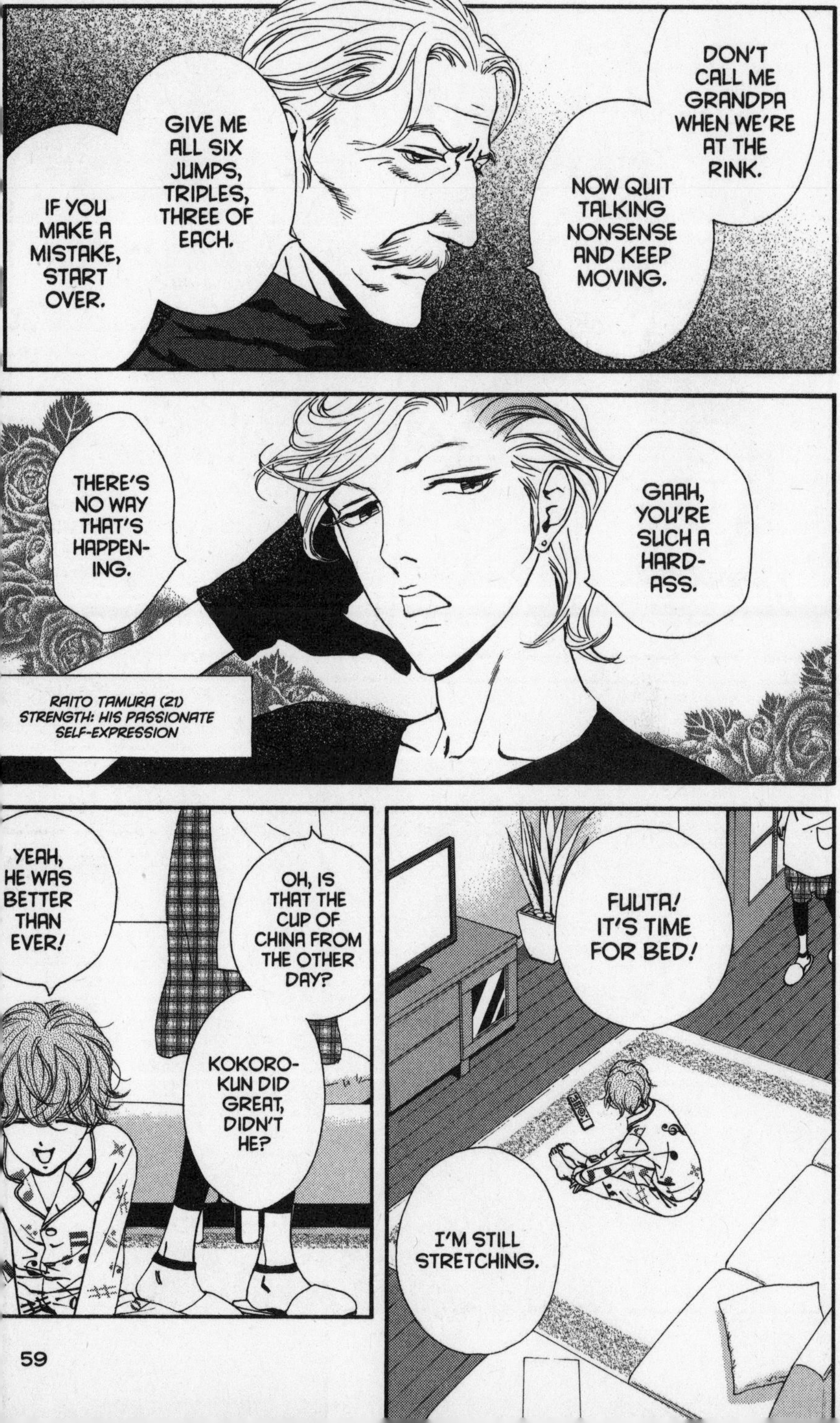
DON'T CALL ME GRANDPA WHEN WE'RE AT THE RINK.
NOW QUIT TALKING NONSENSE AND KEEP MOVING.
GIVE ME ALL SIX JUMPS, TRIPLES, THREE OF EACH.
IF YOU MAKE A MISTAKE, START OVER.
GAAH, YOU'RE SUCH A HARD-ASS.
THERE'S NO WAY THAT'S HAPPEN-ING.
RAITO TAMURA (21) STRENGTH: HIS PASSIONATE SELF-EXPRESSION
FUUTA! IT'S TIME FOR BED!
I'M STILL STRETCHING.
OH, IS THAT THE CUP OF CHINA FROM THE OTHER DAY?
KOKORO-KUN DID GREAT, DIDN'T HE?
YEAH, HE WAS BETTER THAN EVER!

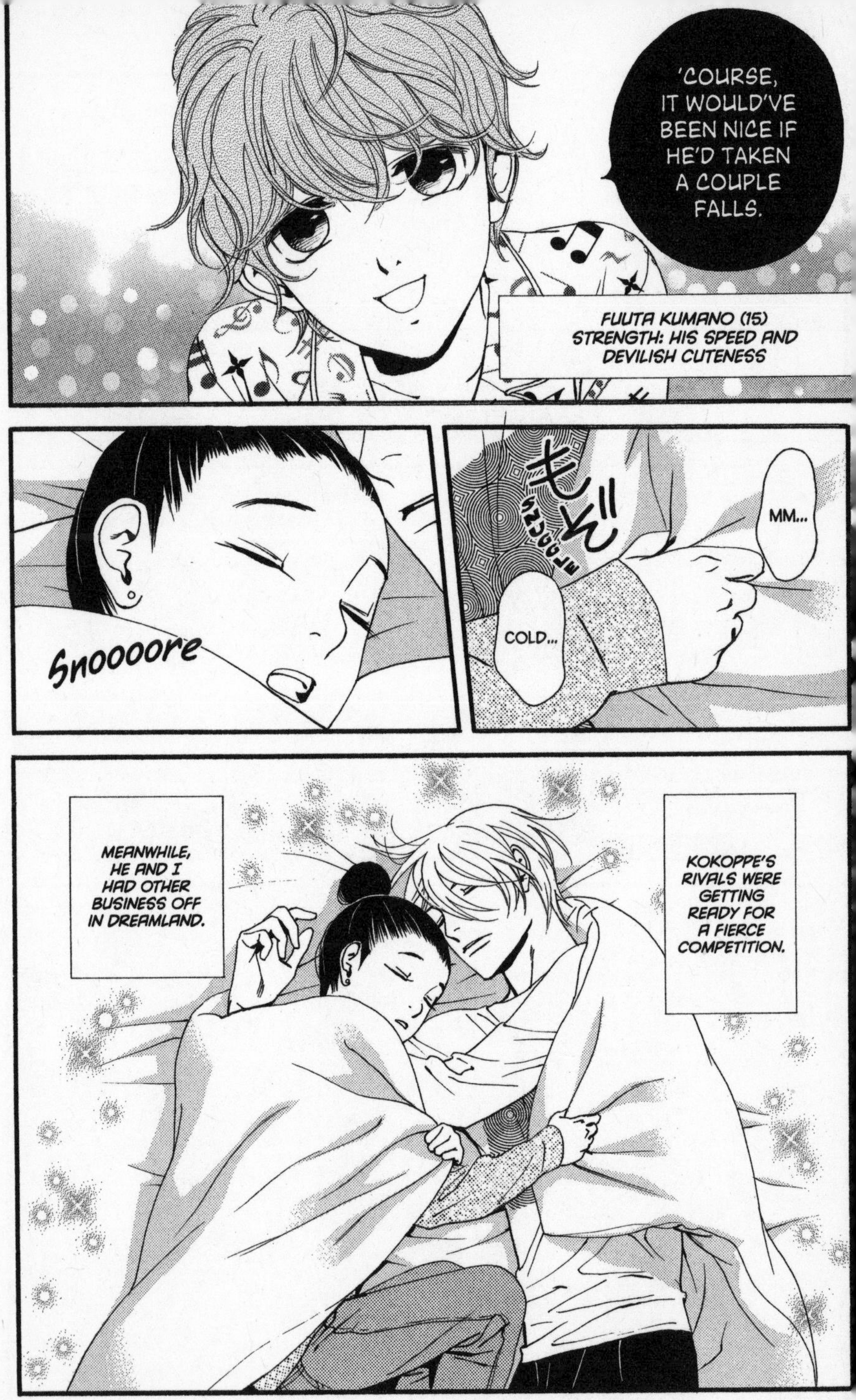
'COURSE, IT WOULD'VE BEEN NICE IF HE'D TAKEN A COUPLE FALLS.
FUUTA KUMANO (15) STRENGTH: HIS SPEED AND DEVILISH CUTENESS
もぞ
SNUGGLE
MM...
COLD...
Snoooore
KOKOPPE'S RIVALS WERE GETTING READY FOR A FIERCE COMPETITION.
MEANWHILE, HE AND I HAD OTHER BUSINESS OFF IN DREAMLAND.

Spell 3
I'd Do Anything

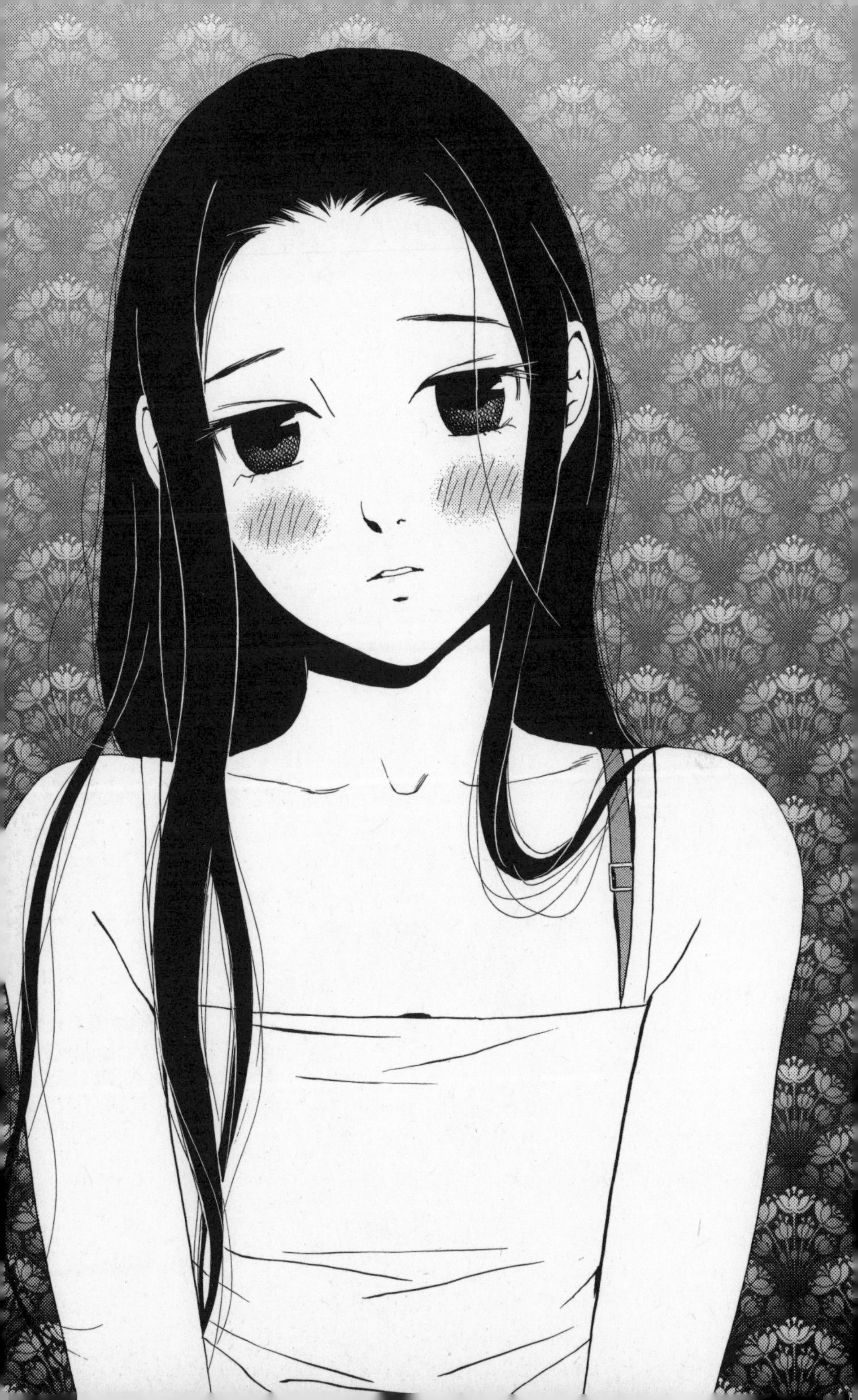

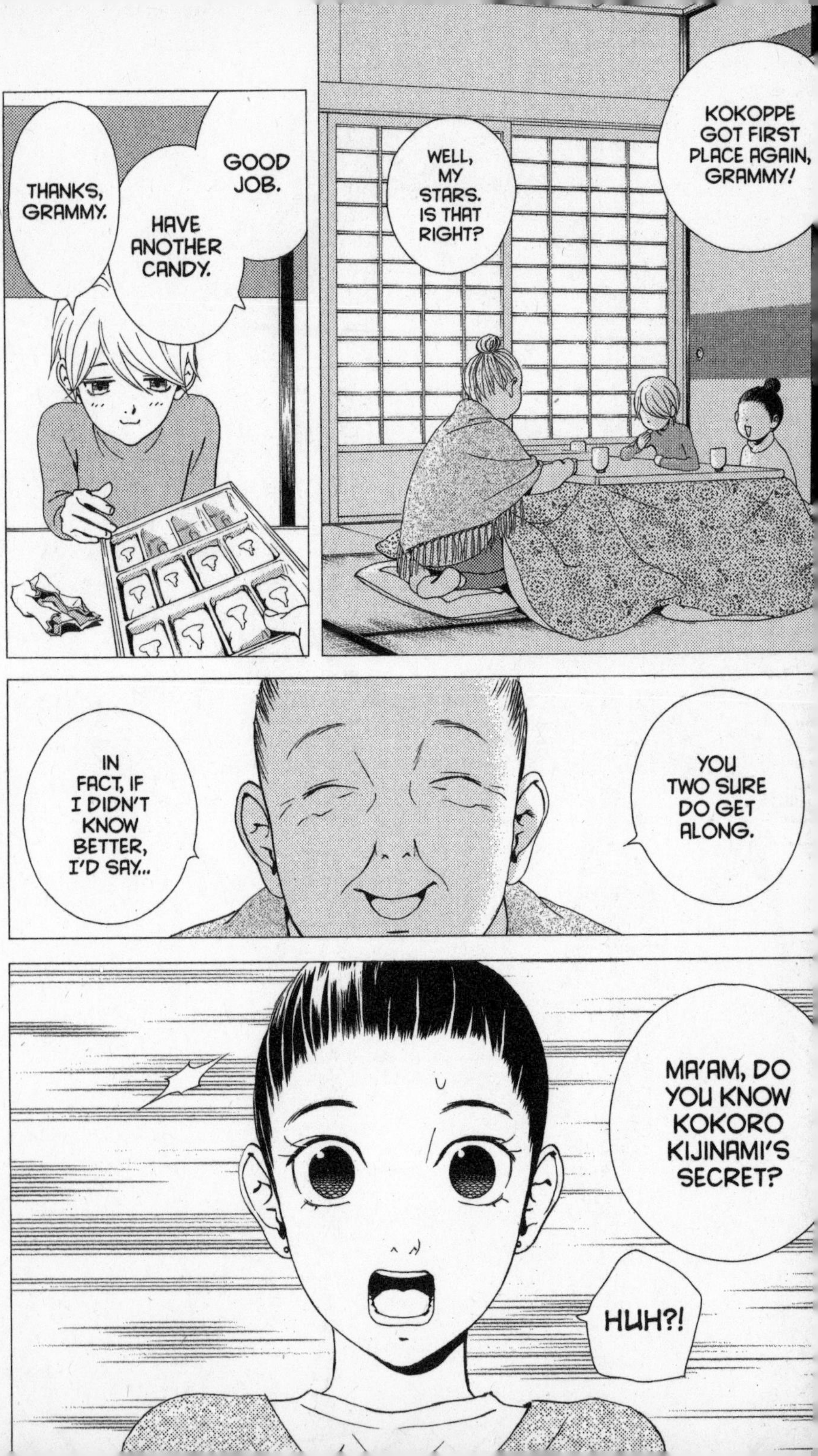
KOKOPPE GOT FIRST PLACE AGAIN, GRAMMY!
WELL, MY STARS. IS THAT RIGHT?
GOOD JOB.
HAVE ANOTHER CANDY.
THANKS, GRAMMY.
YOU TWO SURE DO GET ALONG.
IN FACT, IF I DIDN'T KNOW BETTER, I'D SAY...
MA'AM, DO YOU KNOW KOKORO KIJINAMI'S SECRET?
HUH?!

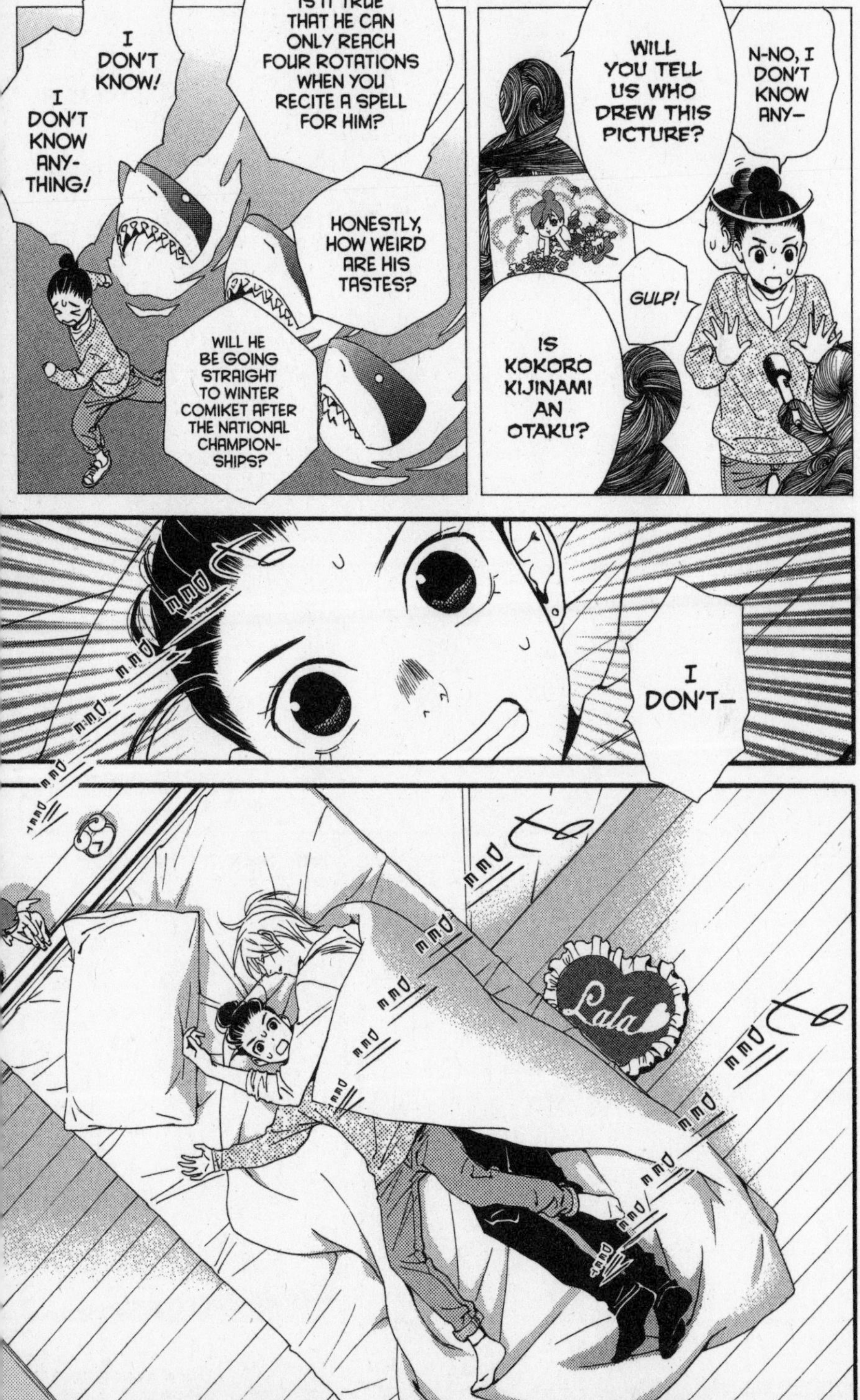
N-NO, I DON'T KNOW ANY—
WILL YOU TELL US WHO DREW THIS PICTURE?
GULP!
IS KOKORO KIJINAMI AN OTAKU?
IS IT TRUE THAT HE CAN ONLY REACH FOUR ROTATIONS WHEN YOU RECITE A SPELL FOR HIM?
I DON'T KNOW!
I DON'T KNOW ANY-THING!
HONESTLY, HOW WEIRD ARE HIS TASTES?
WILL HE BE GOING STRAIGHT TO WINTER COMIKET AFTER THE NATIONAL CHAMPION-SHIPS?
I DON'T—
Lala

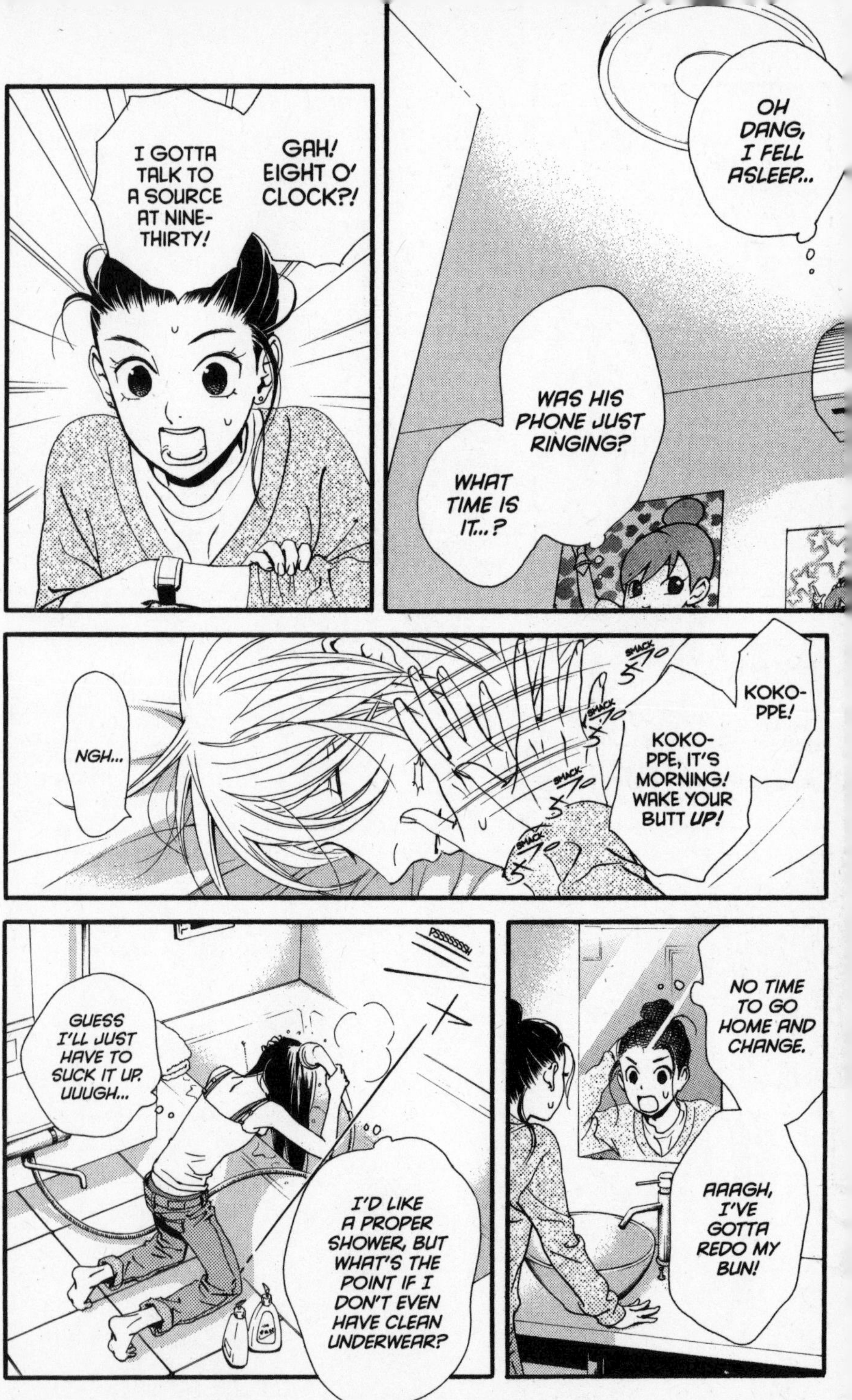
OH DANG, I FELL ASLEEP...
WAS HIS PHONE JUST RINGING?
WHAT TIME IS IT...?
GAH! EIGHT O' CLOCK?!
I GOTTA TALK TO A SOURCE AT NINE-THIRTY!
KOKOPPE!
KOKOPPE, IT'S MORNING! WAKE YOUR BUTT *UP*!
SMACK
SMACK
SMACK
SMACK
NGH...
NO TIME TO GO HOME AND CHANGE.
AAAGH, I'VE GOTTA REDO MY BUN!
PSSSSSSH
GUESS I'LL JUST HAVE TO SUCK IT UP. UUUGH...
I'D LIKE A PROPER SHOWER, BUT WHAT'S THE POINT IF I DON'T EVEN HAVE CLEAN UNDERWEAR?

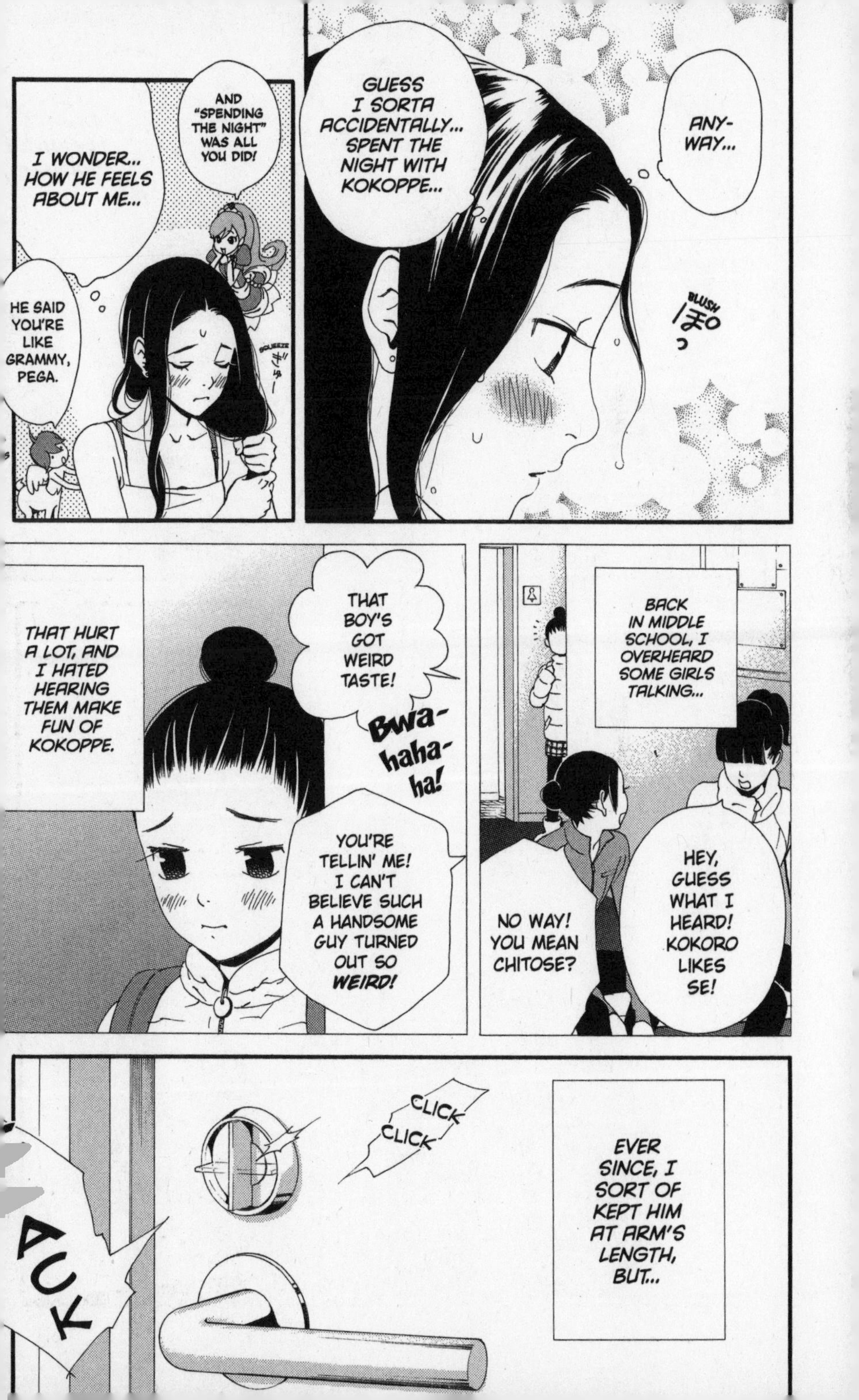
ANY-WAY...
GUESS I SORTA ACCIDENTALLY... SPENT THE NIGHT WITH KOKOPPE...
BLUSH
ぽっ
AND "SPENDING THE NIGHT" WAS ALL YOU DID!
I WONDER... HOW HE FEELS ABOUT ME...
SQUEEZE
HE SAID YOU'RE LIKE GRAMMY, PEGA.
BACK IN MIDDLE SCHOOL, I OVERHEARD SOME GIRLS TALKING...
HEY, GUESS WHAT I HEARD! KOKORO LIKES SE!
NO WAY! YOU MEAN CHITOSE?
THAT BOY'S GOT WEIRD TASTE!
Bwa-haha-ha!
YOU'RE TELLIN' ME! I CAN'T BELIEVE SUCH A HANDSOME GUY TURNED OUT SO *WEIRD!*
THAT HURT A LOT, AND I HATED HEARING THEM MAKE FUN OF KOKOPPE.
EVER SINCE, I SORT OF KEPT HIM AT ARM'S LENGTH, BUT...
CLICK
CLICK
AUCK

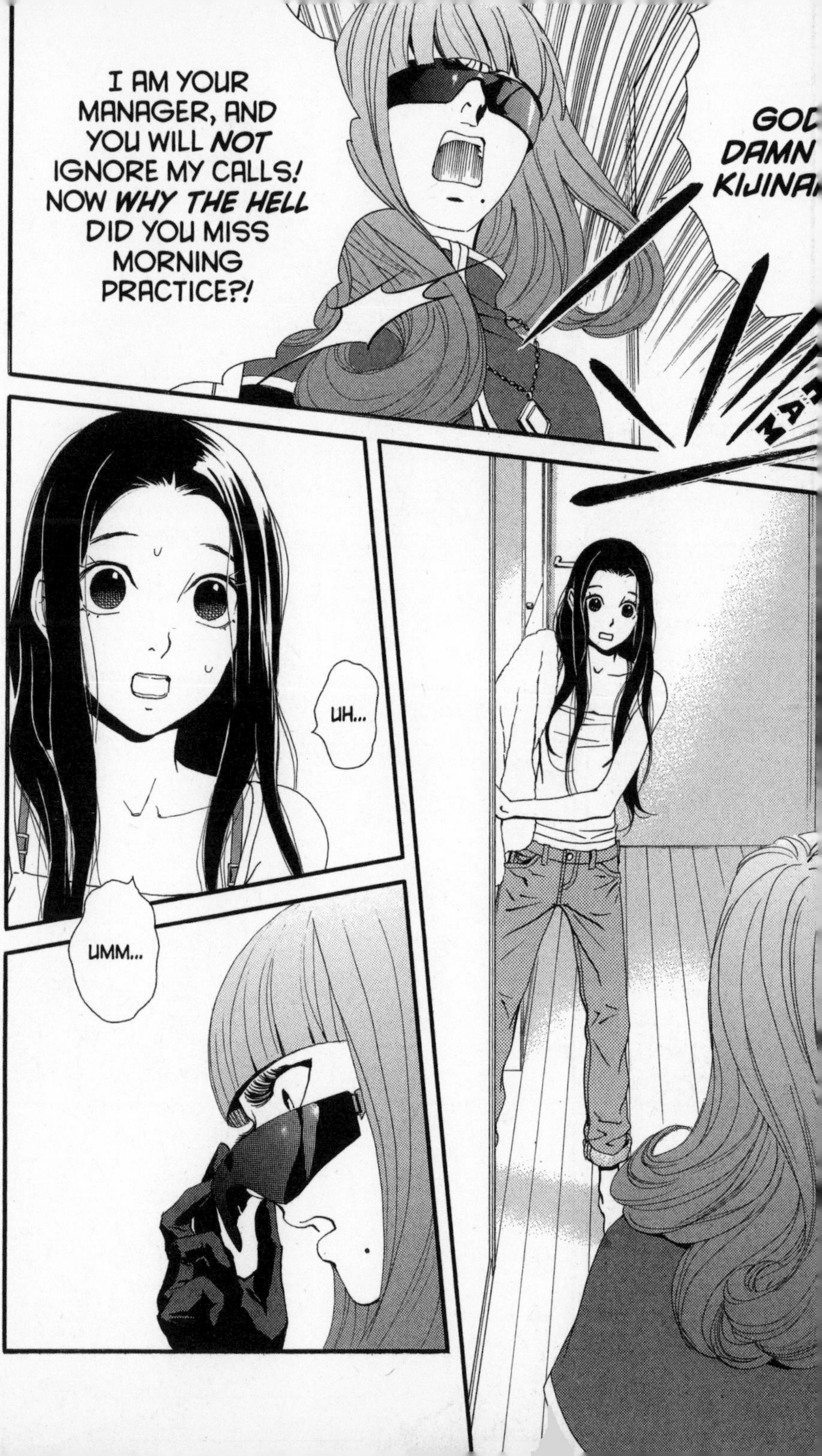
GOD DAMN KIJINA
I AM YOUR MANAGER, AND YOU WILL ***NOT*** IGNORE MY CALLS! NOW ***WHY THE HELL*** DID YOU MISS MORNING PRACTICE?!
UH...
UMM...

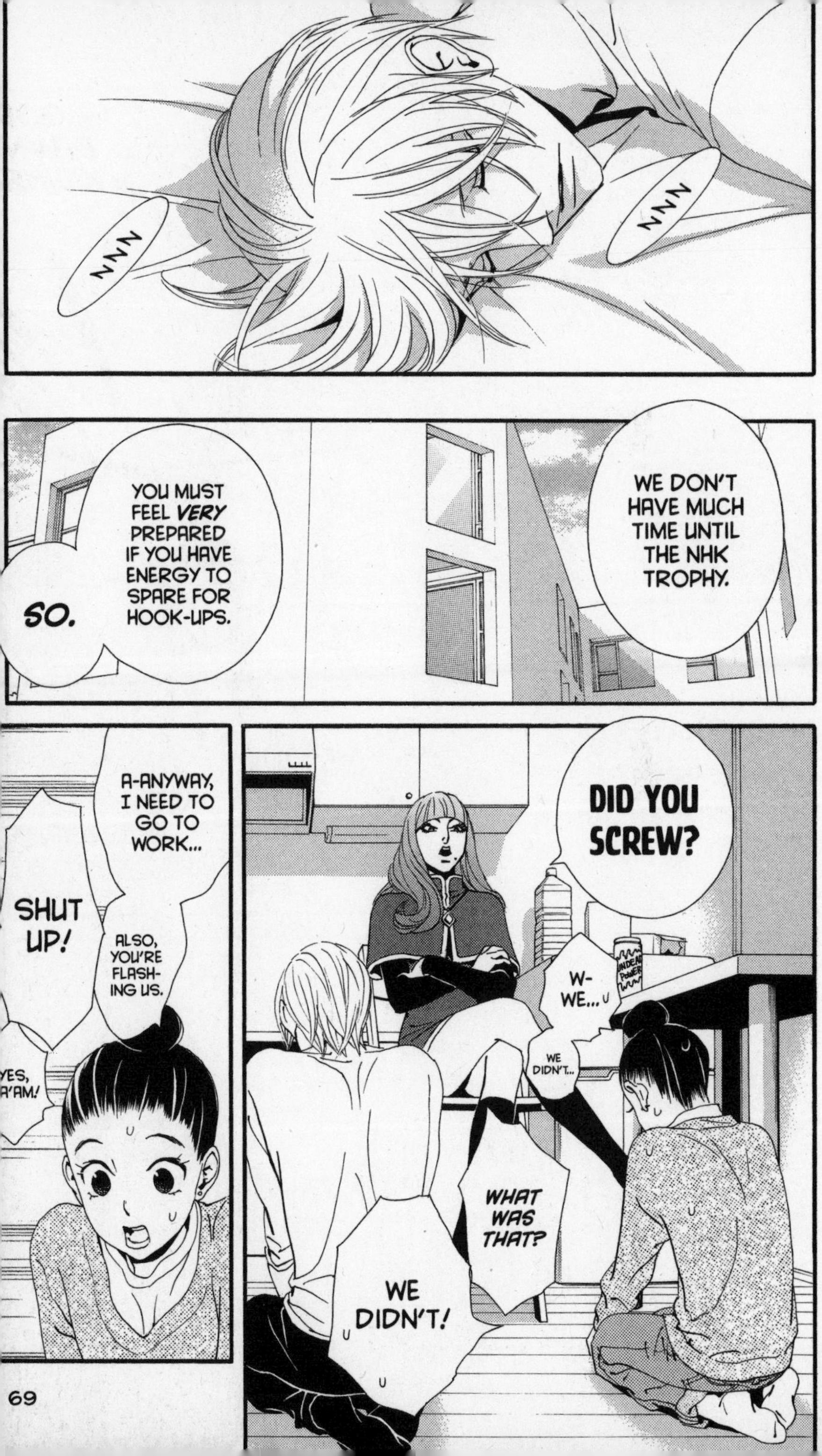
NNN
NNN
WE DON'T HAVE MUCH TIME UNTIL THE NHK TROPHY.
YOU MUST FEEL *VERY* PREPARED IF YOU HAVE ENERGY TO SPARE FOR HOOK-UPS.
SO.
DID YOU SCREW?
UNDEAD POWER
W- WE...
WE DIDN'T...
WHAT WAS THAT?
WE DIDN'T!
A-ANYWAY, I NEED TO GO TO WORK...
ALSO, YOU'RE FLASHING US.
SHUT UP!
YES, A'AM!

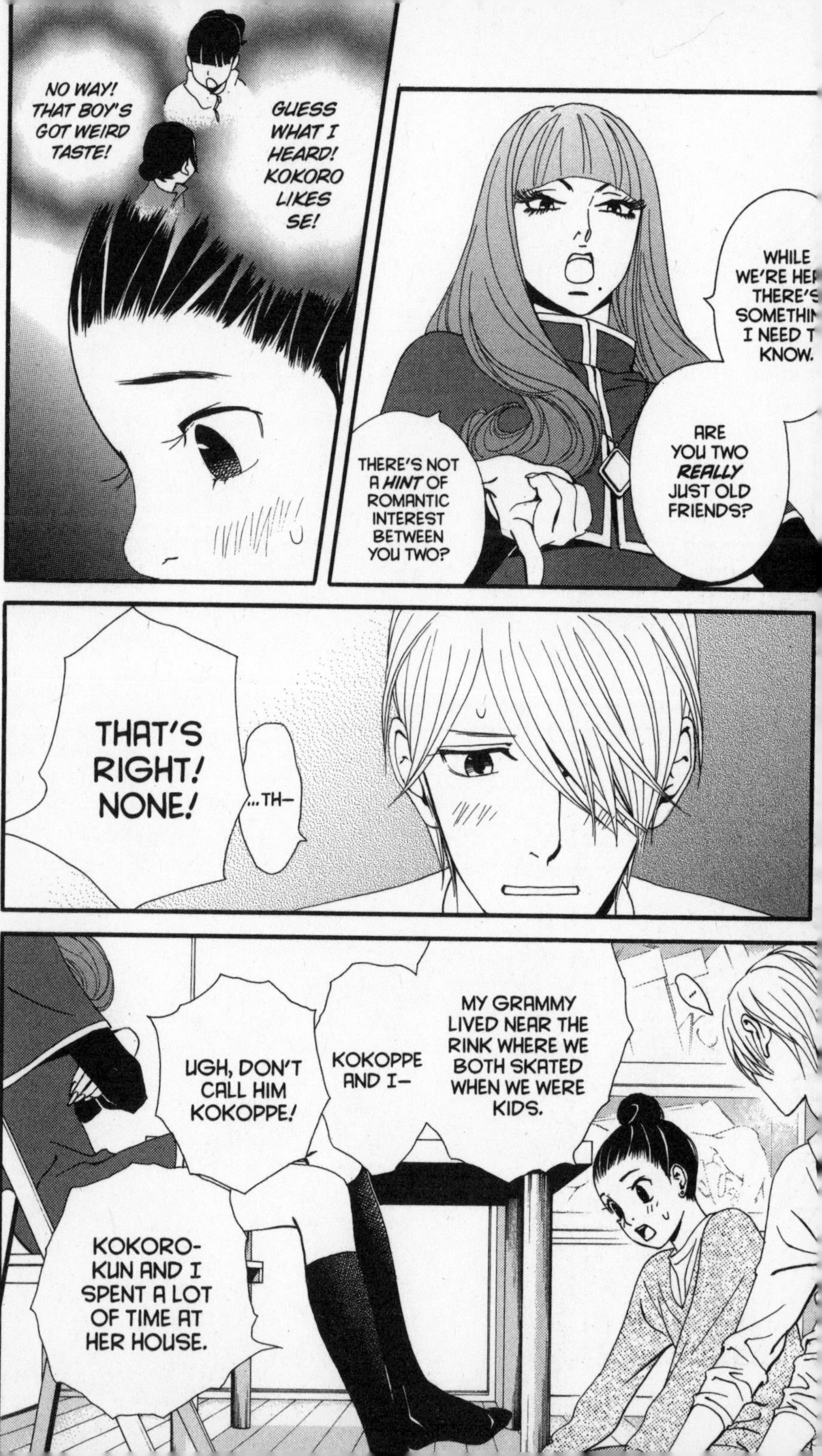
WHILE WE'RE HE THERE'S SOMETHIN I NEED T KNOW.
ARE YOU TWO *REALLY* JUST OLD FRIENDS?
THERE'S NOT A *HINT* OF ROMANTIC INTEREST BETWEEN YOU TWO?
GUESS WHAT I HEARD! KOKORO LIKES SE!
NO WAY! THAT BOY'S GOT WEIRD TASTE!
...TH–
THAT'S RIGHT! NONE!
MY GRAMMY LIVED NEAR THE RINK WHERE WE BOTH SKATED WHEN WE WERE KIDS.
KOKOPPE AND I–
UGH, DON'T CALL HIM KOKOPPE!
KOKORO-KUN AND I SPENT A LOT OF TIME AT HER HOUSE.

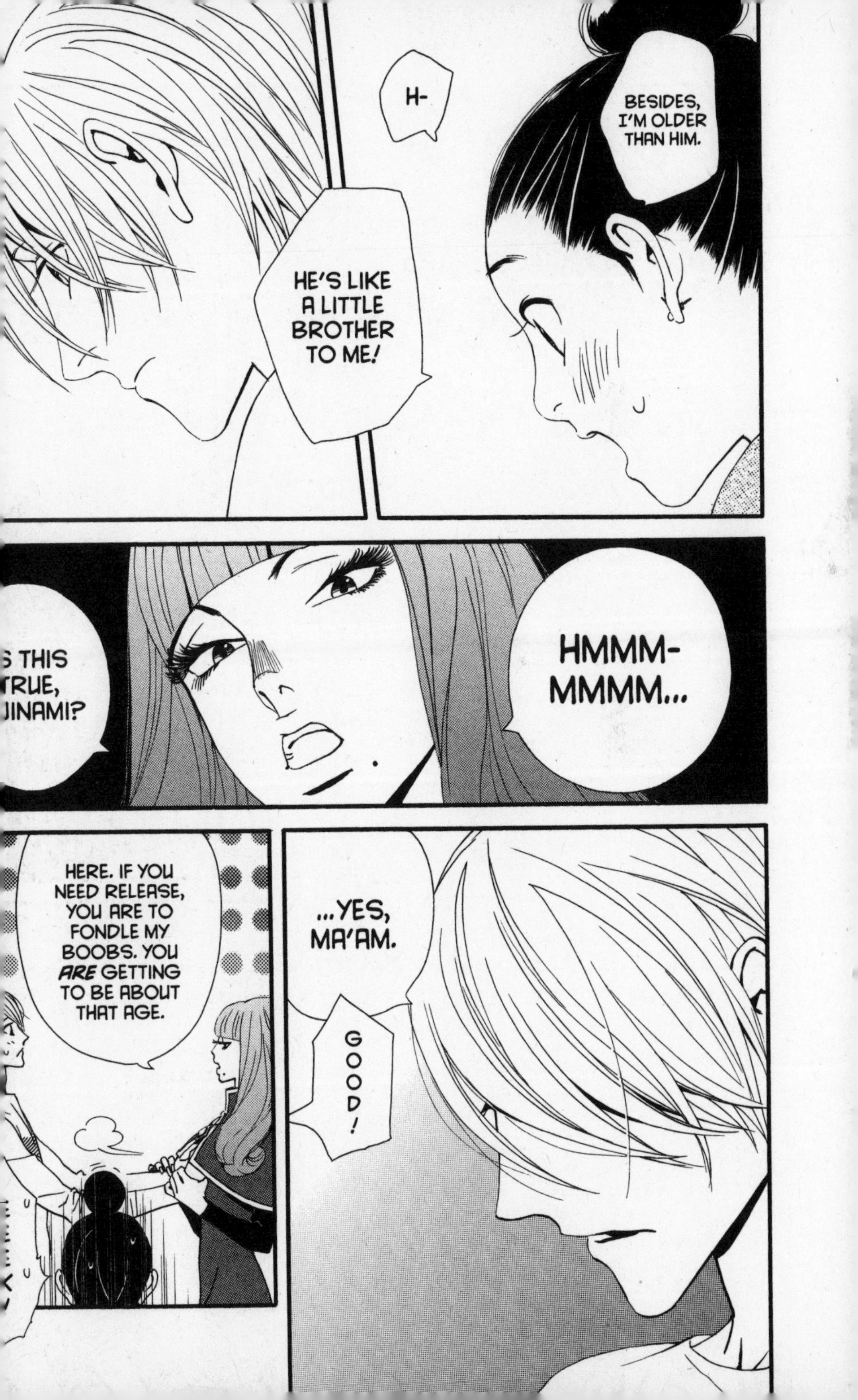
BESIDES, I'M OLDER THAN HIM.
H-
HE'S LIKE A LITTLE BROTHER TO ME!
HMMM-MMMM...
S THIS TRUE, INAMI?
...YES, MA'AM.
GOOD!
HERE. IF YOU NEED RELEASE, YOU ARE TO FONDLE MY BOOBS. YOU *ARE* GETTING TO BE ABOUT THAT AGE.

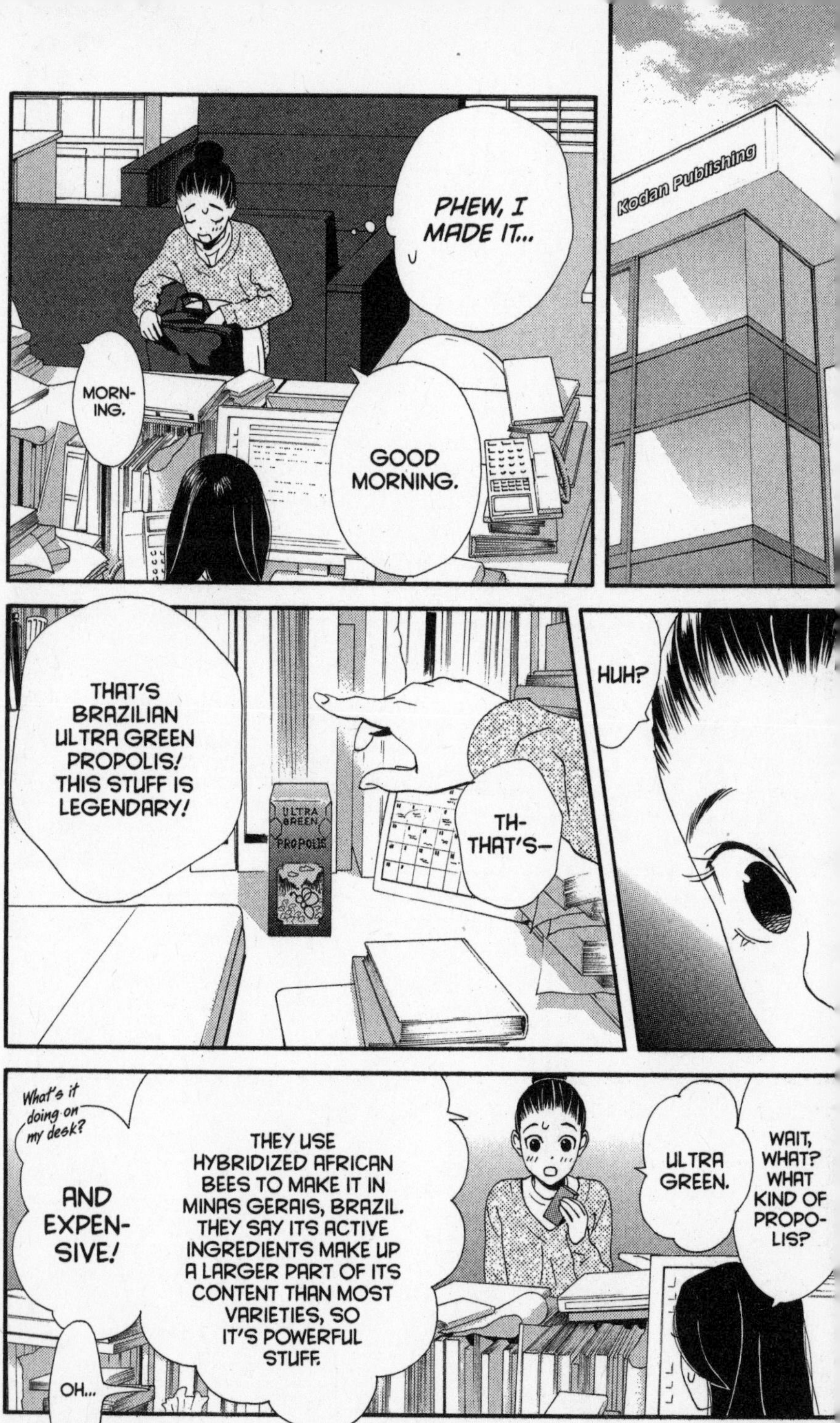
Kodan Publishing
PHEW, I MADE IT...
GOOD MORNING.
MORN-ING.
HUH?
TH- THAT'S—
THAT'S BRAZILIAN ULTRA GREEN PROPOLIS! THIS STUFF IS LEGENDARY!
ULTRA GREEN PROPOLIS
WAIT, WHAT? WHAT KIND OF PROPO-LIS?
ULTRA GREEN.
THEY USE HYBRIDIZED AFRICAN BEES TO MAKE IT IN MINAS GERAIS, BRAZIL. THEY SAY ITS ACTIVE INGREDIENTS MAKE UP A LARGER PART OF ITS CONTENT THAN MOST VARIETIES, SO IT'S POWERFUL STUFF.
What's it doing on my desk?
AND EXPEN-SIVE!
OH...

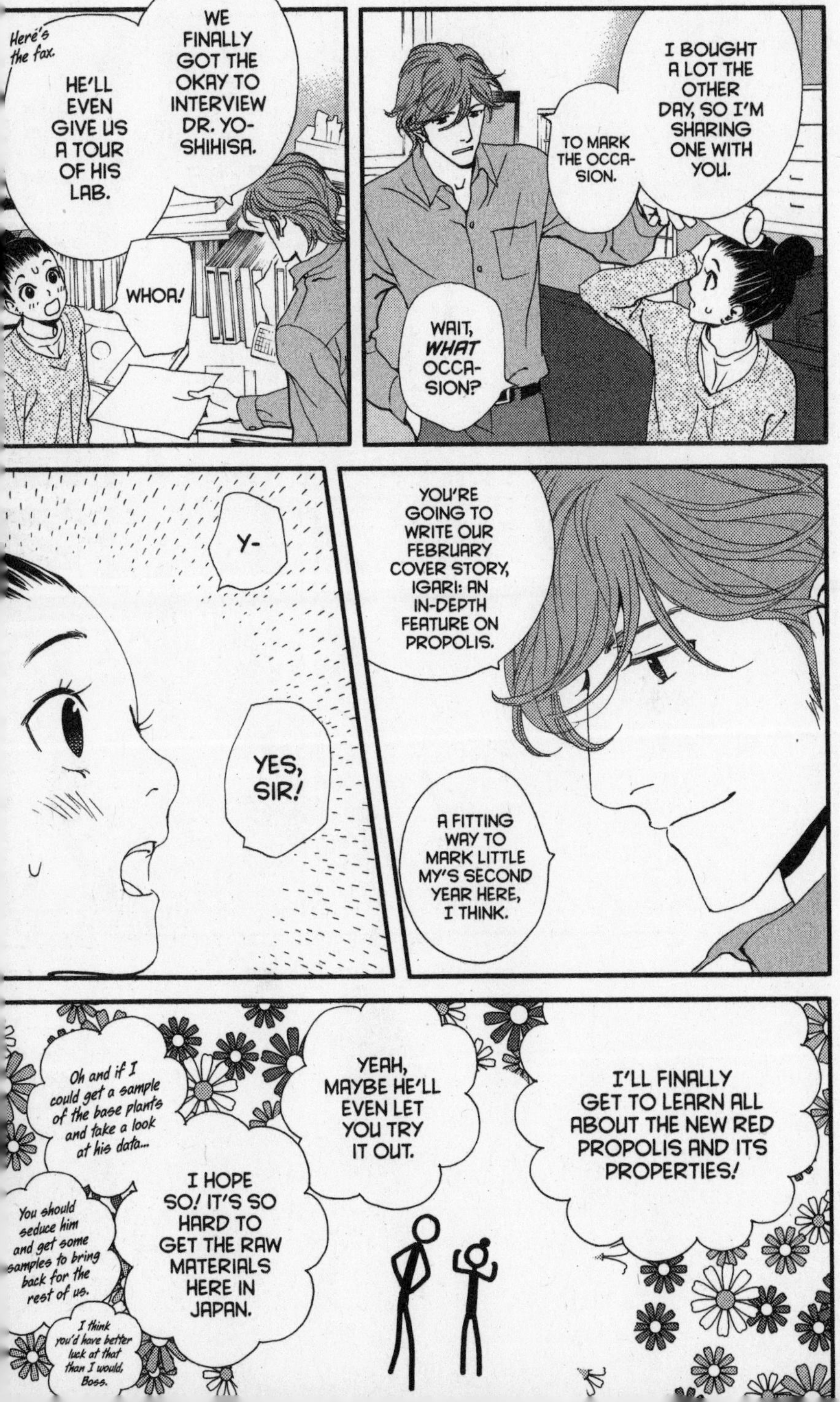
I BOUGHT A LOT THE OTHER DAY, SO I'M SHARING ONE WITH YOU.
TO MARK THE OCCASION.
WAIT, *WHAT* OCCASION?
WE FINALLY GOT THE OKAY TO INTERVIEW DR. YOSHIHISA.
Here's the fax.
HE'LL EVEN GIVE US A TOUR OF HIS LAB.
WHOA!
YOU'RE GOING TO WRITE OUR FEBRUARY COVER STORY, IGARI: AN IN-DEPTH FEATURE ON PROPOLIS.
A FITTING WAY TO MARK LITTLE MY'S SECOND YEAR HERE, I THINK.
Y-
YES, SIR!
I'LL FINALLY GET TO LEARN ALL ABOUT THE NEW RED PROPOLIS AND ITS PROPERTIES!
YEAH, MAYBE HE'LL EVEN LET YOU TRY IT OUT.
I HOPE SO! IT'S SO HARD TO GET THE RAW MATERIALS HERE IN JAPAN.
Oh and if I could get a sample of the base plants and take a look at his data...
You should seduce him and get some samples to bring back for the rest of us.
I think you'd have better luck at that than I would, Boss.

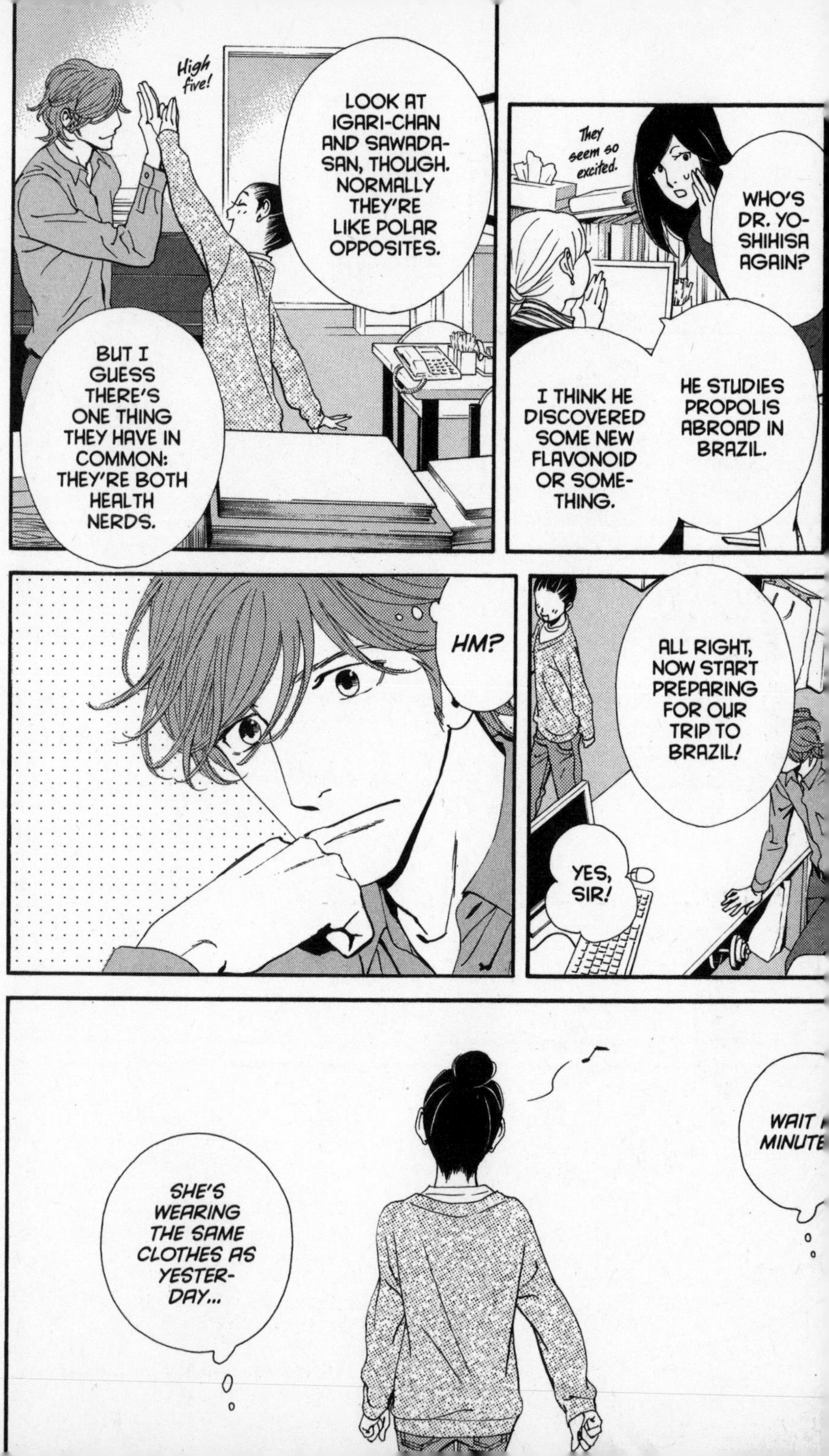
They seem so excited.
WHO'S DR. YOSHIHISA AGAIN?
HE STUDIES PROPOLIS ABROAD IN BRAZIL.
I THINK HE DISCOVERED SOME NEW FLAVONOID OR SOMETHING.
High five!
LOOK AT IGARI-CHAN AND SAWADA-SAN, THOUGH. NORMALLY THEY'RE LIKE POLAR OPPOSITES.
BUT I GUESS THERE'S ONE THING THEY HAVE IN COMMON: THEY'RE BOTH HEALTH NERDS.
ALL RIGHT, NOW START PREPARING FOR OUR TRIP TO BRAZIL!
YES, SIR!
HM?
WAIT MINUTE
SHE'S WEARING THE SAME CLOTHES AS YESTERDAY...

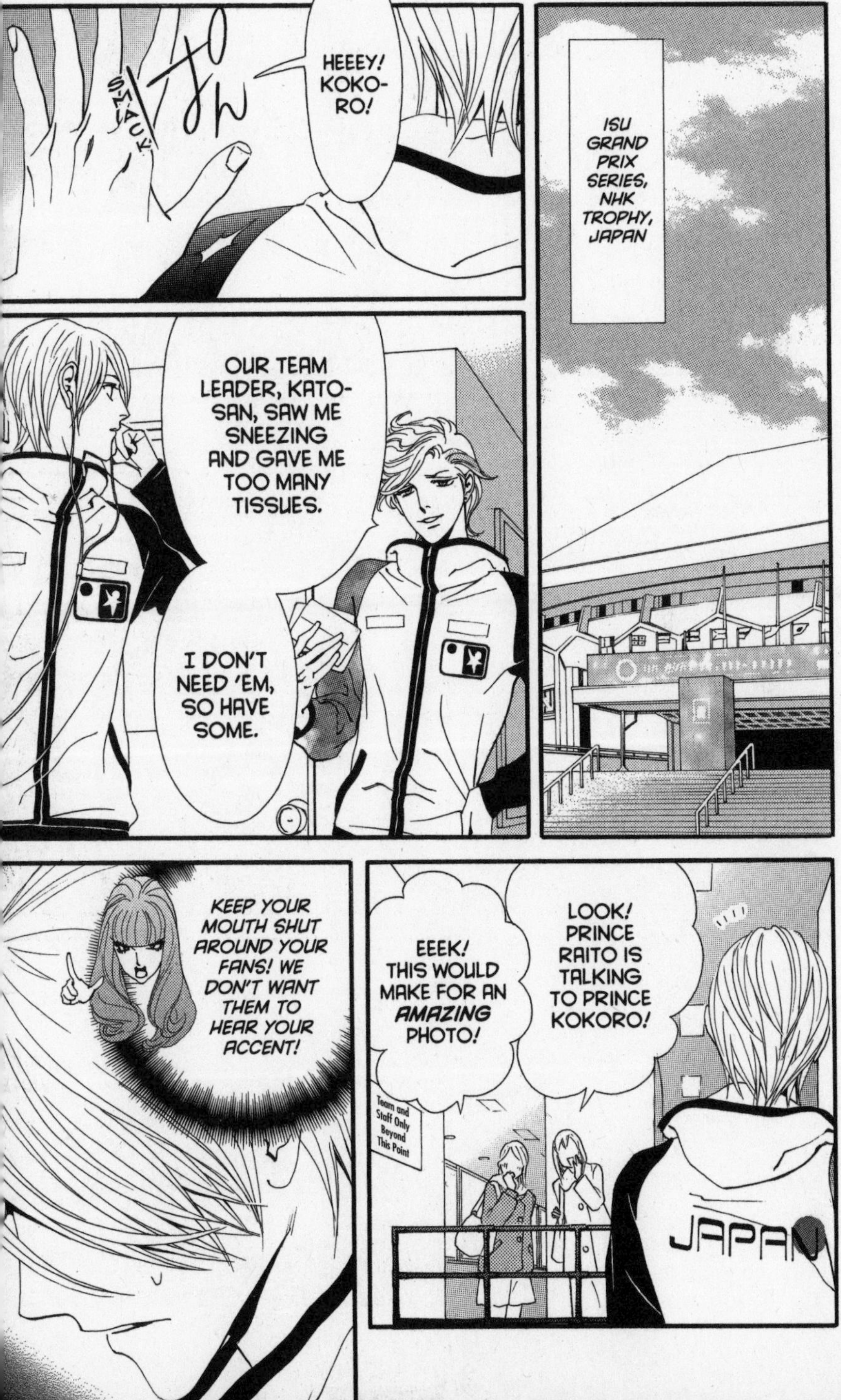
ISU GRAND PRIX SERIES, NHK TROPHY, JAPAN
HEEEY! KOKO-RO!
SMACK
OUR TEAM LEADER, KATO-SAN, SAW ME SNEEZING AND GAVE ME TOO MANY TISSUES.
I DON'T NEED 'EM, SO HAVE SOME.
LOOK! PRINCE RAITO IS TALKING TO PRINCE KOKORO!
EEEK! THIS WOULD MAKE FOR AN AMAZING PHOTO!
Team and Staff Only Beyond This Point
JAPAN
KEEP YOUR MOUTH SHUT AROUND YOUR FANS! WE DON'T WANT THEM TO HEAR YOUR ACCENT!

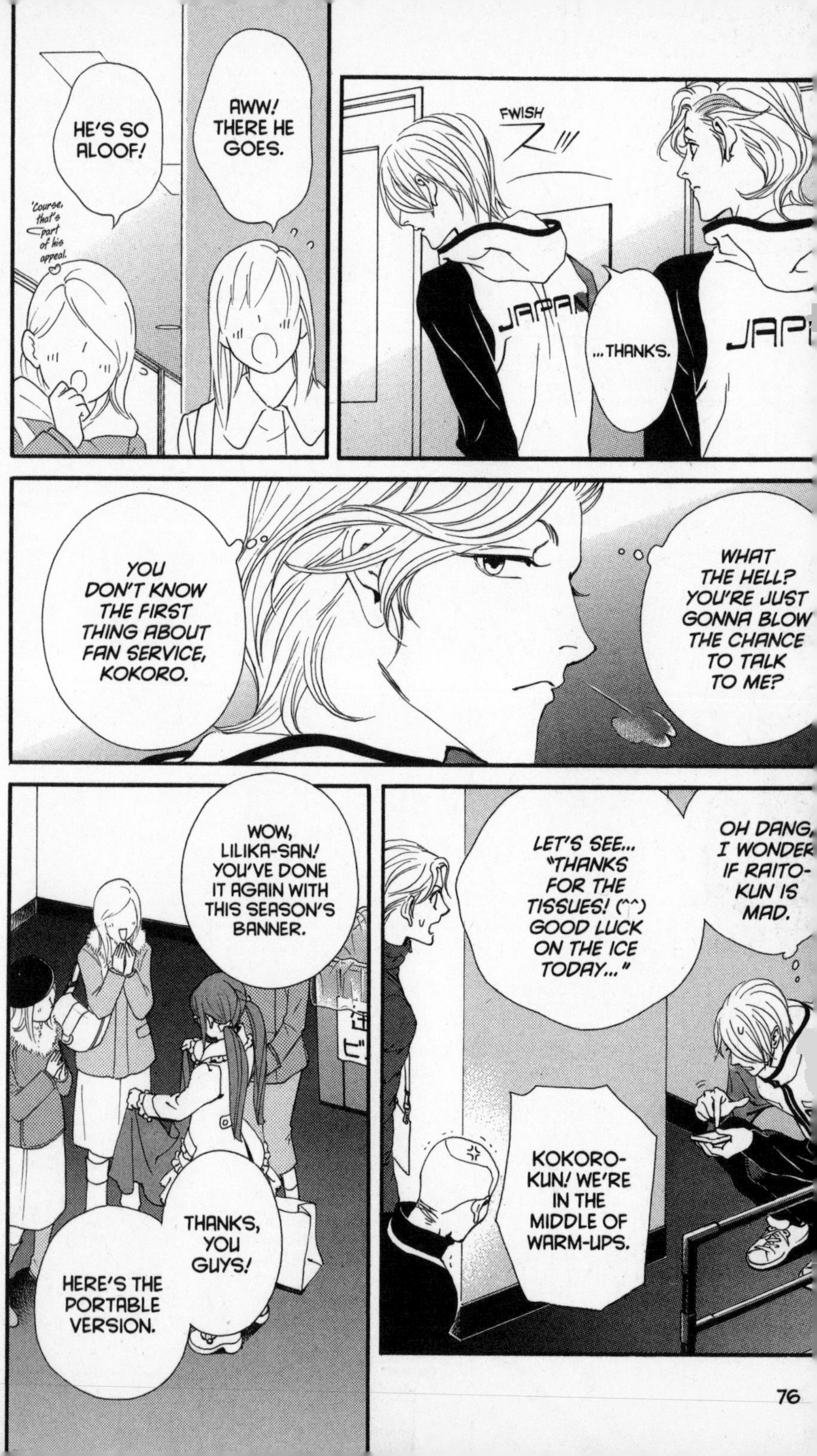
FWISH
...THANKS.
AWW! THERE HE GOES.
HE'S SO ALOOF!
'Course, that's part of his appeal.
WHAT THE HELL? YOU'RE JUST GONNA BLOW THE CHANCE TO TALK TO ME?
YOU DON'T KNOW THE FIRST THING ABOUT FAN SERVICE, KOKORO.
OH DANG, I WONDER IF RAITO-KUN IS MAD.
LET'S SEE... "THANKS FOR THE TISSUES! (^^) GOOD LUCK ON THE ICE TODAY..."
KOKORO-KUN! WE'RE IN THE MIDDLE OF WARM-UPS.
WOW, LILIKA-SAN! YOU'VE DONE IT AGAIN WITH THIS SEASON'S BANNER.
THANKS, YOU GUYS!
HERE'S THE PORTABLE VERSION.

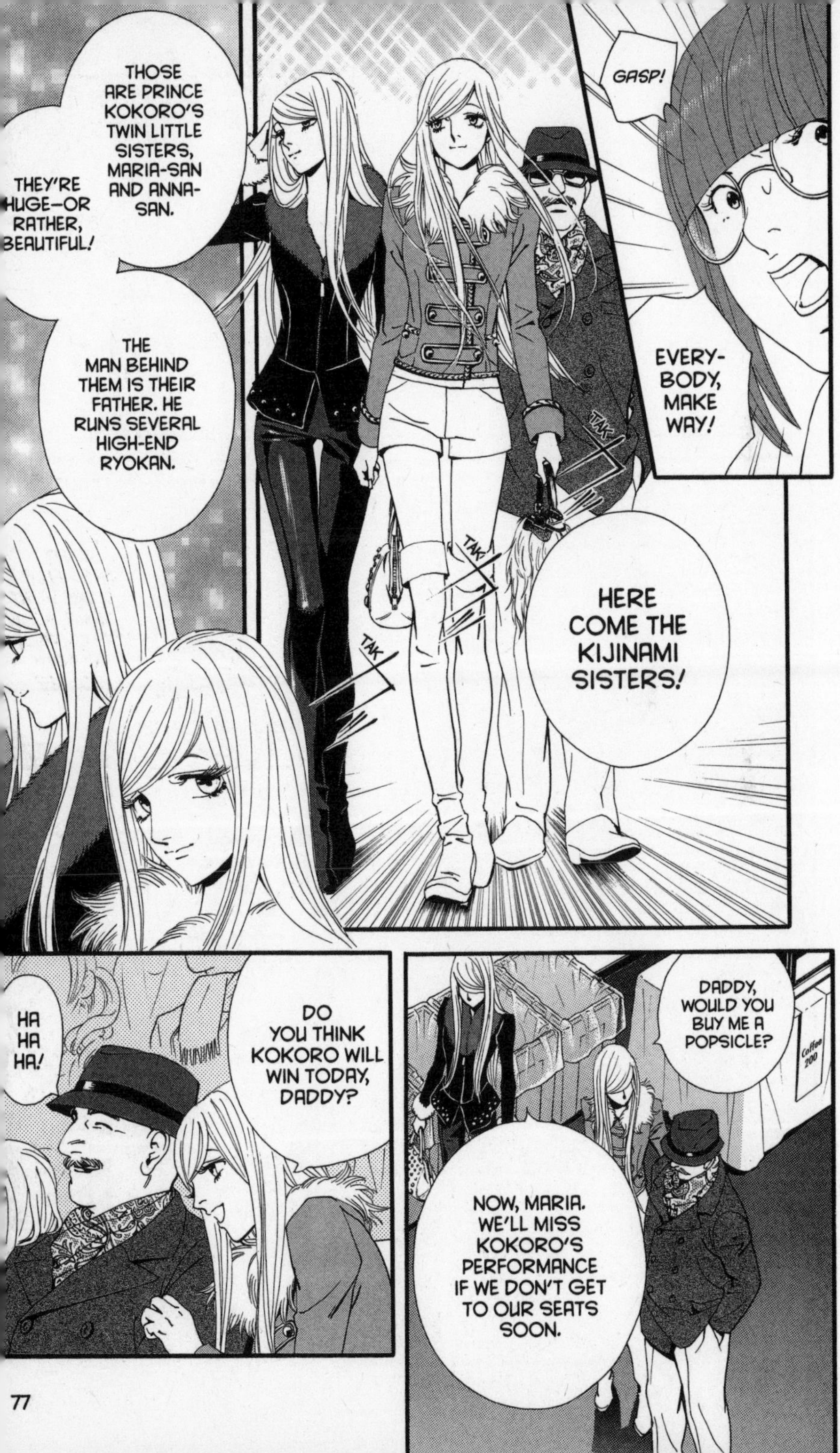
GASP!
EVERYBODY, MAKE WAY!
HERE COME THE KIJINAMI SISTERS!
TAK
TAK
TAK
THOSE ARE PRINCE KOKORO'S TWIN LITTLE SISTERS, MARIA-SAN AND ANNA-SAN.
THEY'RE HUGE—OR RATHER, BEAUTIFUL!
THE MAN BEHIND THEM IS THEIR FATHER. HE RUNS SEVERAL HIGH-END RYOKAN.
DADDY, WOULD YOU BUY ME A POPSICLE?
NOW, MARIA. WE'LL MISS KOKORO'S PERFORMANCE IF WE DON'T GET TO OUR SEATS SOON.
DO YOU THINK KOKORO WILL WIN TODAY, DADDY?
HA HA HA!

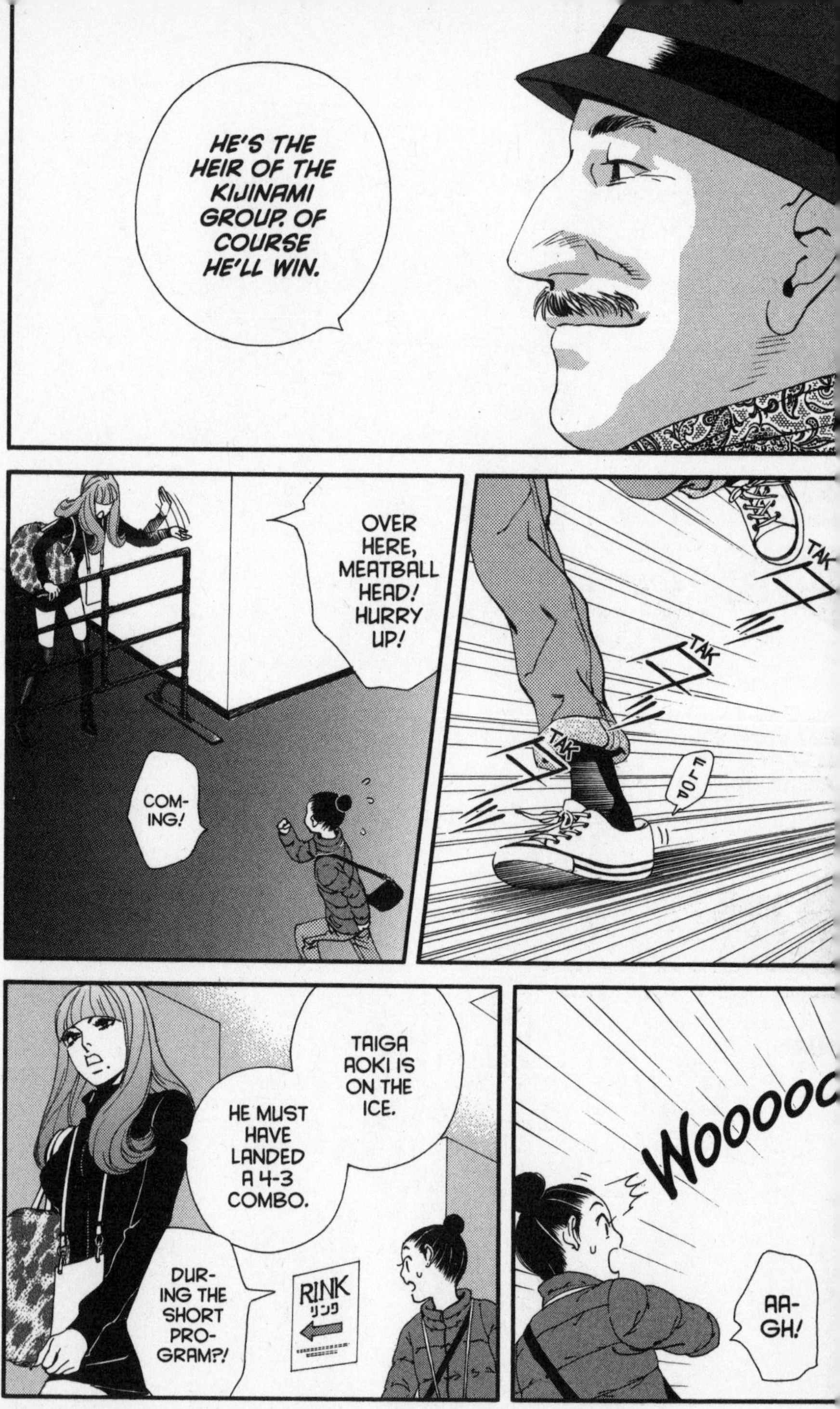
HE'S THE HEIR OF THE KIJINAMI GROUP. OF COURSE HE'LL WIN.
TAK
TAK
TAK
FLOP
OVER HERE, MEATBALL HEAD! HURRY UP!
COMING!
WOOOO
AAGH!
TAIGA AOKI IS ON THE ICE.
HE MUST HAVE LANDED A 4-3 COMBO.
DURING THE SHORT PROGRAM?!
RINK
リンク

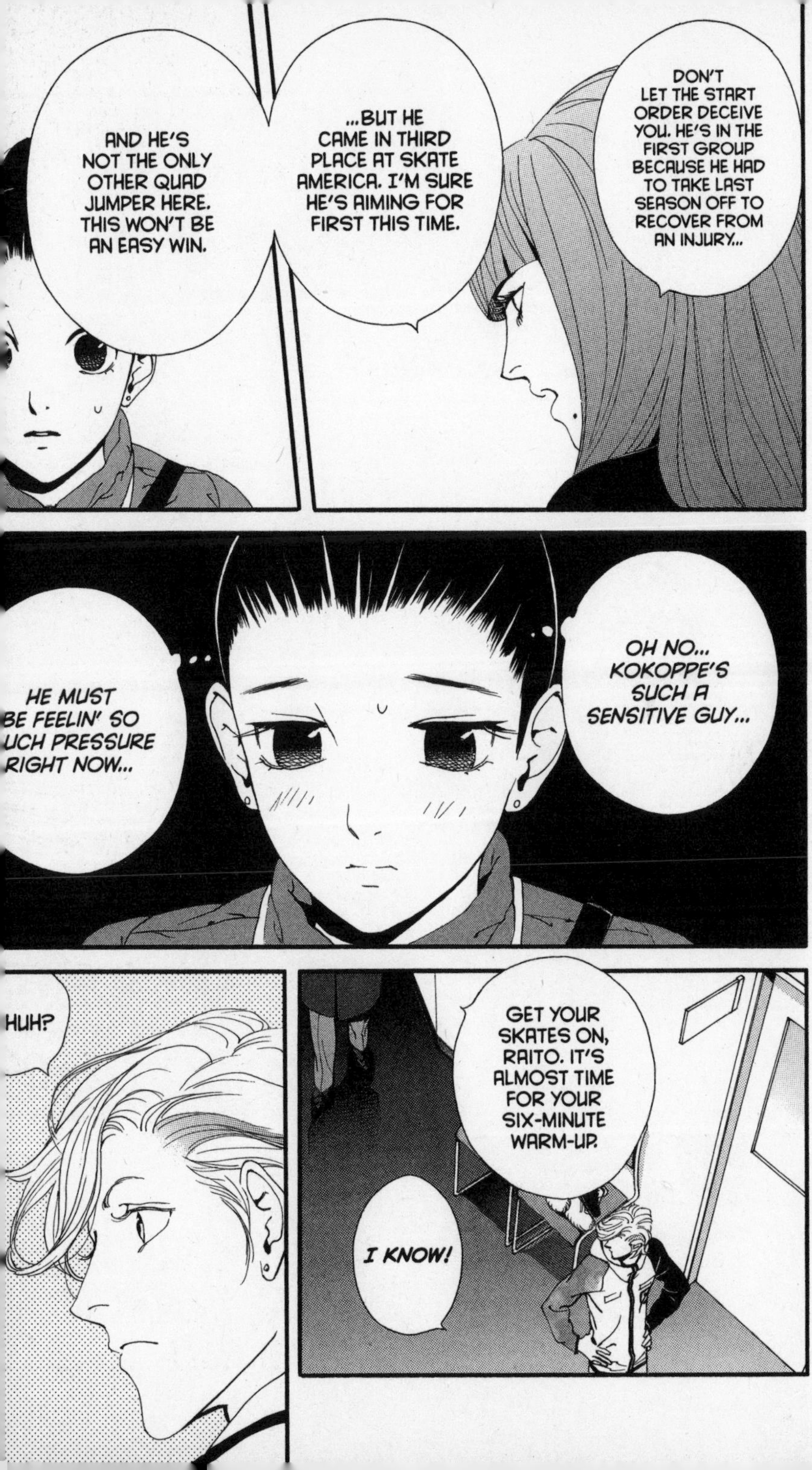
DON'T LET THE START ORDER DECEIVE YOU. HE'S IN THE FIRST GROUP BECAUSE HE HAD TO TAKE LAST SEASON OFF TO RECOVER FROM AN INJURY...
...BUT HE CAME IN THIRD PLACE AT SKATE AMERICA. I'M SURE HE'S AIMING FOR FIRST THIS TIME.
AND HE'S NOT THE ONLY OTHER QUAD JUMPER HERE. THIS WON'T BE AN EASY WIN.
OH NO... KOKOPPE'S SUCH A SENSITIVE GUY...
HE MUST BE FEELIN' SO UCH PRESSURE RIGHT NOW...
GET YOUR SKATES ON, RAITO. IT'S ALMOST TIME FOR YOUR SIX-MINUTE WARM-UP.
I KNOW!
HUH?

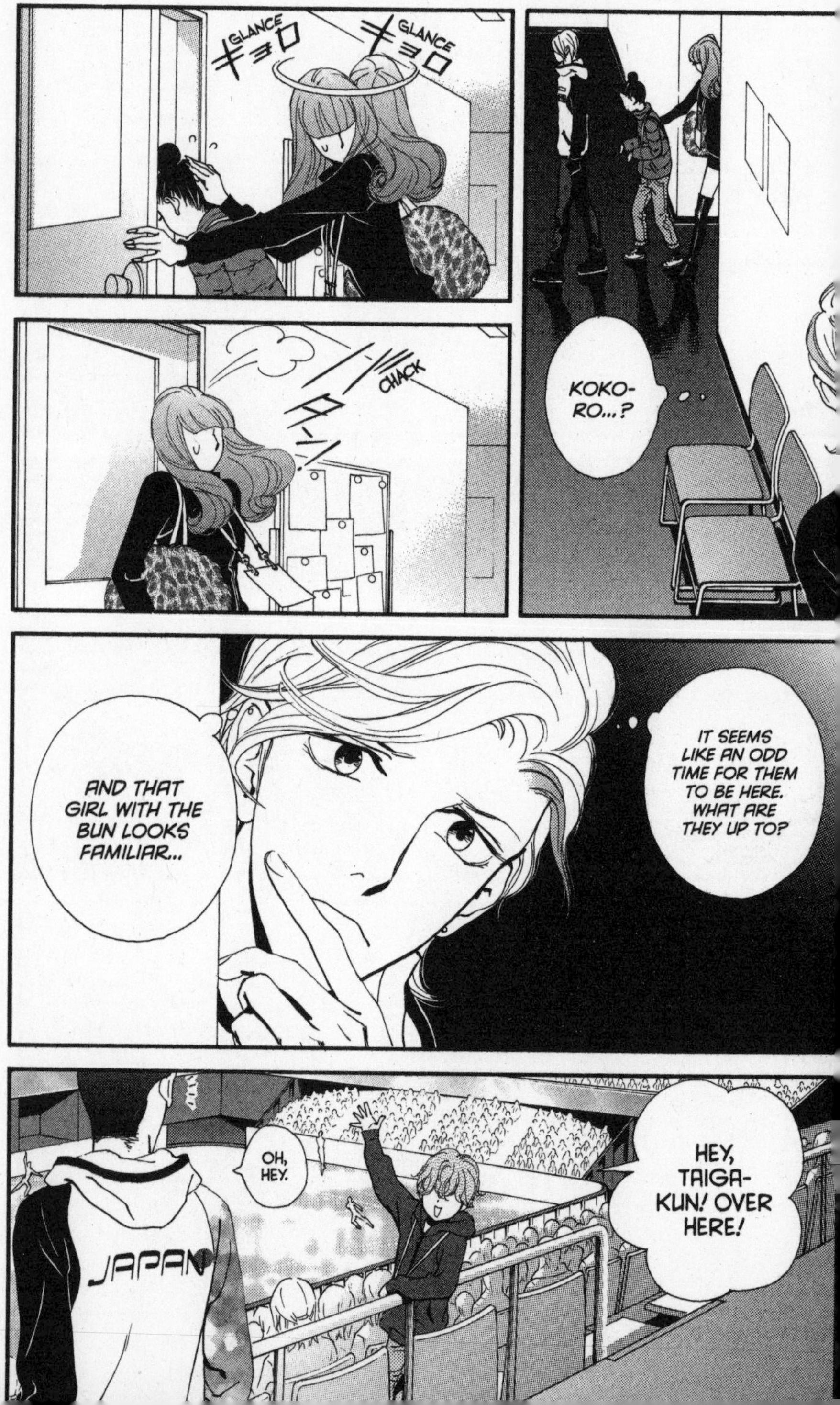
KOKO-RO...?
GLANCE
キョロ
GLANCE
キョロ
CHACK
IT SEEMS LIKE AN ODD TIME FOR THEM TO BE HERE. WHAT ARE THEY UP TO?
AND THAT GIRL WITH THE BUN LOOKS FAMILIAR...
HEY, TAIGA-KUN! OVER HERE!
OH, HEY.
JAPAN

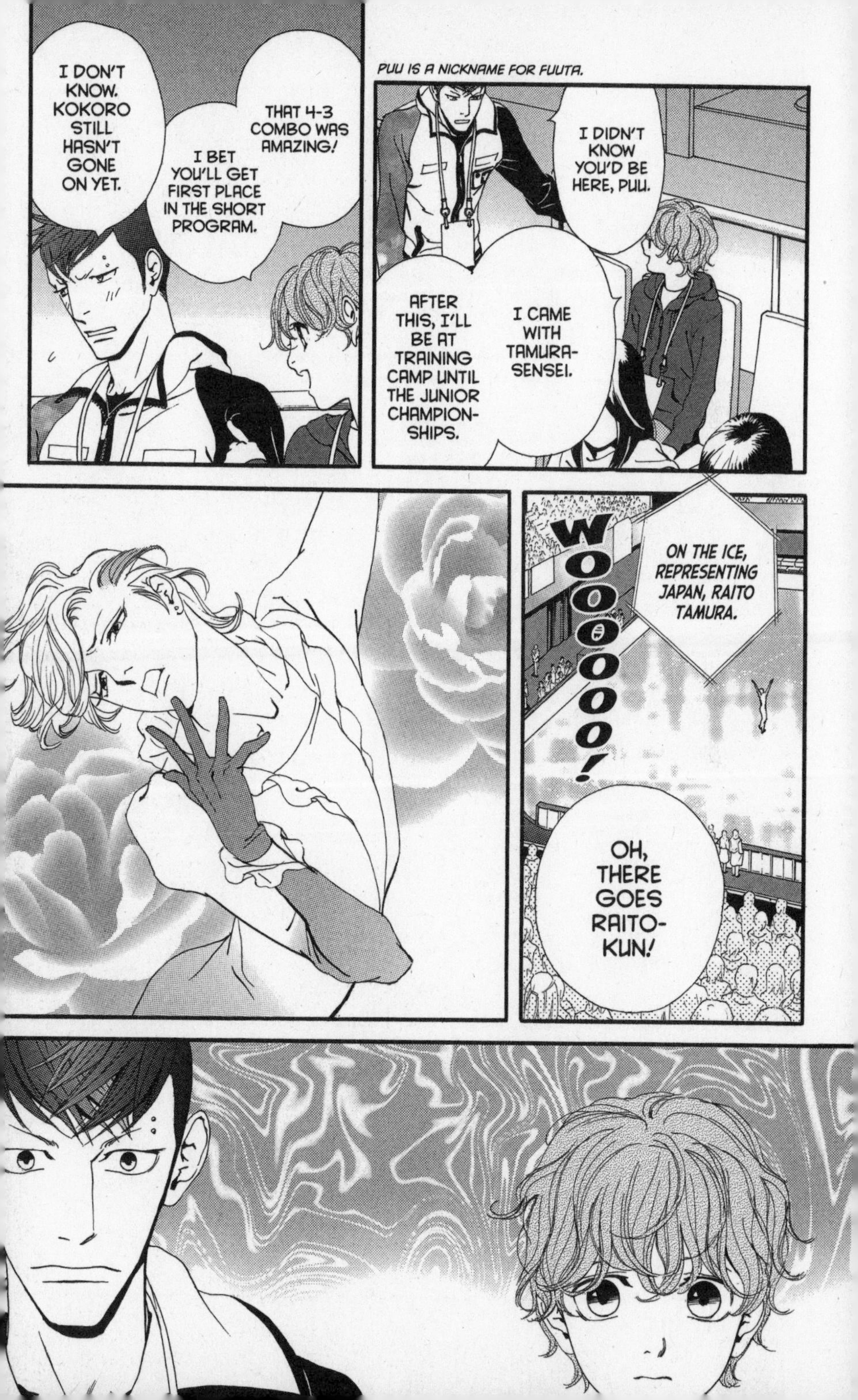
PUU IS A NICKNAME FOR FUUTA.
I DIDN'T KNOW YOU'D BE HERE, PUU.
I CAME WITH TAMURA-SENSEI.
AFTER THIS, I'LL BE AT TRAINING CAMP UNTIL THE JUNIOR CHAMPION-SHIPS.
THAT 4-3 COMBO WAS AMAZING!
I BET YOU'LL GET FIRST PLACE IN THE SHORT PROGRAM.
I DON'T KNOW. KOKORO STILL HASN'T GONE ON YET.
ON THE ICE, REPRESENTING JAPAN, RAITO TAMURA.
WOOOOOOO!
OH, THERE GOES RAITO-KUN!

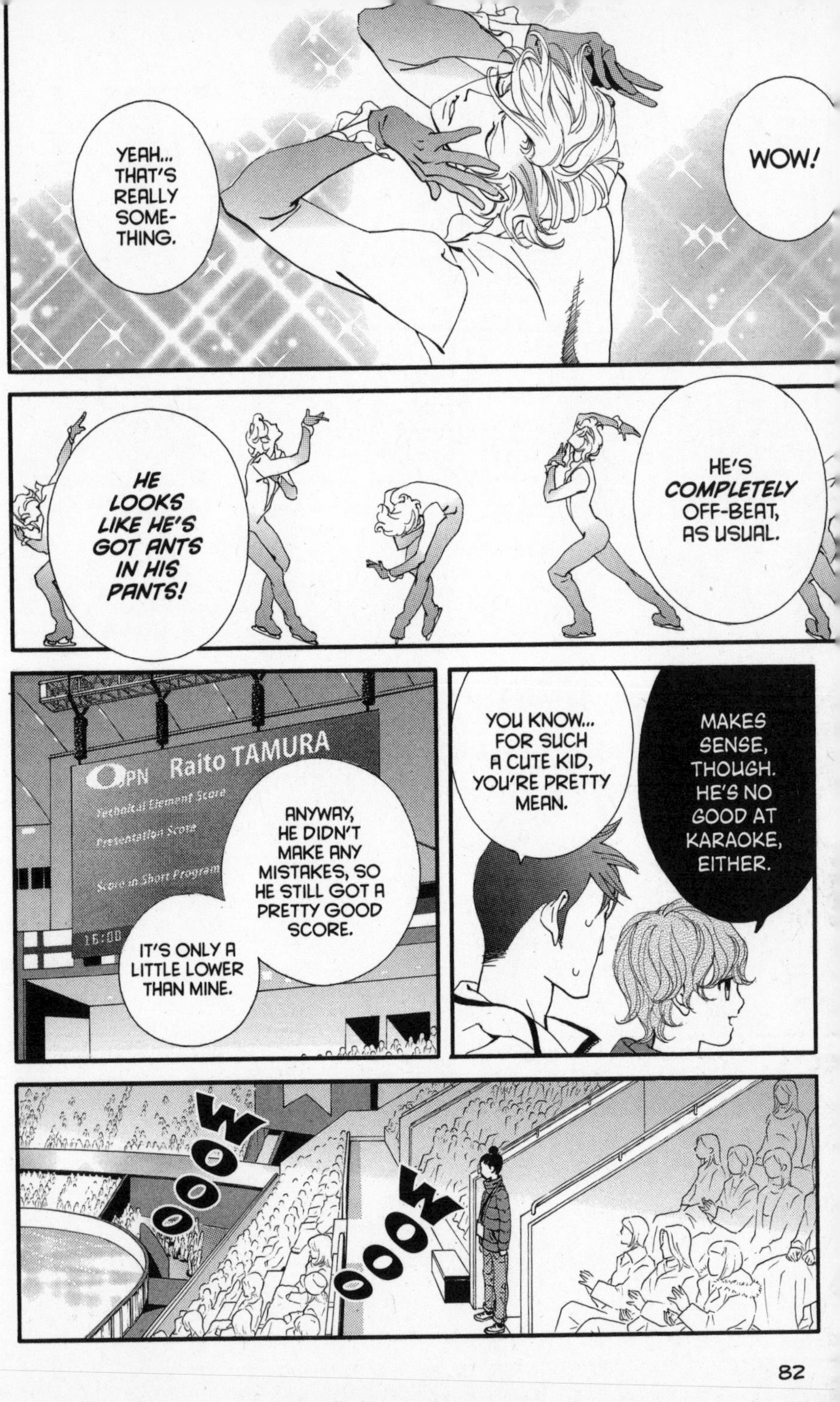
WOW!
YEAH... THAT'S REALLY SOMETHING.
HE'S *COMPLETELY* OFF-BEAT, AS USUAL.
HE LOOKS LIKE HE'S GOT ANTS IN HIS PANTS!
MAKES SENSE, THOUGH. HE'S NO GOOD AT KARAOKE, EITHER.
YOU KNOW... FOR SUCH A CUTE KID, YOU'RE PRETTY MEAN.
Raito TAMURA
ANYWAY, HE DIDN'T MAKE ANY MISTAKES, SO HE STILL GOT A PRETTY GOOD SCORE.
IT'S ONLY A LITTLE LOWER THAN MINE.

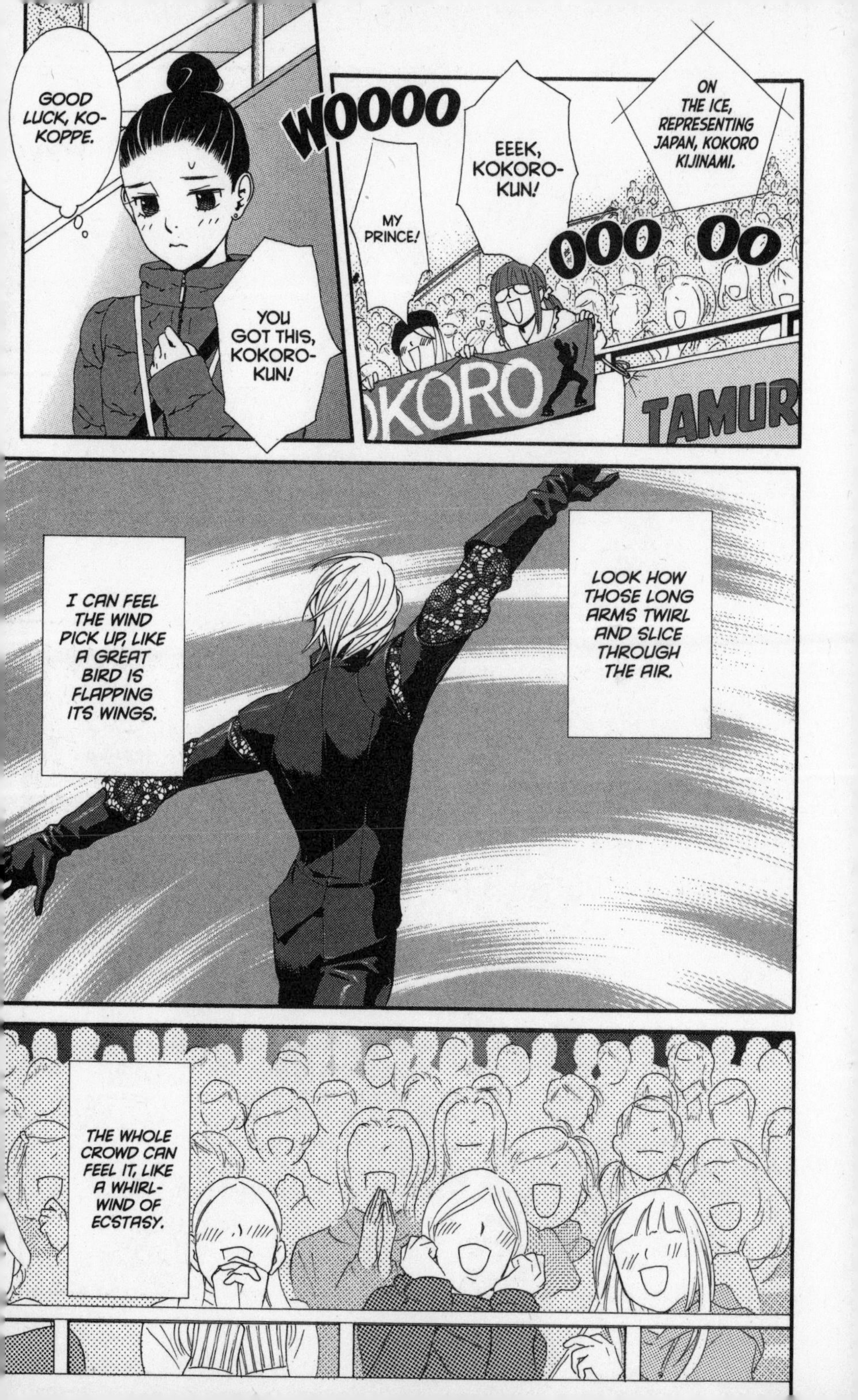
ON THE ICE, REPRESENTING JAPAN, KOKORO KIJINAMI.
WOOOO
EEEK, KOKORO-KUN!
MY PRINCE!
OOO OO
OKORO
TAMUR
GOOD LUCK, KO-KOPPE.
YOU GOT THIS, KOKORO-KUN!
LOOK HOW THOSE LONG ARMS TWIRL AND SLICE THROUGH THE AIR.
I CAN FEEL THE WIND PICK UP, LIKE A GREAT BIRD IS FLAPPING ITS WINGS.
THE WHOLE CROWD CAN FEEL IT, LIKE A WHIRL-WIND OF ECSTASY.

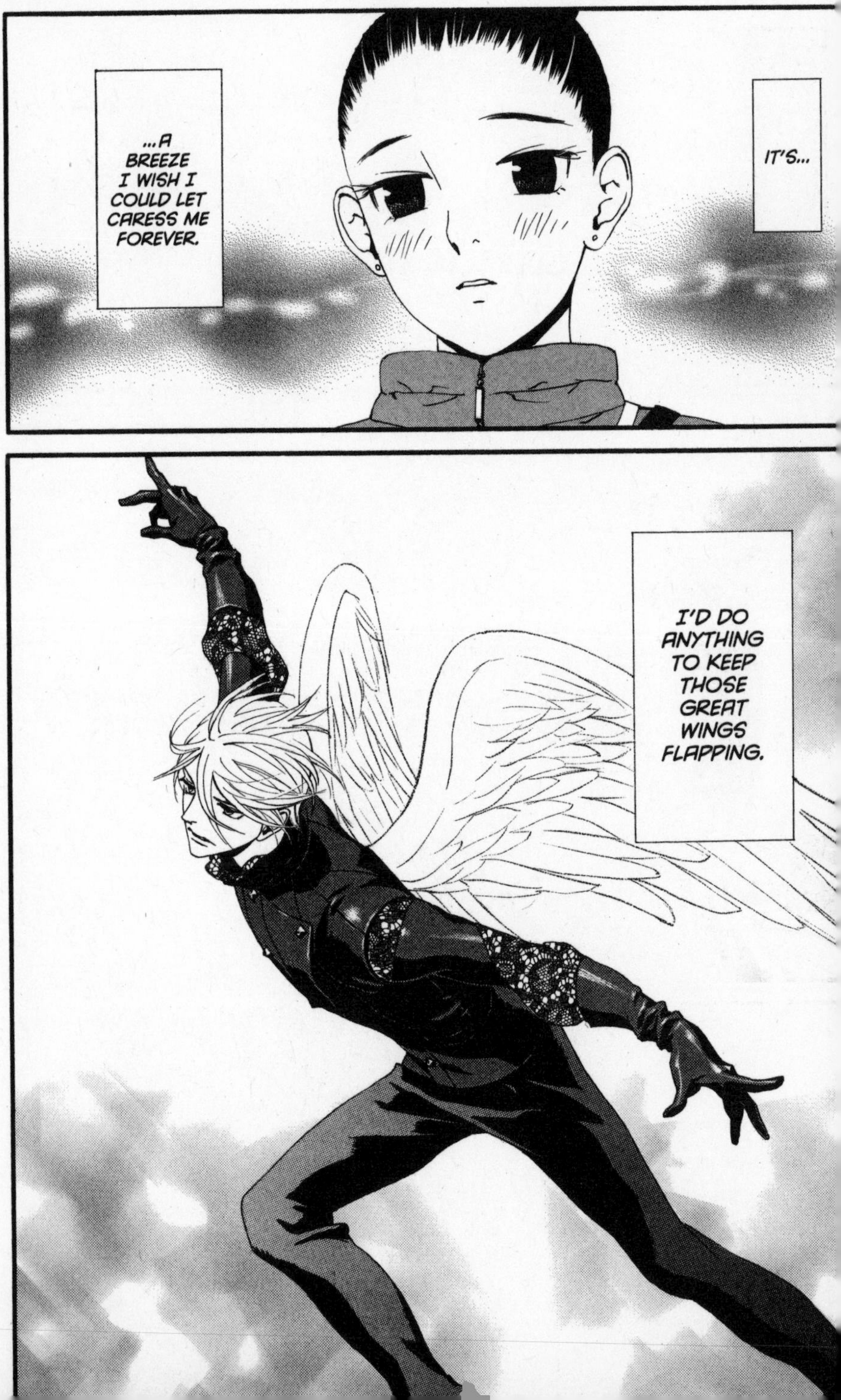
IT'S...
...A BREEZE I WISH I COULD LET CARESS ME FOREVER.
I'D DO ANYTHING TO KEEP THOSE GREAT WINGS FLAPPING.

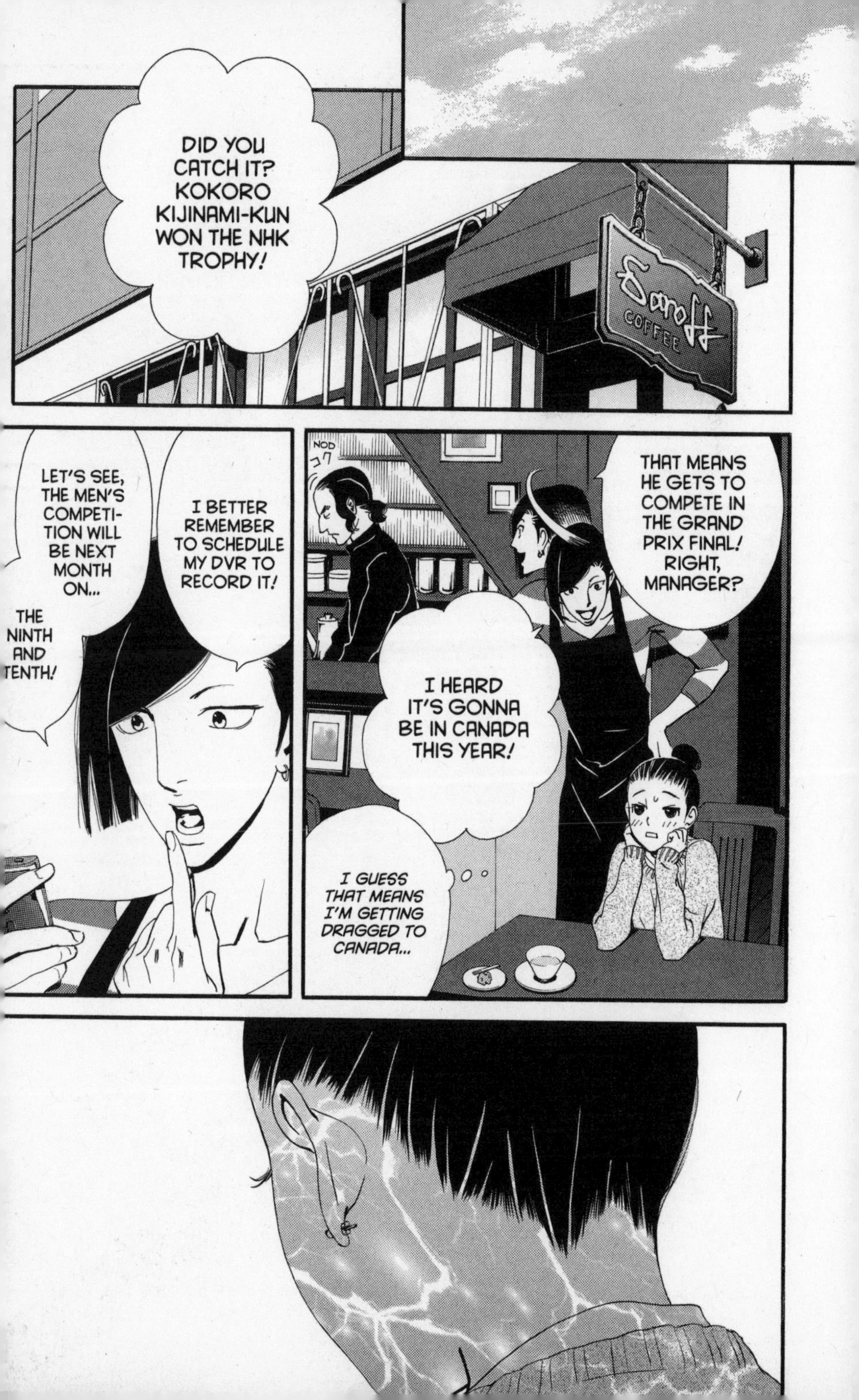
DID YOU CATCH IT? KOKORO KIJINAMI-KUN WON THE NHK TROPHY!
COFFEE
THAT MEANS HE GETS TO COMPETE IN THE GRAND PRIX FINAL! RIGHT, MANAGER?
NOD
I HEARD IT'S GONNA BE IN CANADA THIS YEAR!
I GUESS THAT MEANS I'M GETTING DRAGGED TO CANADA...
I BETTER REMEMBER TO SCHEDULE MY DVR TO RECORD IT!
LET'S SEE, THE MEN'S COMPETITION WILL BE NEXT MONTH ON...
THE NINTH AND TENTH!

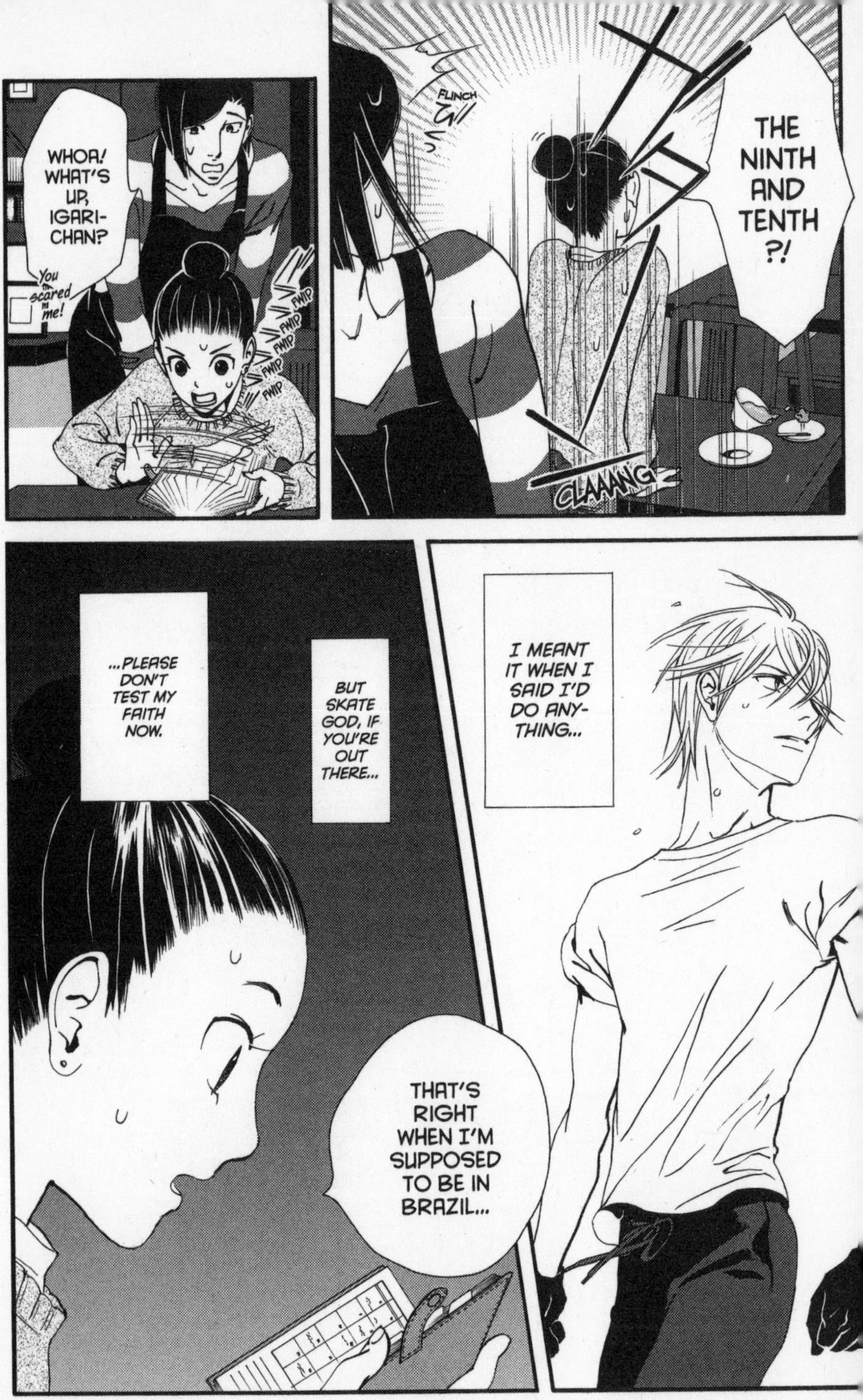
FLINCH
THE NINTH AND TENTH?!
CLAAANG
WHOA! WHAT'S UP, IGARI-CHAN?
You scared me!
FWIP
FWIP
FWIP
FWIP
FWIP
I MEANT IT WHEN I SAID I'D DO ANYTHING...
BUT SKATE GOD, IF YOU'RE OUT THERE...
...PLEASE DON'T TEST MY FAITH NOW.
THAT'S RIGHT WHEN I'M SUPPOSED TO BE IN BRAZIL...

Spell 4
The Magic Kiss

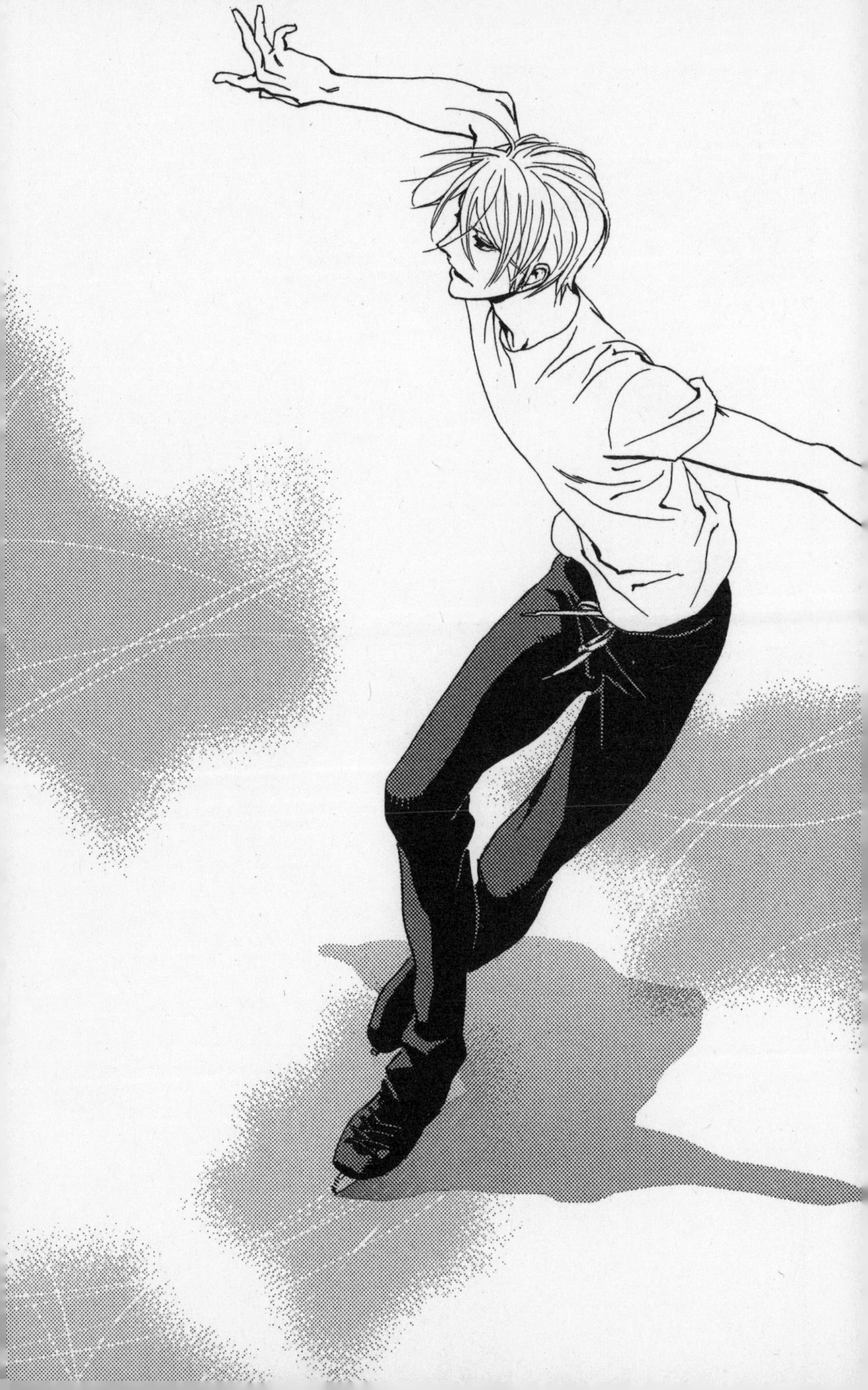

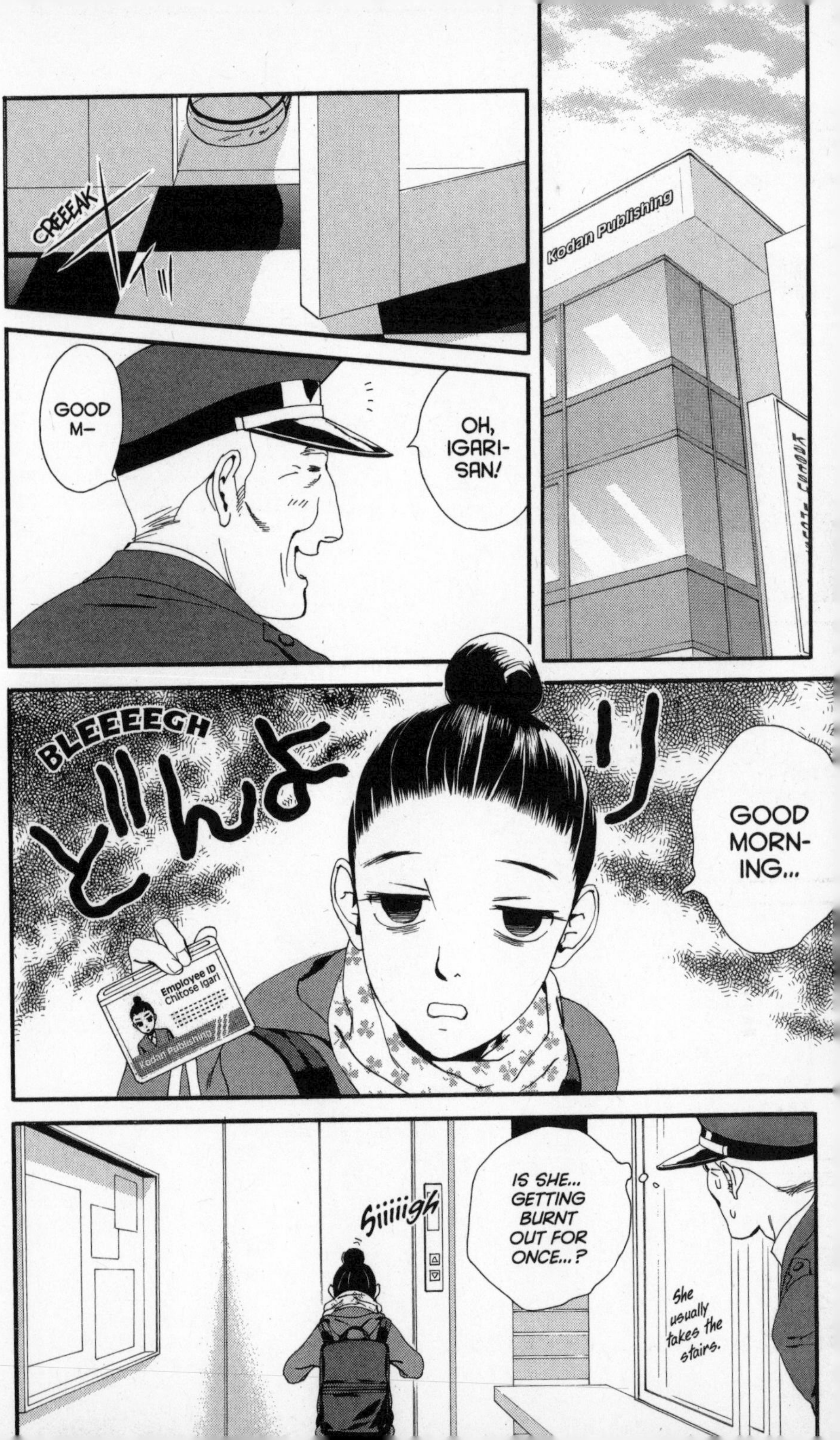
Kodan Publishing
CREEEAK
OH, IGARI-SAN!
GOOD M—
GOOD MORNING...
BLEEEEGH
どんより
Employee ID Chitose Igari
Kodan Publishing
IS SHE... GETTING BURNT OUT FOR ONCE...?
She usually takes the stairs.
Siiiiigh

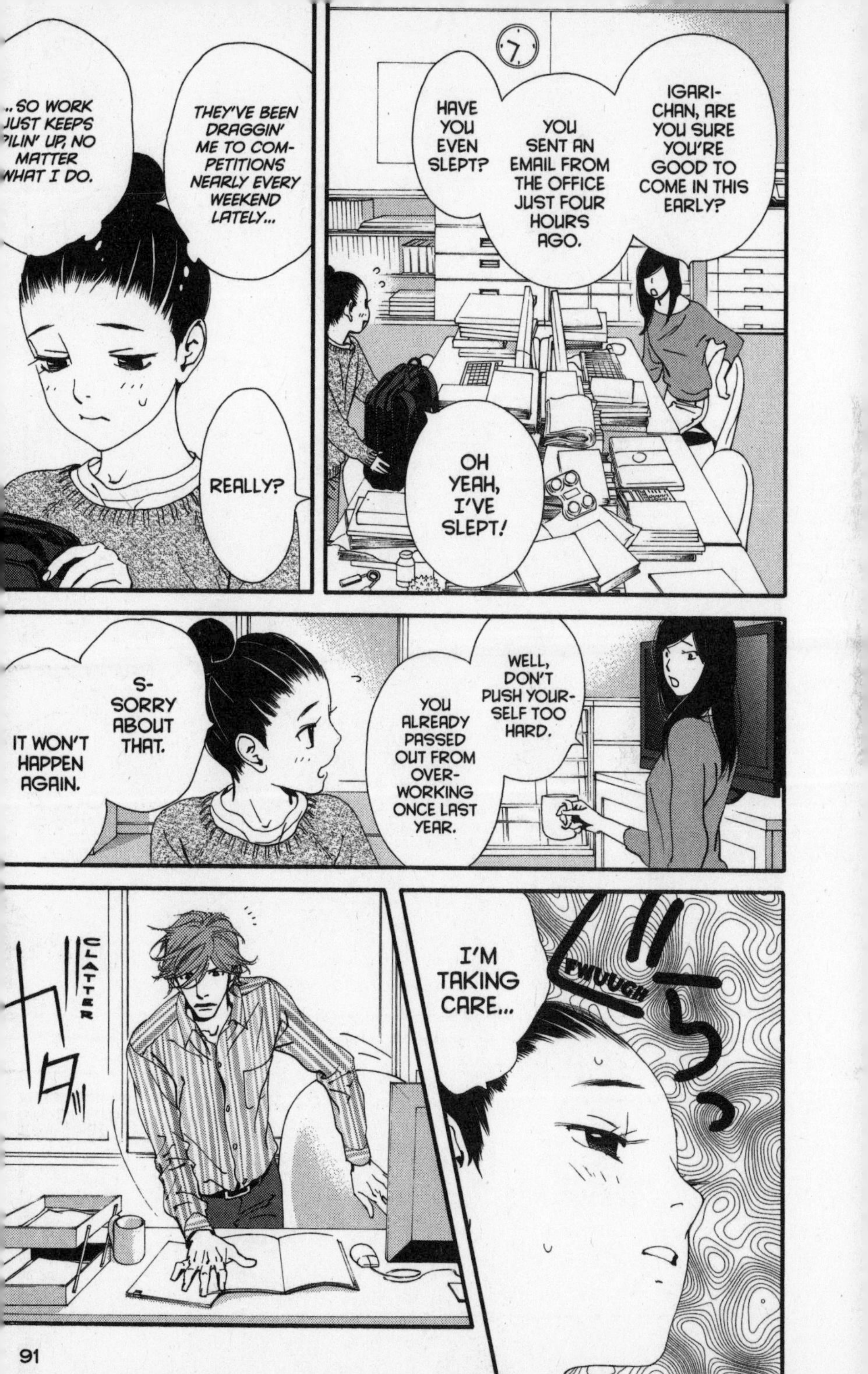
IGARI-CHAN, ARE YOU SURE YOU'RE GOOD TO COME IN THIS EARLY?
YOU SENT AN EMAIL FROM THE OFFICE JUST FOUR HOURS AGO.
HAVE YOU EVEN SLEPT?
OH YEAH, I'VE SLEPT!
THEY'VE BEEN DRAGGIN' ME TO COMPETITIONS NEARLY EVERY WEEKEND LATELY...
..SO WORK JUST KEEPS PILIN' UP, NO MATTER WHAT I DO.
REALLY?
WELL, DON'T PUSH YOURSELF TOO HARD.
YOU ALREADY PASSED OUT FROM OVERWORKING ONCE LAST YEAR.
S-SORRY ABOUT THAT.
IT WON'T HAPPEN AGAIN.
FWUUGH
I'M TAKING CARE...
CLATTER

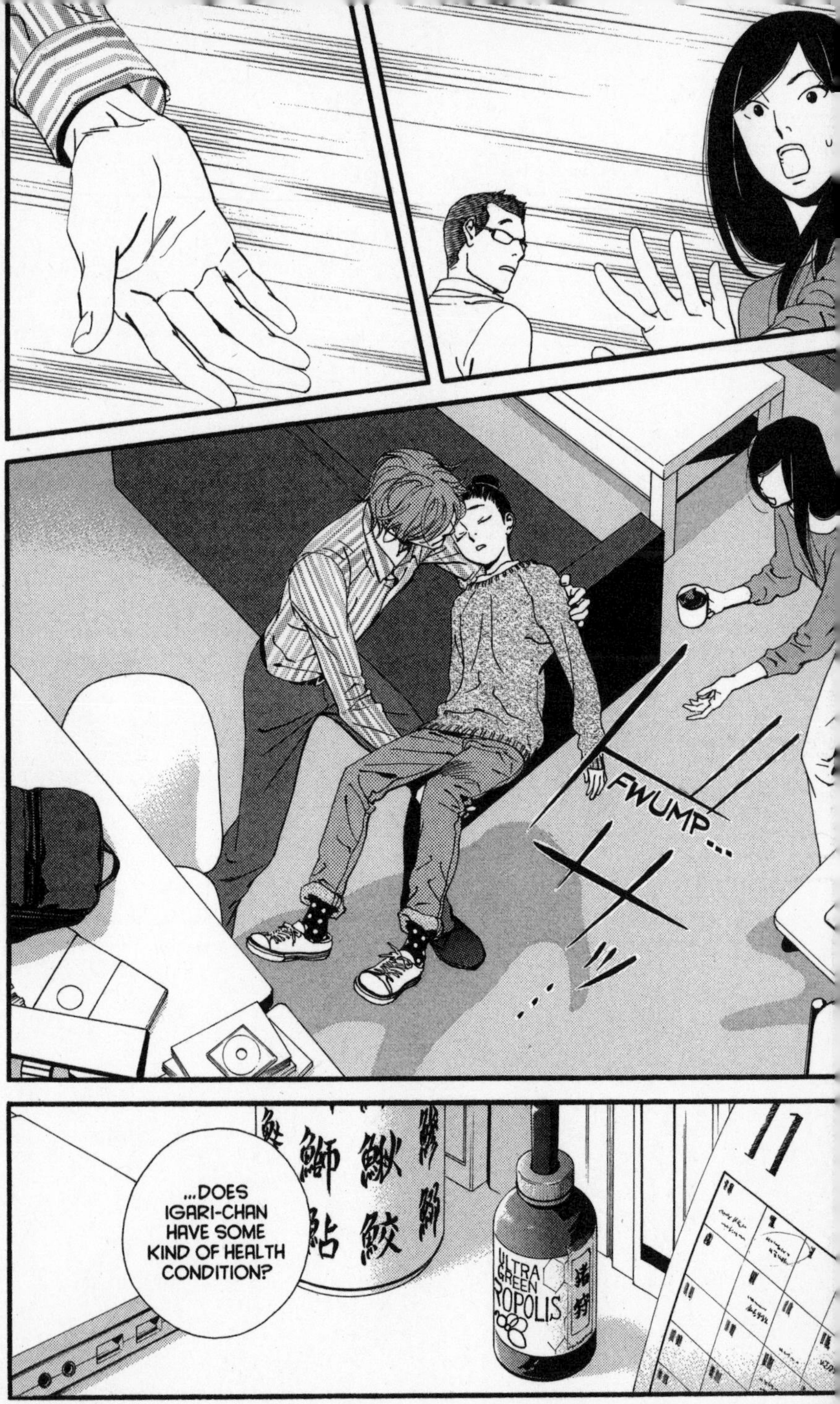
FWUMP...
...
...DOES IGARI-CHAN HAVE SOME KIND OF HEALTH CONDITION?
ULTRA GREEN

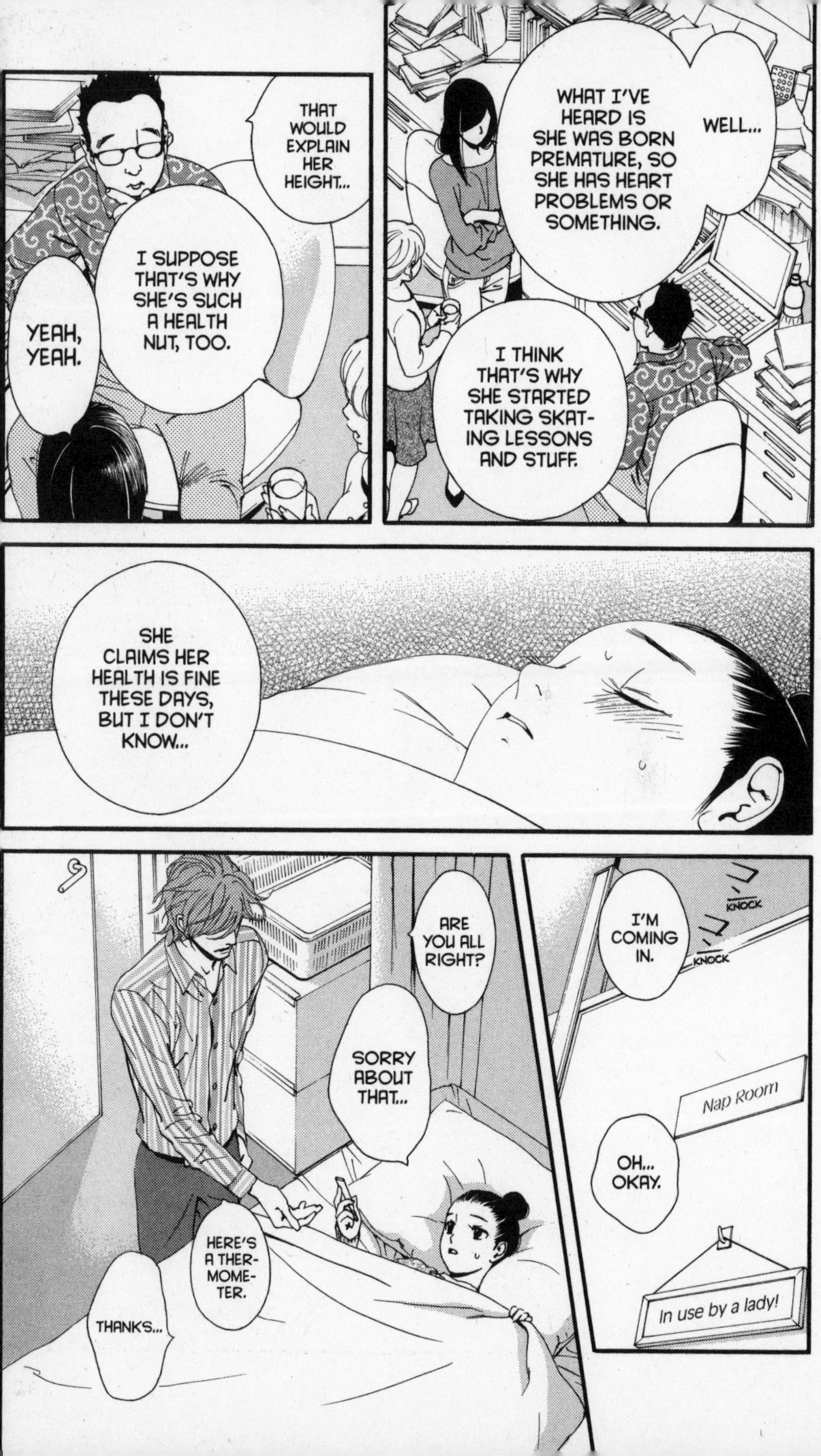
WELL...
WHAT I'VE HEARD IS SHE WAS BORN PREMATURE, SO SHE HAS HEART PROBLEMS OR SOMETHING.
I THINK THAT'S WHY SHE STARTED TAKING SKATING LESSONS AND STUFF.
THAT WOULD EXPLAIN HER HEIGHT...
I SUPPOSE THAT'S WHY SHE'S SUCH A HEALTH NUT, TOO.
YEAH, YEAH.
SHE CLAIMS HER HEALTH IS FINE THESE DAYS, BUT I DON'T KNOW...
KNOCK
KNOCK
I'M COMING IN.
Nap Room
OH... OKAY.
In use by a lady!
ARE YOU ALL RIGHT?
SORRY ABOUT THAT...
HERE'S A THERMOMETER.
THANKS...

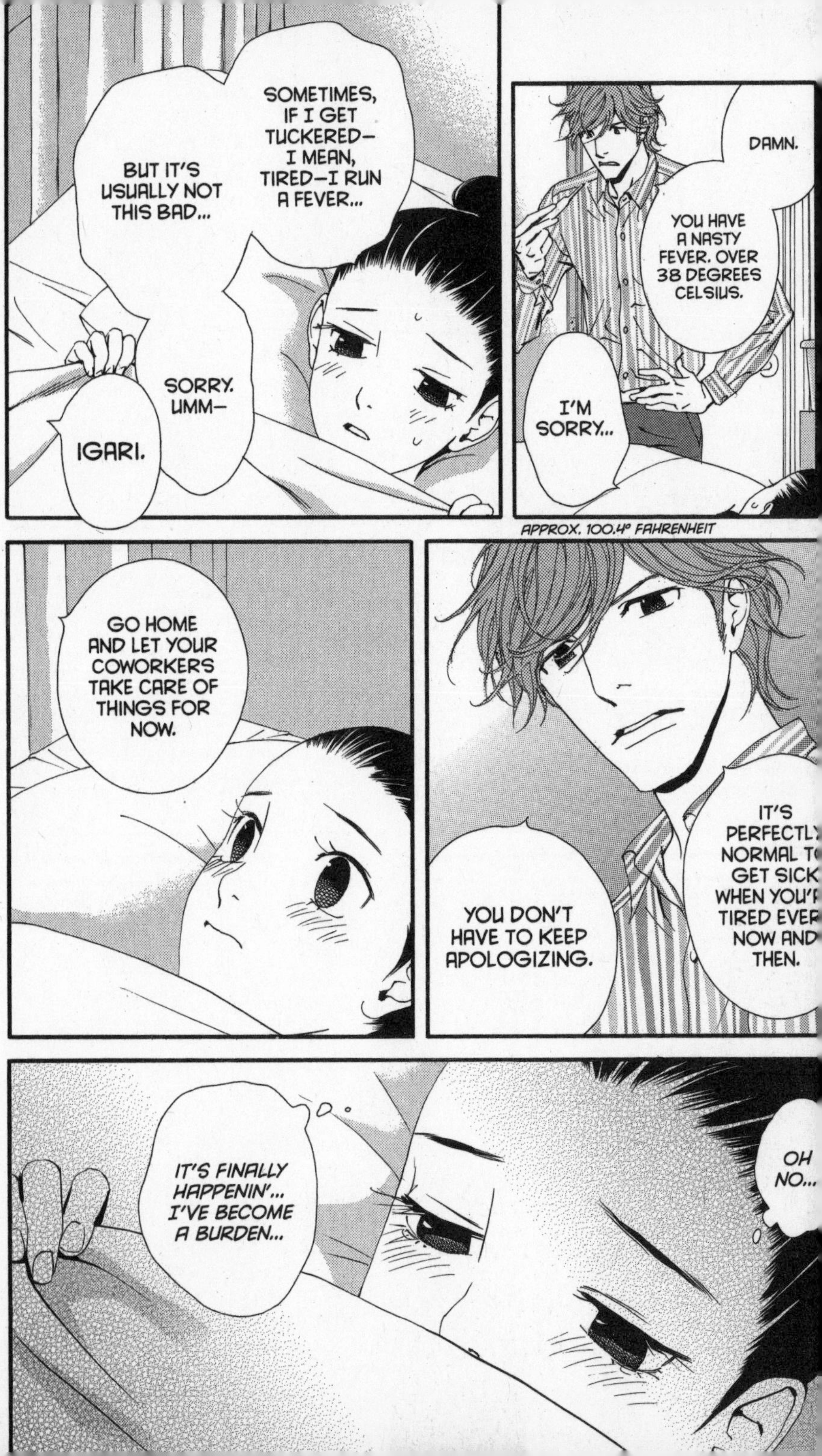
DAMN.
YOU HAVE A NASTY FEVER. OVER 38 DEGREES CELSIUS.
I'M SORRY...
APPROX. 100.4° FAHRENHEIT
SOMETIMES, IF I GET TUCKERED— I MEAN, TIRED—I RUN A FEVER...
BUT IT'S USUALLY NOT THIS BAD...
SORRY. UMM—
IGARI.
IT'S PERFECTL NORMAL T GET SICK WHEN YOU' TIRED EVER NOW AND THEN.
YOU DON'T HAVE TO KEEP APOLOGIZING.
GO HOME AND LET YOUR COWORKERS TAKE CARE OF THINGS FOR NOW.
OH NO...
IT'S FINALLY HAPPENIN'... I'VE BECOME A BURDEN...

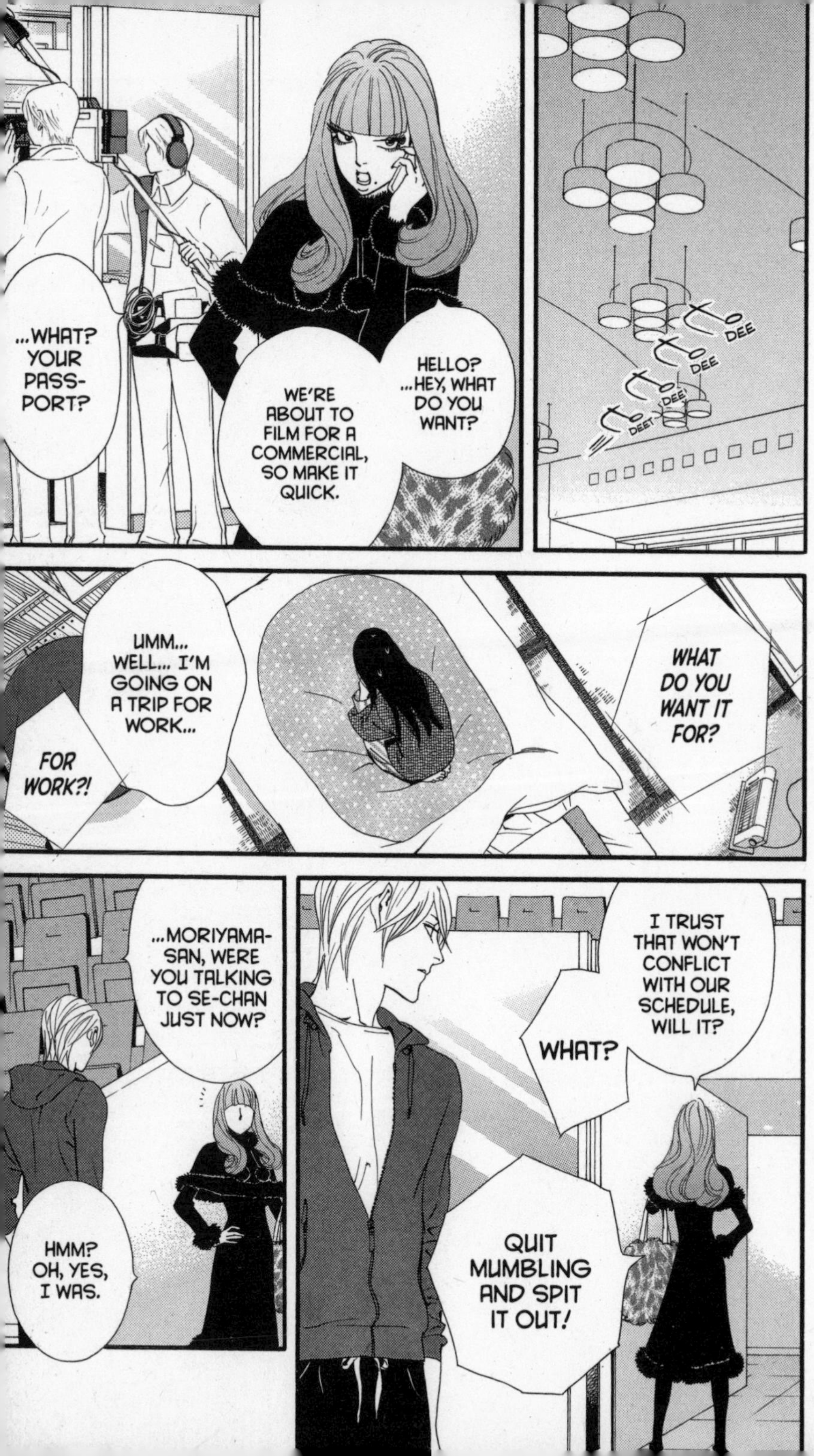
DEE DEE DEE DEE DEET
HELLO? ...HEY, WHAT DO YOU WANT?
WE'RE ABOUT TO FILM FOR A COMMERCIAL, SO MAKE IT QUICK.
...WHAT? YOUR PASSPORT?
WHAT DO YOU WANT IT FOR?
UMM... WELL... I'M GOING ON A TRIP FOR WORK...
FOR WORK?!
I TRUST THAT WON'T CONFLICT WITH OUR SCHEDULE, WILL IT?
WHAT?
QUIT MUMBLING AND SPIT IT OUT!
...MORIYAMA-SAN, WERE YOU TALKING TO SE-CHAN JUST NOW?
HMM? OH, YES, I WAS.

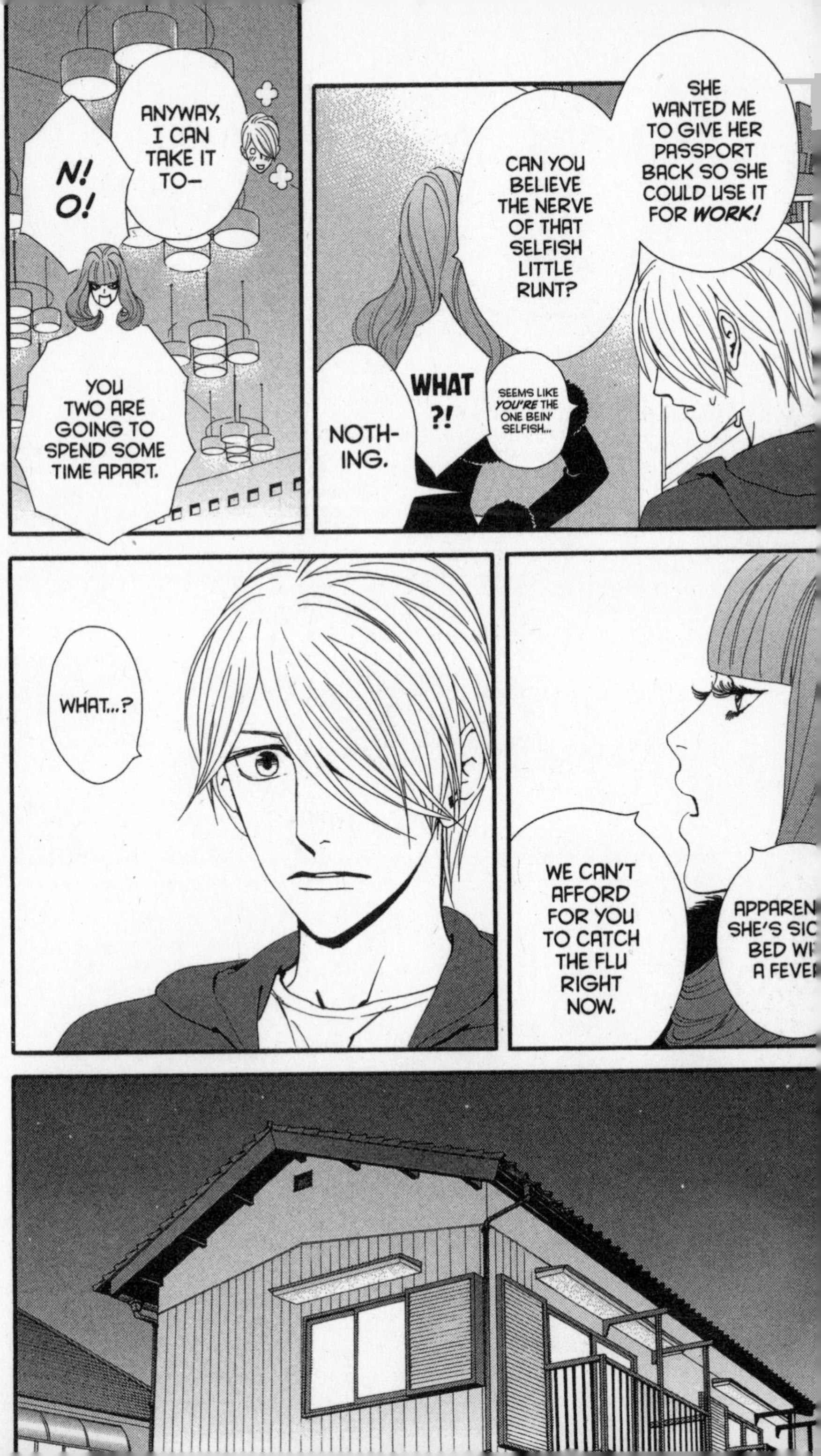
SHE WANTED ME TO GIVE HER PASSPORT BACK SO SHE COULD USE IT FOR *WORK!*
CAN YOU BELIEVE THE NERVE OF THAT SELFISH LITTLE RUNT?
SEEMS LIKE *YOU'RE* THE ONE BEIN' SELFISH...
WHAT ?!
NOTH-ING.
ANYWAY, I CAN TAKE IT TO—
N! O!
YOU TWO ARE GOING TO SPEND SOME TIME APART.
APPAREN SHE'S SIC BED WI A FEVE
WE CAN'T AFFORD FOR YOU TO CATCH THE FLU RIGHT NOW.
WHAT...?

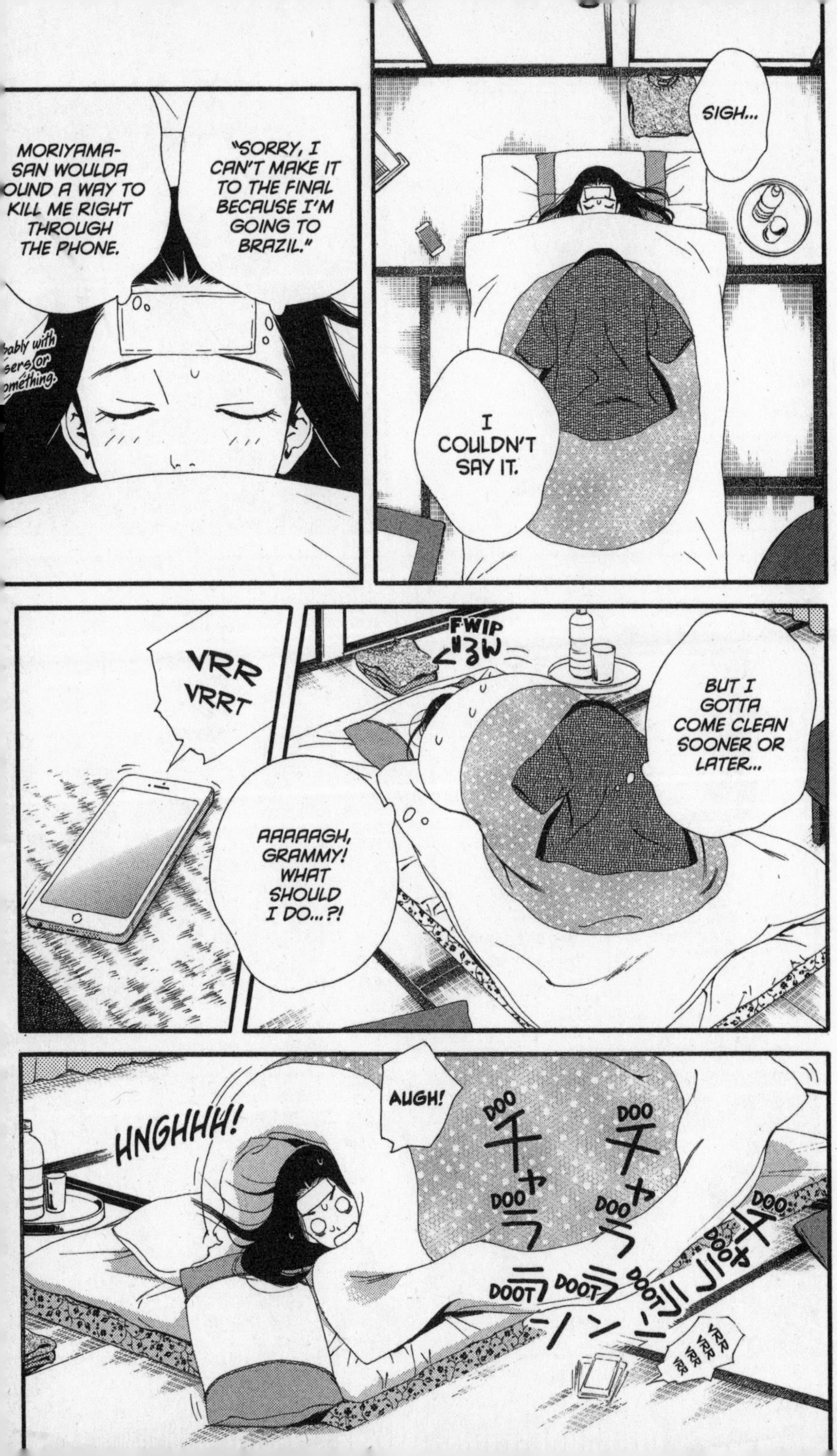
SIGH...
I COULDN'T SAY IT.
"SORRY, I CAN'T MAKE IT TO THE FINAL BECAUSE I'M GOING TO BRAZIL."
MORIYAMA-SAN WOULDA OUND A WAY TO KILL ME RIGHT THROUGH THE PHONE.
bably with sers or omething.
FWIP
BUT I GOTTA COME CLEAN SOONER OR LATER...
AAAAAGH, GRAMMY! WHAT SHOULD I DO...?!
VRR VRRT
AUGH!
DOO DOO DOO DOO DOO
HNGHHH!
DOOT DOOT DOOT DOOT
VRR VRR VRR

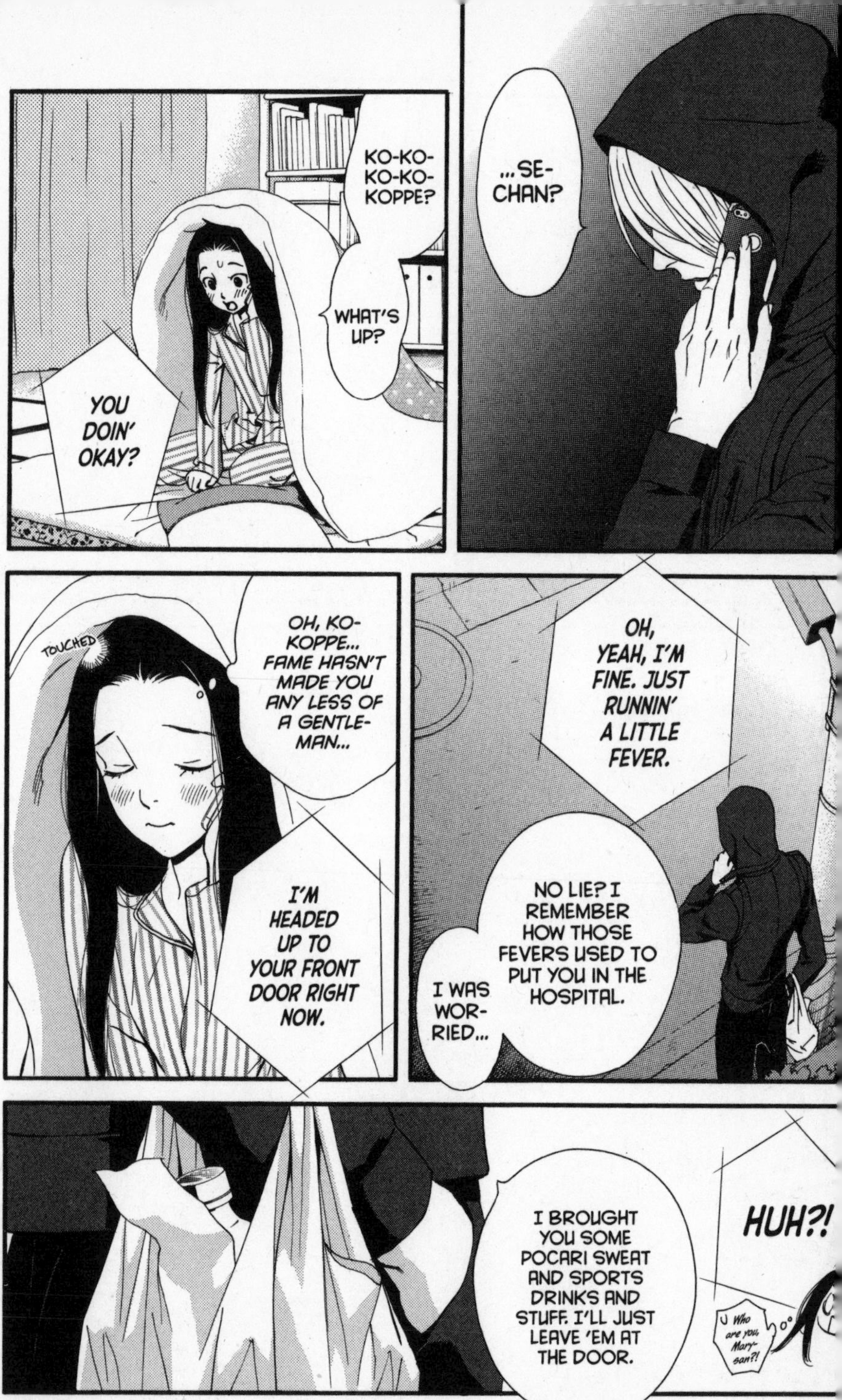
...SE-CHAN?
KO-KO-KO-KO-KOPPE?
WHAT'S UP?
YOU DOIN' OKAY?
OH, YEAH, I'M FINE. JUST RUNNIN' A LITTLE FEVER.
NO LIE? I REMEMBER HOW THOSE FEVERS USED TO PUT YOU IN THE HOSPITAL.
I WAS WOR-RIED...
TOUCHED
OH, KO-KOPPE... FAME HASN'T MADE YOU ANY LESS OF A GENTLE-MAN...
I'M HEADED UP TO YOUR FRONT DOOR RIGHT NOW.
HUH?!
Who are you, Mary-san?!
I BROUGHT YOU SOME POCARI SWEAT AND SPORTS DRINKS AND STUFF. I'LL JUST LEAVE 'EM AT THE DOOR.

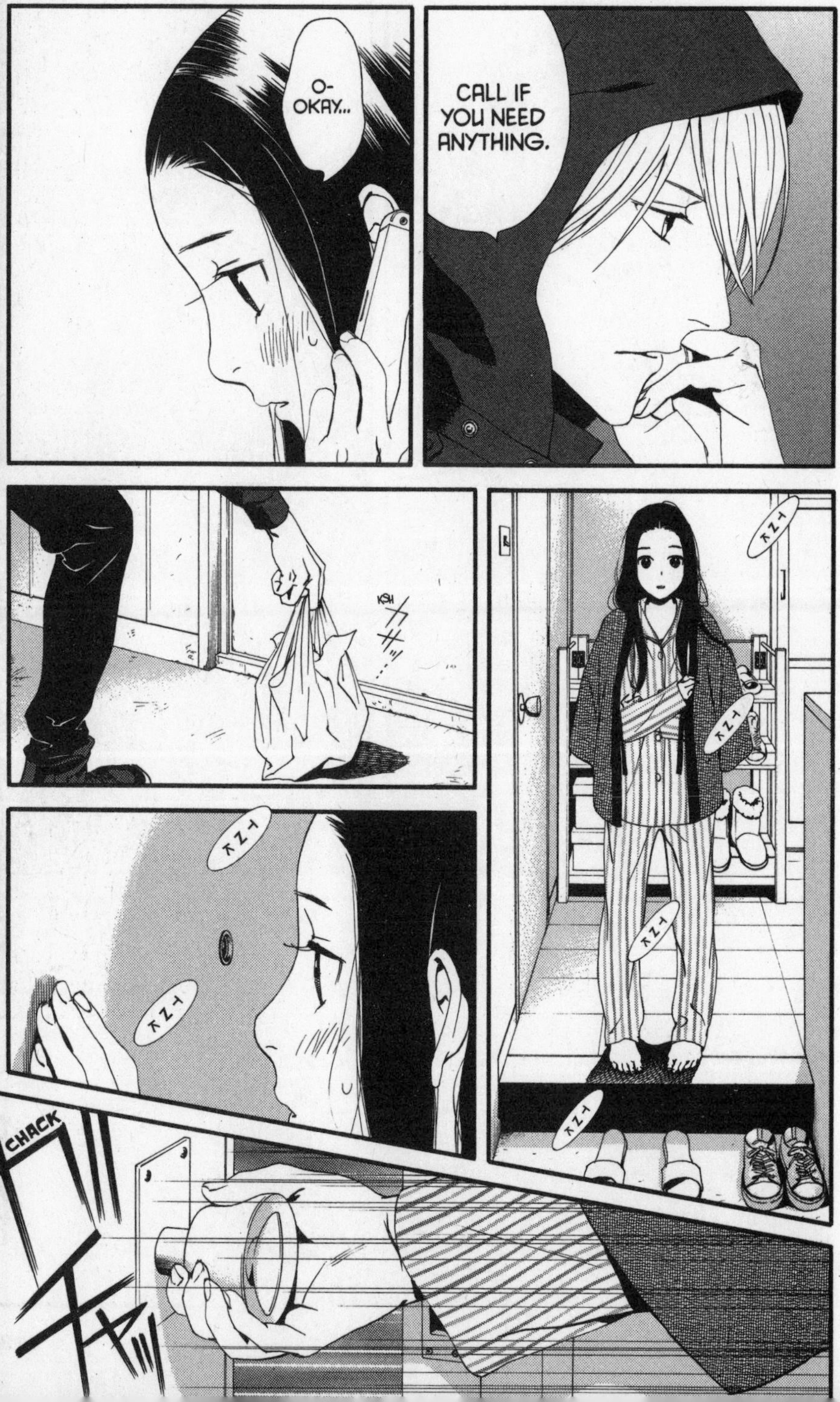
CALL IF YOU NEED ANYTHING.
O- OKAY...
KSH
CHACK

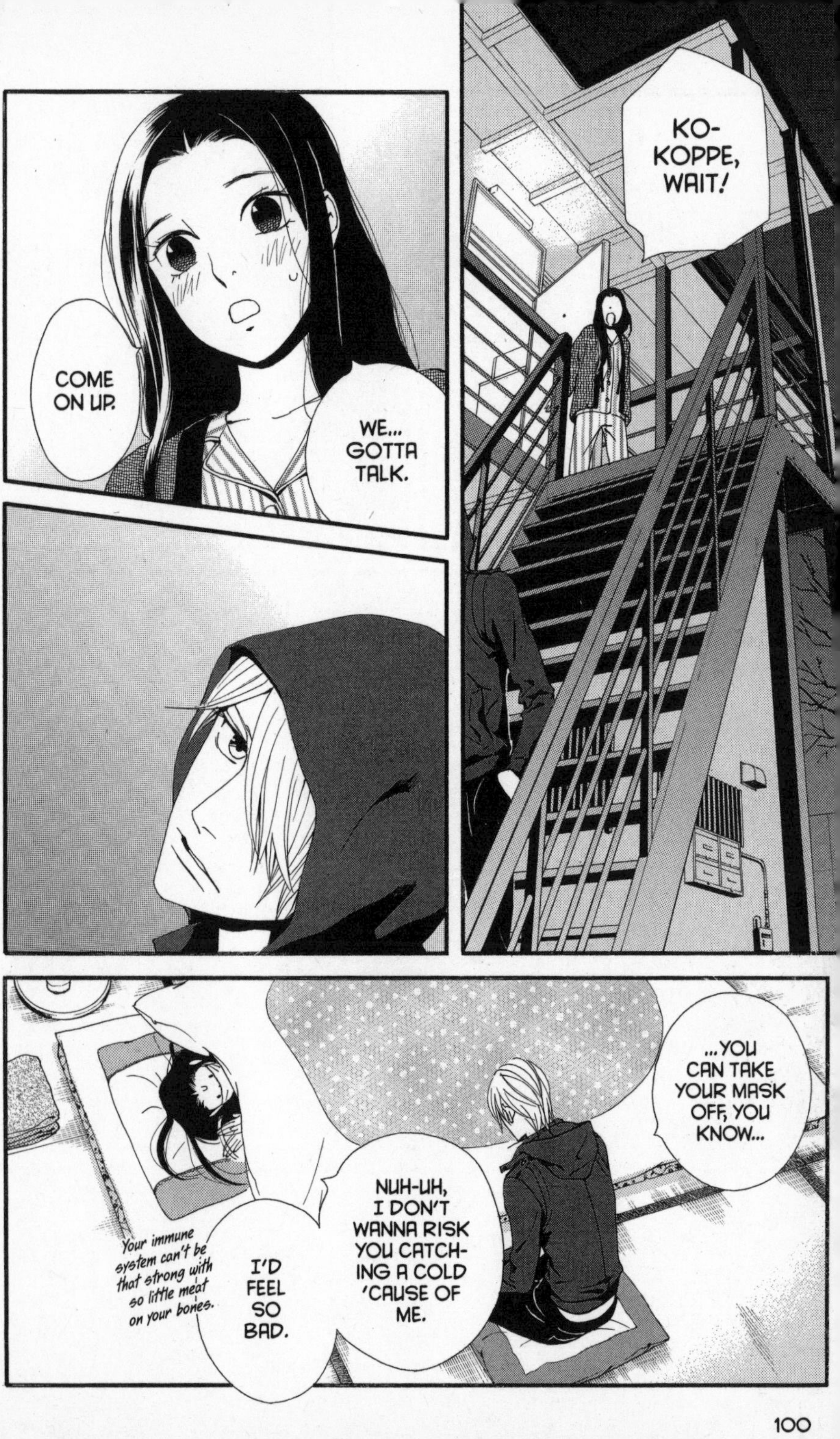
KO-KOPPE, WAIT!
COME ON UP.
WE... GOTTA TALK.
...YOU CAN TAKE YOUR MASK OFF, YOU KNOW...
NUH-UH, I DON'T WANNA RISK YOU CATCHING A COLD 'CAUSE OF ME.
I'D FEEL SO BAD.
Your immune system can't be that strong with so little meat on your bones.

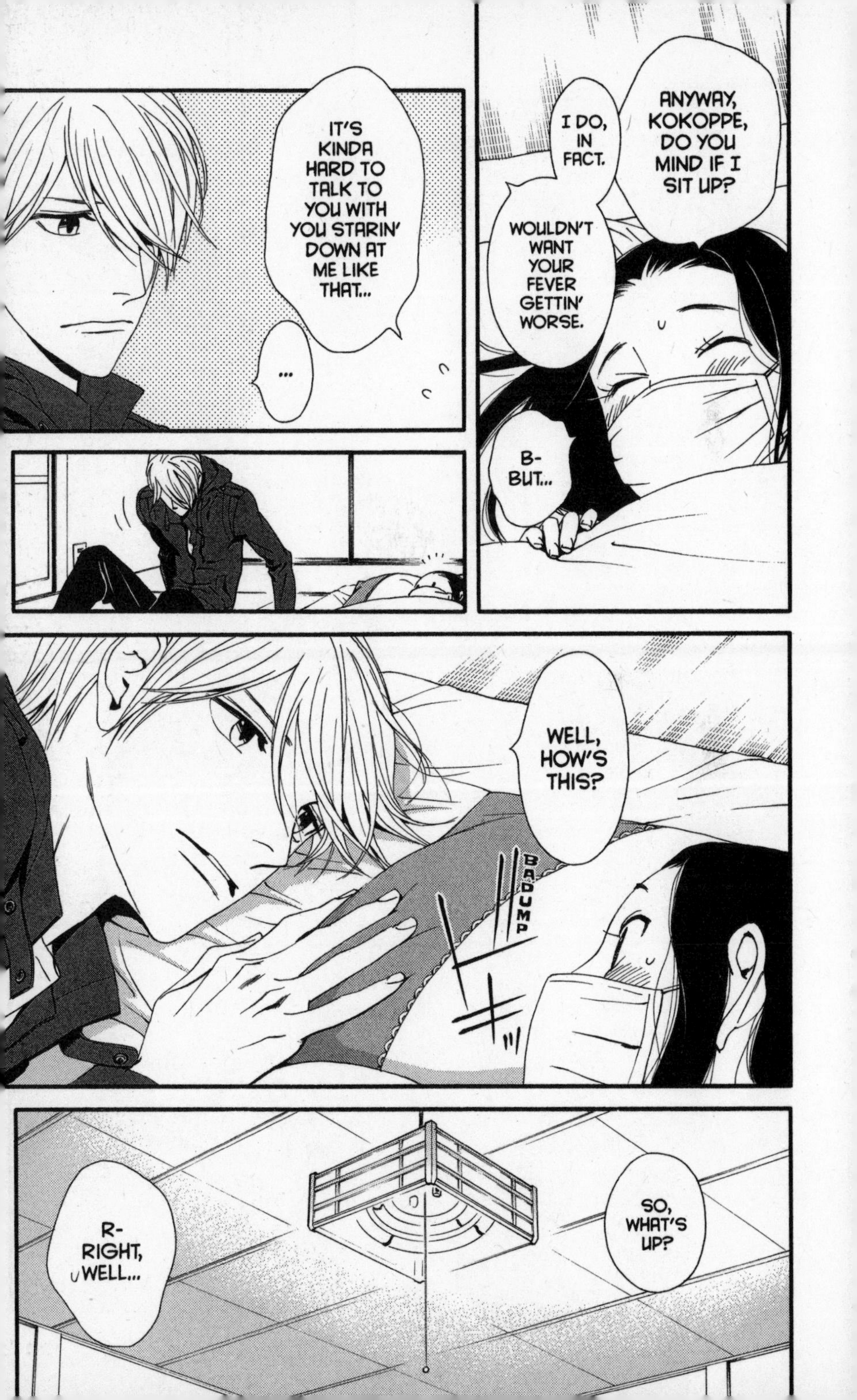
ANYWAY, KOKOPPE, DO YOU MIND IF I SIT UP?
I DO, IN FACT.
WOULDN'T WANT YOUR FEVER GETTIN' WORSE.
B-BUT...
IT'S KINDA HARD TO TALK TO YOU WITH YOU STARIN' DOWN AT ME LIKE THAT...
...
WELL, HOW'S THIS?
BADUMP
SO, WHAT'S UP?
R-RIGHT, WELL...

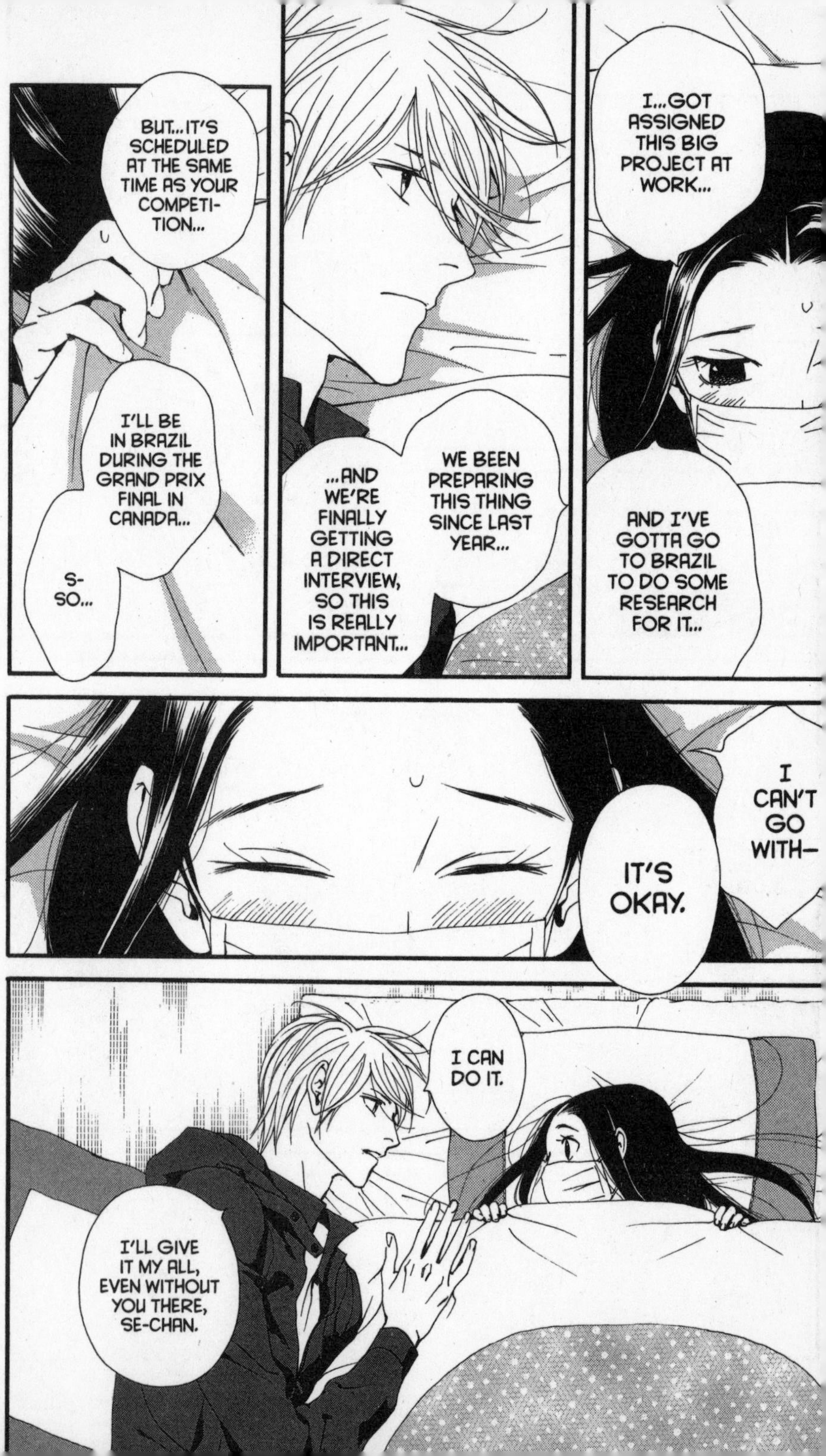
I...GOT ASSIGNED THIS BIG PROJECT AT WORK...
AND I'VE GOTTA GO TO BRAZIL TO DO SOME RESEARCH FOR IT...
WE BEEN PREPARING THIS THING SINCE LAST YEAR...
...AND WE'RE FINALLY GETTING A DIRECT INTERVIEW, SO THIS IS REALLY IMPORTANT...
BUT...IT'S SCHEDULED AT THE SAME TIME AS YOUR COMPETITION...
I'LL BE IN BRAZIL DURING THE GRAND PRIX FINAL IN CANADA...
S-SO...
I CAN'T GO WITH—
IT'S OKAY.
I CAN DO IT.
I'LL GIVE IT MY ALL, EVEN WITHOUT YOU THERE, SE-CHAN.

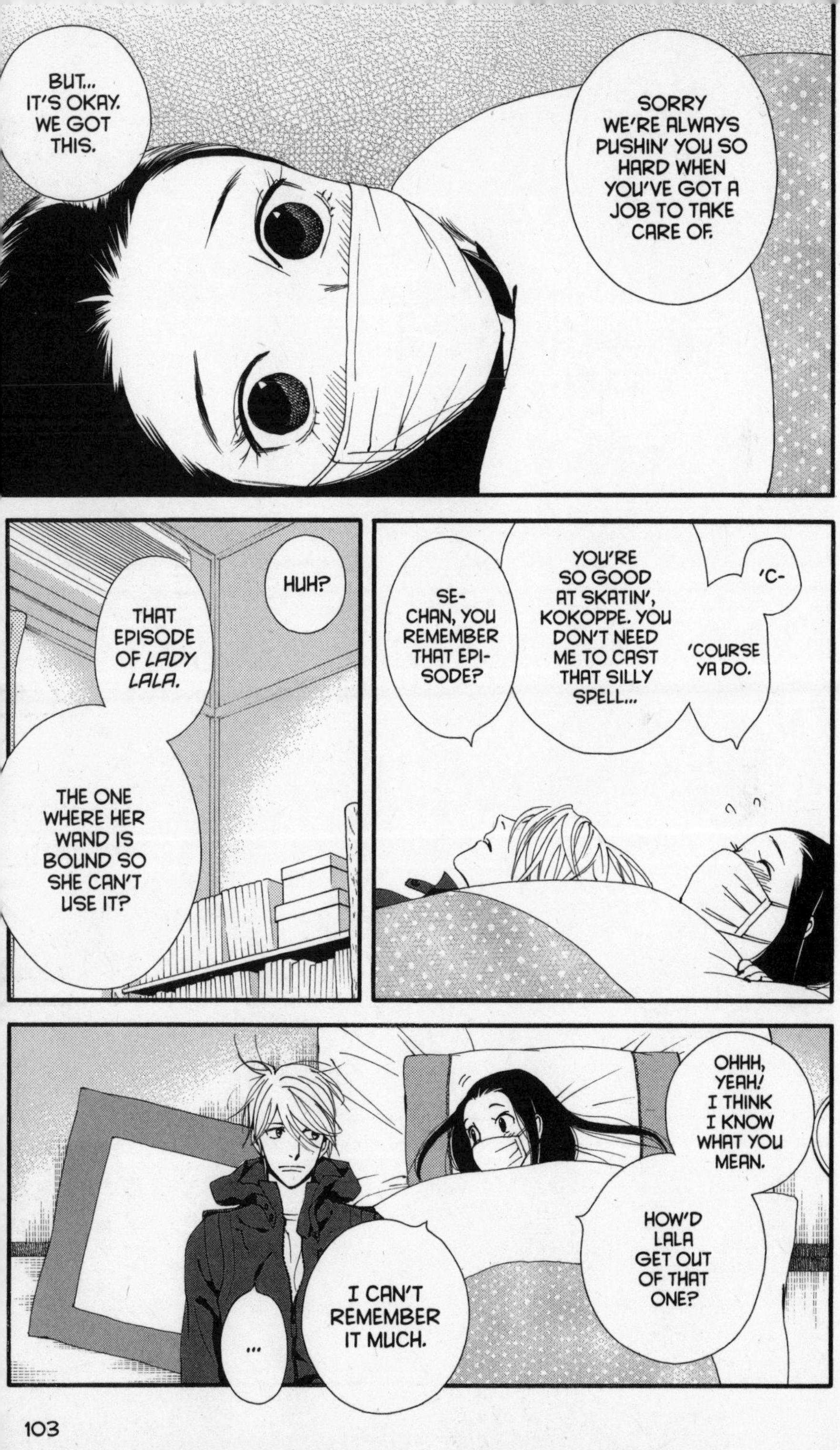
SORRY WE'RE ALWAYS PUSHIN' YOU SO HARD WHEN YOU'VE GOT A JOB TO TAKE CARE OF.
BUT... IT'S OKAY. WE GOT THIS.
'C-
'COURSE YA DO.
YOU'RE SO GOOD AT SKATIN', KOKOPPE. YOU DON'T NEED ME TO CAST THAT SILLY SPELL...
SE-CHAN, YOU REMEMBER THAT EPISODE?
HUH?
THAT EPISODE OF *LADY LALA*.
THE ONE WHERE HER WAND IS BOUND SO SHE CAN'T USE IT?
OHHH, YEAH! I THINK I KNOW WHAT YOU MEAN.
HOW'D LALA GET OUT OF THAT ONE?
I CAN'T REMEMBER IT MUCH.
...

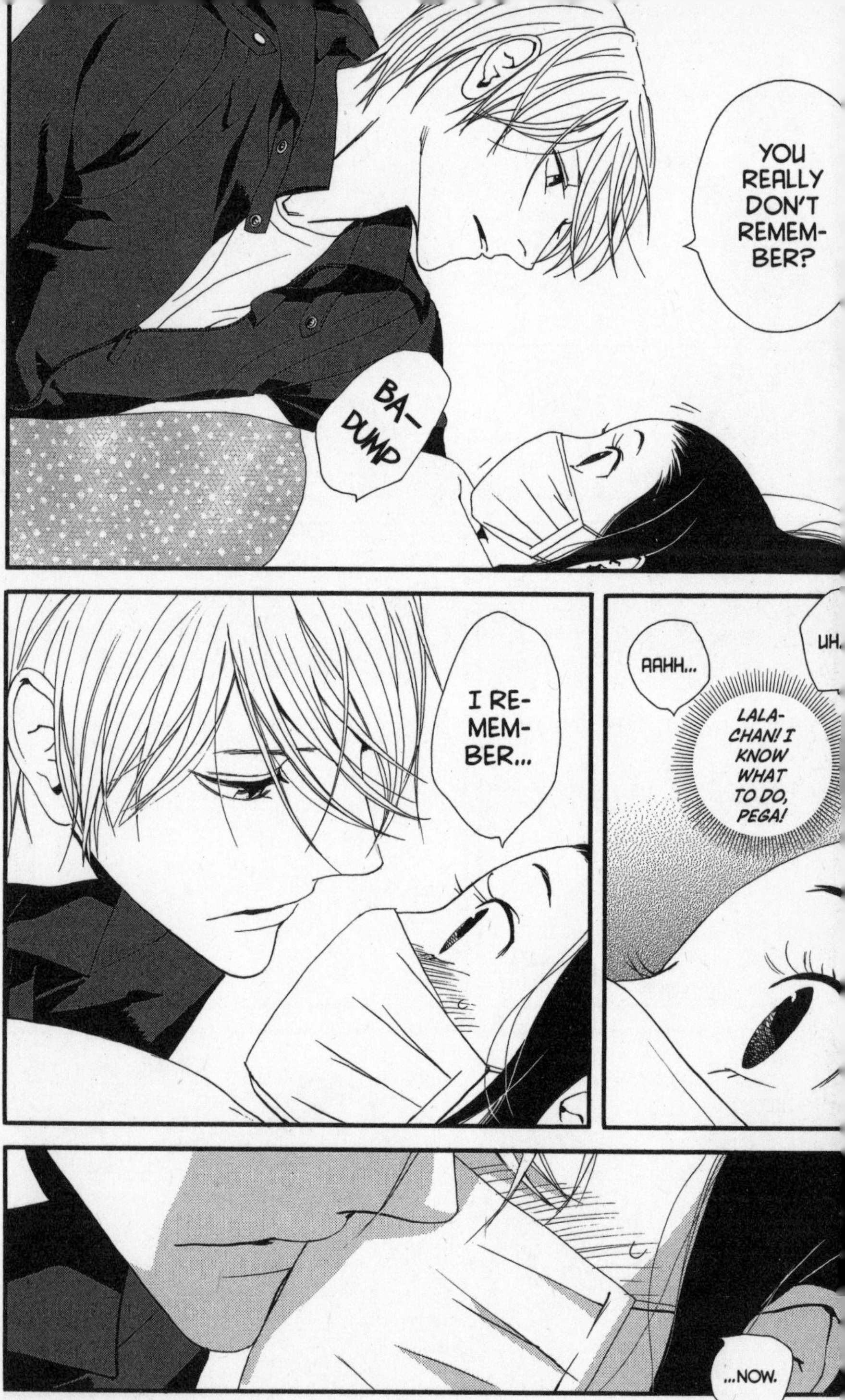
YOU REALLY DON'T REMEMBER?
BA-DUMP
UH..
AAHH...
LALA-CHAN! I KNOW WHAT TO DO, PEGA!
I RE-MEMBER...
...NOW.

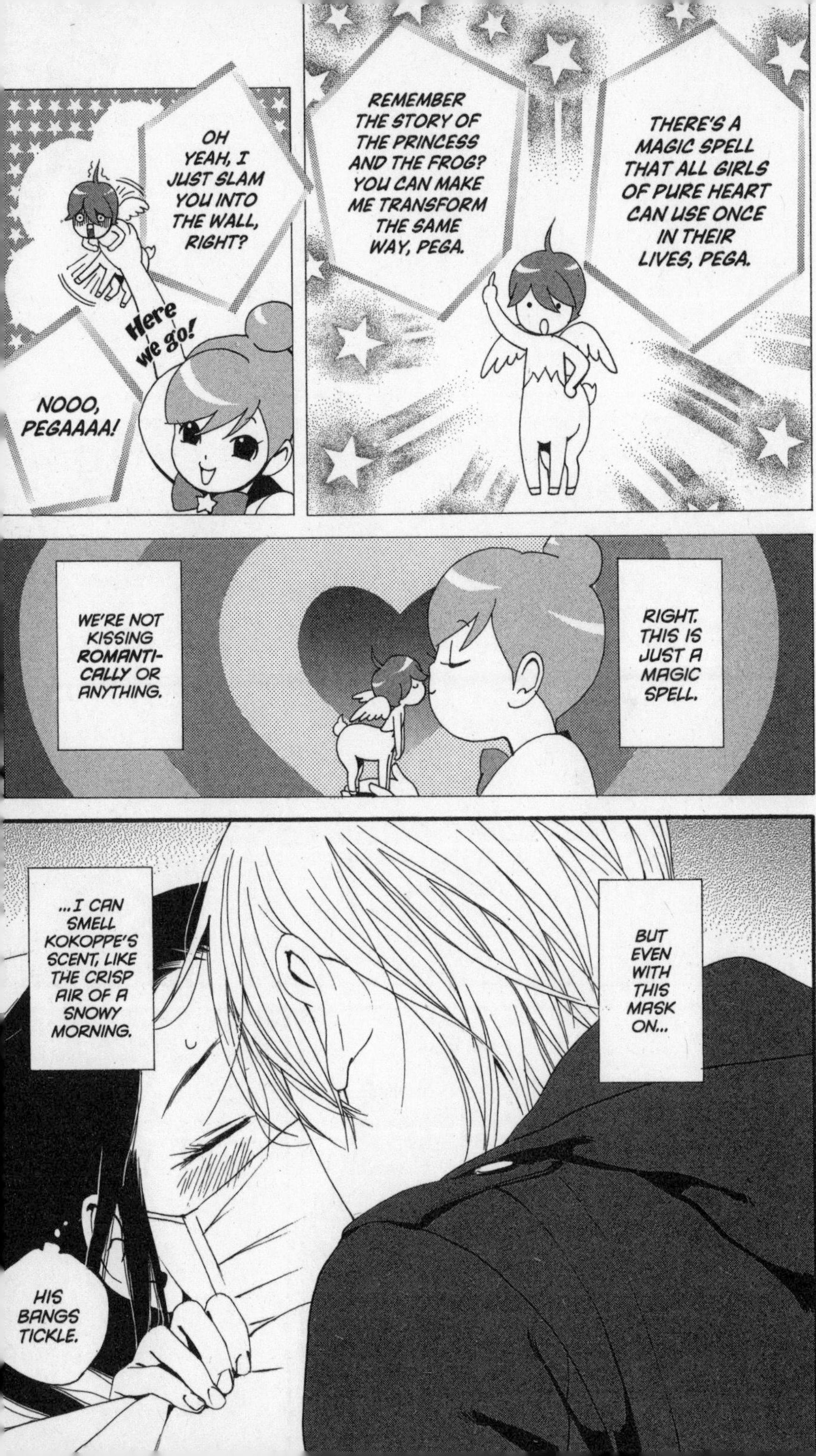
THERE'S A MAGIC SPELL THAT ALL GIRLS OF PURE HEART CAN USE ONCE IN THEIR LIVES, PEGA.
REMEMBER THE STORY OF THE PRINCESS AND THE FROG? YOU CAN MAKE ME TRANSFORM THE SAME WAY, PEGA.
OH YEAH, I JUST SLAM YOU INTO THE WALL, RIGHT?
Here we go!
NOOO, PEGAAAA!
RIGHT. THIS IS JUST A MAGIC SPELL.
WE'RE NOT KISSING ROMANTICALLY OR ANYTHING.
BUT EVEN WITH THIS MASK ON...
...I CAN SMELL KOKOPPE'S SCENT, LIKE THE CRISP AIR OF A SNOWY MORNING.
HIS BANGS TICKLE.

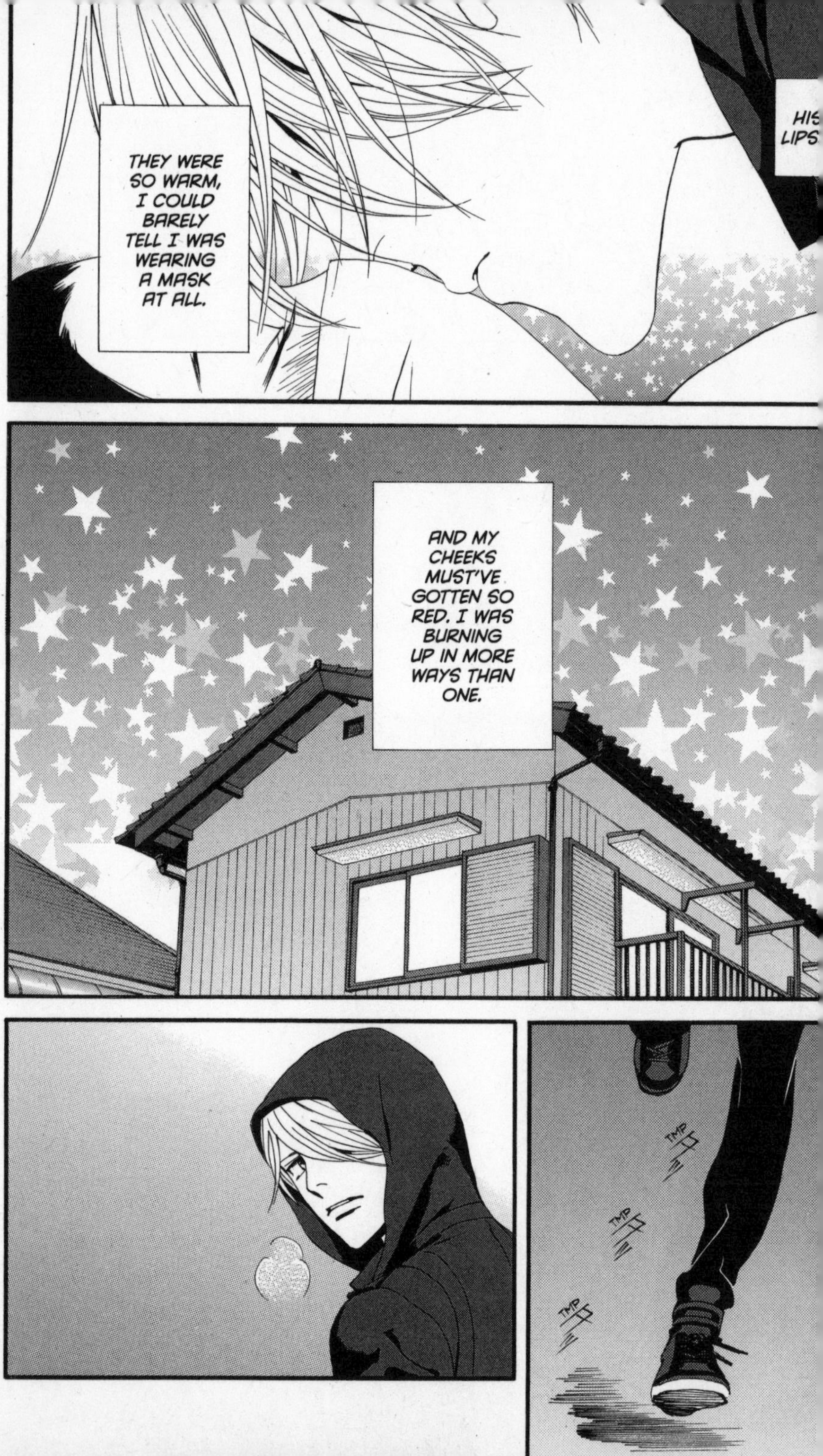
HIS LIPS
THEY WERE SO WARM, I COULD BARELY TELL I WAS WEARING A MASK AT ALL.
AND MY CHEEKS MUST'VE GOTTEN SO RED. I WAS BURNING UP IN MORE WAYS THAN ONE.
TMP
TMP
TMP

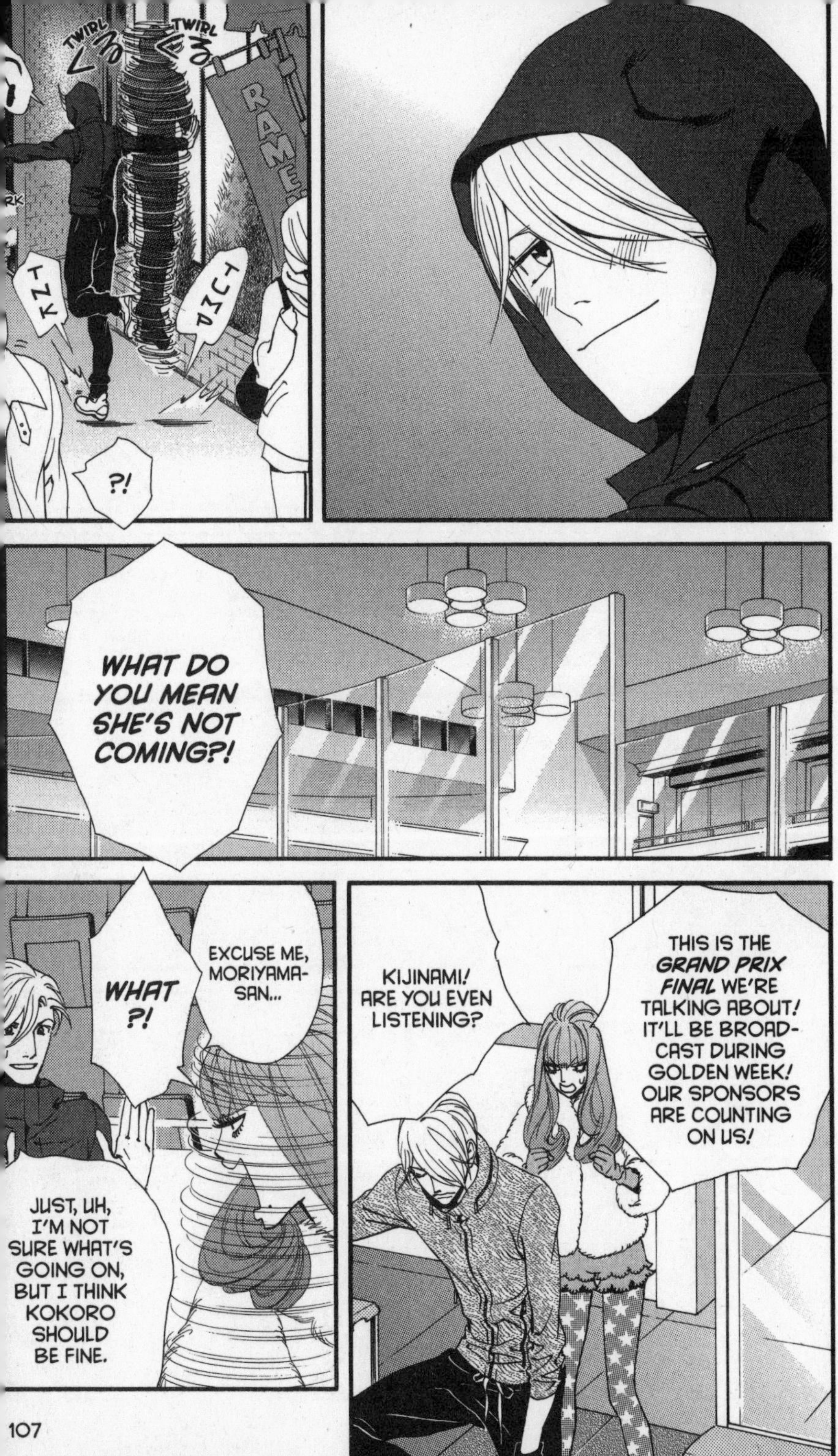

TWIRL
TWIRL
TNK
TUMP
?!
WHAT DO YOU MEAN SHE'S NOT COMING?!
THIS IS THE *GRAND PRIX FINAL* WE'RE TALKING ABOUT! IT'LL BE BROAD-CAST DURING GOLDEN WEEK! OUR SPONSORS ARE COUNTING ON US!
KIJINAMI! ARE YOU EVEN LISTENING?
EXCUSE ME, MORIYAMA-SAN...
WHAT?!
JUST, UH, I'M NOT SURE WHAT'S GOING ON, BUT I THINK KOKORO SHOULD BE FINE.

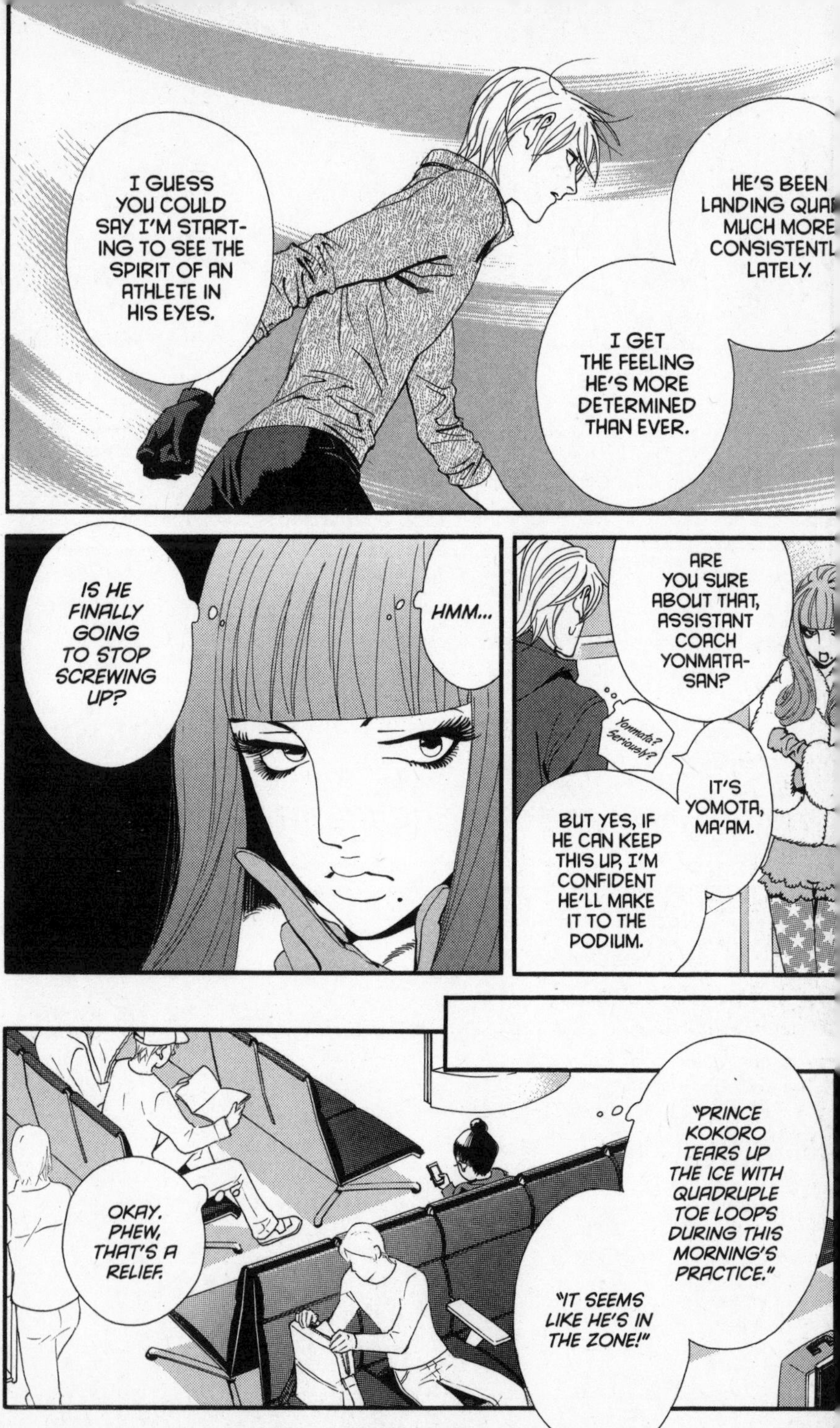
HE'S BEEN LANDING QUA MUCH MORE CONSISTENTL LATELY.
I GET THE FEELING HE'S MORE DETERMINED THAN EVER.
I GUESS YOU COULD SAY I'M START-ING TO SEE THE SPIRIT OF AN ATHLETE IN HIS EYES.
ARE YOU SURE ABOUT THAT, ASSISTANT COACH YONMATA-SAN?
Yonmata? Seriously?
IT'S YOMOTA, MA'AM.
BUT YES, IF HE CAN KEEP THIS UP, I'M CONFIDENT HE'LL MAKE IT TO THE PODIUM.
HMM...
IS HE FINALLY GOING TO STOP SCREWING UP?
"PRINCE KOKORO TEARS UP THE ICE WITH QUADRUPLE TOE LOOPS DURING THIS MORNING'S PRACTICE."
"IT SEEMS LIKE HE'S IN THE ZONE!"
OKAY. PHEW, THAT'S A RELIEF.

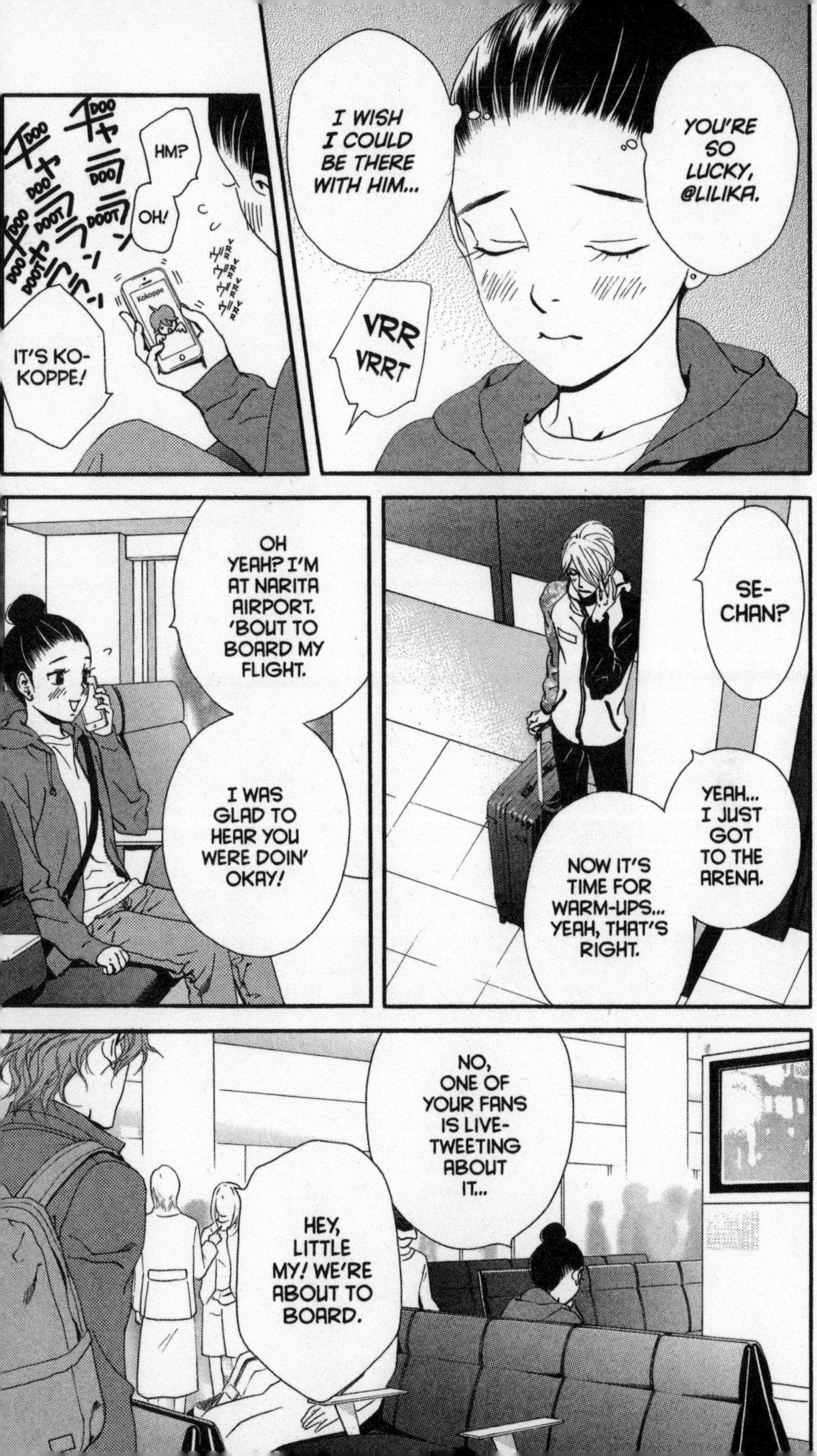
YOU'RE SO LUCKY, @LILIKA.
I WISH I COULD BE THERE WITH HIM...
VRR VRRT
DOO DOO DOOT
DOO DOO DOOT
HM?
OH!
Kokoppe
IT'S KO-KOPPE!
SE-CHAN?
YEAH... I JUST GOT TO THE ARENA.
NOW IT'S TIME FOR WARM-UPS... YEAH, THAT'S RIGHT.
OH YEAH? I'M AT NARITA AIRPORT. 'BOUT TO BOARD MY FLIGHT.
I WAS GLAD TO HEAR YOU WERE DOIN' OKAY!
NO, ONE OF YOUR FANS IS LIVE-TWEETING ABOUT IT...
HEY, LITTLE MY! WE'RE ABOUT TO BOARD.

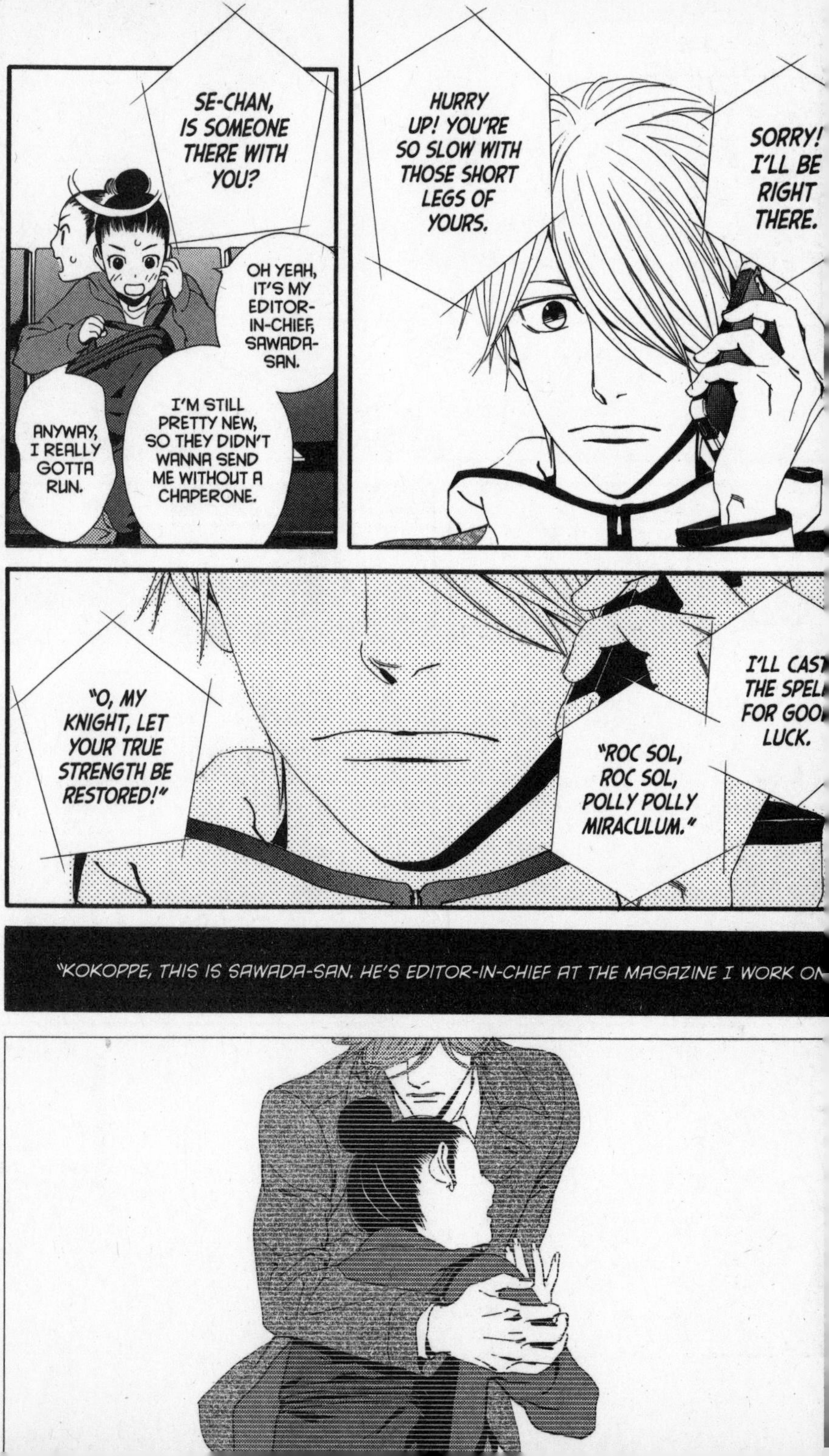
HURRY UP! YOU'RE SO SLOW WITH THOSE SHORT LEGS OF YOURS.
SORRY! I'LL BE RIGHT THERE.
SE-CHAN, IS SOMEONE THERE WITH YOU?
OH YEAH, IT'S MY EDITOR-IN-CHIEF, SAWADA-SAN.
I'M STILL PRETTY NEW, SO THEY DIDN'T WANNA SEND ME WITHOUT A CHAPERONE.
ANYWAY, I REALLY GOTTA RUN.
I'LL CAST THE SPEL FOR GOO LUCK.
"ROC SOL, ROC SOL, POLLY POLLY MIRACULUM."
"O, MY KNIGHT, LET YOUR TRUE STRENGTH BE RESTORED!"
"KOKOPPE, THIS IS SAWADA-SAN. HE'S EDITOR-IN-CHIEF AT THE MAGAZINE I WORK ON

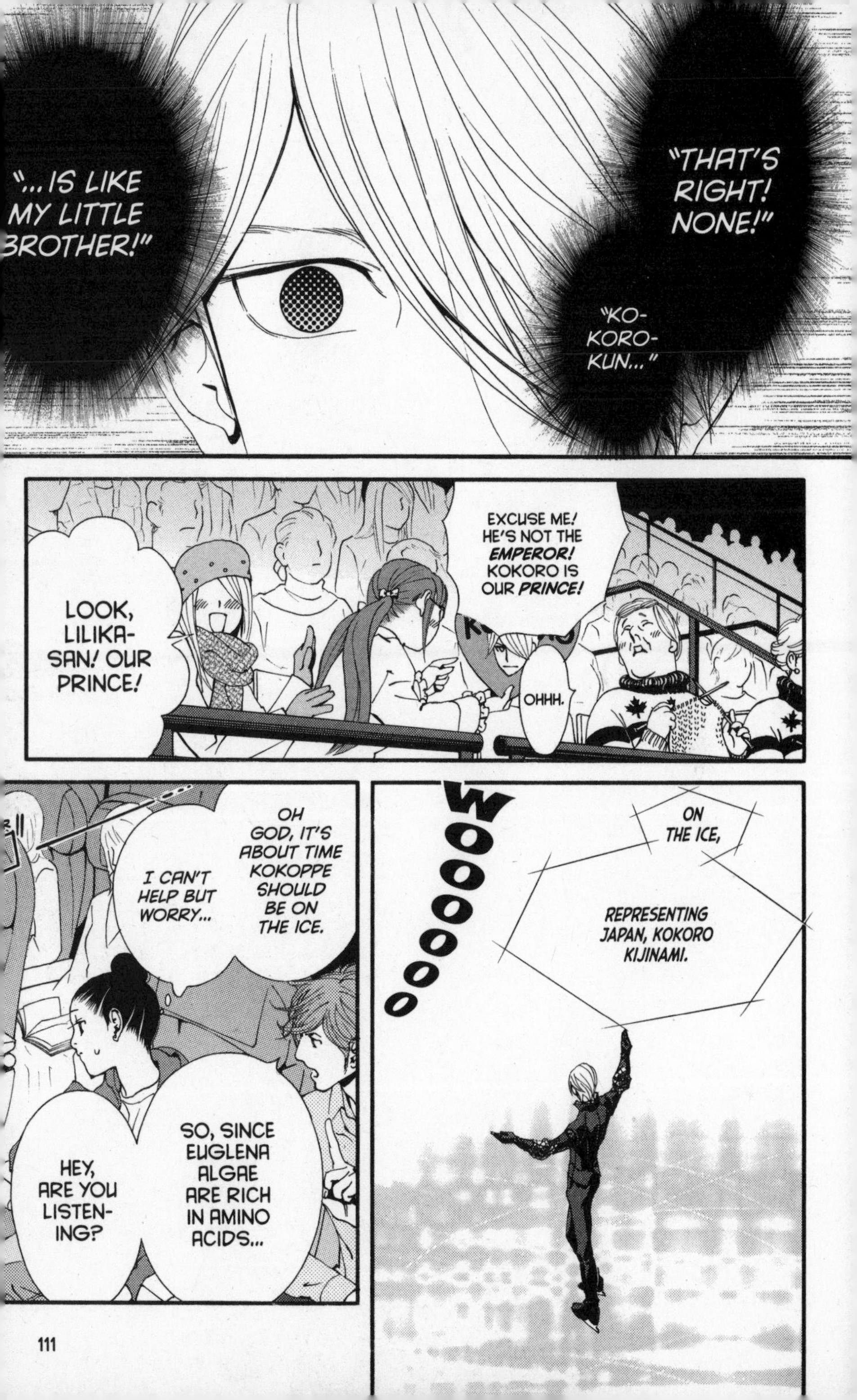
"THAT'S RIGHT! NONE!"
"KO-KORO-KUN..."
"...IS LIKE MY LITTLE BROTHER!"
EXCUSE ME! HE'S NOT THE EMPEROR! KOKORO IS OUR PRINCE!
OHHH.
LOOK, LILIKA-SAN! OUR PRINCE!
WOOOOOOO
ON THE ICE,
REPRESENTING JAPAN, KOKORO KIJINAMI.
OH GOD, IT'S ABOUT TIME KOKOPPE SHOULD BE ON THE ICE.
I CAN'T HELP BUT WORRY...
SO, SINCE EUGLENA ALGAE ARE RICH IN AMINO ACIDS...
HEY, ARE YOU LISTEN-ING?

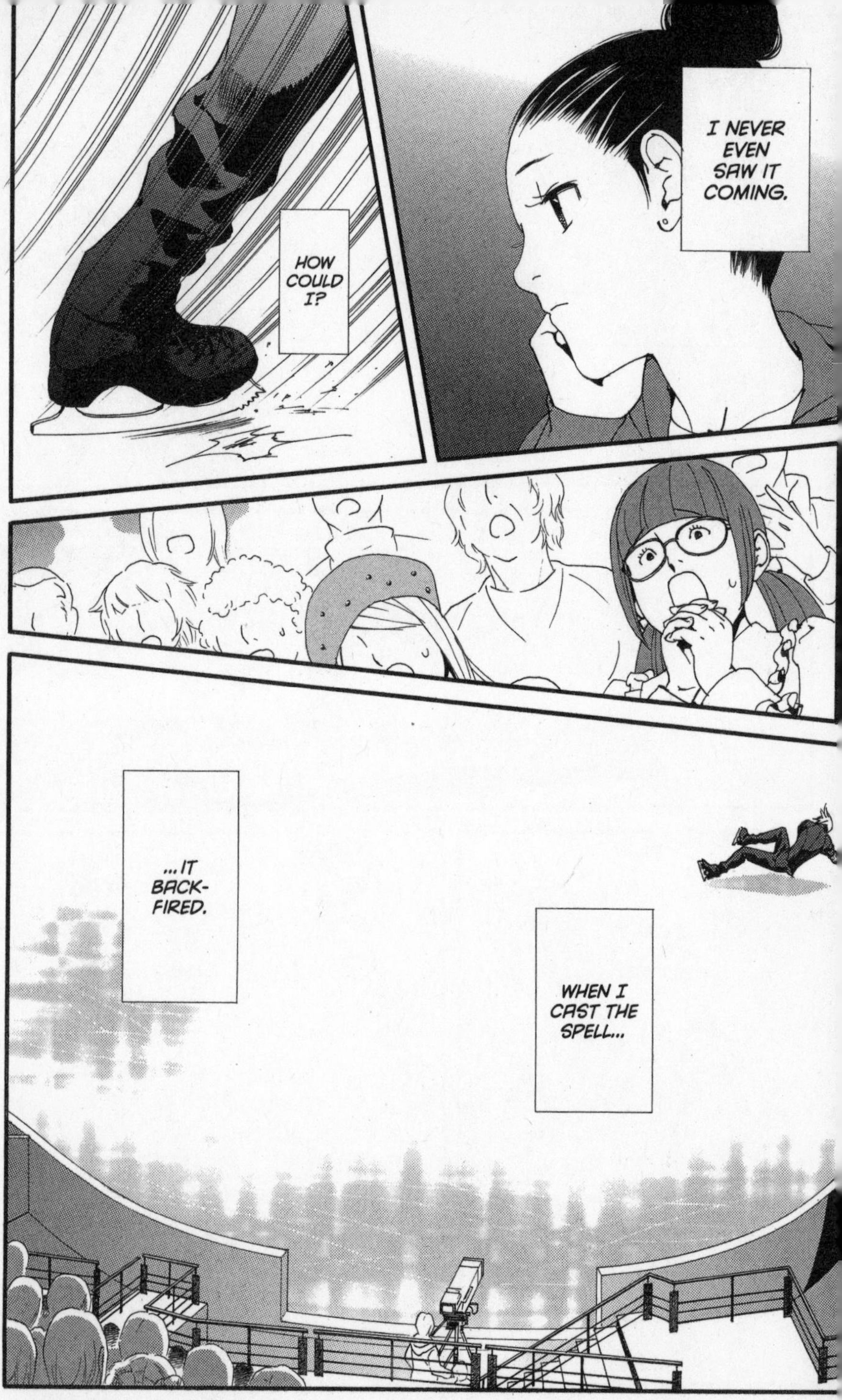
I NEVER EVEN SAW IT COMING.
HOW COULD I?
WHEN I CAST THE SPELL...
...IT BACK-FIRED.

Spell 5
I Want to Grow Up

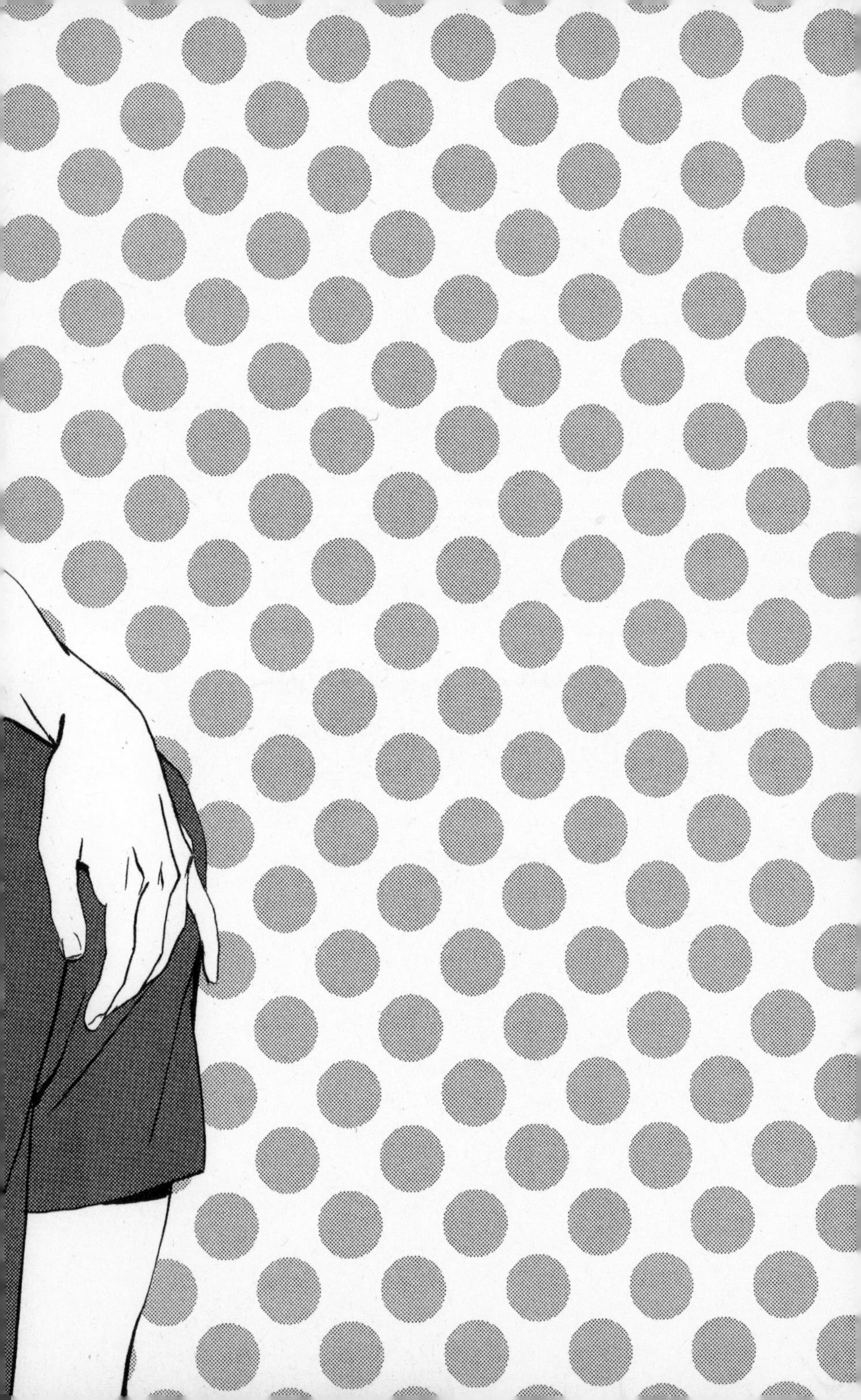

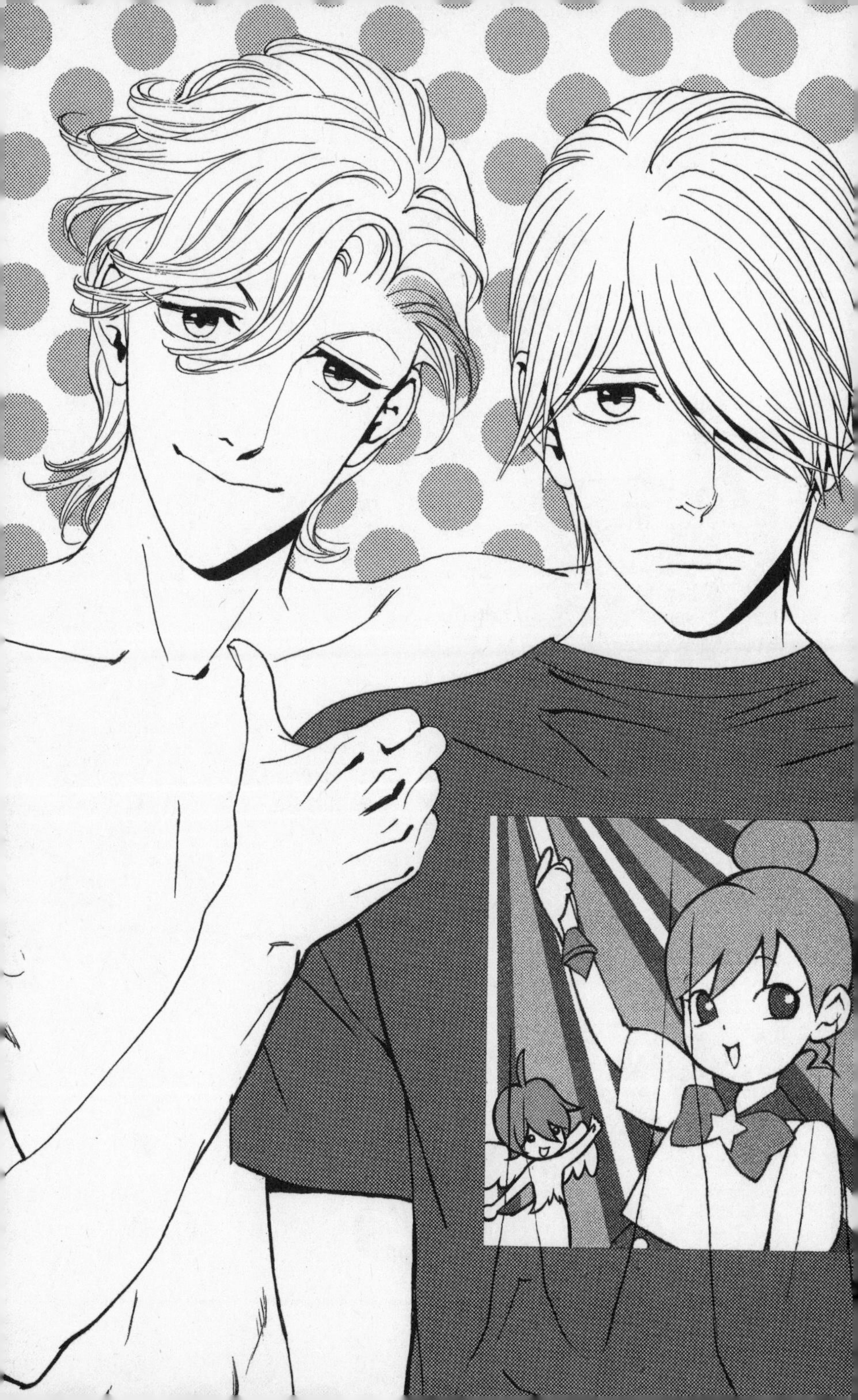

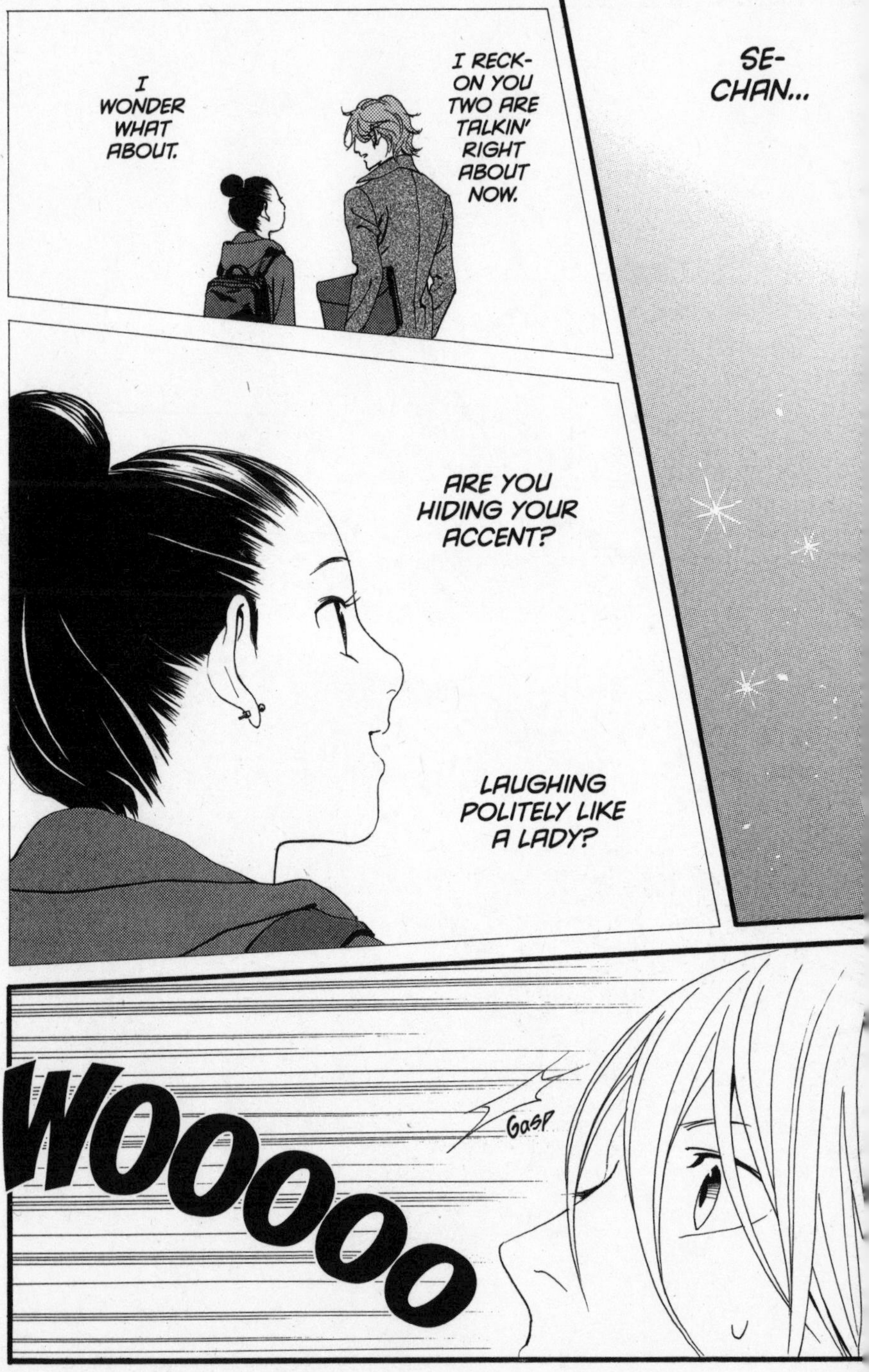
SE-CHAN...
I RECK-ON YOU TWO ARE TALKIN' RIGHT ABOUT NOW.
I WONDER WHAT ABOUT.
ARE YOU HIDING YOUR ACCENT?
LAUGHING POLITELY LIKE A LADY?
Gasp
WOOOOO

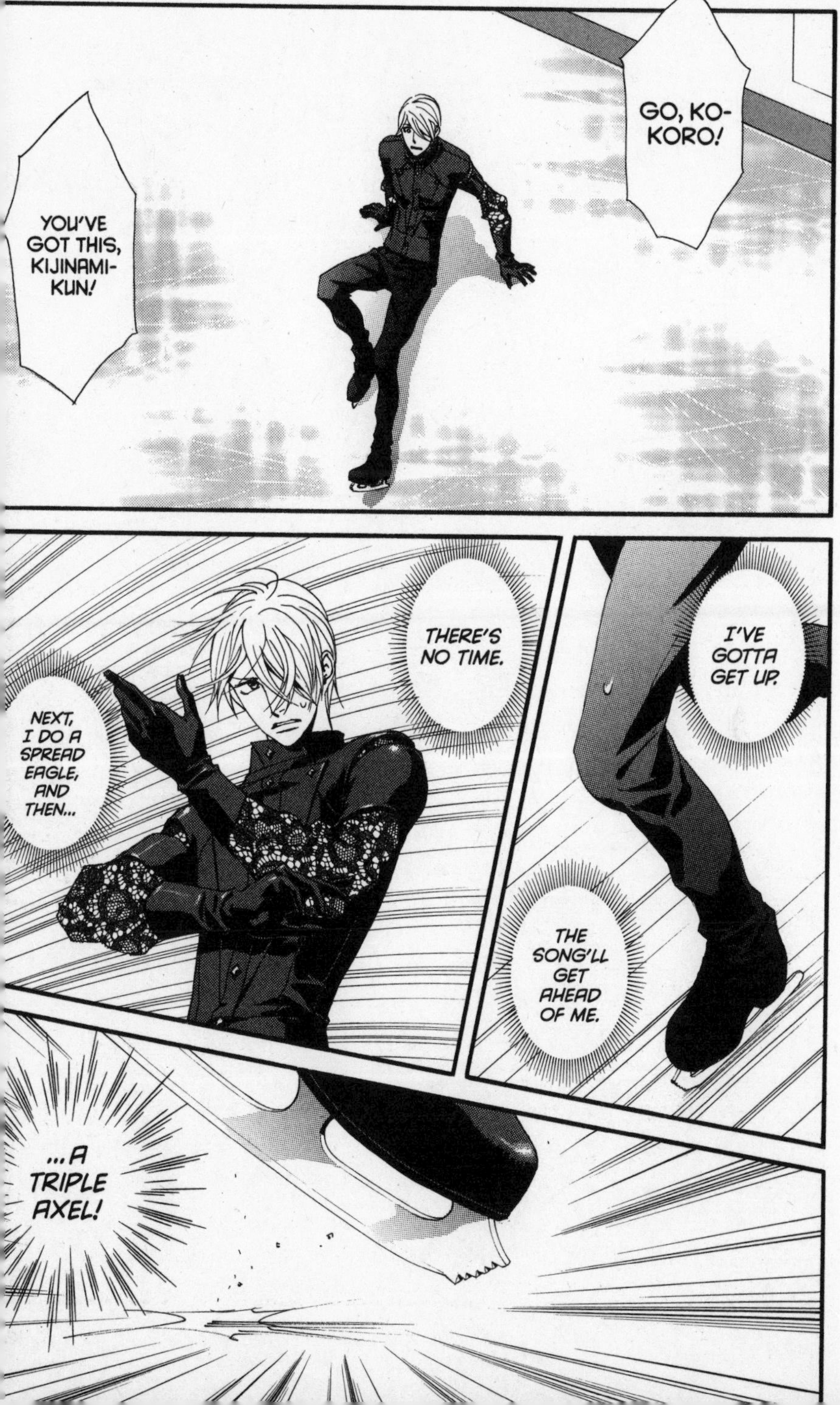
GO, KO-KORO!
YOU'VE GOT THIS, KIJINAMI-KUN!
I'VE GOTTA GET UP.
THE SONG'LL GET AHEAD OF ME.
THERE'S NO TIME.
NEXT, I DO A SPREAD EAGLE, AND THEN...
...A TRIPLE AXEL!

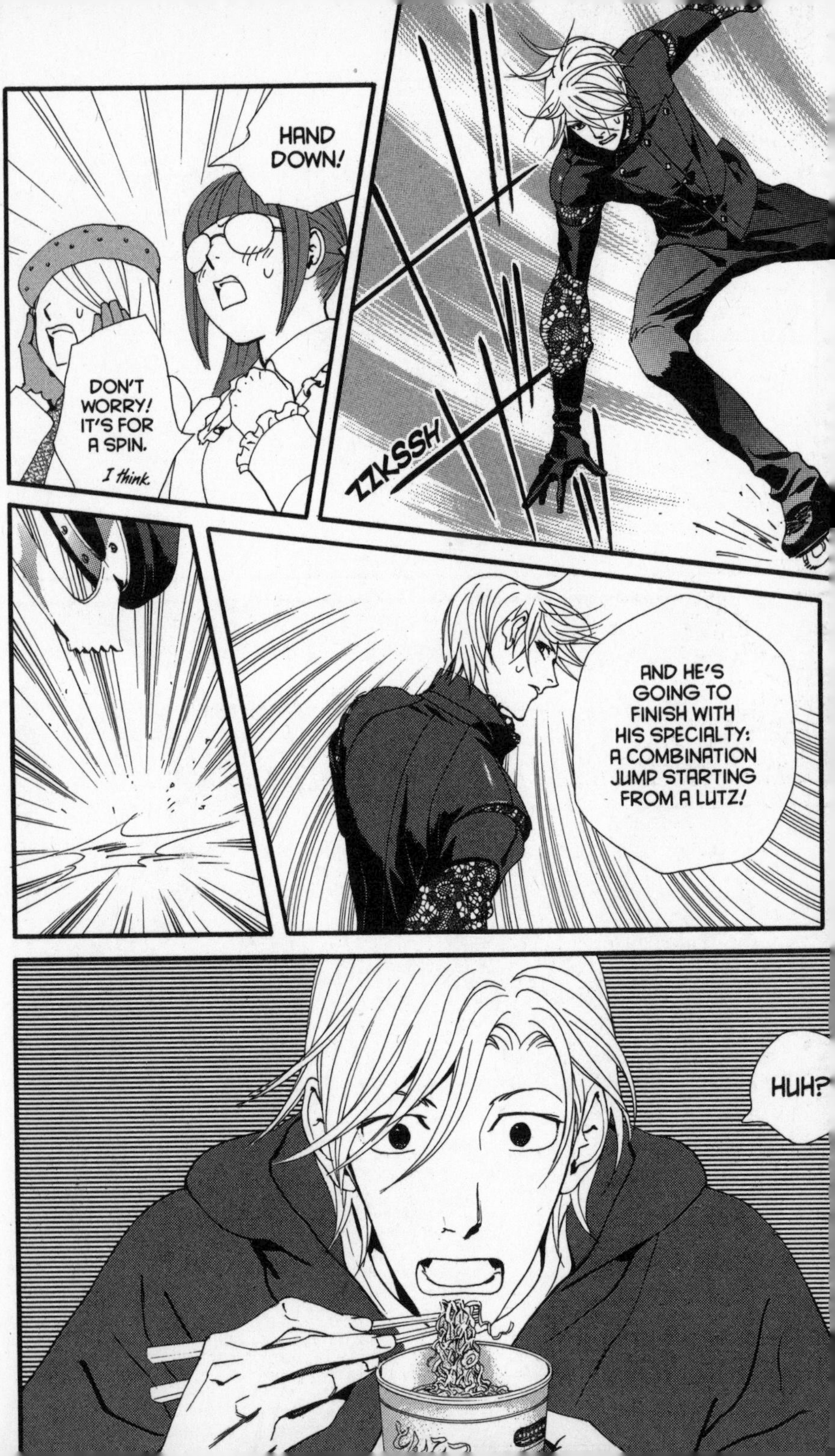
ZZKSSH
HAND DOWN!
DON'T WORRY! IT'S FOR A SPIN.
I think.
AND HE'S GOING TO FINISH WITH HIS SPECIALTY: A COMBINATION JUMP STARTING FROM A LUTZ!
HUH?

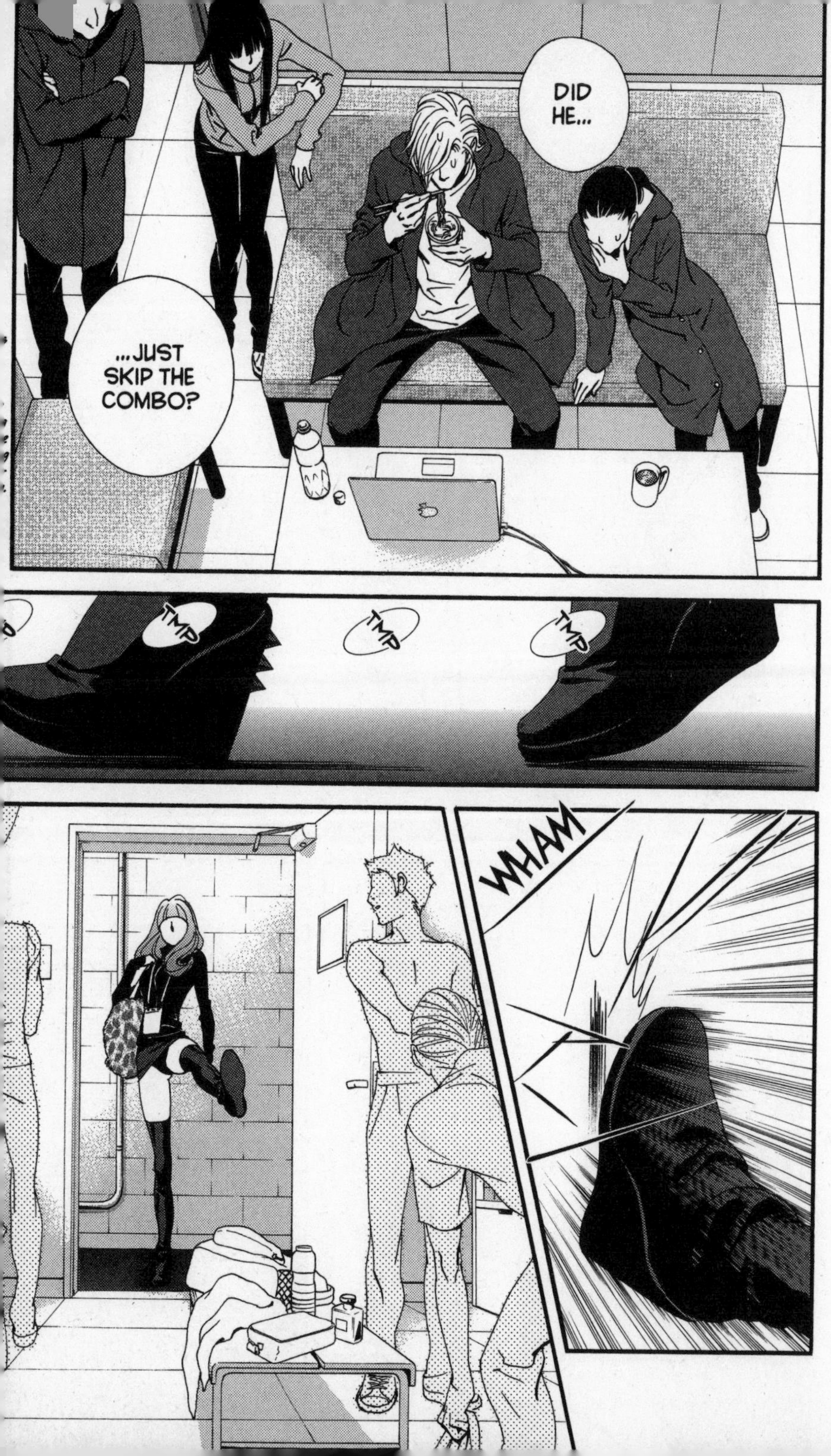
DID HE...
...JUST SKIP THE COMBO?
TMP
TMP
TMP
WHAM

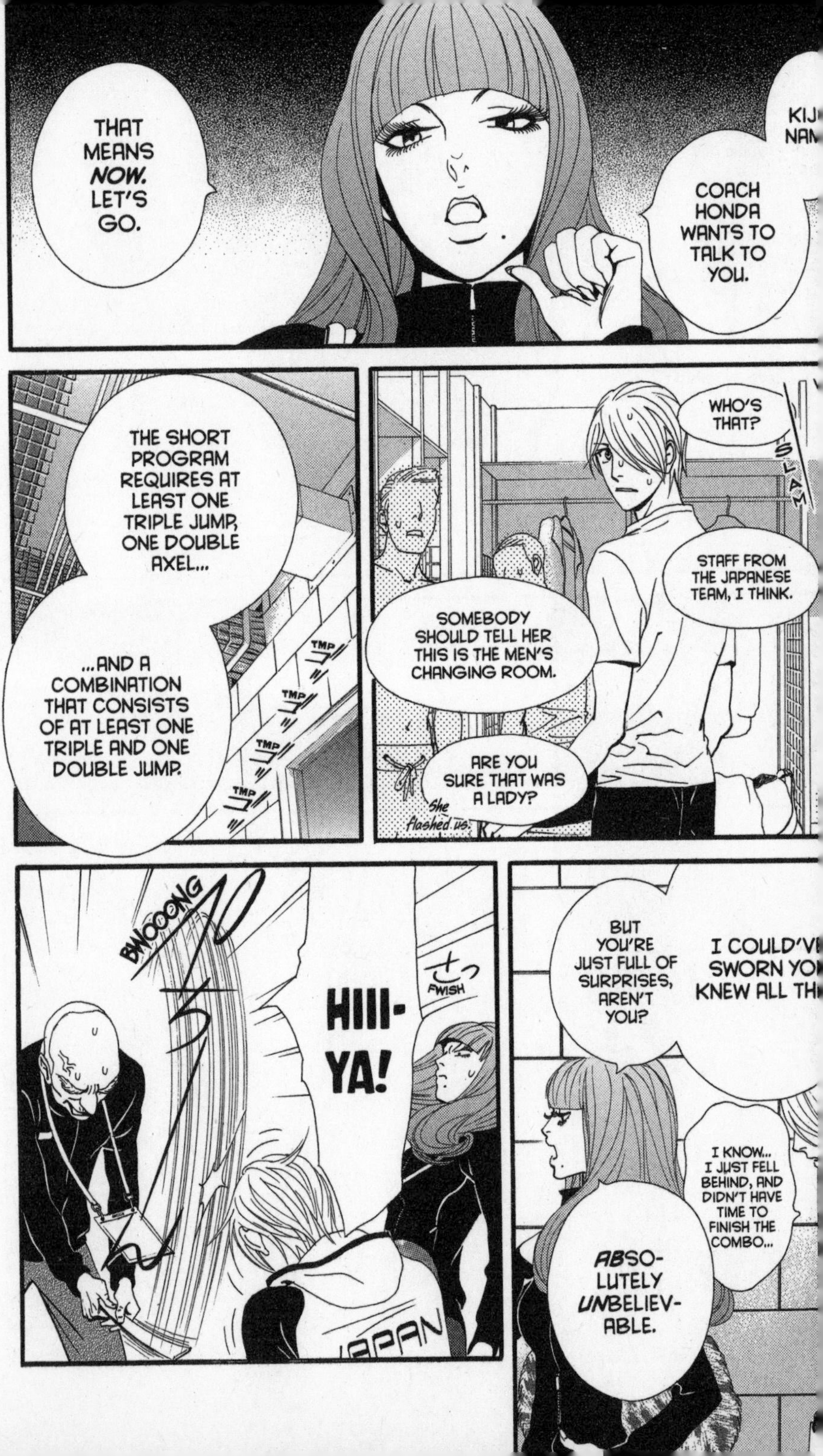
COACH HONDA WANTS TO TALK TO YOU.
THAT MEANS NOW. LET'S GO.
WHO'S THAT?
SLAM
STAFF FROM THE JAPANESE TEAM, I THINK.
SOMEBODY SHOULD TELL HER THIS IS THE MEN'S CHANGING ROOM.
ARE YOU SURE THAT WAS A LADY?
She flashed us.
THE SHORT PROGRAM REQUIRES AT LEAST ONE TRIPLE JUMP, ONE DOUBLE AXEL...
...AND A COMBINATION THAT CONSISTS OF AT LEAST ONE TRIPLE AND ONE DOUBLE JUMP.
TMP
TMP
TMP
TMP
BUT YOU'RE JUST FULL OF SURPRISES, AREN'T YOU?
I KNOW... I JUST FELL BEHIND, AND DIDN'T HAVE TIME TO FINISH THE COMBO...
ABSO-LUTELY UNBELIEV-ABLE.
FWISH
HIII-YA!
BWOOONG

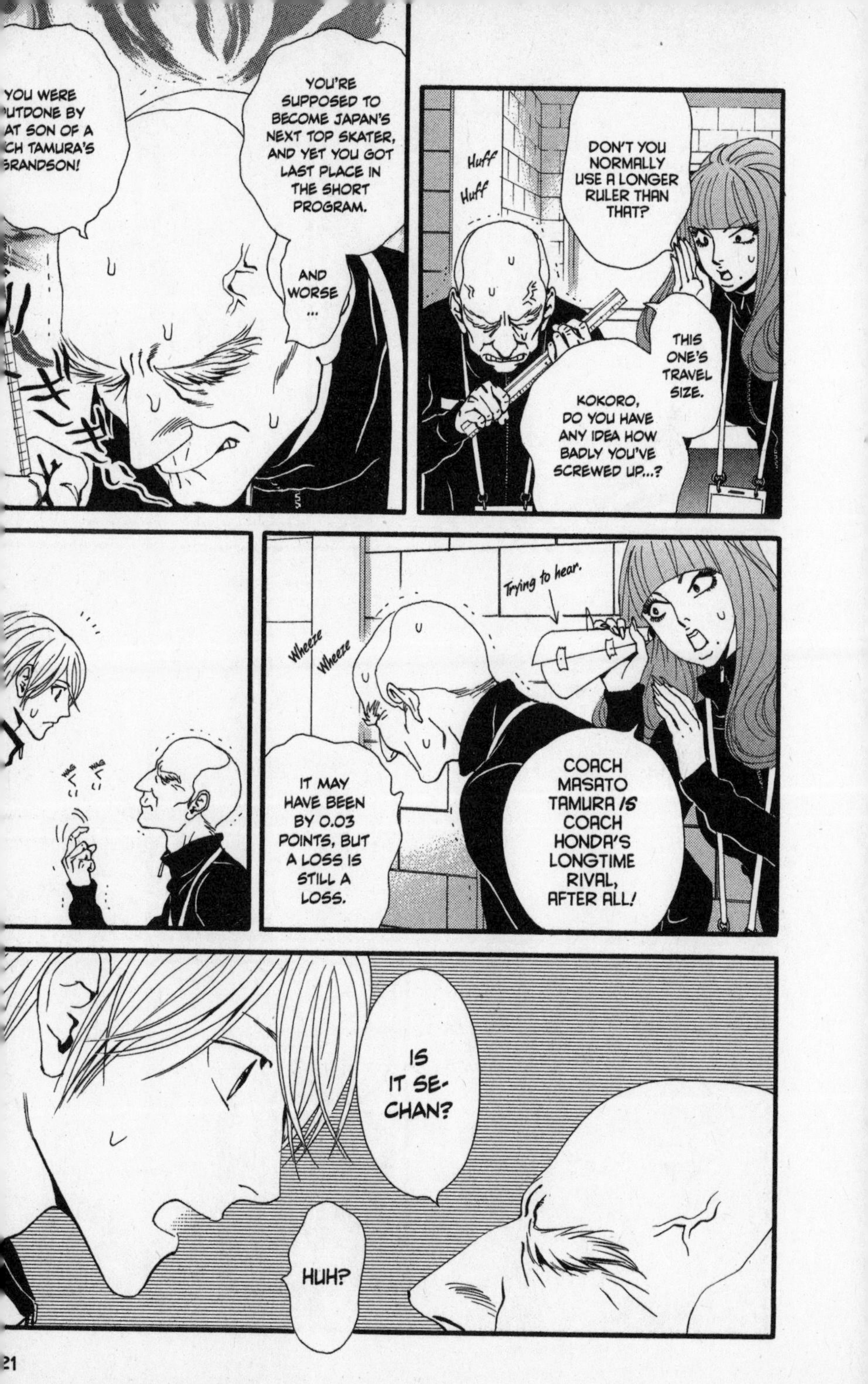
Huff
Huff
DON'T YOU NORMALLY USE A LONGER RULER THAN THAT?
THIS ONE'S TRAVEL SIZE.
KOKORO, DO YOU HAVE ANY IDEA HOW BADLY YOU'VE SCREWED UP...?
YOU'RE SUPPOSED TO BECOME JAPAN'S NEXT TOP SKATER, AND YET YOU GOT LAST PLACE IN THE SHORT PROGRAM.
AND WORSE ...
YOU WERE UTDONE BY AT SON OF A CH TAMURA'S RANDSON!
Trying to hear.
Wheeze
Wheeze
COACH MASATO TAMURA *IS* COACH HONDA'S LONGTIME RIVAL, AFTER ALL!
IT MAY HAVE BEEN BY 0.03 POINTS, BUT A LOSS IS STILL A LOSS.
WAG
WAG
IS IT SE-CHAN?
HUH?

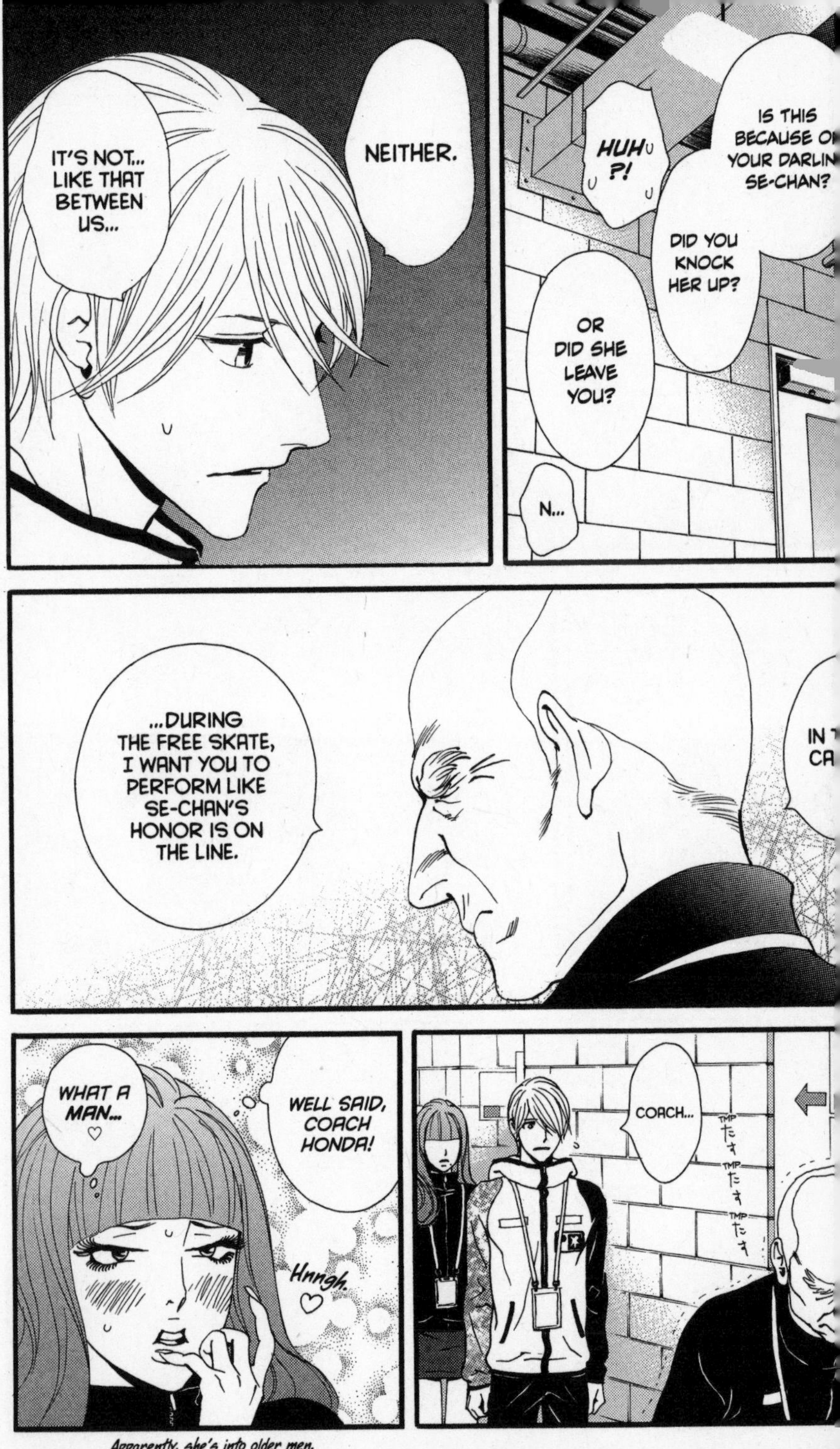
IS THIS BECAUSE O YOUR DARLIN SE-CHAN?
HUH ?!
DID YOU KNOCK HER UP?
OR DID SHE LEAVE YOU?
N...
NEITHER.
IT'S NOT... LIKE THAT BETWEEN US...
...DURING THE FREE SKATE, I WANT YOU TO PERFORM LIKE SE-CHAN'S HONOR IS ON THE LINE.
COACH...
TMP たす
TMP たす
TMP たす
WELL SAID, COACH HONDA!
WHAT A MAN... ♡
Hnngh. ♡

Apparently, she's into older men.

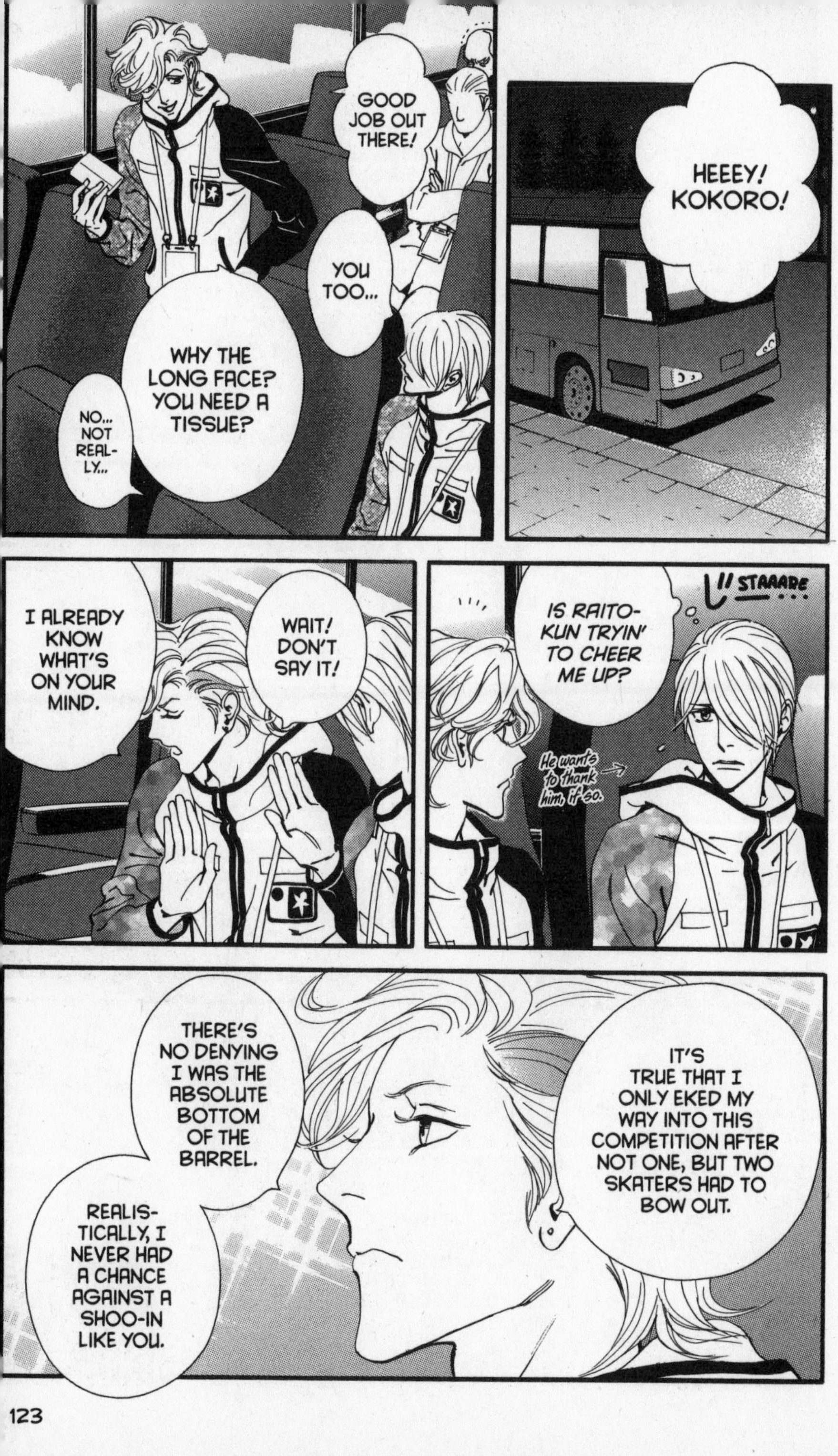
HEEEY! KOKORO!
GOOD JOB OUT THERE!
YOU TOO...
WHY THE LONG FACE? YOU NEED A TISSUE?
NO... NOT REAL-LY...
STAAARE
IS RAITO-KUN TRYIN' TO CHEER ME UP?
He wants to thank him, if so.
WAIT! DON'T SAY IT!
I ALREADY KNOW WHAT'S ON YOUR MIND.
IT'S TRUE THAT I ONLY EKED MY WAY INTO THIS COMPETITION AFTER NOT ONE, BUT TWO SKATERS HAD TO BOW OUT.
THERE'S NO DENYING I WAS THE ABSOLUTE BOTTOM OF THE BARREL.
REALIS-TICALLY, I NEVER HAD A CHANCE AGAINST A SHOO-IN LIKE YOU.

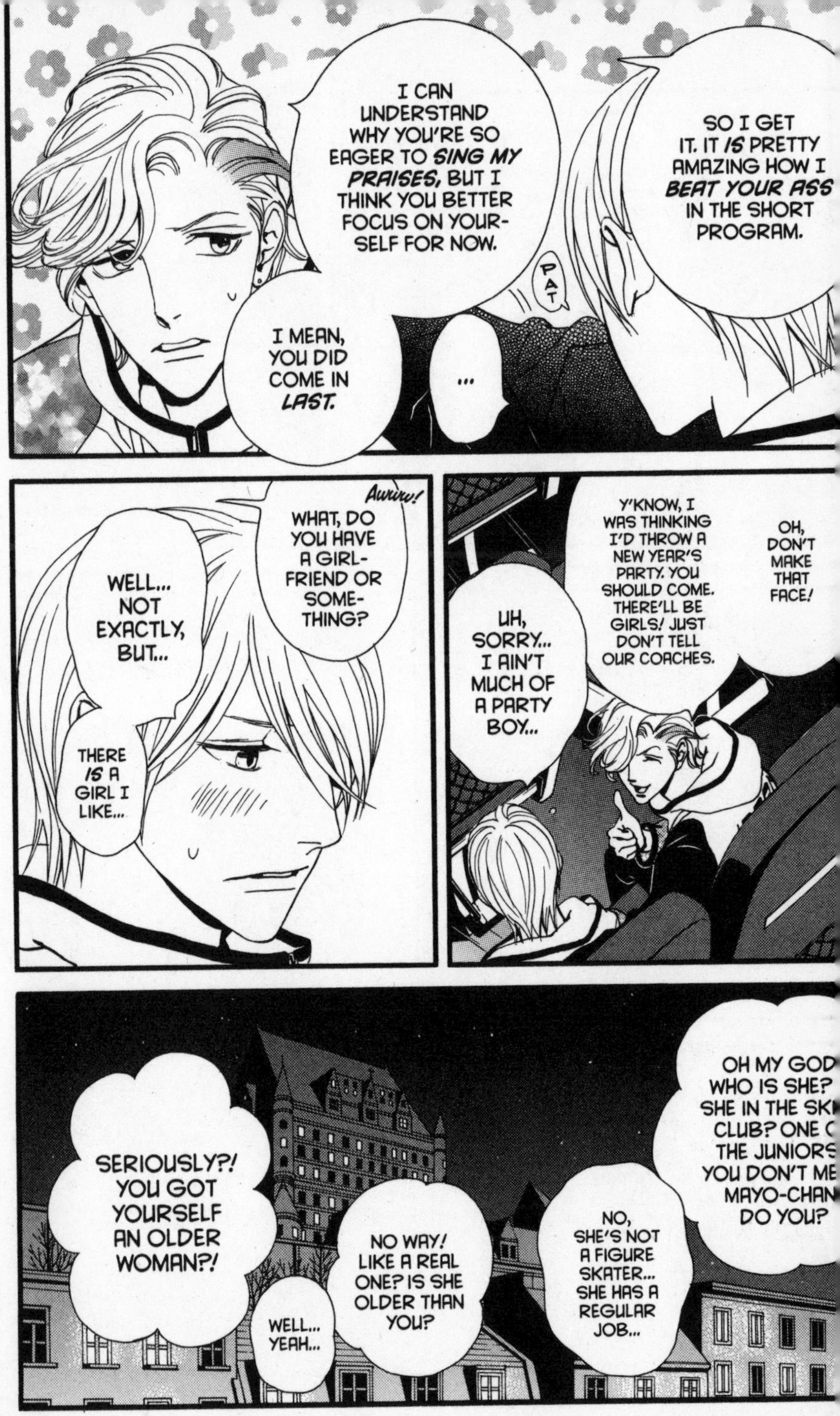
SO I GET IT. IT *IS* PRETTY AMAZING HOW I *BEAT YOUR ASS* IN THE SHORT PROGRAM.
I CAN UNDERSTAND WHY YOU'RE SO EAGER TO *SING MY PRAISES,* BUT I THINK YOU BETTER FOCUS ON YOURSELF FOR NOW.
PAT
...
I MEAN, YOU DID COME IN *LAST.*
OH, DON'T MAKE THAT FACE!
Y'KNOW, I WAS THINKING I'D THROW A NEW YEAR'S PARTY. YOU SHOULD COME. THERE'LL BE GIRLS! JUST DON'T TELL OUR COACHES.
UH, SORRY... I AIN'T MUCH OF A PARTY BOY...
Awww!
WHAT, DO YOU HAVE A GIRLFRIEND OR SOMETHING?
WELL... NOT EXACTLY, BUT...
THERE *IS* A GIRL I LIKE...
OH MY GOD WHO IS SHE? SHE IN THE SK CLUB? ONE O THE JUNIORS YOU DON'T ME MAYO-CHAN DO YOU?
NO, SHE'S NOT A FIGURE SKATER... SHE HAS A REGULAR JOB...
NO WAY! LIKE A REAL ONE? IS SHE OLDER THAN YOU?
WELL... YEAH...
SERIOUSLY?! YOU GOT YOURSELF AN OLDER WOMAN?!

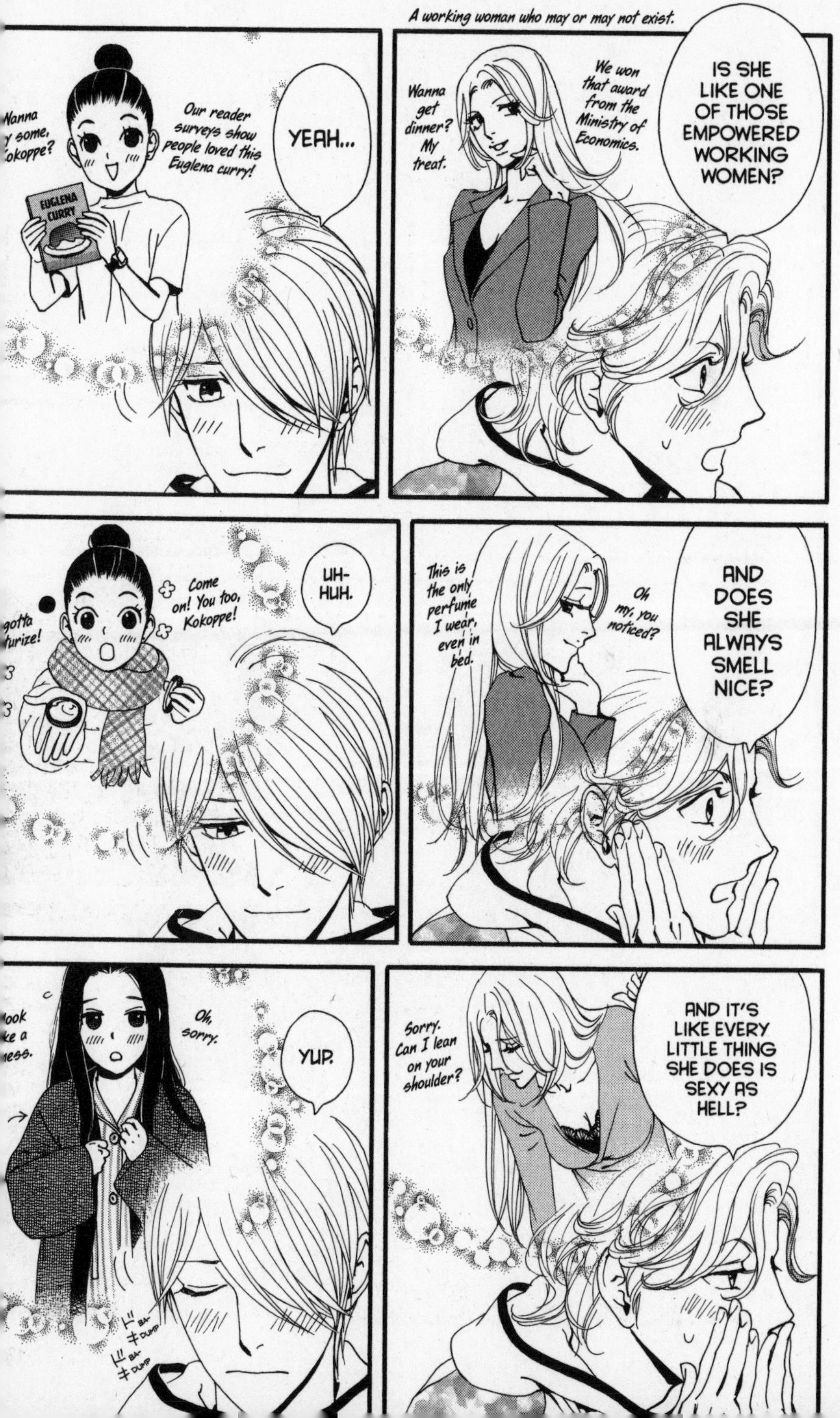
A working woman who may or may not exist.
IS SHE LIKE ONE OF THOSE EMPOWERED WORKING WOMEN?
We won that award from the Ministry of Economics.
Wanna get dinner? My treat.
YEAH...
Our reader surveys show people loved this Euglena curry!
Wanna y some, okoppe?
EUGLENA CURRY
AND DOES SHE ALWAYS SMELL NICE?
Oh my, you noticed?
This is the only perfume I wear, even in bed.
UH-HUH.
Come on! You too, Kokoppe!
gotta urize!
AND IT'S LIKE EVERY LITTLE THING SHE DOES IS SEXY AS HELL?
Sorry. Can I lean on your shoulder?
YUP.
Oh, sorry.
look ke a ness.
ドキ BA-DUMP
ドキ BA-DUMP

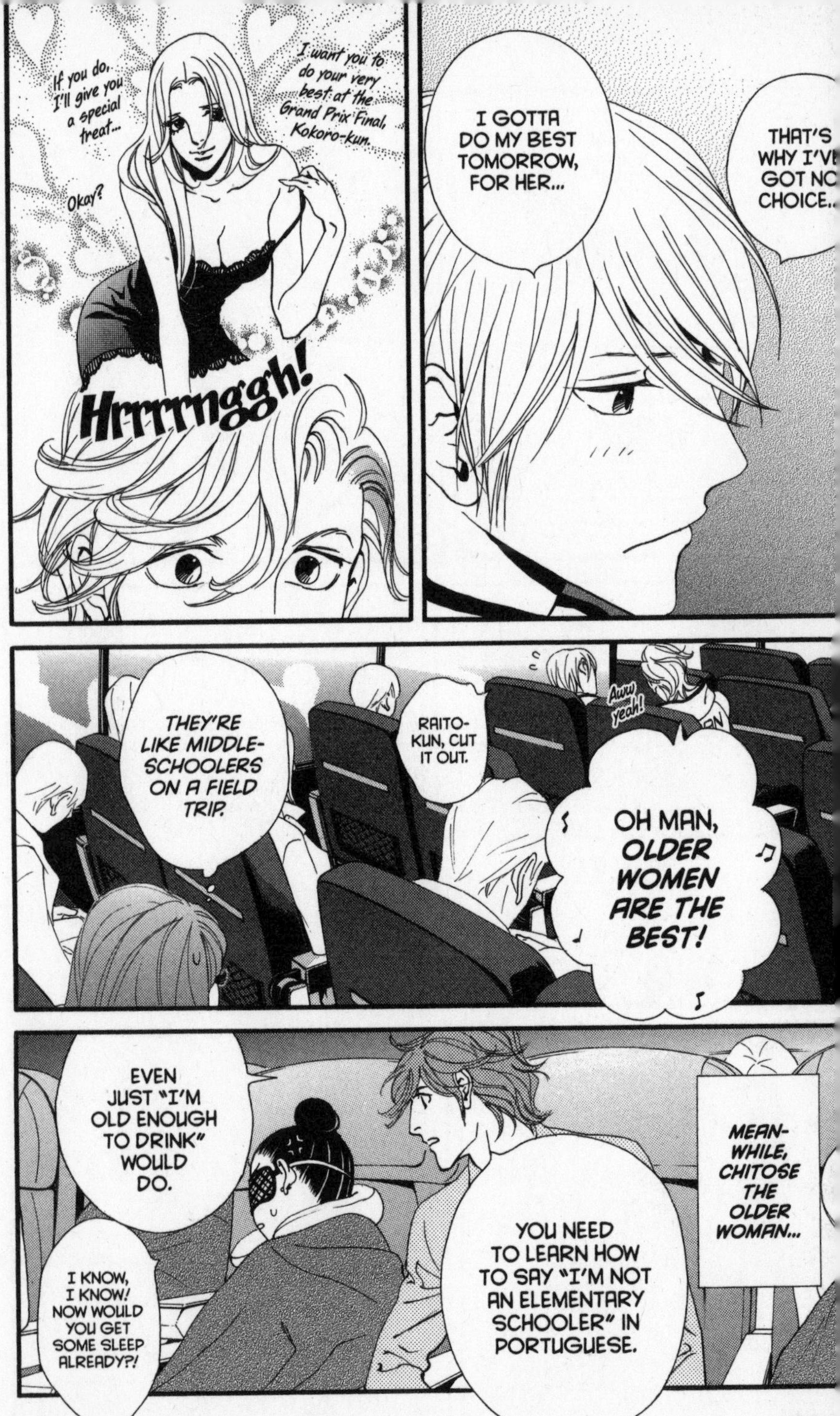
THAT'S WHY I'V GOT NO CHOICE...
I GOTTA DO MY BEST TOMORROW, FOR HER...
I want you to do your very best at the Grand Prix Final, Kokoro-kun.
If you do, I'll give you a special treat...
Okay?
Hrrrrnggh!
OH MAN, OLDER WOMEN ARE THE BEST!
Aww yeah!
RAITO-KUN, CUT IT OUT.
THEY'RE LIKE MIDDLE-SCHOOLERS ON A FIELD TRIP.
MEAN-WHILE, CHITOSE THE OLDER WOMAN...
YOU NEED TO LEARN HOW TO SAY "I'M NOT AN ELEMENTARY SCHOOLER" IN PORTUGUESE.
EVEN JUST "I'M OLD ENOUGH TO DRINK" WOULD DO.
I KNOW, I KNOW! NOW WOULD YOU GET SOME SLEEP ALREADY?!

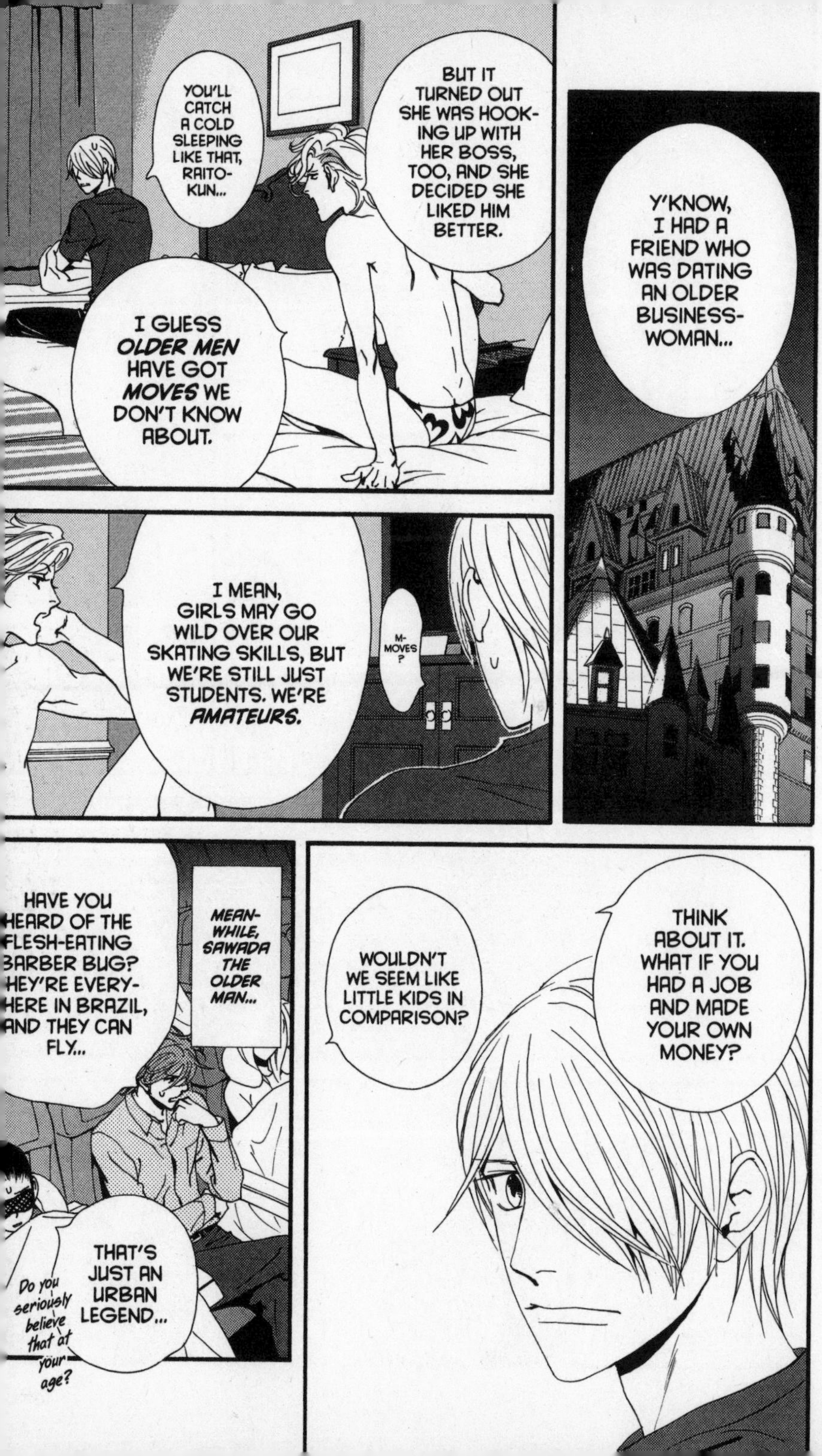
Y'KNOW, I HAD A FRIEND WHO WAS DATING AN OLDER BUSINESS-WOMAN...
BUT IT TURNED OUT SHE WAS HOOK-ING UP WITH HER BOSS, TOO, AND SHE DECIDED SHE LIKED HIM BETTER.
YOU'LL CATCH A COLD SLEEPING LIKE THAT, RAITO-KUN...
I GUESS *OLDER MEN* HAVE GOT *MOVES* WE DON'T KNOW ABOUT.
M-MOVES?
I MEAN, GIRLS MAY GO WILD OVER OUR SKATING SKILLS, BUT WE'RE STILL JUST STUDENTS. WE'RE *AMATEURS.*
THINK ABOUT IT. WHAT IF YOU HAD A JOB AND MADE YOUR OWN MONEY?
WOULDN'T WE SEEM LIKE LITTLE KIDS IN COMPARISON?
MEAN-WHILE, SAWADA THE OLDER MAN...
HAVE YOU HEARD OF THE FLESH-EATING BARBER BUG? HEY'RE EVERY-HERE IN BRAZIL, AND THEY CAN FLY...
THAT'S JUST AN URBAN LEGEND...
Do you seriously believe that at your age?

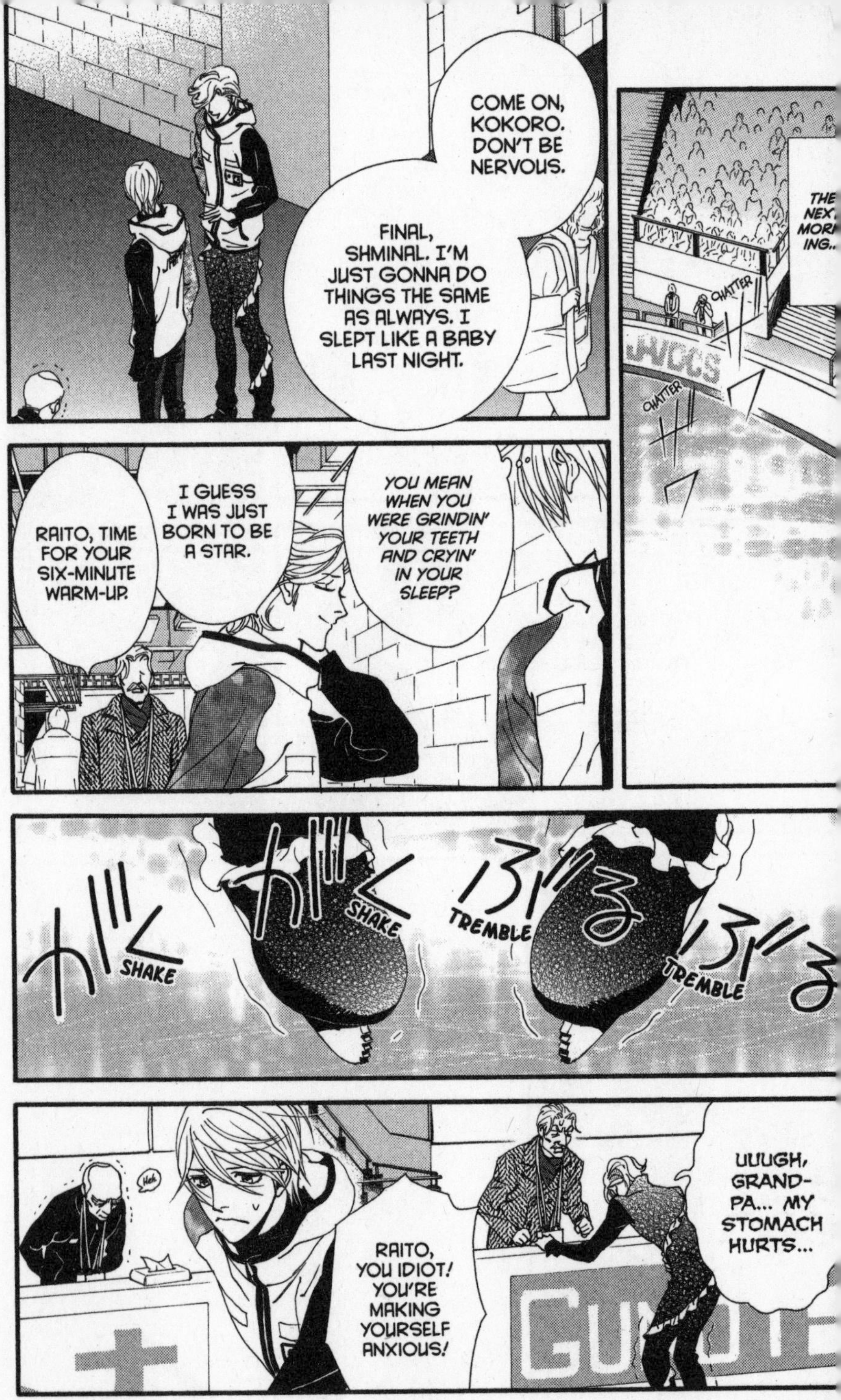
THE NEX
MORN
ING..
CHATTER
CHATTER
COME ON, KOKORO. DON'T BE NERVOUS.
FINAL, SHMINAL. I'M JUST GONNA DO THINGS THE SAME AS ALWAYS. I SLEPT LIKE A BABY LAST NIGHT.
YOU MEAN WHEN YOU WERE GRINDIN' YOUR TEETH AND CRYIN' IN YOUR SLEEP?
I GUESS I WAS JUST BORN TO BE A STAR.
RAITO, TIME FOR YOUR SIX-MINUTE WARM-UP.
TREMBLE
TREMBLE
SHAKE
SHAKE
UUUGH, GRANDPA... MY STOMACH HURTS...
RAITO, YOU IDIOT! YOU'RE MAKING YOURSELF ANXIOUS!
Heh

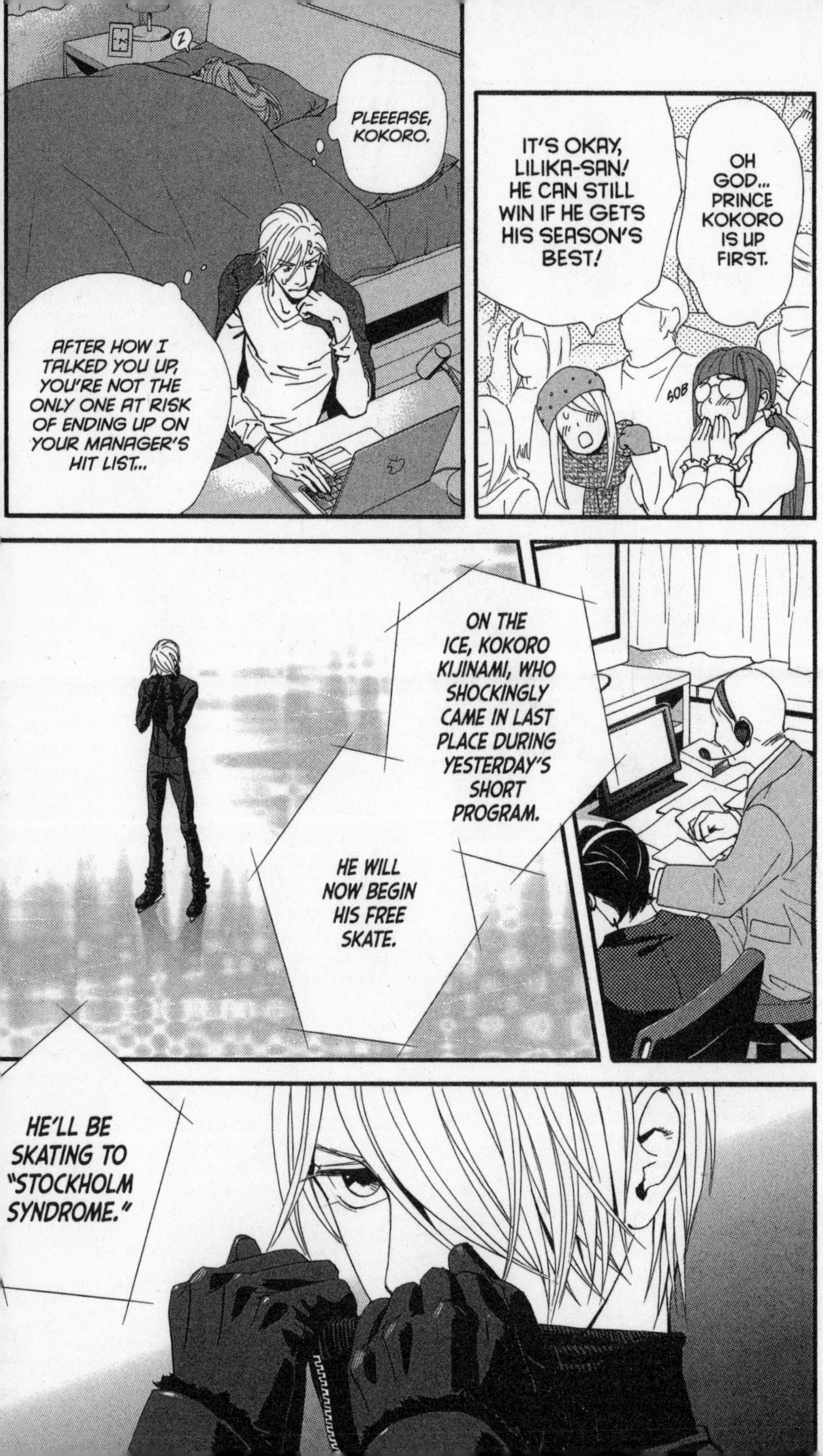
OH GOD... PRINCE KOKORO IS UP FIRST.
IT'S OKAY, LILIKA-SAN! HE CAN STILL WIN IF HE GETS HIS SEASON'S BEST!
SOB
Z
PLEEEASE, KOKORO.
AFTER HOW I TALKED YOU UP, YOU'RE NOT THE ONLY ONE AT RISK OF ENDING UP ON YOUR MANAGER'S HIT LIST...
ON THE ICE, KOKORO KIJINAMI, WHO SHOCKINGLY CAME IN LAST PLACE DURING YESTERDAY'S SHORT PROGRAM.
HE WILL NOW BEGIN HIS FREE SKATE.
HE'LL BE SKATING TO "STOCKHOLM SYNDROME."

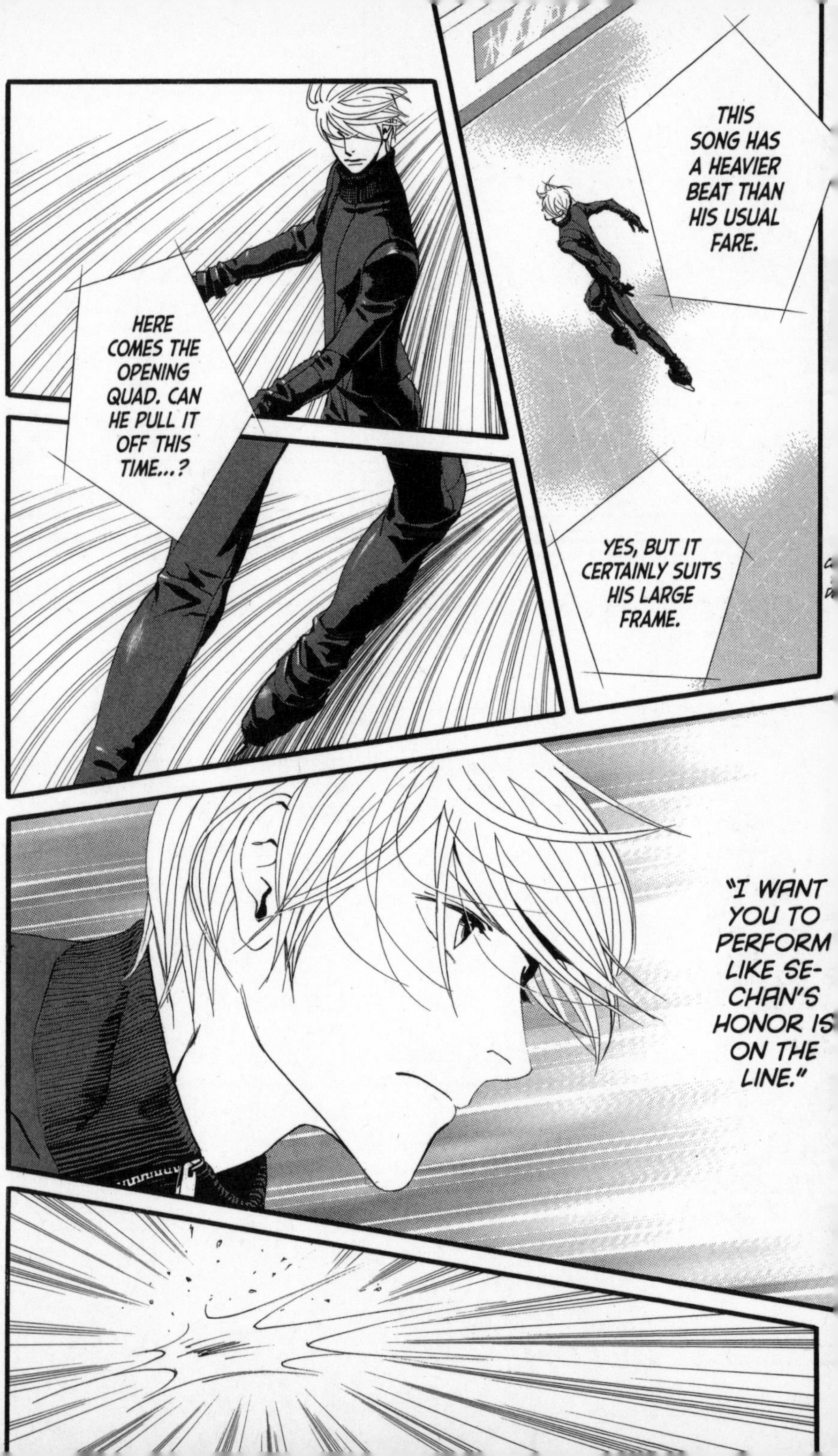
THIS SONG HAS A HEAVIER BEAT THAN HIS USUAL FARE.
YES, BUT IT CERTAINLY SUITS HIS LARGE FRAME.
HERE COMES THE OPENING QUAD. CAN HE PULL IT OFF THIS TIME...?
"I WANT YOU TO PERFORM LIKE SE-CHAN'S HONOR IS ON THE LINE."

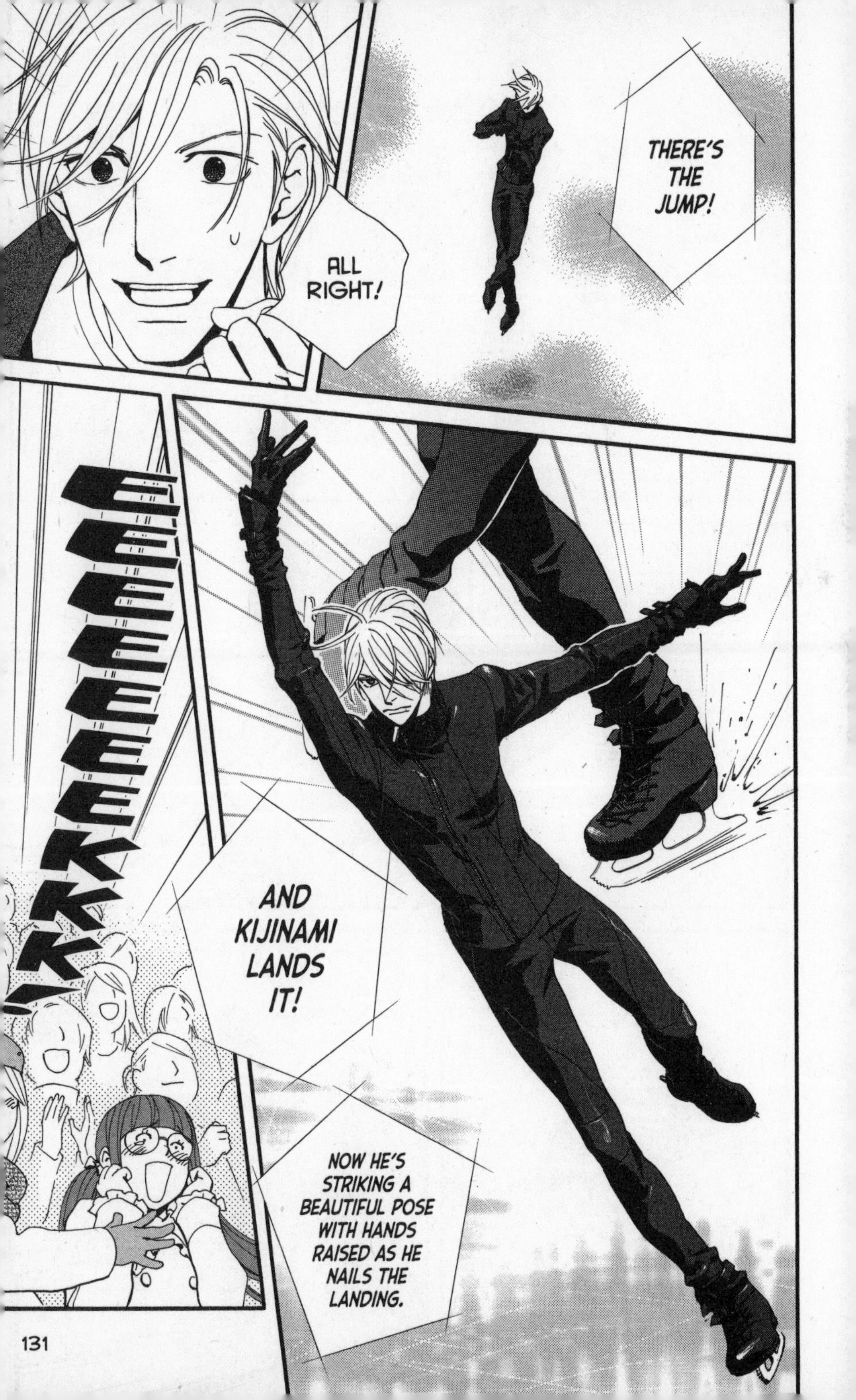
THERE'S THE JUMP!
ALL RIGHT!
AND KIJINAMI LANDS IT!
NOW HE'S STRIKING A BEAUTIFUL POSE WITH HANDS RAISED AS HE NAILS THE LANDING.
EEEEEEEKKK!

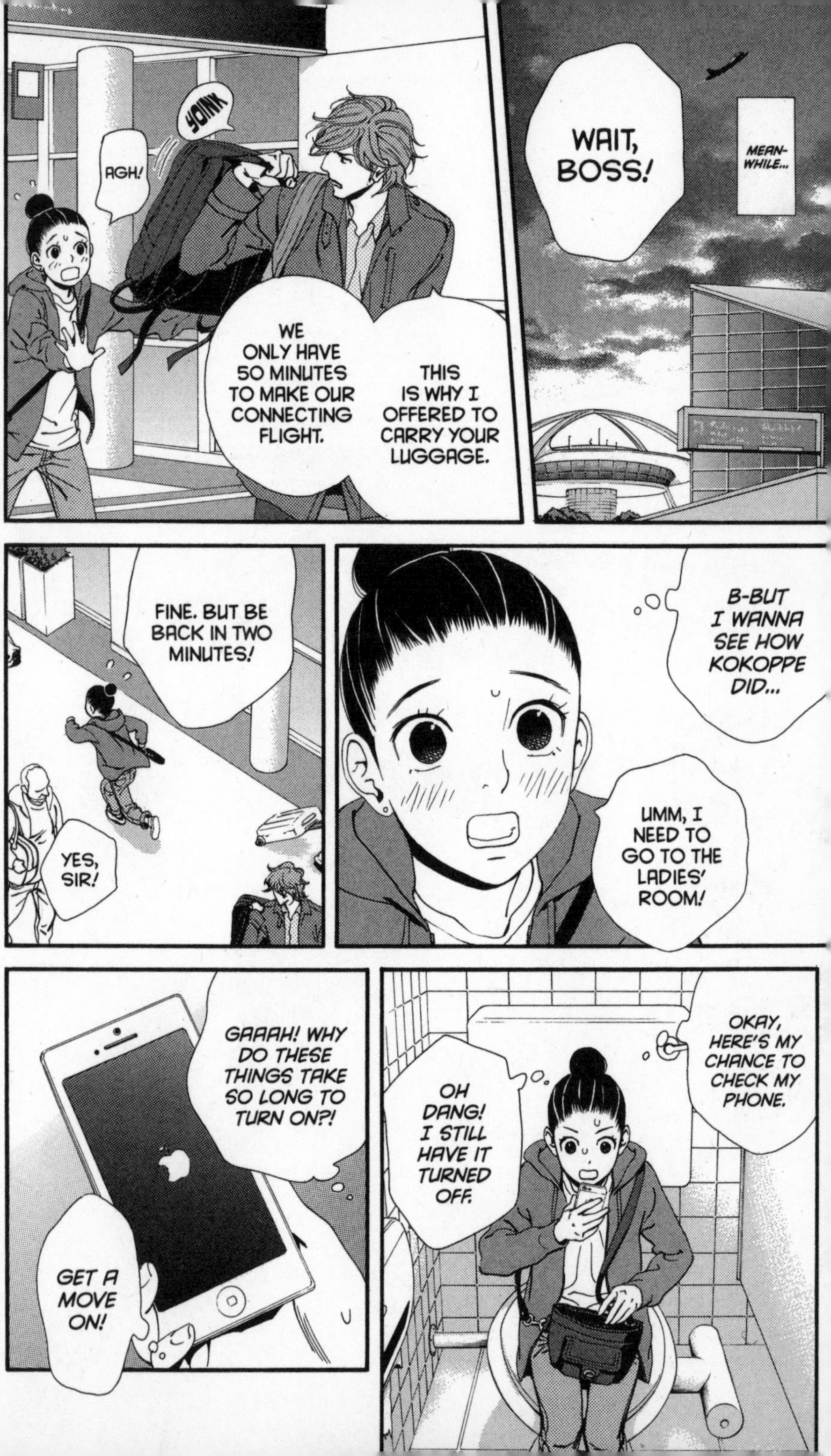
MEAN-WHILE...
WAIT, BOSS!
YOINK
AGH!
THIS IS WHY I OFFERED TO CARRY YOUR LUGGAGE.
WE ONLY HAVE 50 MINUTES TO MAKE OUR CONNECTING FLIGHT.
B-BUT I WANNA SEE HOW KOKOPPE DID...
UMM, I NEED TO GO TO THE LADIES' ROOM!
FINE. BUT BE BACK IN TWO MINUTES!
YES, SIR!
OKAY, HERE'S MY CHANCE TO CHECK MY PHONE.
OH DANG! I STILL HAVE IT TURNED OFF.
GAAAH! WHY DO THESE THINGS TAKE SO LONG TO TURN ON?!
GET A MOVE ON!

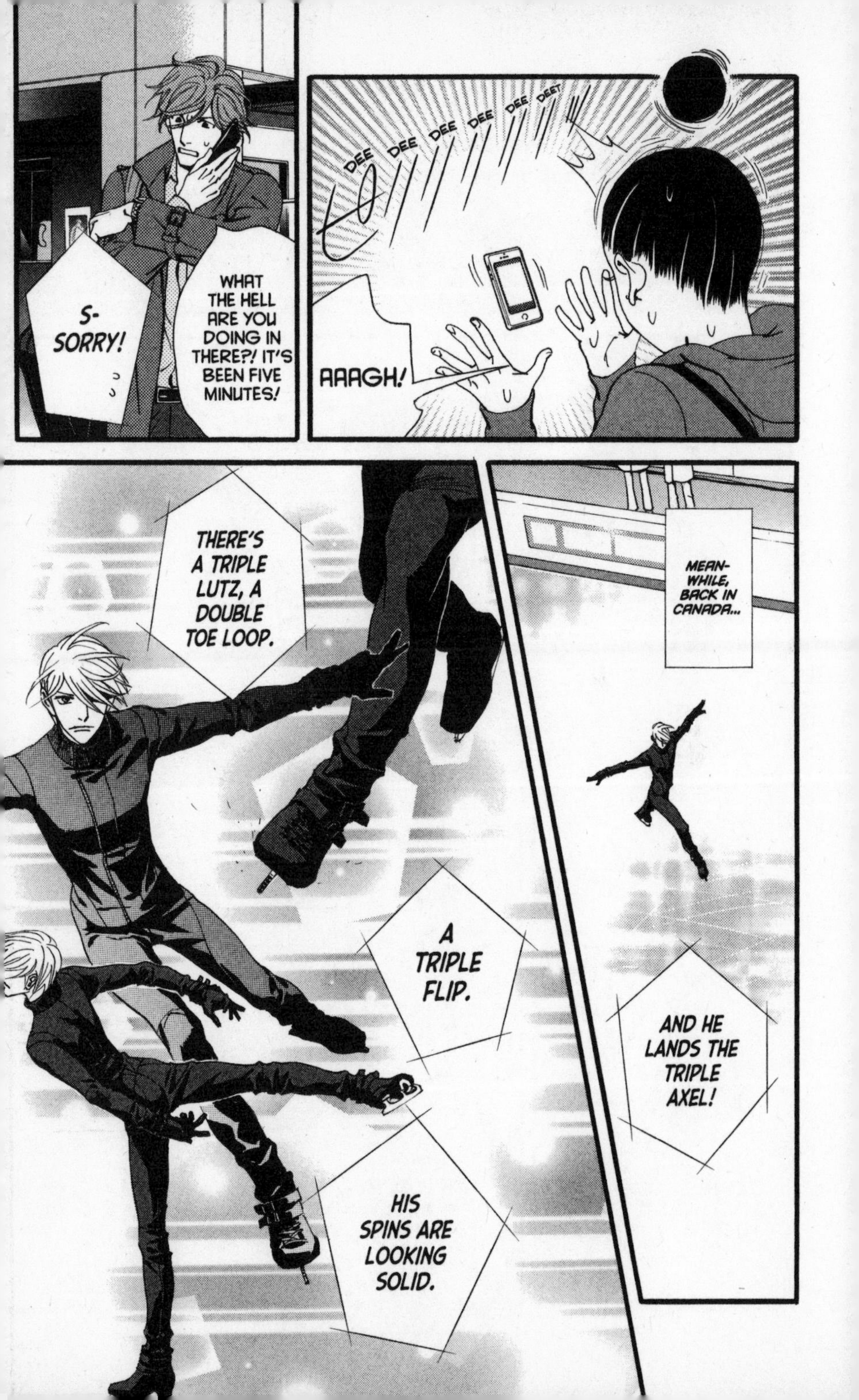
DEE DEE DEE DEE DEE DEET
AAAGH!
WHAT THE HELL ARE YOU DOING IN THERE?! IT'S BEEN FIVE MINUTES!
S-SORRY!
MEAN-WHILE, BACK IN CANADA...
AND HE LANDS THE TRIPLE AXEL!
THERE'S A TRIPLE LUTZ, A DOUBLE TOE LOOP.
A TRIPLE FLIP.
HIS SPINS ARE LOOKING SOLID.

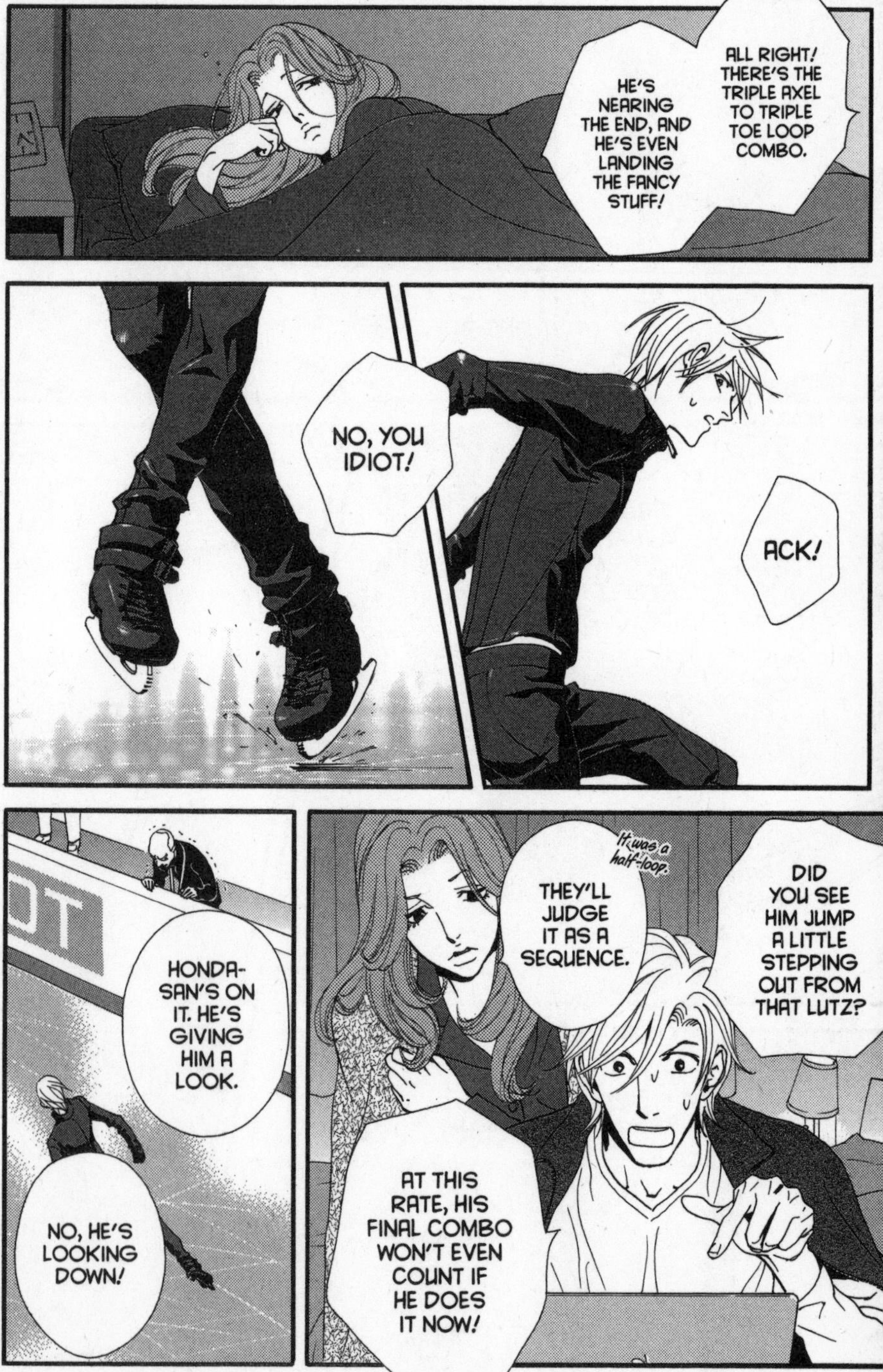
ALL RIGHT! THERE'S THE TRIPLE AXEL TO TRIPLE TOE LOOP COMBO.
HE'S NEARING THE END, AND HE'S EVEN LANDING THE FANCY STUFF!
ACK!
NO, YOU IDIOT!
DID YOU SEE HIM JUMP A LITTLE STEPPING OUT FROM THAT LUTZ?
It was a half-loop.
THEY'LL JUDGE IT AS A SEQUENCE.
AT THIS RATE, HIS FINAL COMBO WON'T EVEN COUNT IF HE DOES IT NOW!
HONDA-SAN'S ON IT. HE'S GIVING HIM A LOOK.
NO, HE'S LOOKING DOWN!

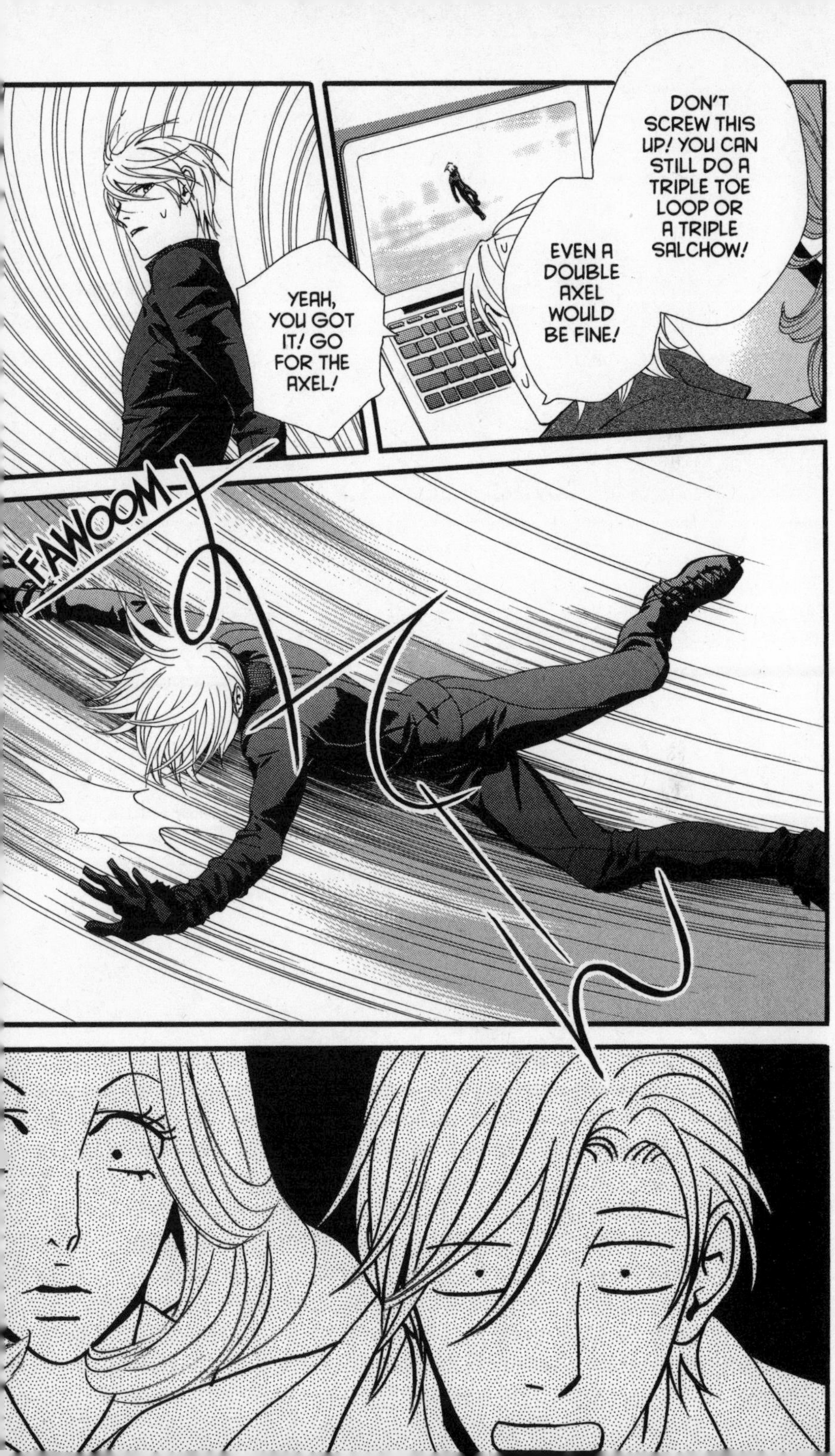
DON'T SCREW THIS UP! YOU CAN STILL DO A TRIPLE TOE LOOP OR A TRIPLE SALCHOW!
EVEN A DOUBLE AXEL WOULD BE FINE!
YEAH, YOU GOT IT! GO FOR THE AXEL!
FAWOOM

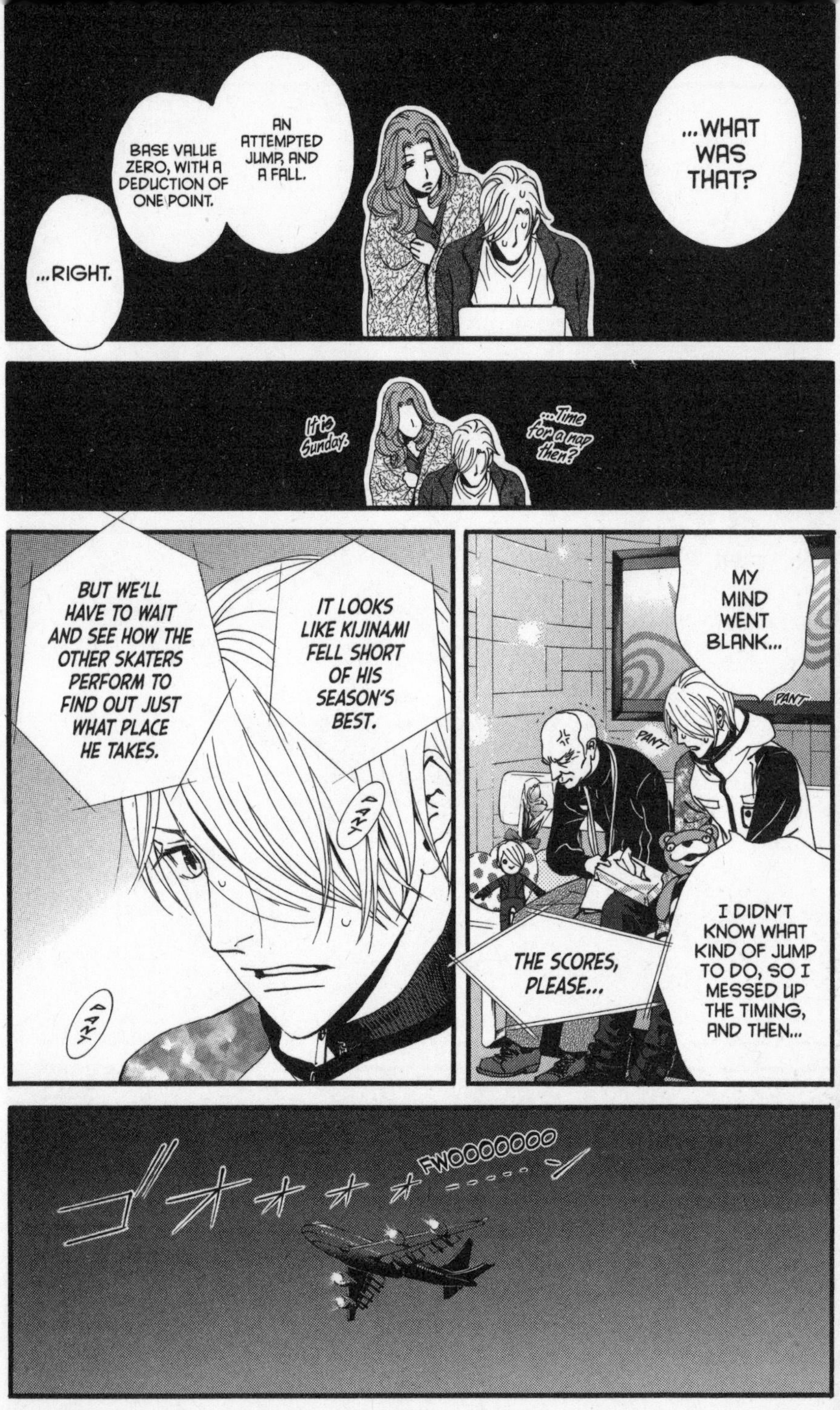
...WHAT WAS THAT?
AN ATTEMPTED JUMP, AND A FALL.
BASE VALUE ZERO, WITH A DEDUCTION OF ONE POINT.
...RIGHT.
...Time for a nap then?
It is Sunday.
MY MIND WENT BLANK...
PANT
PANT
I DIDN'T KNOW WHAT KIND OF JUMP TO DO, SO I MESSED UP THE TIMING, AND THEN...
THE SCORES, PLEASE...
IT LOOKS LIKE KIJINAMI FELL SHORT OF HIS SEASON'S BEST.
BUT WE'LL HAVE TO WAIT AND SEE HOW THE OTHER SKATERS PERFORM TO FIND OUT JUST WHAT PLACE HE TAKES.
PANT
PANT
FWOOOOOOO

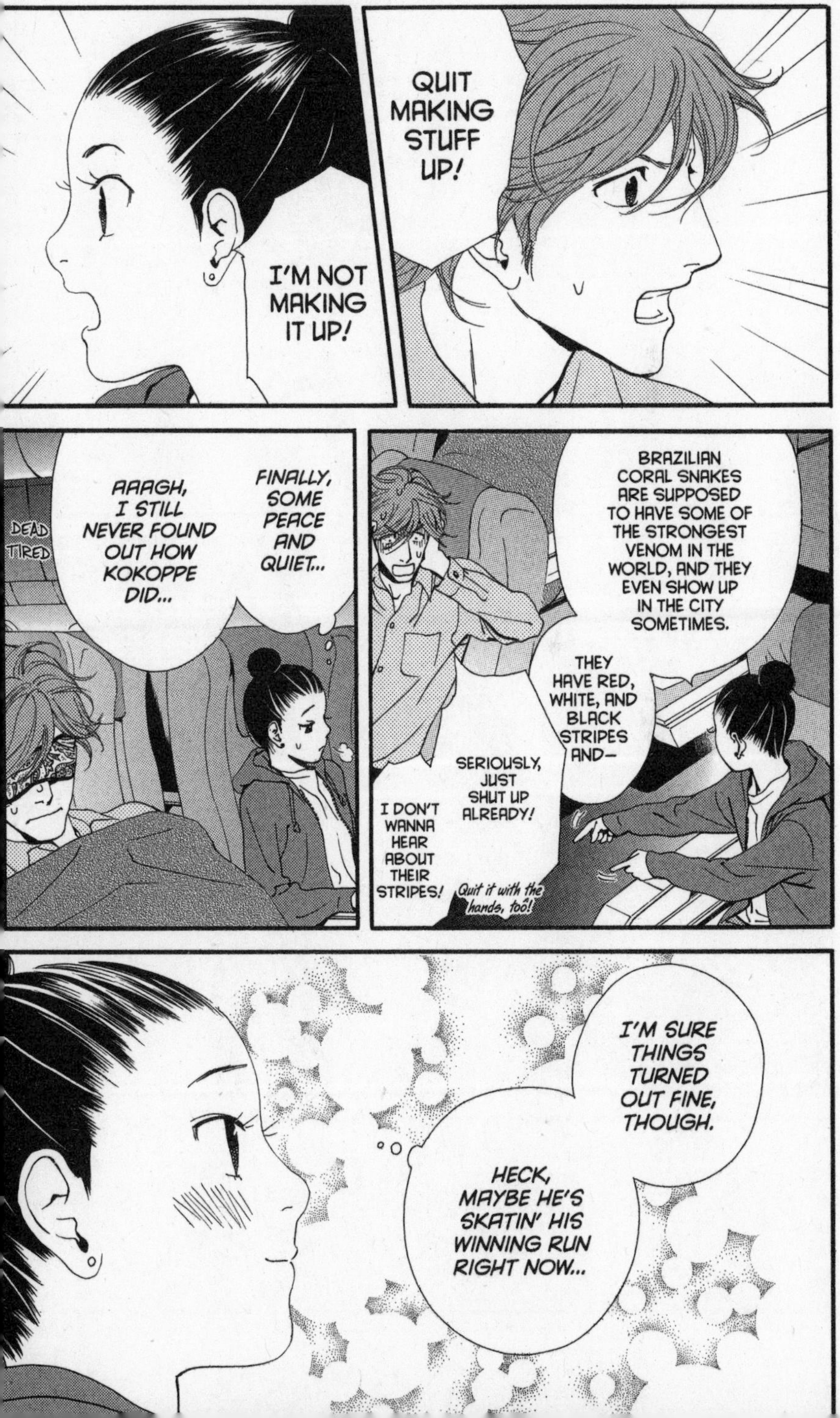
QUIT MAKING STUFF UP!
I'M NOT MAKING IT UP!
BRAZILIAN CORAL SNAKES ARE SUPPOSED TO HAVE SOME OF THE STRONGEST VENOM IN THE WORLD, AND THEY EVEN SHOW UP IN THE CITY SOMETIMES.
THEY HAVE RED, WHITE, AND BLACK STRIPES AND—
SERIOUSLY, JUST SHUT UP ALREADY!
I DON'T WANNA HEAR ABOUT THEIR STRIPES!
Quit it with the hands, too!
FINALLY, SOME PEACE AND QUIET...
AAAGH, I STILL NEVER FOUND OUT HOW KOKOPPE DID...
DEAD TIRED
I'M SURE THINGS TURNED OUT FINE, THOUGH.
HECK, MAYBE HE'S SKATIN' HIS WINNING RUN RIGHT NOW...

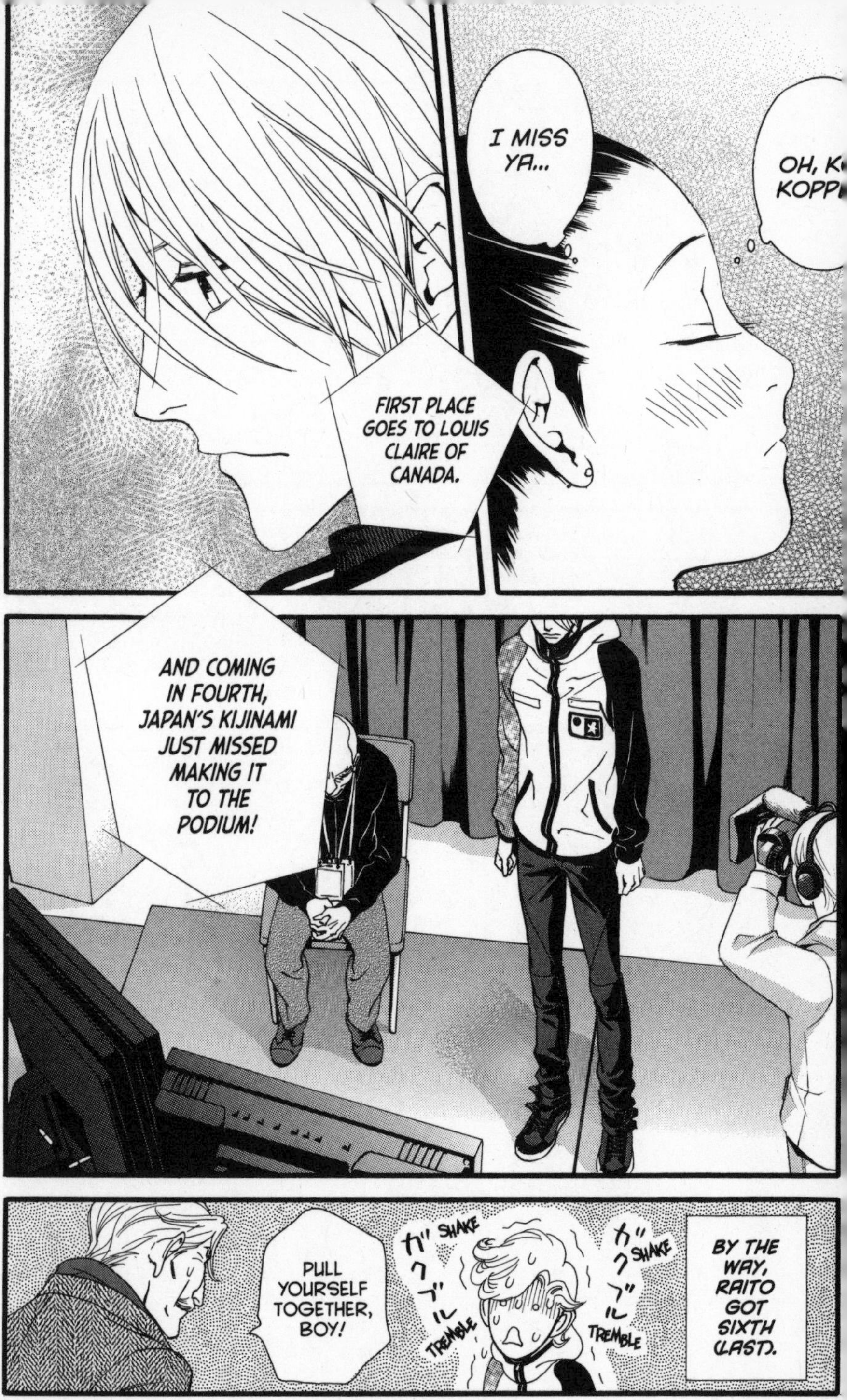

OH, K KOPP
I MISS YA...
FIRST PLACE GOES TO LOUIS CLAIRE OF CANADA.
AND COMING IN FOURTH, JAPAN'S KIJINAMI JUST MISSED MAKING IT TO THE PODIUM!
BY THE WAY, RAITO GOT SIXTH (LAST).
ガクブル SHAKE TREMBLE
ガクブル SHAKE TREMBLE
PULL YOURSELF TOGETHER, BOY!

Spell 6
The Distance
Between Us

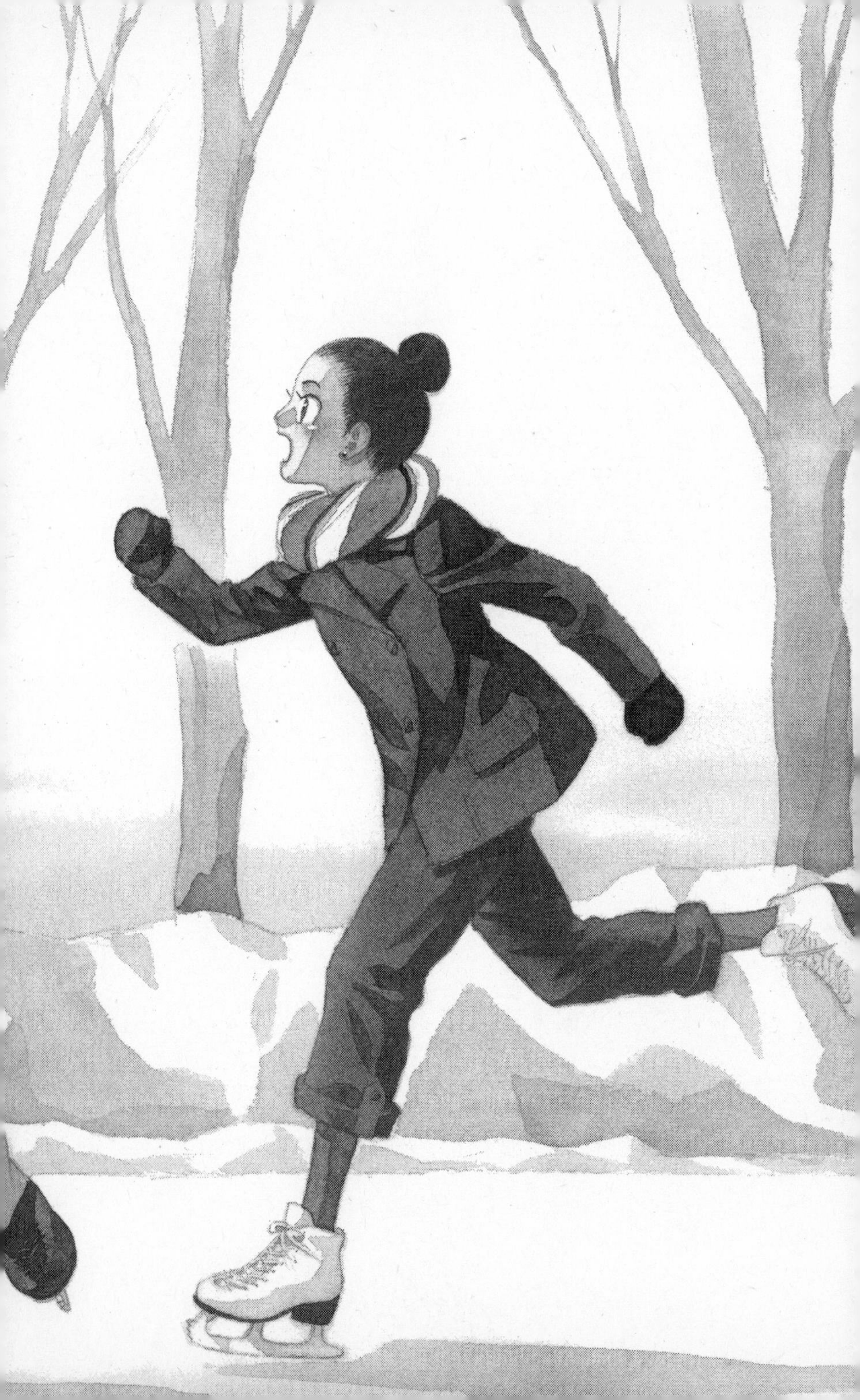

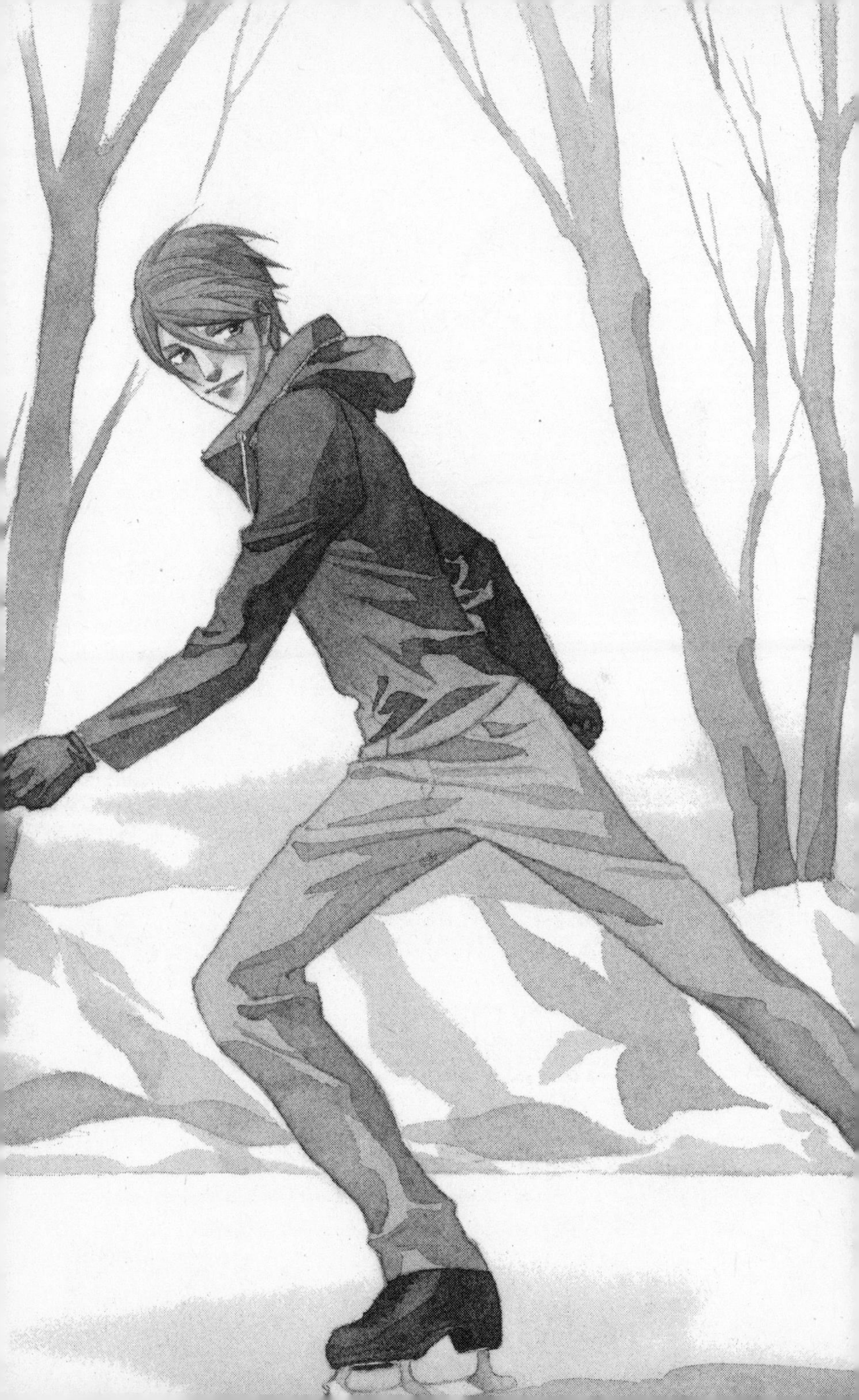

So! What's the story so far?☆

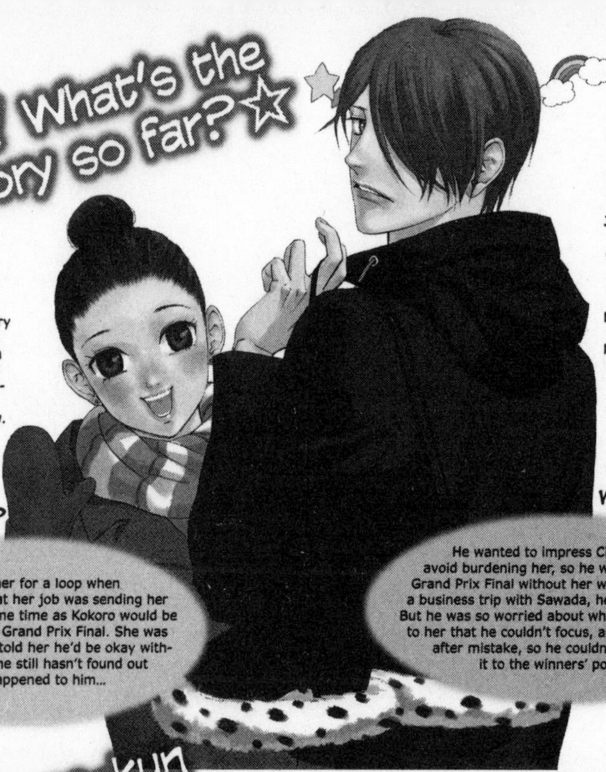

Chitose Igari
Chitose's our main character. She's so short that she gets mistaken for an elementary schooler a lot, but she's actually 23 and has been working for the editorial department of the health-and-lifestyle magazine *SASSO* for two years now. She's also Kokoro's childhood friend.

Kokoro Kijina
Kokoro is the nu one candidate t Japan's next top figure skater. can't handle pres though, so his re vary wildly. Lat however, Chitose begun reciting a spell for him fron longtime favorite *Magical Princess Lala*, and he's go more consistent his quadruple ju as a result.

What's up with Chitose?

It threw her for a loop when she found out that her job was sending her to Brazil at the same time as Kokoro would be competing in the Grand Prix Final. She was relieved when he told her he'd be okay without her, but she still hasn't found out what happened to him...

What's with Kokor

He wanted to impress Chitose and avoid burdening her, so he went to the ISU Grand Prix Final without her while she went on a business trip with Sawada, her editor-in-chief. But he was so worried about what her boss mear to her that he couldn't focus, and made mistake after mistake, so he couldn't even make it to the winners' podium.

Pega-kun Explains!

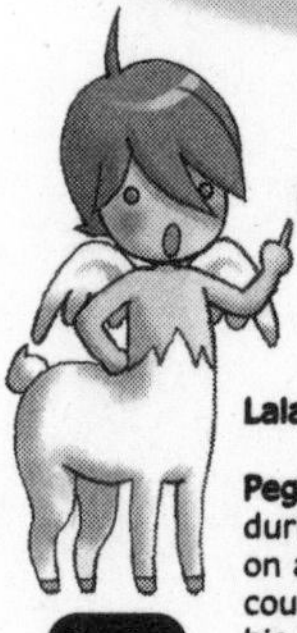

Pega-kun

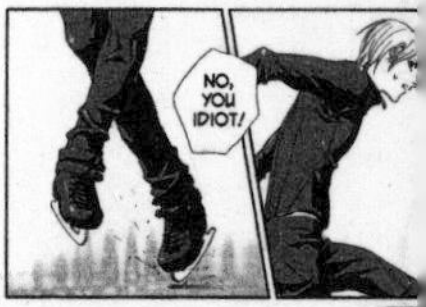
NO, YOU IDIOT!

Lala: So why'd Kokoppe lose?

Pega-kun: You're only allowed three combination jumps during the free skate, pega. When he messed up the landing on a triple jump, he accidentally jumped again, and that got counted as his third combo, pega. That meant if he stuck to his plan, his next combo wouldn't count at all, pega. So, he needed to score what points he could by doing a regular jump he hadn't done yet, pega! This is known as the Zayak Rule, pega.

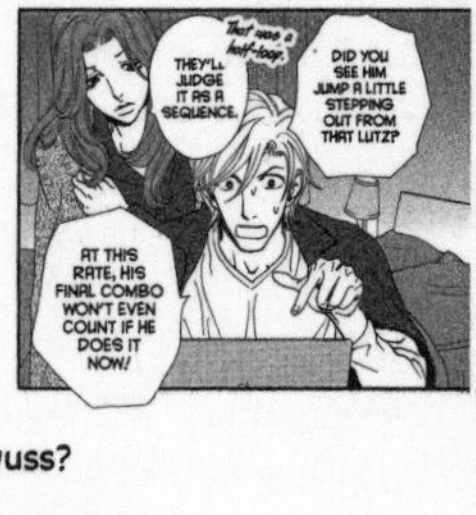
DID YOU SEE HIM JUMP A LITTLE STEPPING OUT FROM THAT LUTZ?
That was a half-loop.
THEY'LL JUDGE IT AS A SEQUENCE.
AT THIS RATE, HIS FINAL COMBO WON'T EVEN COUNT IF HE DOES IT NOW!

Lala: I have no idea what you're talking about.

Pega-kun: Well, you don't really need to understand, pega... Anyway, Kokoppe couldn't decide on what jump to do next, so his posture faltered, and he fell on his face, pega.

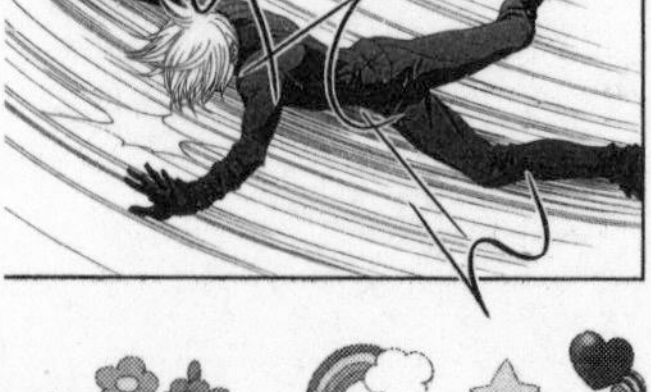
FWOOM

Lala: In other words, he's a hopeless wuss?

Pega-kun: Th-That's one way of putting it, pega...

Lala: Keep an eye out for the next episode of *Pega-kun Explains!*

Pega-kun: Now let's get back to the story, pega!

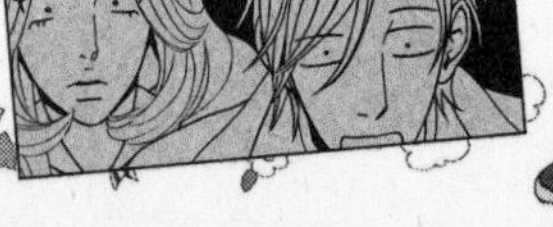

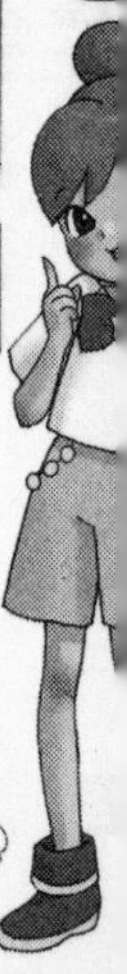

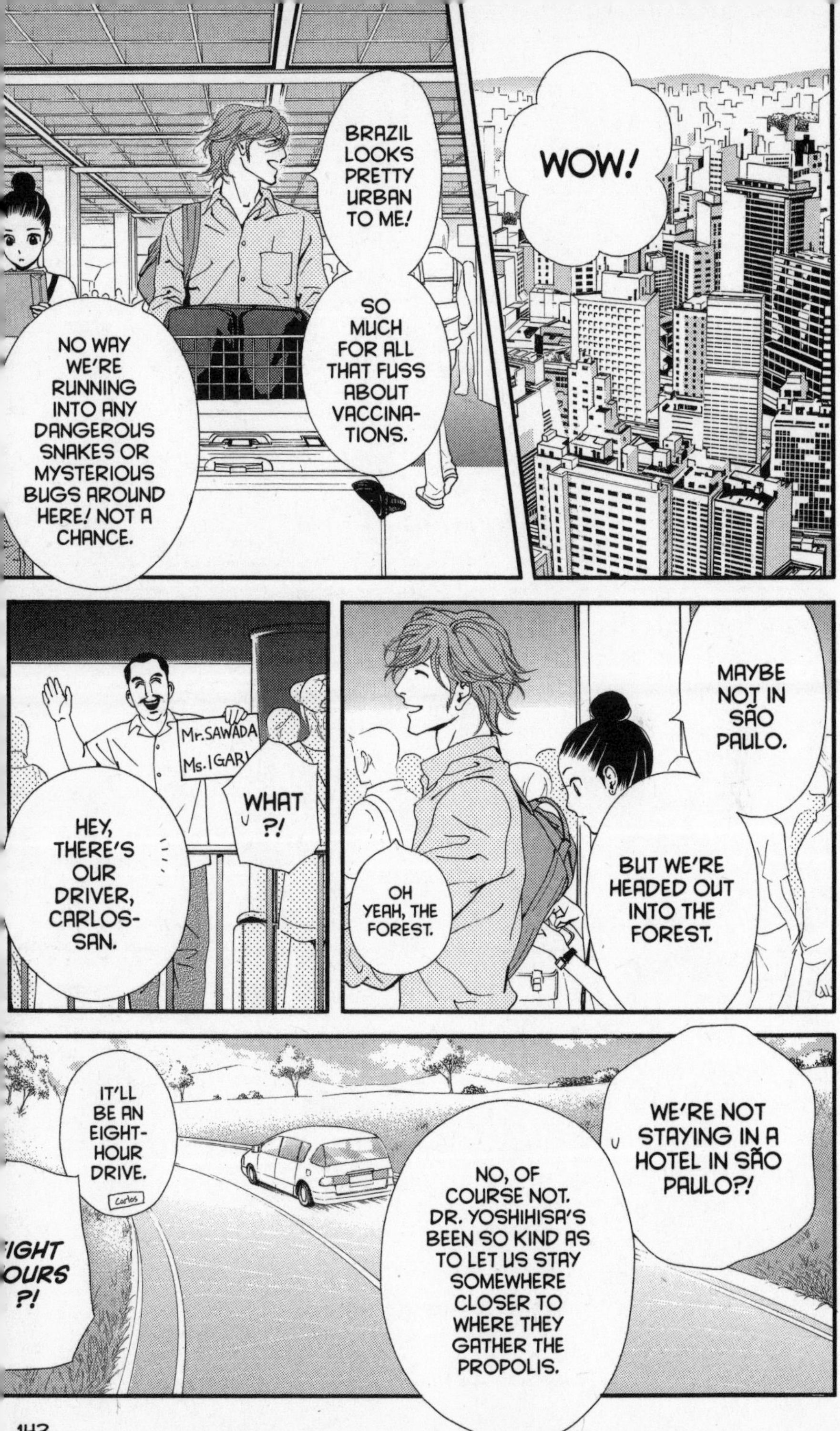
WOW!
BRAZIL LOOKS PRETTY URBAN TO ME!
SO MUCH FOR ALL THAT FUSS ABOUT VACCINA-TIONS.
NO WAY WE'RE RUNNING INTO ANY DANGEROUS SNAKES OR MYSTERIOUS BUGS AROUND HERE! NOT A CHANCE.
MAYBE NOT IN SÃO PAULO.
BUT WE'RE HEADED OUT INTO THE FOREST.
OH YEAH, THE FOREST.
WHAT ?!
Mr.SAWADA
Ms.IGAR
HEY, THERE'S OUR DRIVER, CARLOS-SAN.
WE'RE NOT STAYING IN A HOTEL IN SÃO PAULO?!
NO, OF COURSE NOT. DR. YOSHIHISA'S BEEN SO KIND AS TO LET US STAY SOMEWHERE CLOSER TO WHERE THEY GATHER THE PROPOLIS.
IT'LL BE AN EIGHT-HOUR DRIVE.
Carlos
IGHT OURS ?!

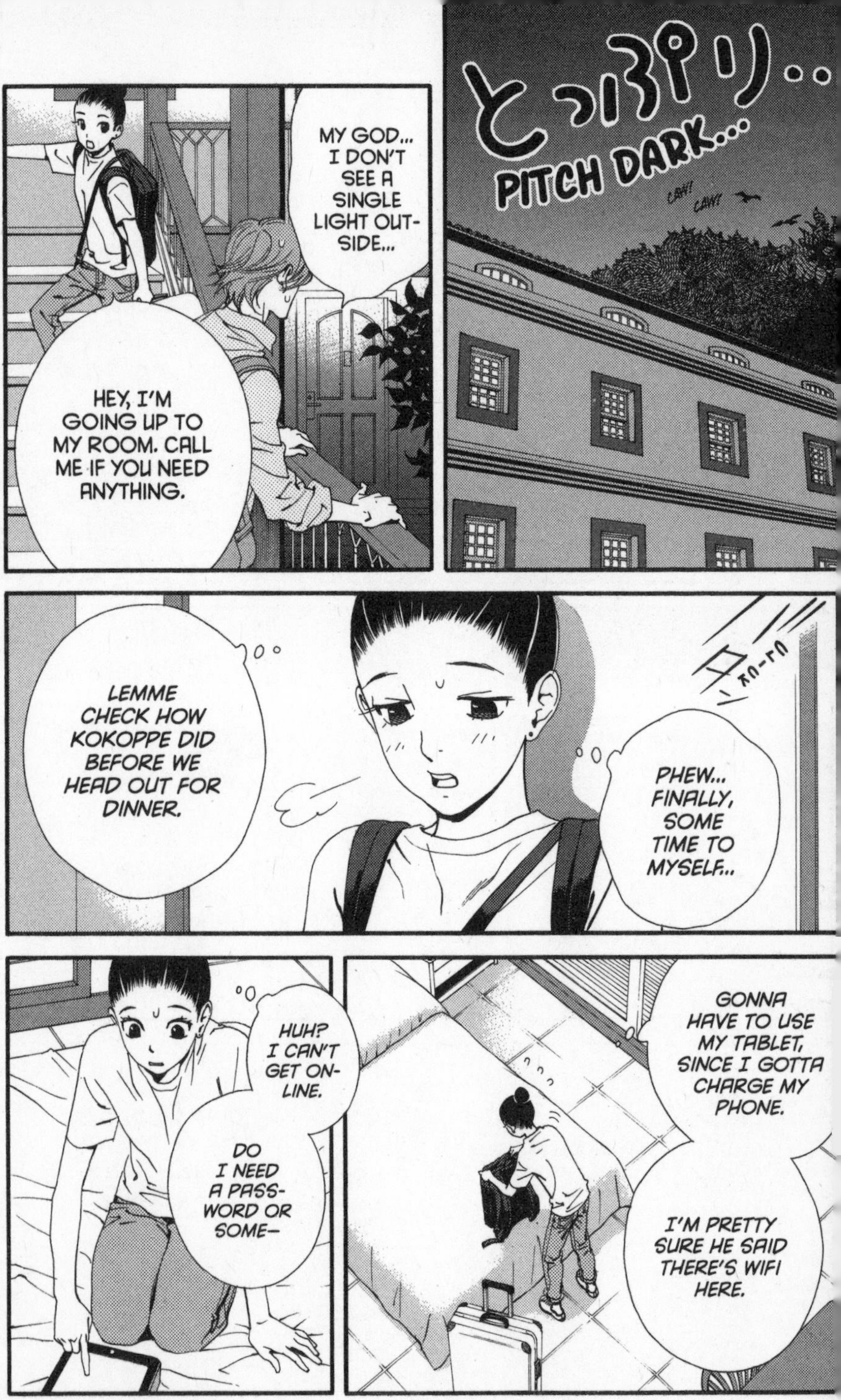
とっぷり…
PITCH DARK…
CAW!
CAW!
MY GOD… I DON'T SEE A SINGLE LIGHT OUT-SIDE…
HEY, I'M GOING UP TO MY ROOM. CALL ME IF YOU NEED ANYTHING.
PHEW… FINALLY, SOME TIME TO MYSELF…
LEMME CHECK HOW KOKOPPE DID BEFORE WE HEAD OUT FOR DINNER.
GONNA HAVE TO USE MY TABLET, SINCE I GOTTA CHARGE MY PHONE.
I'M PRETTY SURE HE SAID THERE'S WIFI HERE.
HUH? I CAN'T GET ON-LINE.
DO I NEED A PASS-WORD OR SOME–

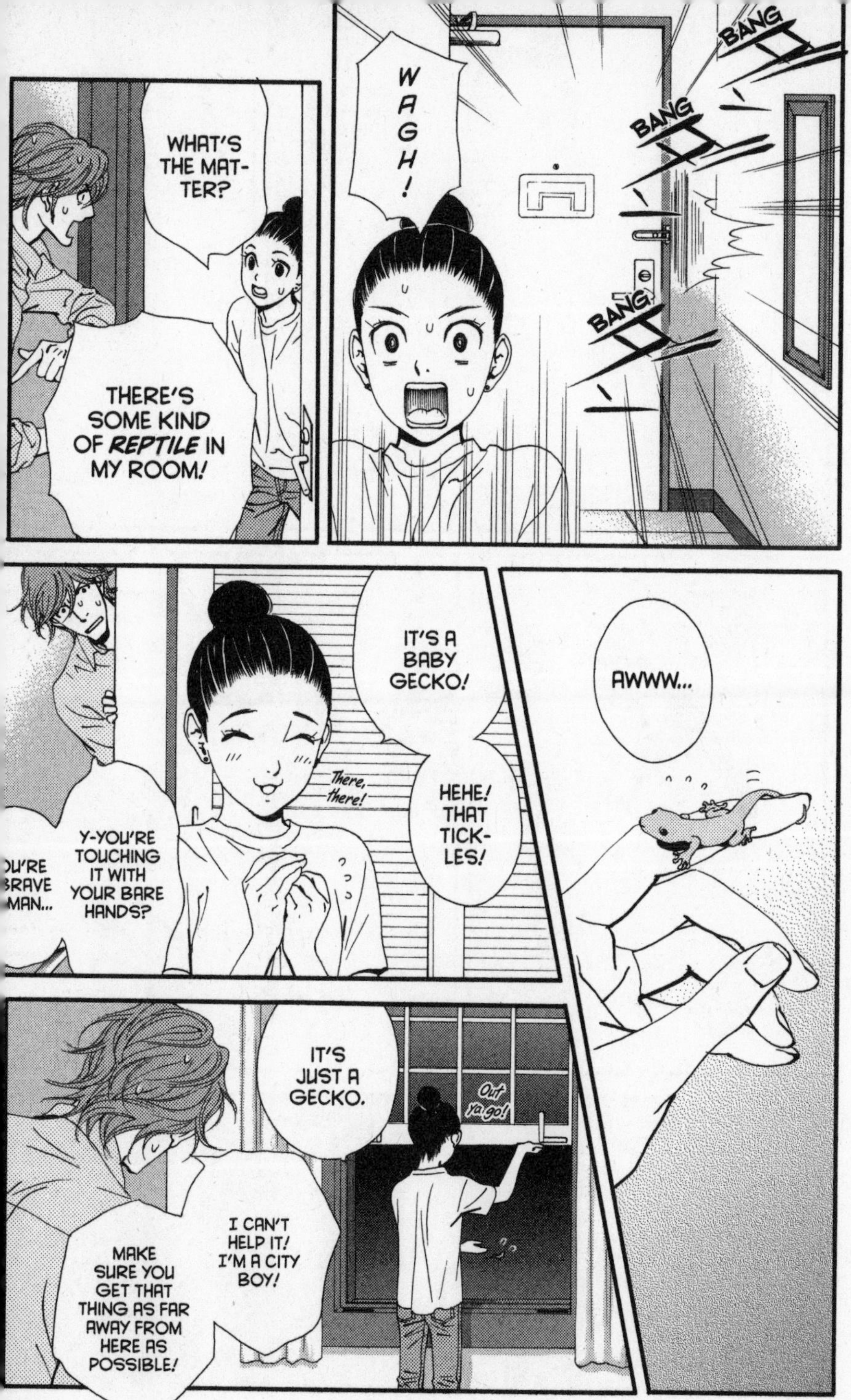

WAGH!
BANG
BANG
BANG
WHAT'S THE MAT-TER?
THERE'S SOME KIND OF *REPTILE* IN MY ROOM!
AWWW...
IT'S A BABY GECKO!
HEHE! THAT TICK-LES!
There, there!
Y-YOU'RE TOUCHING IT WITH YOUR BARE HANDS?
OU'RE BRAVE MAN...
IT'S JUST A GECKO.
Out ya go!
I CAN'T HELP IT! I'M A CITY BOY!
MAKE SURE YOU GET THAT THING AS FAR AWAY FROM HERE AS POSSIBLE!

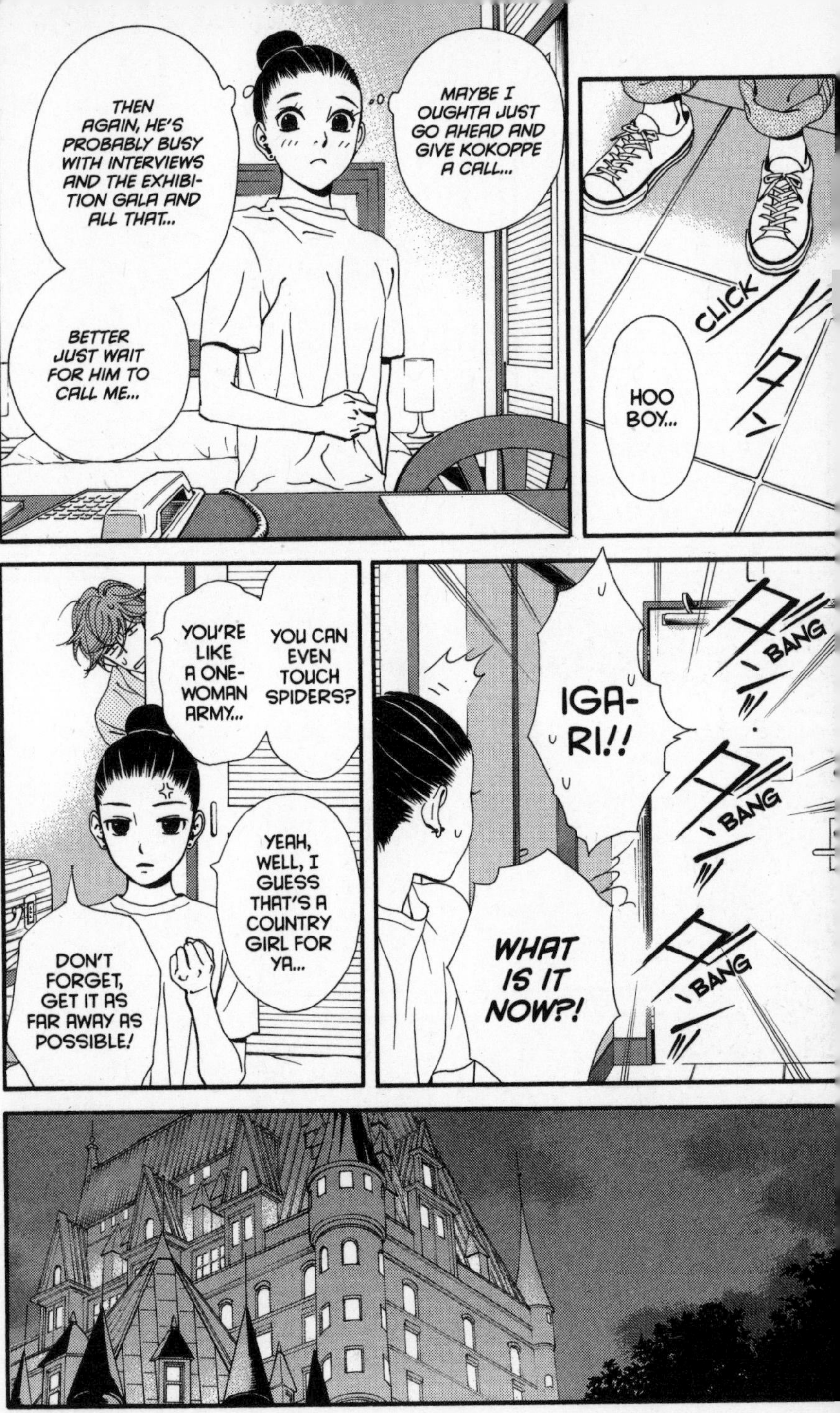
CLICK
HOO BOY...
MAYBE I OUGHTA JUST GO AHEAD AND GIVE KOKOPPE A CALL...
THEN AGAIN, HE'S PROBABLY BUSY WITH INTERVIEWS AND THE EXHIBITION GALA AND ALL THAT...
BETTER JUST WAIT FOR HIM TO CALL ME...
BANG
BANG
BANG
IGA-RI!!
WHAT IS IT NOW?!
YOU CAN EVEN TOUCH SPIDERS?
YOU'RE LIKE A ONE-WOMAN ARMY...
YEAH, WELL, I GUESS THAT'S A COUNTRY GIRL FOR YA...
DON'T FORGET, GET IT AS FAR AWAY AS POSSIBLE!

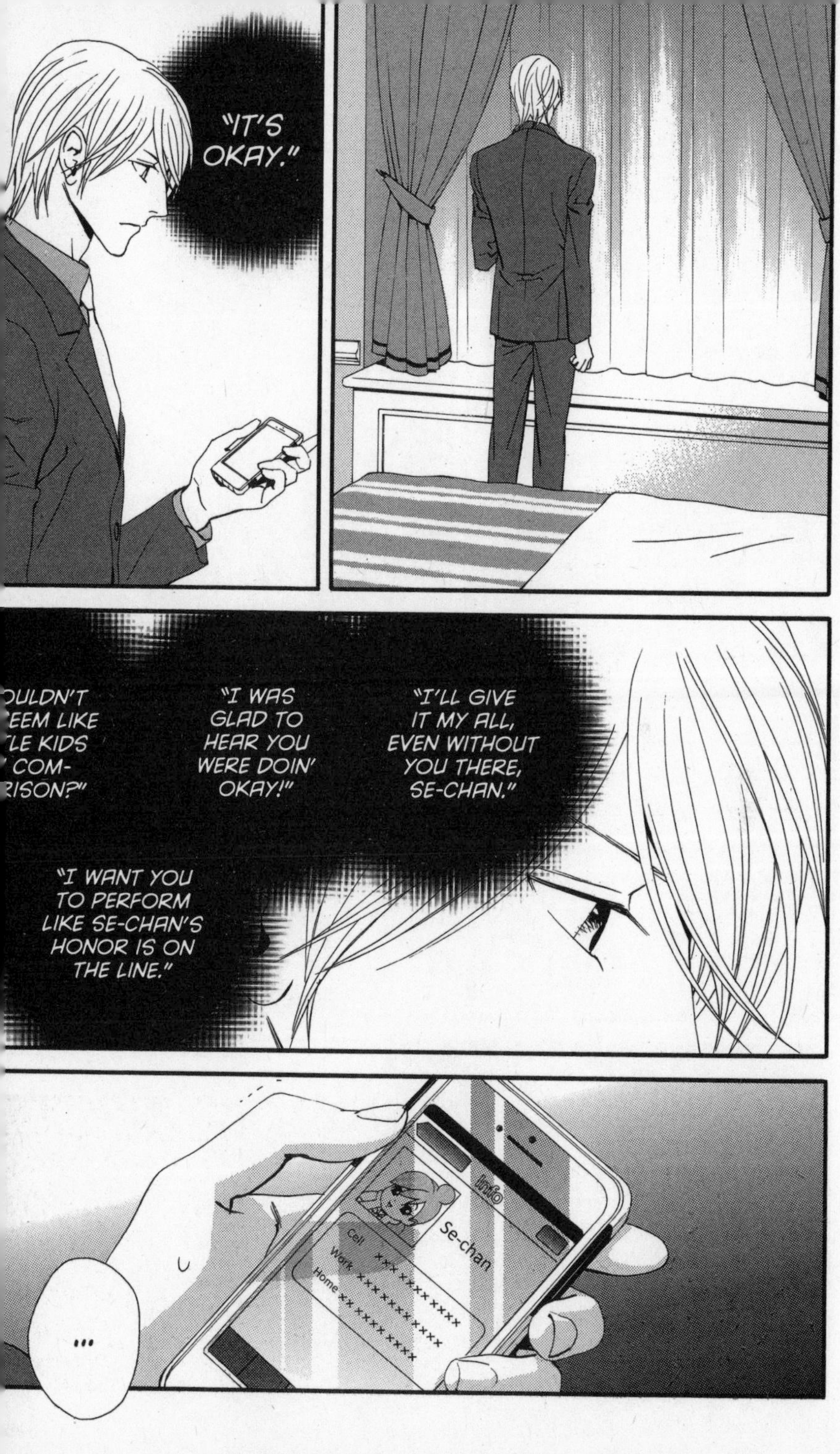
"IT'S OKAY."
"I'LL GIVE IT MY ALL, EVEN WITHOUT YOU THERE, SE-CHAN."
"I WAS GLAD TO HEAR YOU WERE DOIN' OKAY!"
OULDN'T EEM LIKE LE KIDS COM- RISON?"
"I WANT YOU TO PERFORM LIKE SE-CHAN'S HONOR IS ON THE LINE."
Info
Se-chan
Cell
Work
Home
...

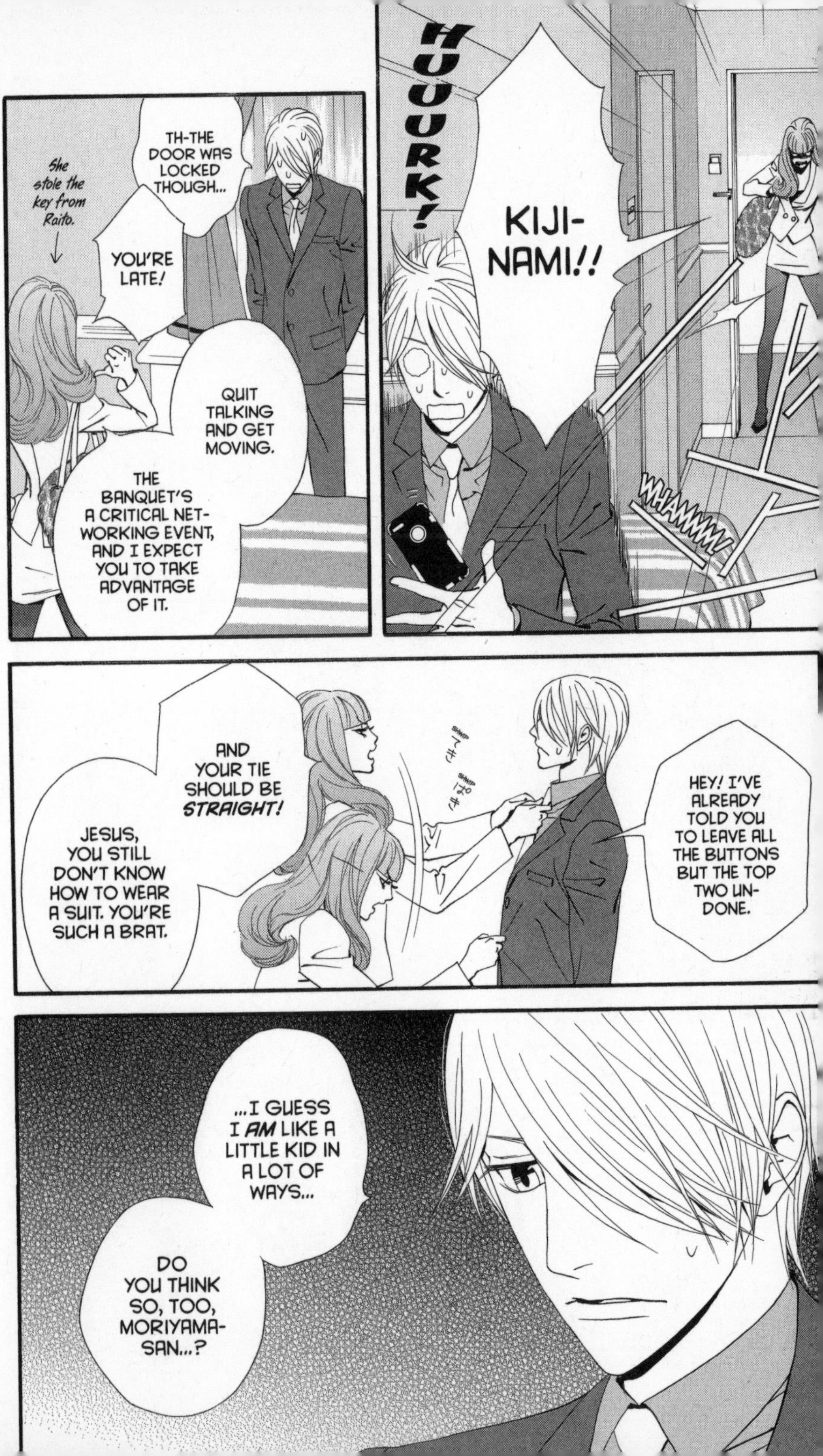
HUUURK!
KIJI-NAMI!!
WHAMMM!
TH-THE DOOR WAS LOCKED THOUGH...
She stole the key from Raito.
YOU'RE LATE!
QUIT TALKING AND GET MOVING.
THE BANQUET'S A CRITICAL NET-WORKING EVENT, AND I EXPECT YOU TO TAKE ADVANTAGE OF IT.
HEY! I'VE ALREADY TOLD YOU TO LEAVE ALL THE BUTTONS BUT THE TOP TWO UN-DONE.
SHWIP てき
SHWIP ぱき
AND YOUR TIE SHOULD BE STRAIGHT!
JESUS, YOU STILL DON'T KNOW HOW TO WEAR A SUIT. YOU'RE SUCH A BRAT.
...I GUESS I AM LIKE A LITTLE KID IN A LOT OF WAYS...
DO YOU THINK SO, TOO, MORIYAMA-SAN...?

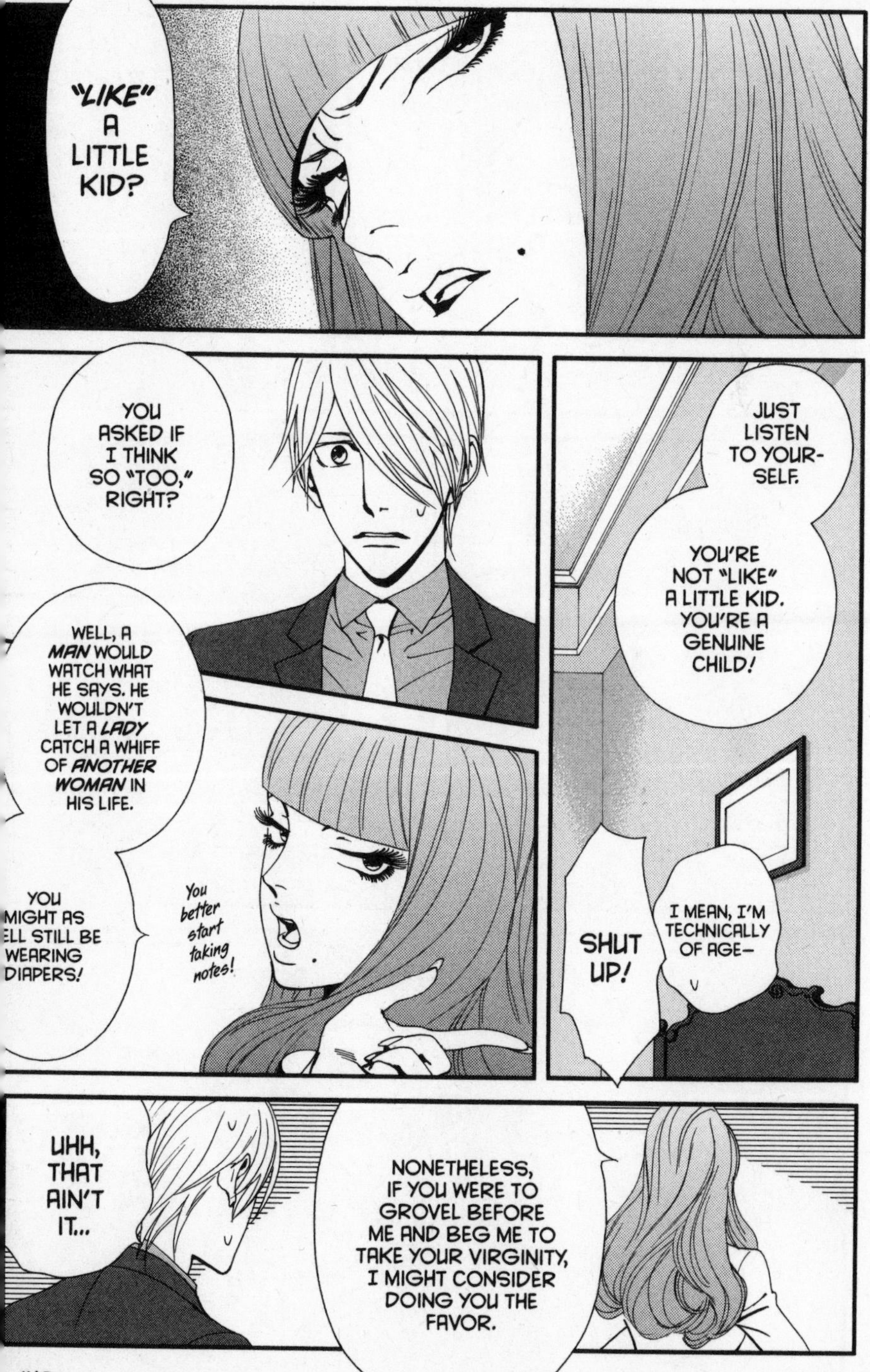

"LIKE" A LITTLE KID?
JUST LISTEN TO YOUR-SELF.
YOU'RE NOT "LIKE" A LITTLE KID. YOU'RE A GENUINE CHILD!
I MEAN, I'M TECHNICALLY OF AGE—
SHUT UP!
YOU ASKED IF I THINK SO "TOO," RIGHT?
WELL, A *MAN* WOULD WATCH WHAT HE SAYS. HE WOULDN'T LET A *LADY* CATCH A WHIFF OF *ANOTHER WOMAN* IN HIS LIFE.
You better start taking notes!
YOU MIGHT AS ELL STILL BE WEARING DIAPERS!
NONETHELESS, IF YOU WERE TO GROVEL BEFORE ME AND BEG ME TO TAKE YOUR VIRGINITY, I MIGHT CONSIDER DOING YOU THE FAVOR.
UHH, THAT AIN'T IT...

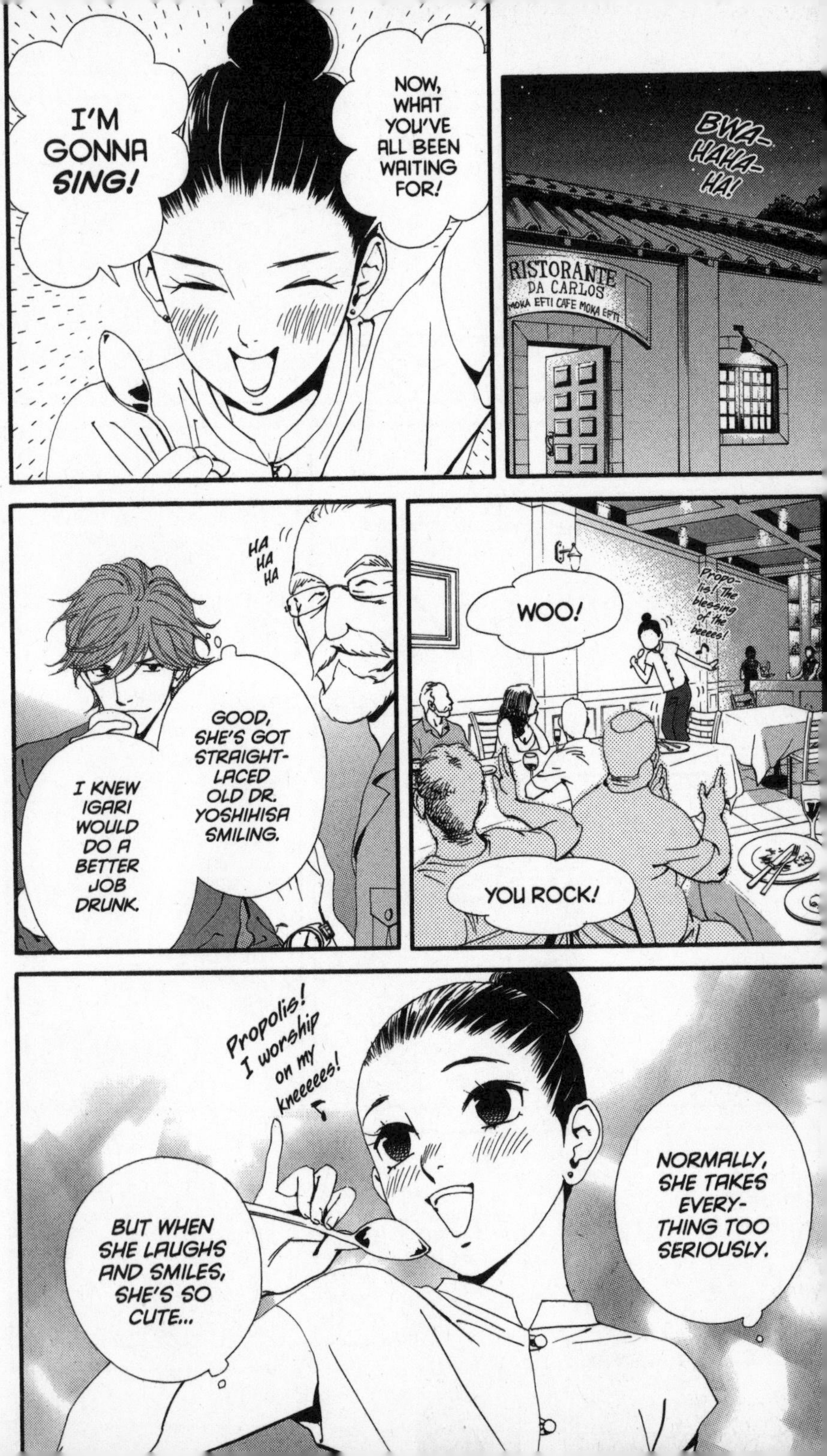
BWA-HAHAHA-HA!
RISTORANTE DA CARLOS
MOKA EFTI CAFE MOKA EFTI
NOW, WHAT YOU'VE ALL BEEN WAITING FOR!
I'M GONNA SING!
Propolis! The blessing of the beeees!
WOO!
YOU ROCK!
HA HA HA
GOOD, SHE'S GOT STRAIGHT-LACED OLD DR. YOSHIHISA SMILING.
I KNEW IGARI WOULD DO A BETTER JOB DRUNK.
NORMALLY, SHE TAKES EVERY-THING TOO SERIOUSLY.
Propolis! I worship on my kneeeees!
BUT WHEN SHE LAUGHS AND SMILES, SHE'S SO CUTE...

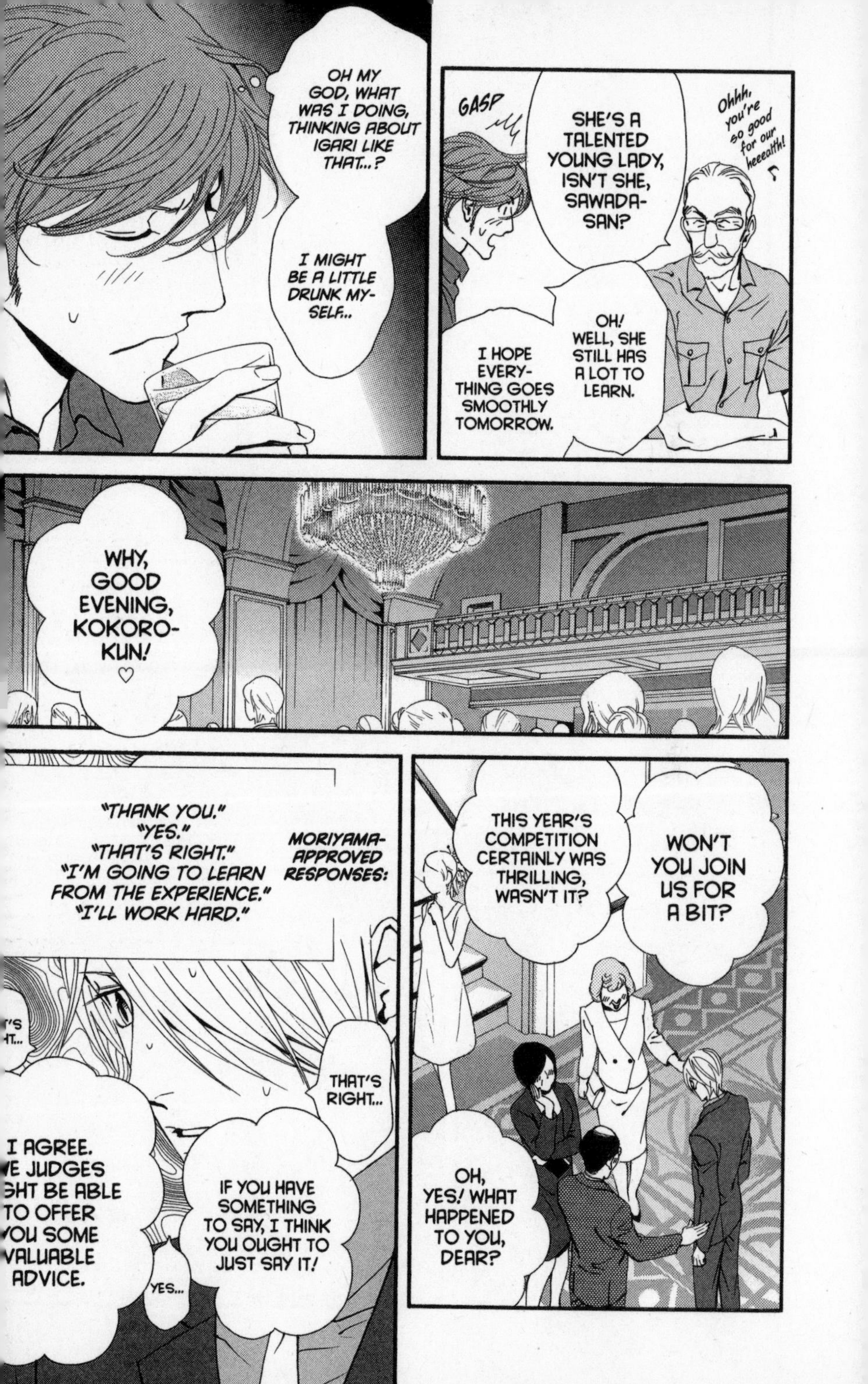
Ohhh, you're so good for our heeeealth! ♪
SHE'S A TALENTED YOUNG LADY, ISN'T SHE, SAWADA-SAN?
GASP
OH! WELL, SHE STILL HAS A LOT TO LEARN.
I HOPE EVERYTHING GOES SMOOTHLY TOMORROW.
OH MY GOD, WHAT WAS I DOING, THINKING ABOUT IGARI LIKE THAT...?
I MIGHT BE A LITTLE DRUNK MY-SELF...
WHY, GOOD EVENING, KOKORO-KUN! ♡
WON'T YOU JOIN US FOR A BIT?
THIS YEAR'S COMPETITION CERTAINLY WAS THRILLING, WASN'T IT?
OH, YES! WHAT HAPPENED TO YOU, DEAR?
MORIYAMA-APPROVED RESPONSES:
"THANK YOU." "YES." "THAT'S RIGHT." "I'M GOING TO LEARN FROM THE EXPERIENCE." "I'LL WORK HARD."
THAT'S RIGHT...
IF YOU HAVE SOMETHING TO SAY, I THINK YOU OUGHT TO JUST SAY IT!
I AGREE. E JUDGES GHT BE ABLE TO OFFER YOU SOME VALUABLE ADVICE.
YES...

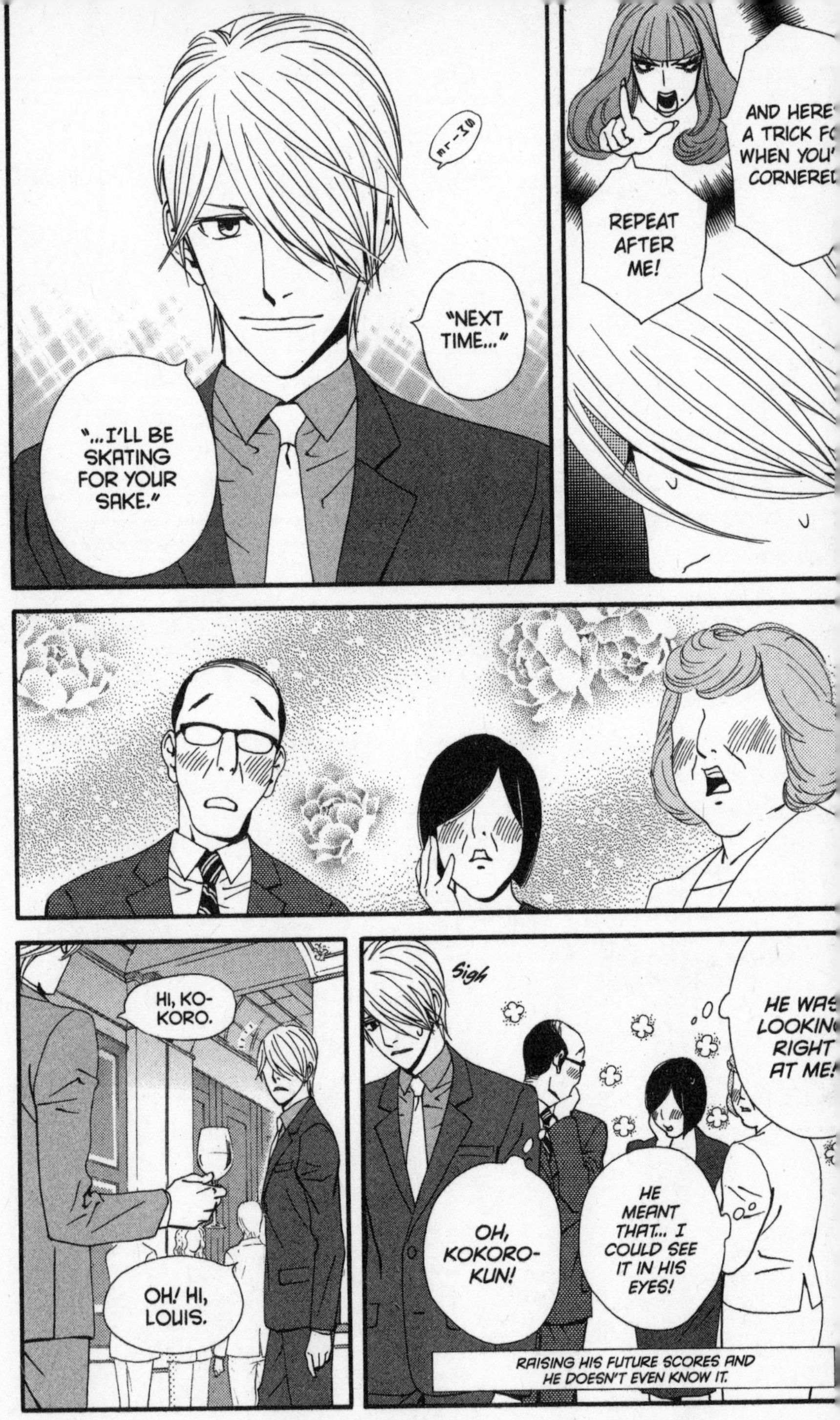
AND HERE' A TRICK FO WHEN YOU' CORNERED
REPEAT AFTER ME!
"NEXT TIME..."
"...I'LL BE SKATING FOR YOUR SAKE."
HE WAS LOOKING RIGHT AT ME!
HE MEANT THAT... I COULD SEE IT IN HIS EYES!
Sigh
OH, KOKORO-KUN!
RAISING HIS FUTURE SCORES AND HE DOESN'T EVEN KNOW IT.
HI, KO-KORO.
OH! HI, LOUIS.

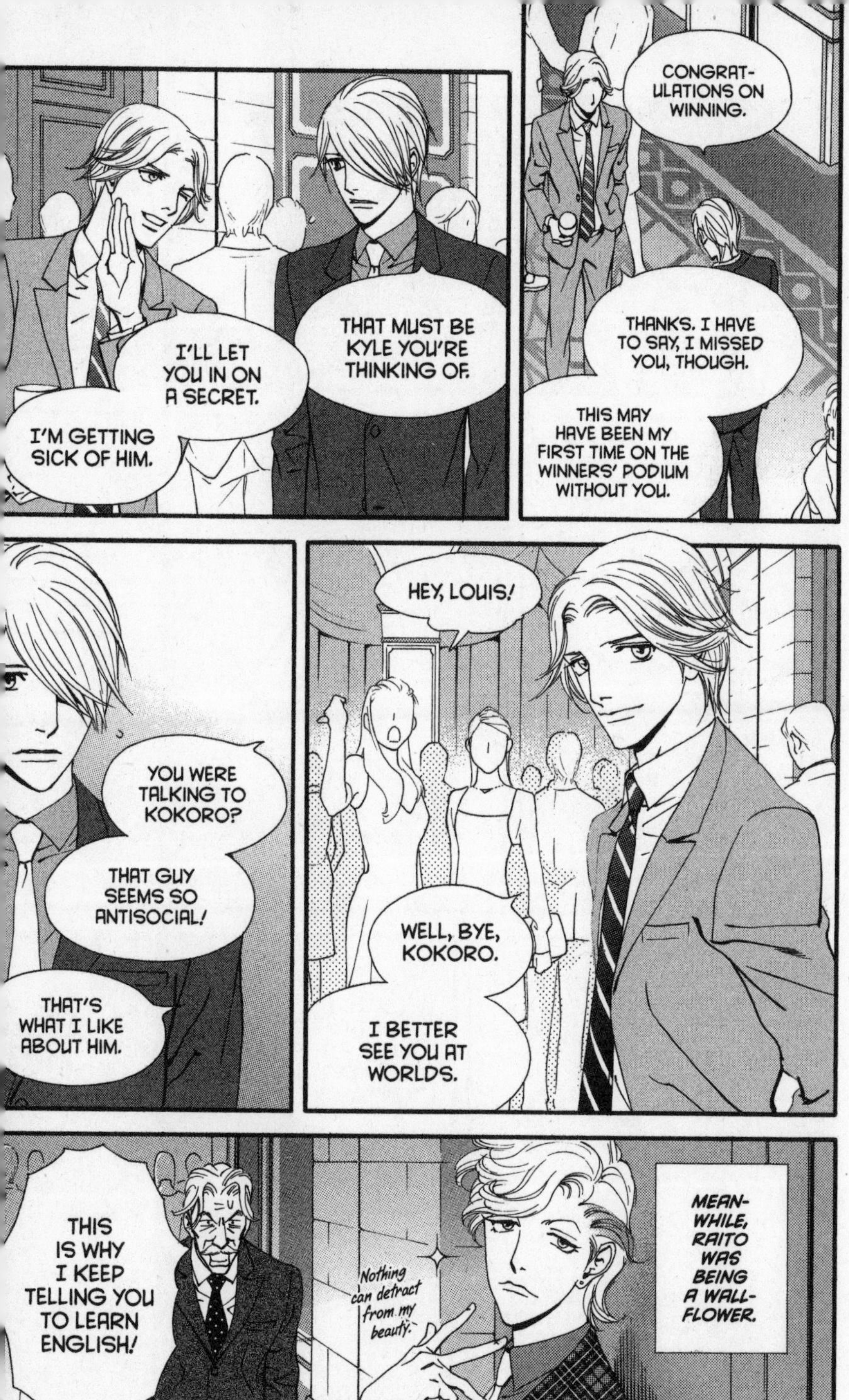
CONGRAT-ULATIONS ON WINNING.
THANKS. I HAVE TO SAY, I MISSED YOU, THOUGH.
THIS MAY HAVE BEEN MY FIRST TIME ON THE WINNERS' PODIUM WITHOUT YOU.
I'LL LET YOU IN ON A SECRET.
I'M GETTING SICK OF HIM.
THAT MUST BE KYLE YOU'RE THINKING OF.
HEY, LOUIS!
WELL, BYE, KOKORO.
I BETTER SEE YOU AT WORLDS.
YOU WERE TALKING TO KOKORO?
THAT GUY SEEMS SO ANTISOCIAL!
THAT'S WHAT I LIKE ABOUT HIM.
MEAN-WHILE, RAITO WAS BEING A WALL-FLOWER.
Nothing can detract from my beauty.
THIS IS WHY I KEEP TELLING YOU TO LEARN ENGLISH!

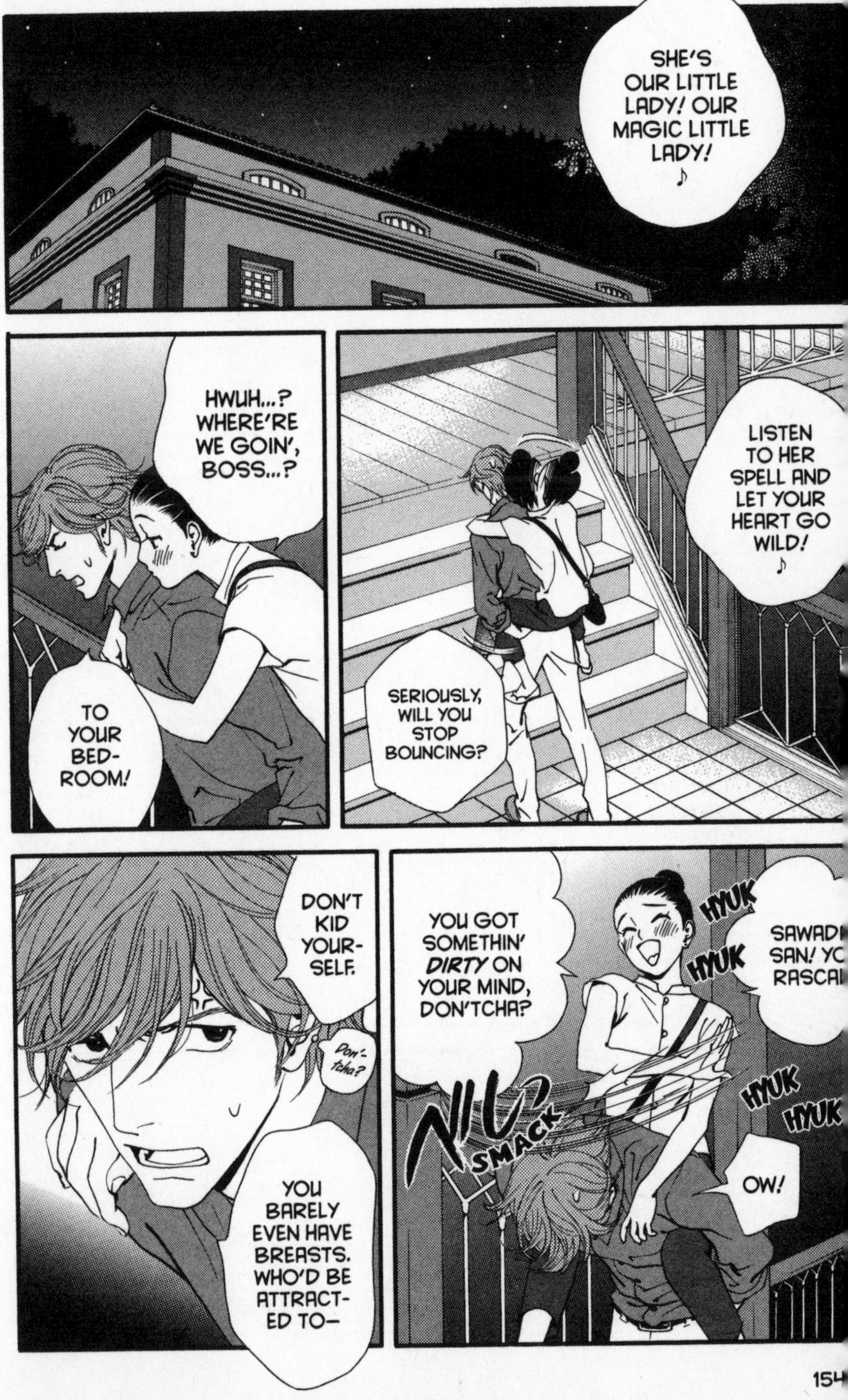
SHE'S OUR LITTLE LADY! OUR MAGIC LITTLE LADY! ♪
LISTEN TO HER SPELL AND LET YOUR HEART GO WILD! ♪
SERIOUSLY, WILL YOU STOP BOUNCING?
HWUH...? WHERE'RE WE GOIN', BOSS...?
TO YOUR BED-ROOM!
SAWAD SAN! YO RASCA
HYUK HYUK
YOU GOT SOMETHIN' *DIRTY* ON YOUR MIND, DON'TCHA?
HYUK HYUK
SMACK
OW!
DON'T KID YOUR-SELF.
Don'-tcha?
YOU BARELY EVEN HAVE BREASTS. WHO'D BE ATTRACT-ED TO—

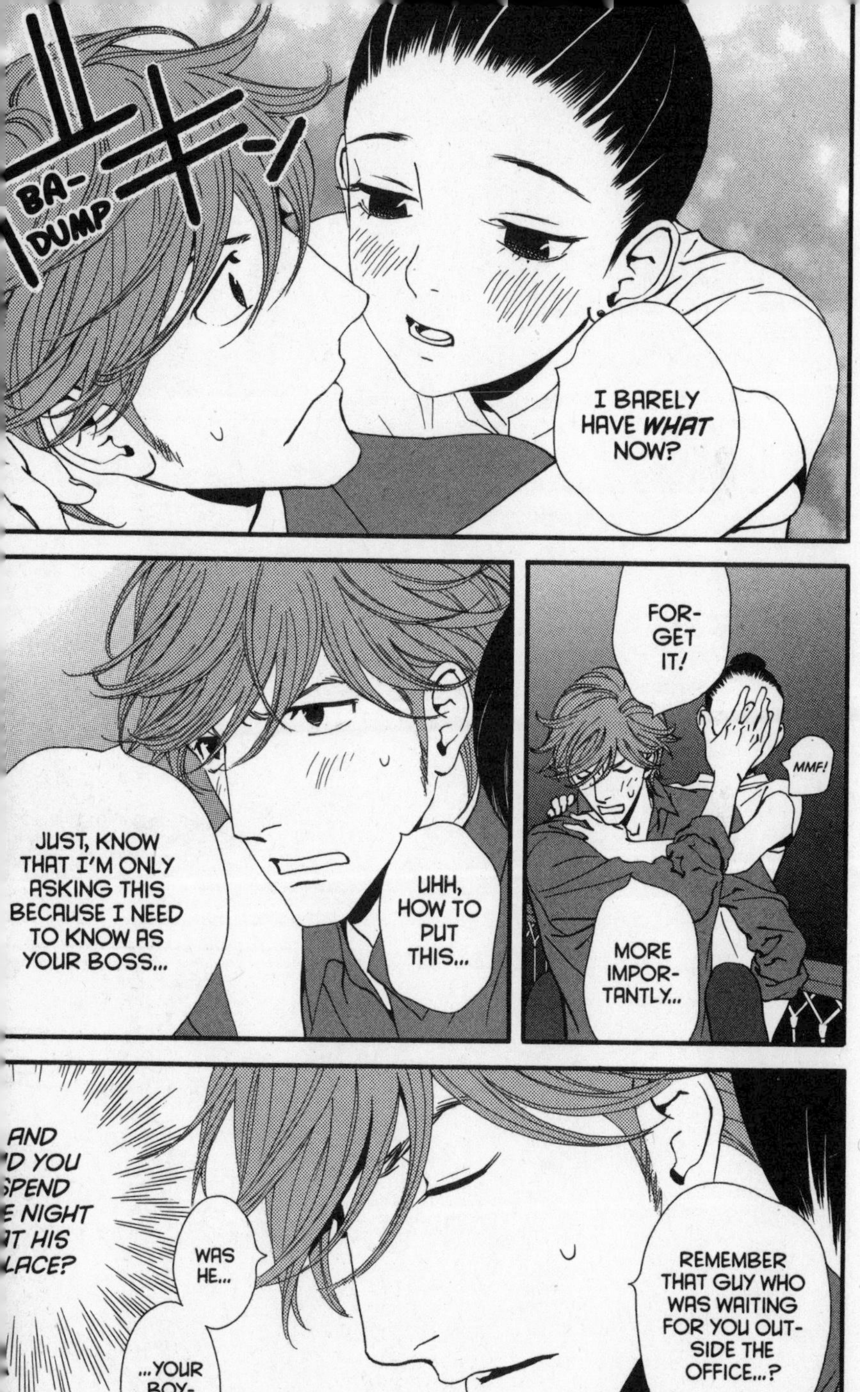
BA-DUMP
I BARELY HAVE *WHAT* NOW?
FOR-GET IT!
MMF!
MORE IMPORTANTLY...
UHH, HOW TO PUT THIS...
JUST, KNOW THAT I'M ONLY ASKING THIS BECAUSE I NEED TO KNOW AS YOUR BOSS...
REMEMBER THAT GUY WHO WAS WAITING FOR YOU OUT-SIDE THE OFFICE...?
WAS HE...
...YOUR BOY-FRIEND?
AND D YOU SPEND E NIGHT AT HIS LACE?

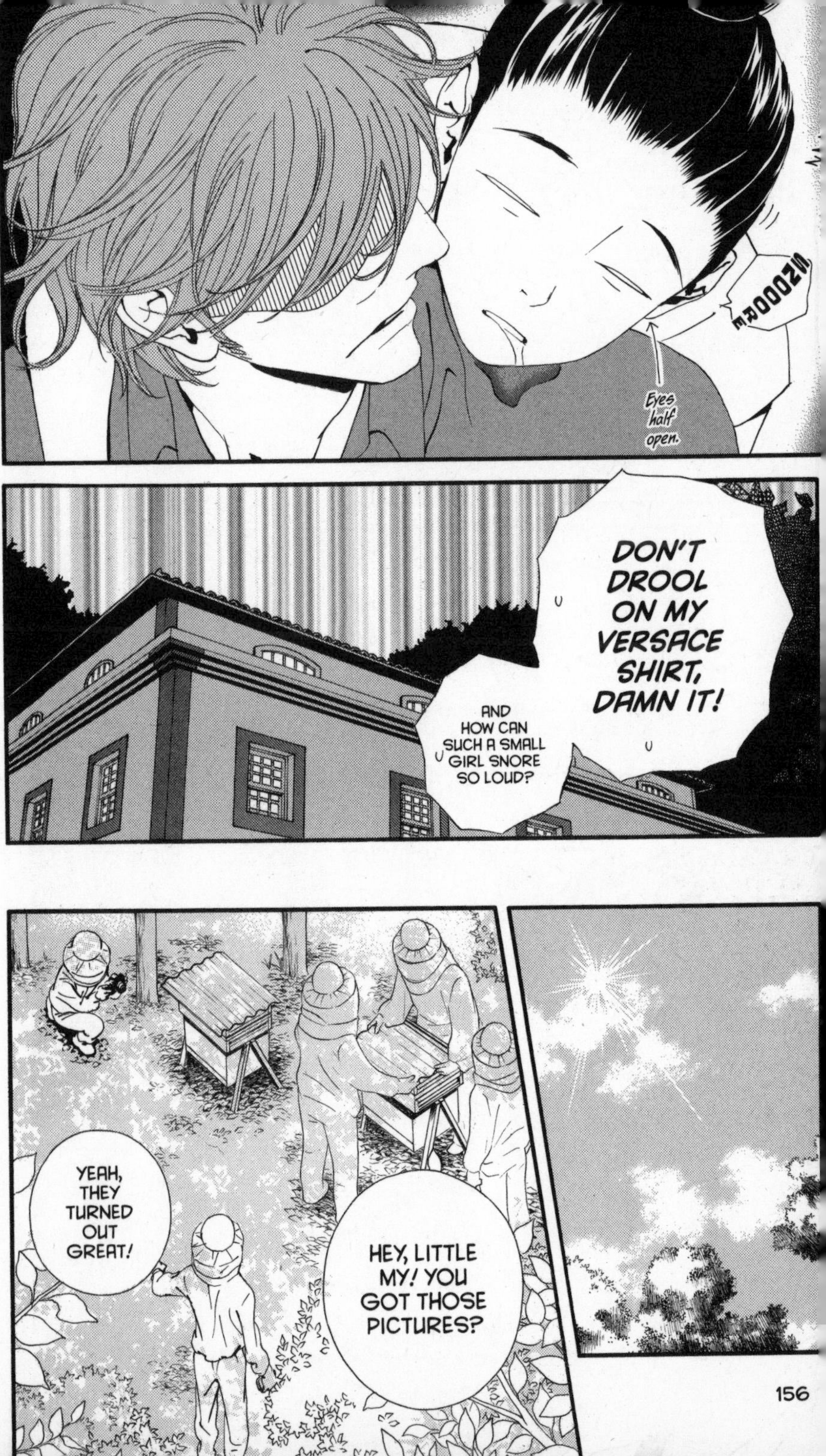
SNOOORE
Eyes half open.
DON'T DROOL ON MY VERSACE SHIRT, DAMN IT!
AND HOW CAN SUCH A SMALL GIRL SNORE SO LOUD?
HEY, LITTLE MY! YOU GOT THOSE PICTURES?
YEAH, THEY TURNED OUT GREAT!

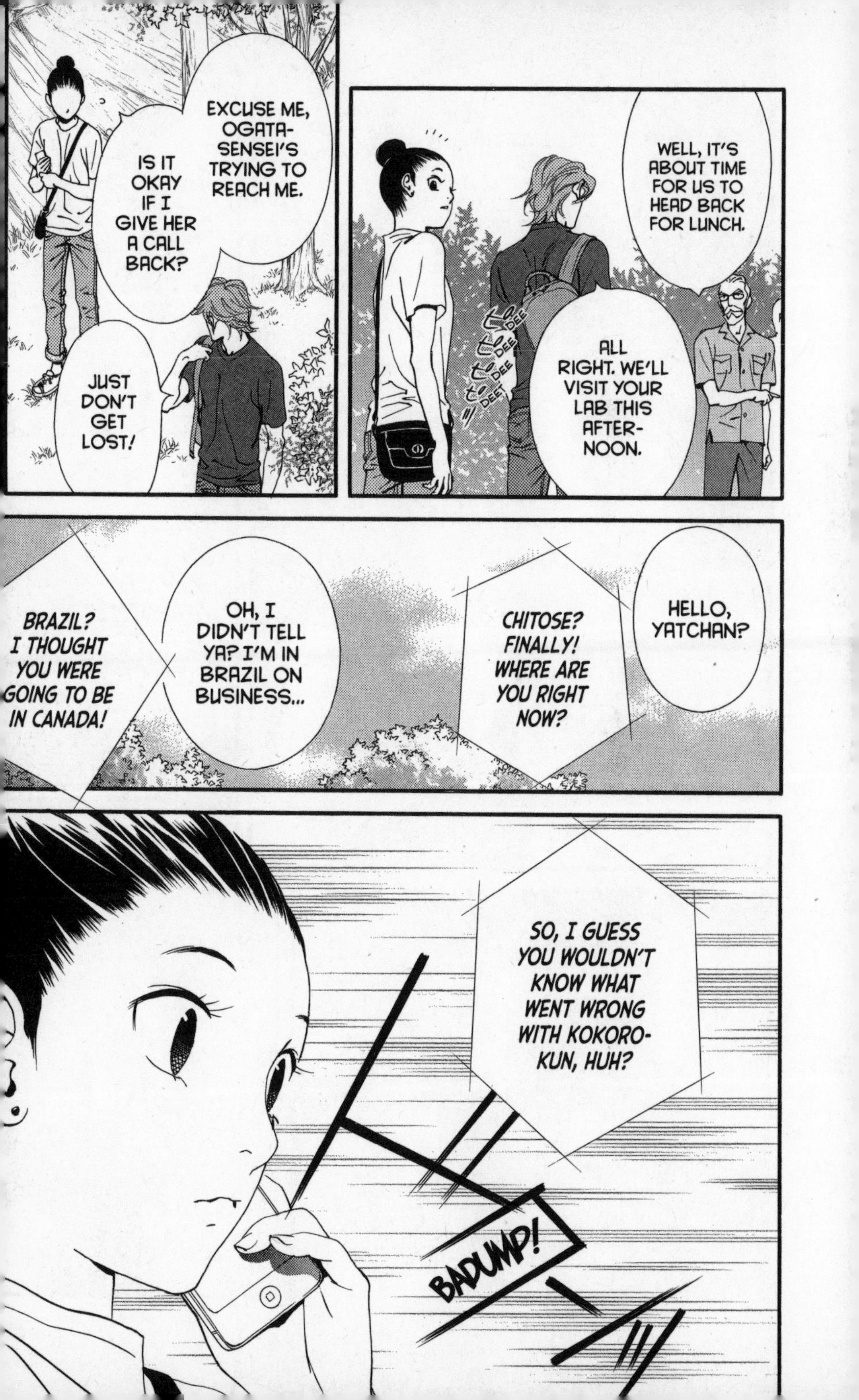
WELL, IT'S ABOUT TIME FOR US TO HEAD BACK FOR LUNCH.
DEE DEE DEE DEET
ALL RIGHT. WE'LL VISIT YOUR LAB THIS AFTERNOON.
EXCUSE ME, OGATA-SENSEI'S TRYING TO REACH ME.
IS IT OKAY IF I GIVE HER A CALL BACK?
JUST DON'T GET LOST!
HELLO, YATCHAN?
CHITOSE? FINALLY! WHERE ARE YOU RIGHT NOW?
OH, I DIDN'T TELL YA? I'M IN BRAZIL ON BUSINESS...
BRAZIL? I THOUGHT YOU WERE GOING TO BE IN CANADA!
SO, I GUESS YOU WOULDN'T KNOW WHAT WENT WRONG WITH KOKORO-KUN, HUH?
BADUMP!

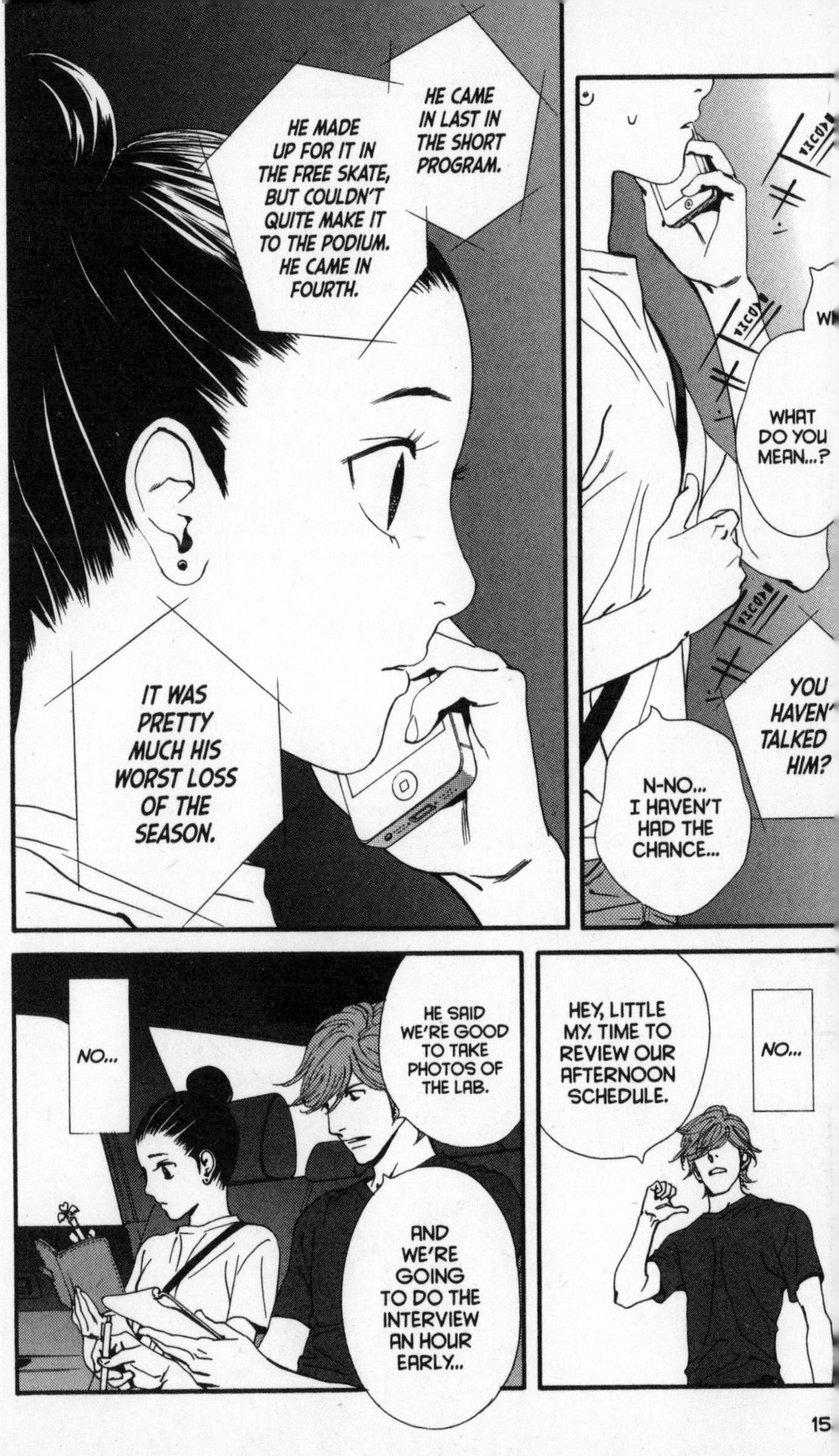
WHAT DO YOU MEAN...?
YOU HAVEN' TALKED HIM?
N-NO... I HAVEN'T HAD THE CHANCE...
HE CAME IN LAST IN THE SHORT PROGRAM.
HE MADE UP FOR IT IN THE FREE SKATE, BUT COULDN'T QUITE MAKE IT TO THE PODIUM. HE CAME IN FOURTH.
IT WAS PRETTY MUCH HIS WORST LOSS OF THE SEASON.
NO...
HEY, LITTLE MY. TIME TO REVIEW OUR AFTERNOON SCHEDULE.
HE SAID WE'RE GOOD TO TAKE PHOTOS OF THE LAB.
NO...
AND WE'RE GOING TO DO THE INTERVIEW AN HOUR EARLY...

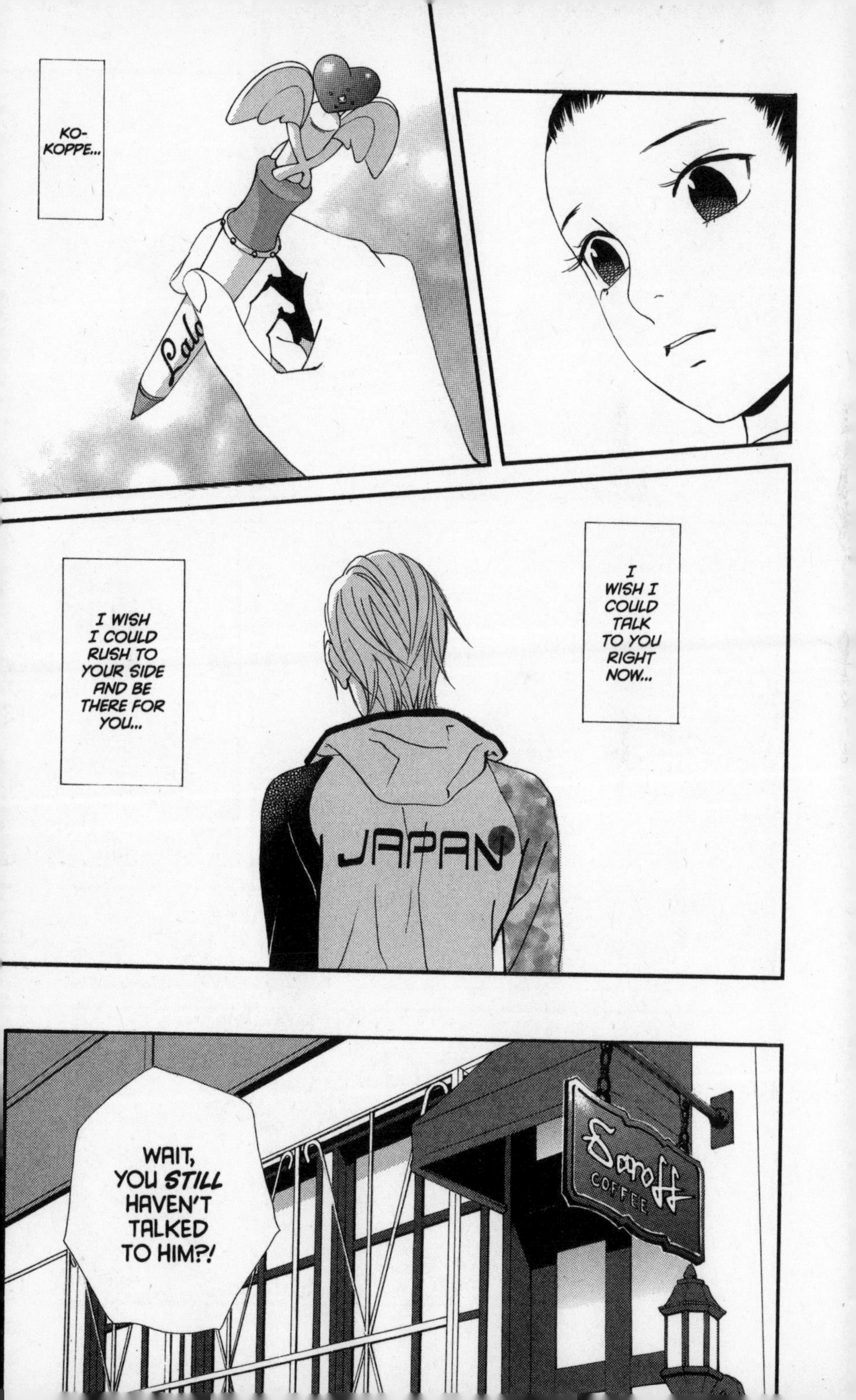
KO-KOPPE...
I WISH I COULD TALK TO YOU RIGHT NOW...
I WISH I COULD RUSH TO YOUR SIDE AND BE THERE FOR YOU...
JAPAN
COFFEE
WAIT, YOU *STILL* HAVEN'T TALKED TO HIM?!

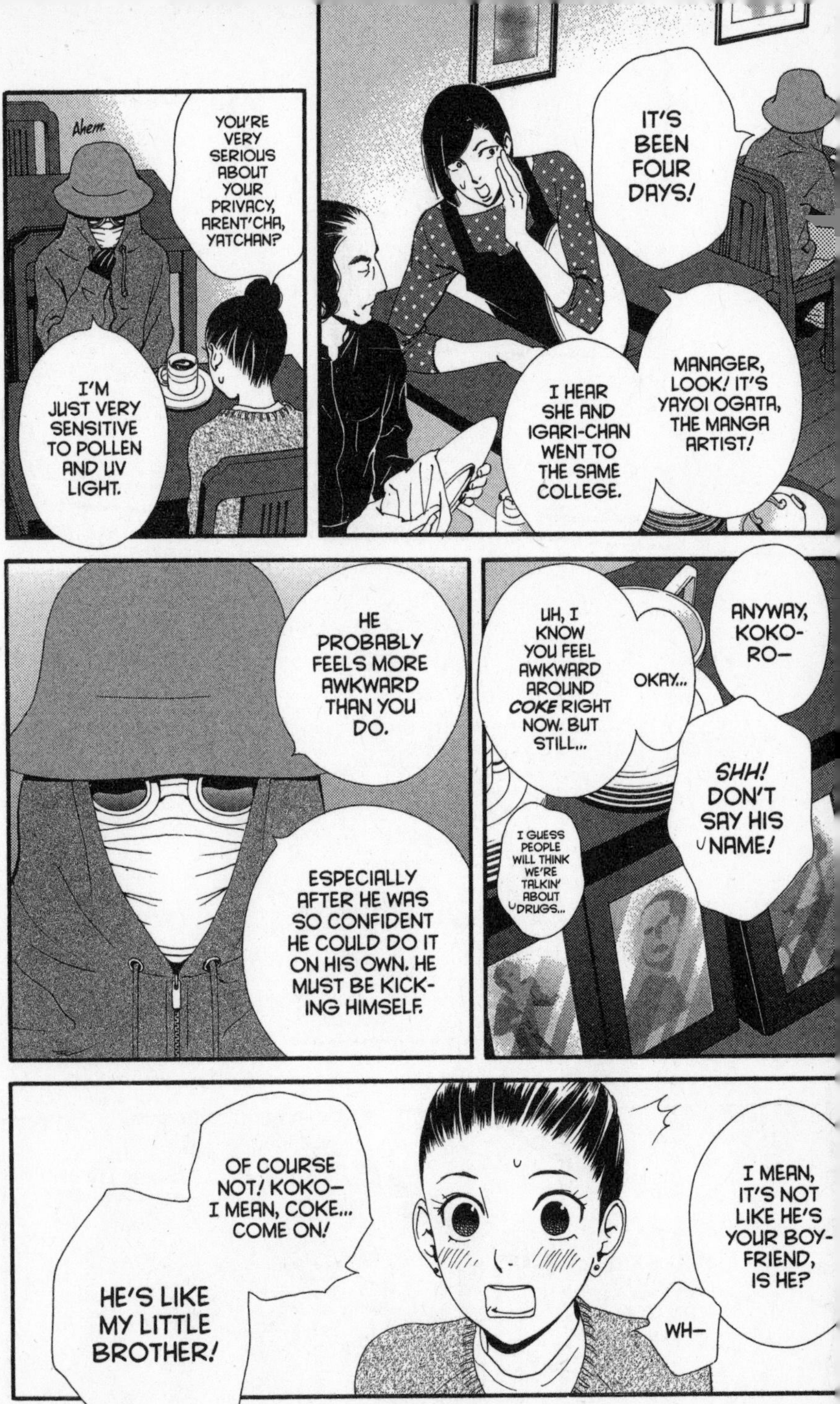
IT'S BEEN FOUR DAYS!
MANAGER, LOOK! IT'S YAYOI OGATA, THE MANGA ARTIST!
I HEAR SHE AND IGARI-CHAN WENT TO THE SAME COLLEGE.
Ahem.
YOU'RE VERY SERIOUS ABOUT YOUR PRIVACY, ARENT'CHA, YATCHAN?
I'M JUST VERY SENSITIVE TO POLLEN AND UV LIGHT.
ANYWAY, KOKO-RO—
OKAY...
UH, I KNOW YOU FEEL AWKWARD AROUND COKE RIGHT NOW. BUT STILL...
SHH! DON'T SAY HIS NAME!
I GUESS PEOPLE WILL THINK WE'RE TALKIN' ABOUT DRUGS...
HE PROBABLY FEELS MORE AWKWARD THAN YOU DO.
ESPECIALLY AFTER HE WAS SO CONFIDENT HE COULD DO IT ON HIS OWN. HE MUST BE KICK-ING HIMSELF.
I MEAN, IT'S NOT LIKE HE'S YOUR BOY-FRIEND, IS HE?
WH—
OF COURSE NOT! KOKO— I MEAN, COKE... COME ON!
HE'S LIKE MY LITTLE BROTHER!

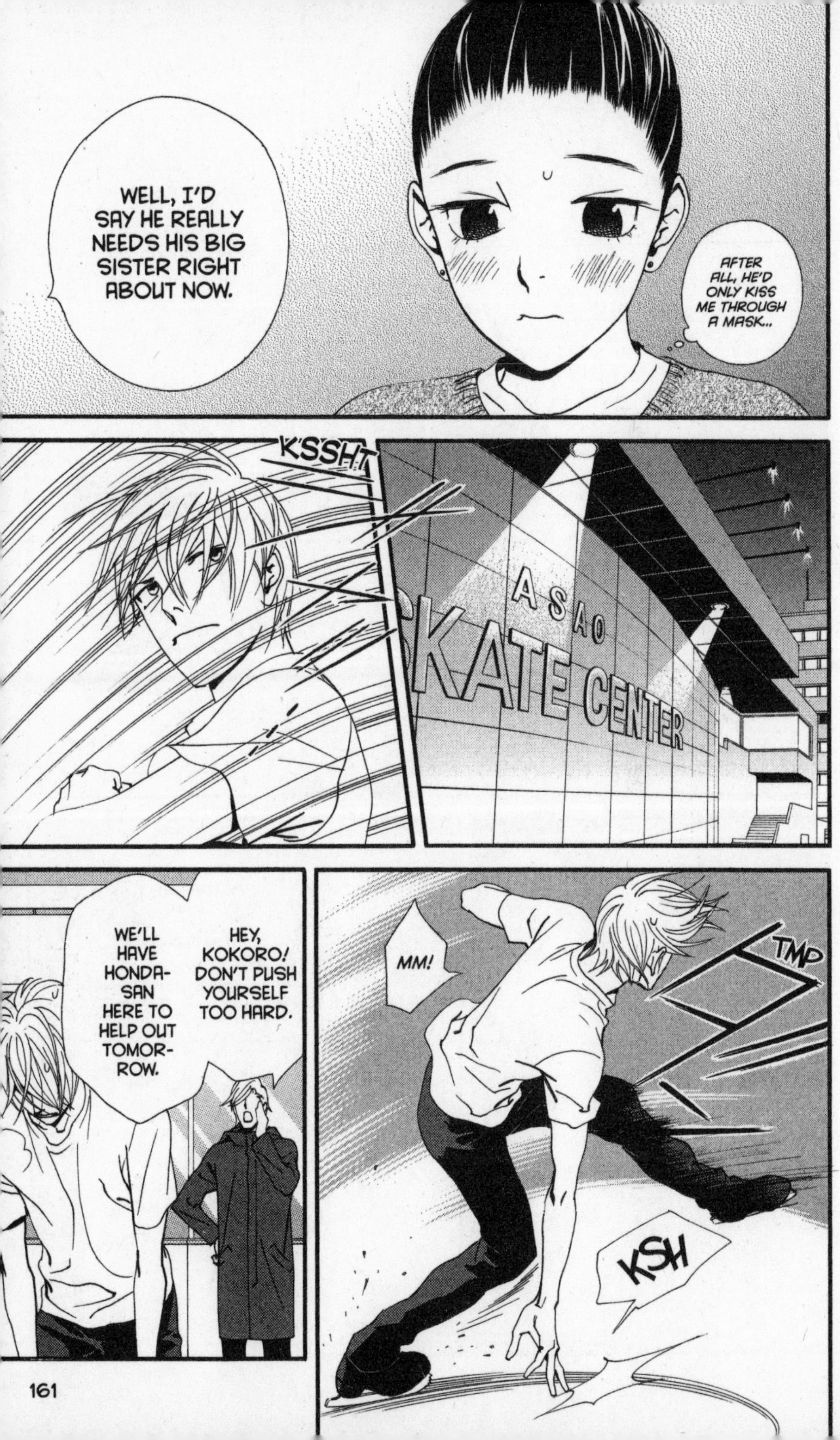
WELL, I'D SAY HE REALLY NEEDS HIS BIG SISTER RIGHT ABOUT NOW.
AFTER ALL, HE'D ONLY KISS ME THROUGH A MASK...
ASAO SKATE CENTER
KSSHT
MM!
TMP
KSH
HEY, KOKORO! DON'T PUSH YOURSELF TOO HARD.
WE'LL HAVE HONDA-SAN HERE TO HELP OUT TOMOR-ROW.

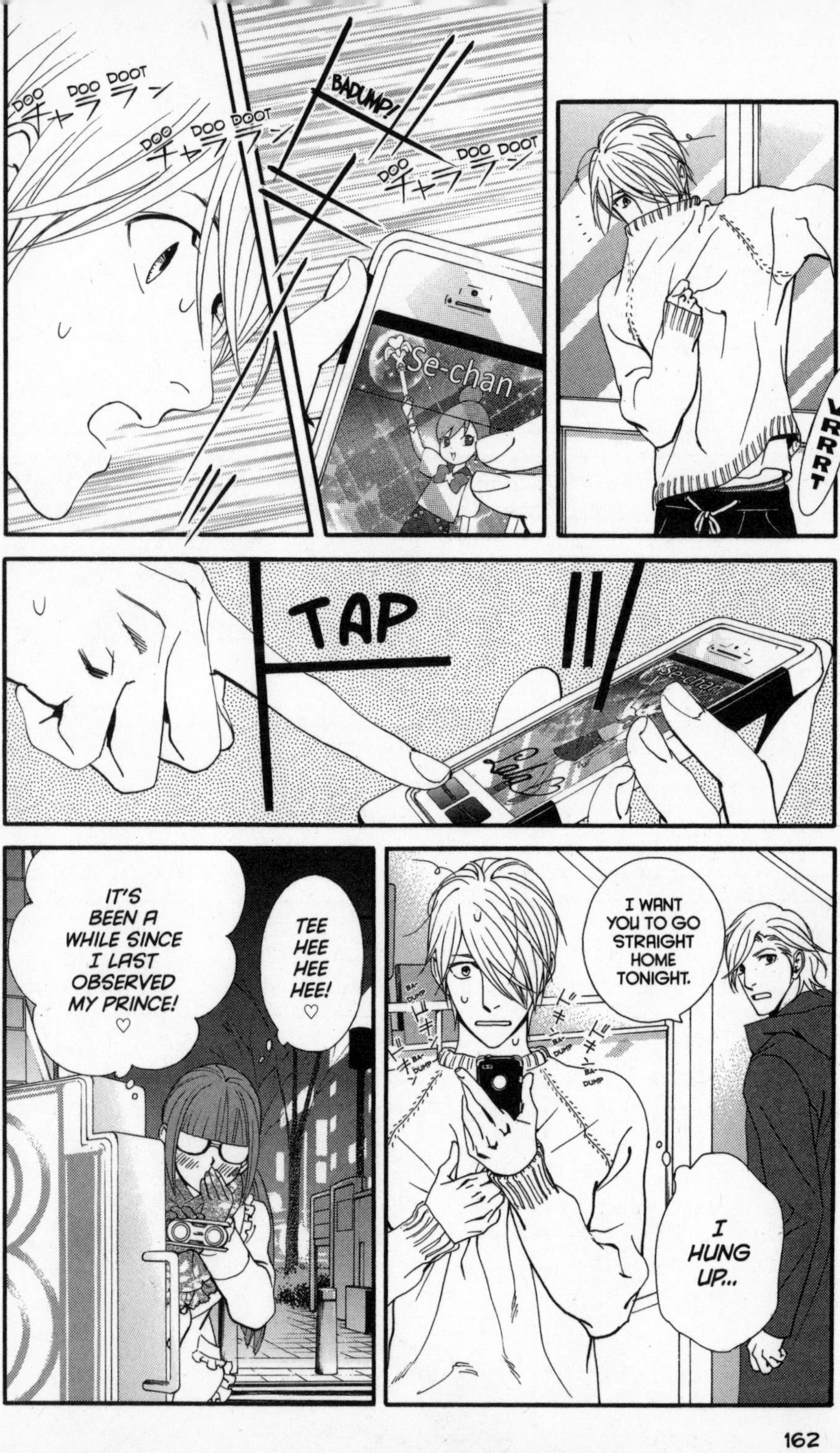
VRRRT
DOO DOO DOOT
DOO DOO DOOT
BADUMP!
DOO DOO DOOT
TAP
I WANT YOU TO GO STRAIGHT HOME TONIGHT.
BA-DUMP
BA-DUMP
BA-DUMP
BA-DUMP
I HUNG UP...
IT'S BEEN A WHILE SINCE I LAST OBSERVED MY PRINCE! ♡
TEE HEE HEE HEE! ♡

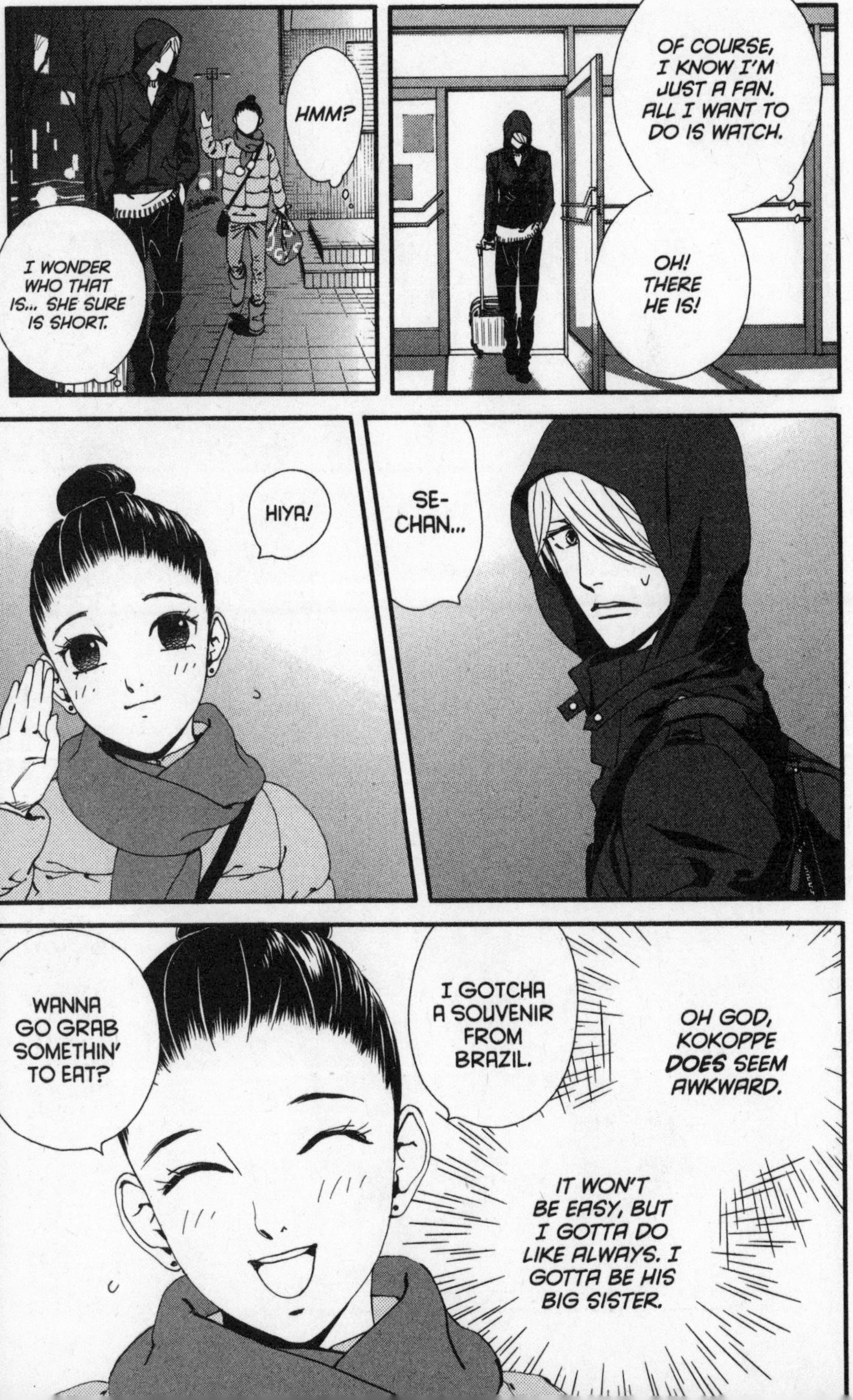
OF COURSE, I KNOW I'M JUST A FAN. ALL I WANT TO DO IS WATCH.
OH! THERE HE IS!
HMM?
I WONDER WHO THAT IS... SHE SURE IS SHORT.
SE-CHAN...
HIYA!
OH GOD, KOKOPPE **DOES** SEEM AWKWARD.
I GOTCHA A SOUVENIR FROM BRAZIL.
WANNA GO GRAB SOMETHIN' TO EAT?
IT WON'T BE EASY, BUT I GOTTA DO LIKE ALWAYS. I GOTTA BE HIS BIG SISTER.

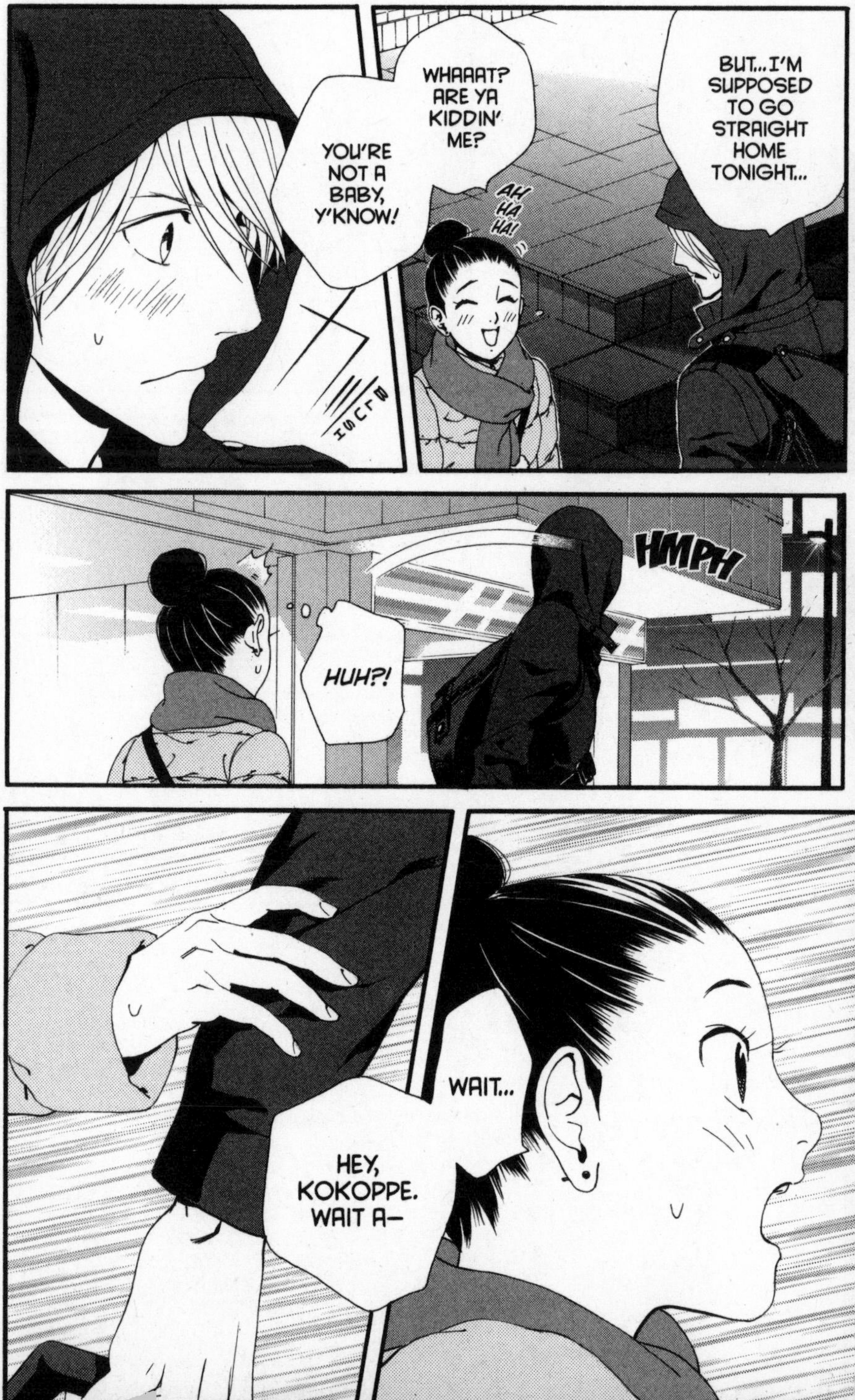
BUT...I'M SUPPOSED TO GO STRAIGHT HOME TONIGHT...
WHAAAT? ARE YA KIDDIN' ME?
AH HA HA!
YOU'RE NOT A BABY, Y'KNOW!
HMPH
HUH?!
WAIT...
HEY, KOKOPPE. WAIT A—

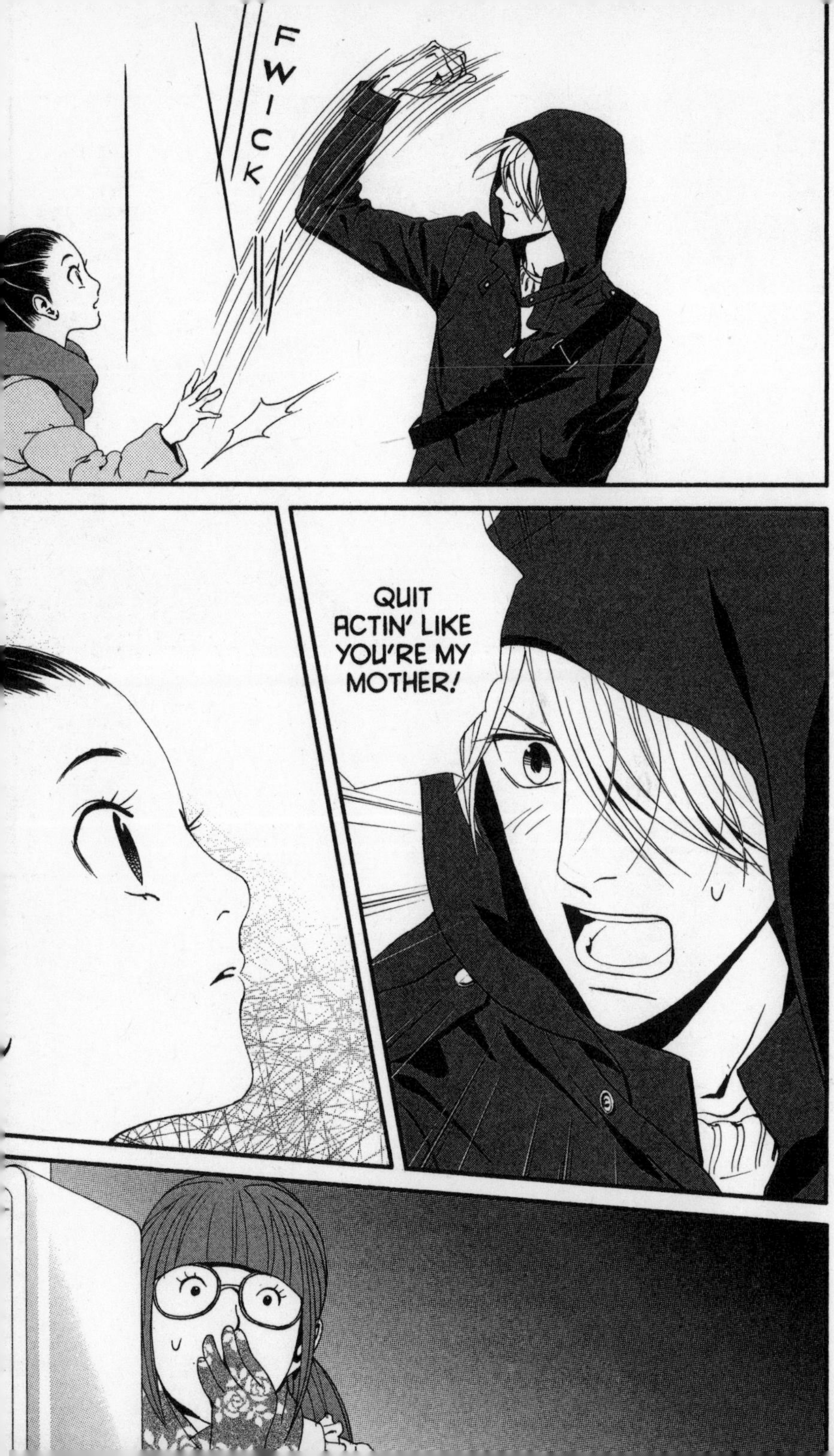
FWICK
QUIT ACTIN' LIKE YOU'RE MY MOTHER!

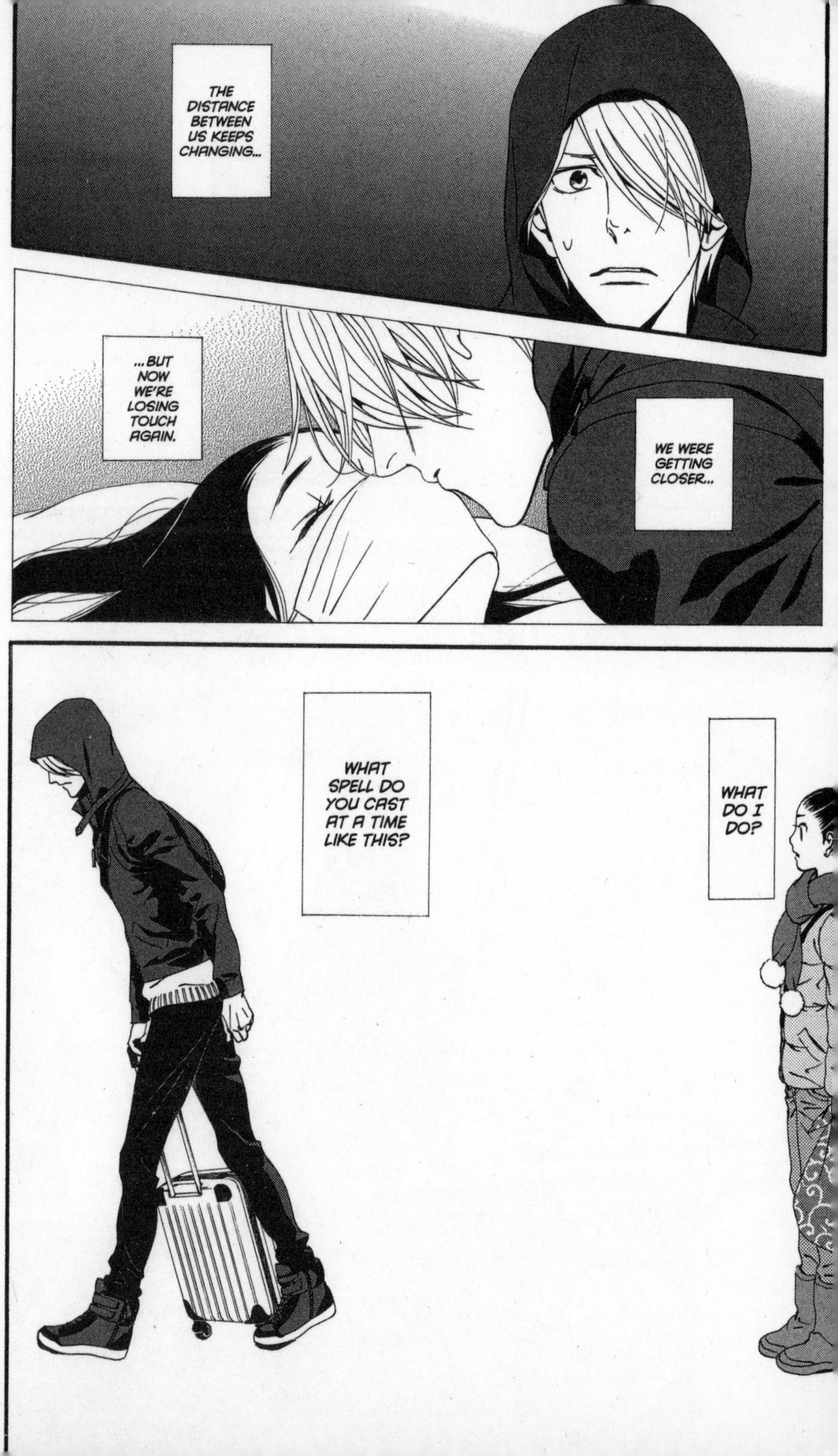
THE DISTANCE BETWEEN US KEEPS CHANGING...
WE WERE GETTING CLOSER...
...BUT NOW WE'RE LOSING TOUCH AGAIN.
WHAT DO I DO?
WHAT SPELL DO YOU CAST AT A TIME LIKE THIS?

To be continued...

TRANSLATION NOTES

LITTLE MY, PAGE 11

Sawada's nickname for Chitose, pronounced "Mii," is inspired by the Japanese name of the character Little My from the *Moomin* series by Tove Jansson. With a below-average height and a topknot bun, Chitose resembles the cartoon character in appearance, hence the nickname.

DENSUKE TANAHASHI, PAGE 12

The fictional Densuke Tanahashi is based on the world-renowned Japanese figure skater Daisuke Takahashi. Born in 1986, Takahashi excelled at multiple international competitions, including the World Figure Skating Championships and Grand Prix Final. At the 2010 Vancouver Winter Olympics, he made history by becoming the first person to win an Olympic medal for Japan and for Asia in the men's singles program. After a legendary sports career, he retired in 2014 due to injuries. In 2018, at age 32, Takahashi announced his comeback to competitive figure skating.

KOKORO'S ACCENT, PAGE 21, AND SE-CHAN AND KOKOPPE, PAGE 24

Both Kokoro and Chitose were raised in Fukushima Prefecture, so they naturally speak its local dialect, and, as Moriyama notes, often slip into it when they are not paying close attention. In comparison with standard Japanese, the Fukushima dialect uses a larger number of stop consonants, such as "-pe," "-ge," and "-be." Their ways of addressing each other—Chitose calling Kokoro "Kokoppe" and Kokoro calling Chitose "Se-chan"—are perfect examples of the Fukushima dialect. When Kokoro and Chitose are talking to one other in the story, they often speak in a Fukushima dialect.

MAMADOR CAKES, PAGE 24

Mamador cakes are a famous snack local to Fukushima Prefecture, where Kokoro grew up. The dough is made of wheat, milk, and butter, and the cakes are filled with sweet bean paste. Known for their strong milk and butter flavor, mamador cakes are a longtime favorite of many Japanese people and a preferred souvenir choice when visiting Fukushima. The confection's name is derived from the Spanish word *mamador*, which means "children who drink their mother's milk."

MOOMINVALLEY AND MYMBLES, PAGE 41

In the *Moomin* series, Little My, the cartoon character that inspired Sawada's nickname for Chitose, is part of the Mymbles family living in Moominvalley. All female members of the Mymbles family share the same hairstyle, with a bun on top of their heads—a look which reminds everyone of Chitose.

Otaku, page 51

Often rendered in English as "nerd" or "geek," an *otaku* is an obsessive fan who hoards information and merchandise of their favorite things. There are train *otaku*, jellyfish *otaku*, and, most famously, anime and manga *otaku*, as is the case with Kokoro. Before acquiring its slang meaning, the word "otaku" was just a formal way of saying "you" that literally translates to "your home." Hence, when one otaku calls another person an "otaku," they are indicating that person is an "insider." Sometimes, *otaku* face social stigma, which is why Kokoro hides his obsession with *Lady Lala* from the public.

Pixiv, page 51

Pixiv.net is an online platform where artists can upload their original illustrations, fan art, and fan fictions, mostly based on manga and anime.

Comiket, page 65

Comiket, short for Comic Market, is a massive convention where authors sell self-published comics and zines (*doujinshi*), and cosplayers show off their costumes. Held twice a year in the summer and winter, Comiket is the largest comics convention in the world, attracting over 500,000 attendees over its three days.

Ryokan, page 77

A *ryokan* is a traditional Japanese inn. Many *ryokan* feature amenities such as tatami mat floors, Japanese-style futons to sleep in, and communal baths. They also often provide their guests with *yukata* robes to wear. The price of a *ryokan* may also include meals, as well as offer the use of a *rotenburo,* or outdoor bath.

Who are you, Mary-san?!, page 98

Mary-san, also known as Mary-san's Phone Call, is a Japanese urban legend about a young girl who loses her favorite doll, Mary. After some time, the girl begins to receive strange phone calls, presumably from Mary, who claims to be right outside her door.

Pocari Sweat, page 98

Pocari Sweat is a popular Japanese sports drink, supposedly formulated to replenish all of the nutrients, ions, and electrolytes lost from sweating.

"You can take your mask off, you know." PAGE 100
In Japan, it's customary for people to cover their mouths with a medical mask when sick, in order to prevent their germs from spreading to other people.

Golden Week, PAGE 107
Golden Week is the week, starting April 29th each year, when a long string of public holidays follow one after another. These holidays are: April 29th (Shōwa Day), May 3rd (Constitution Memorial Day), May 4th (Greenery Day), and May 5th (Children's Day). Most people take the full week off to travel or relax.

A working woman who may or may not exist, PAGE 125
Fans of Yayoi Ogawa's previous series may recognize that Raito's idea of a "working woman who may or may not exist" bears a striking resemblance to Sumire Iwaya, the hardworking, career-focused main female protagonist of Ogawa's cult classic series *You're My Pet* (available now in digital from comiXology and Kodansha Comics).

Hanten, PAGE 125
A *hanten* is a traditional Japanese jacket worn by common people during the Edo Period. Compared with other types of traditional clothing, *hanten* are shorter and feature shorter sleeves, and do not require an *obi*, or sash, as the more formal kimonos do. As a result, a *hanten* gives a casual and intimate impression when it is worn. These days, *hanten* are usually padded and lined with a thick layer of cotton, and are worn as indoor jackets to keep warm during the winter.

Zayak Rule, PAGE 142
The Zayak Rule was enacted by the International Skating Union (ISU) in 1982, after figure skater Elaine Zayak performed six jumps, four of which were triple toe loops, at the World Championships. The rule restricts skaters from performing the same kind of regular jump more than twice, and is thus intended to encourage the skaters to aim for more varieties and techniques during their programs. The Zayak Rule also states that if a jump or spin is repeated, it has to be incorporated into a combination in order to score high points. In Kokoro's case here, he couldn't proceed with his original plan, since he accidentally did three combos consecutively, so he had to come up with a new move which he had not performed in the program.

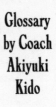

Glossary by Coach Akiyuki Kido

ISU Grand Prix (page 13)
A series of six competitions held between October and December, including Skate America, Skate Canada, the Cup of China, the Trophée Eric Bompard (France), the Rostelecom Cup (Russia), and the NHK Trophy (Japan). The six highest-ranking skaters go on to compete in the Grand Prix Final.

Free skate (page 16)
In the free skating competition, skaters get to choose what elements and moves to use. Still, there are rules about what jumps, spins, and steps are required, as well as restrictions on the number of them allowed. In women's singles, this segment lasts four minutes, and in men's singles, it lasts four minutes and thirty seconds.

Short program (page 17)
The short program is a segment in which the skaters have up to two minutes and fifty seconds to perform eight predetermined elements, such as jumps, spins, or steps.

Triple Axel (page 20)
There are six different jumps in figure skating. An axel is one that begins with the skater facing directly forward. It's the most difficult jump, and a triple axel requires three and a half midair rotations. Midori Ito was the first woman in Japan to successfully execute this jump.

Triple toe loop (page 20)
The toe loop is considered to be the easiest jump. The skater uses their left toe to launch themselves into the air from their right skate's back outside edge. To date, no one has managed to execute this jump with more than four rotations, and only a select few skaters can do even that.

Sit spin (page 22)
This is a spin where the skater crouches with their legs bent at an angle of at least 90 degrees. They must perform three or more rotations for it to count.

Level (page 22)
Elements such as lifts, steps, twizzles, and dance spins are categorized into levels on the basis of certain features. An element with a higher level has a higher base value in scoring, and the highest level is four. World-class skaters perform most elements at level four.

Coach (page 27)
A coach can be someone who belongs to the Figure Skating Instructor Association or someone who just works at a particular ice rink. To work as a professional coach, even talented skaters are typically required to start by helping to teach beginners in a club or classroom setting.

Personal trainer (page 28)
A trainer works to improve a skater's condition and to make them more competitive by providing support and guidance to improve their physical fitness, psychological resilience, and overall health.

National Championships (page 42)
The Japan Figure Skating Championships are held every year near the end of December to determine the best skater in Japan. This competition doubles as the qualifying event to represent Japan at the Olympics.

Technical score (page 42)

The technical score is determined by the technical elements included in the program and their quality. Jumps, spins, steps, and other elements each have a base value, which is modified by a grade of execution (GOE) to get the technical score. The GOE is the average of the modifiers assigned by the judges, excluding the highest and lowest. These modifiers have one of seven values between negative and positive three.

Landing (page 42)

The landing is when the skater lands on the ice after a jump.

Season (page 42)

Each year's skating season begins in July and ends in June of the following year.

Salchow (page 58)

This jump is executed from the left foot's back inside edge by lifting the right foot forward and to the left. The way both feet face outward just before takeoff is a unique feature of the Salchow jump. It was named after the Swedish skater Ulrich Salchow.

Worlds (page 58)

Worlds refers to the World Figure Skating Championships. It's the biggest event of the skating season, excluding the Olympics. The winner earns the title of World champion for that season.

The six jumps (page 59)

In order from most to least difficult, these are the Axel, Lutz, flip, loop, Salchow, and toe loop.

NHK Trophy (page 69)

This is one of the competitions in the ISU Grand Prix.

Team leader (page 75)

At international competitions, each country's team has a leader. These leaders are responsible for facilitating communication between the team members and the hosts of the competition, facilitating communication between the team members and their national skating federation, and supporting their team members in a variety of ways. This tends to be a very busy job, since the leader has to respond to their team's needs on the fly.

Start order (page 79)

This is the order in which the skaters perform. It can be determined either by random draw or by reverse order of ranking.

First group (page 79)

In the free skate, the first group to skate is made up of the skaters who scored the lowest in the short program, and the last group is made up of the skaters who scored the highest.

Six-minute warm-up (page 79)

Each group of skaters gets six minutes to warm up before the competition begins.

Junior Championships (page 81)

The Japan Junior Figure Skating Championships are a competition held toward the end of November to determine the best junior figure skater in Japan. The winner can earn the opportunity to compete in the next Senior Championships.

Spread eagle (page 117)

A spread eagle is a move in which the skater keeps both skates on the ice with the toes of each foot facing straight out to the sides.

Hand down (page 118)

This is when a skater touches the ice with a hand on a landing. It's the second-most serious error after a fall.

Season's best (page 129)

This term refers to a given skater's highest score of the season.

Flip (page 133)

To perform this jump, the skater uses their right toe to launch themselves from their left skate's back inside edge.

Spin (page 133)

A spin involves rotating in place on one leg. Spins are scored on the basis of factors such as the number of rotations, the aesthetic quality of the posture, and the difficulty of the pose.

Sequence (page 134)

A jump sequence differs from a combination, in that the skater does not go directly from landing one jump to performing another, but instead weaves two jumps together with a step (which would include a jump of less than one full rotation) in between. A step sequence is when a skater performs a series of steps while moving in a straight, winding, diagonal, or circular line.

Base value (page 136)

Each element—such as a step, a spin, or a jump—has a base value. Three people—the technical specialist, the assistant technical specialist, and the technical controller—work together to do things like identify elements, count jump rotations, and distinguish the level and type of each spin or step. These determinations result in the assignment of a base score.

Deduction (page 136)

The rules specify certain errors and violations that result in the deduction of points.

Winning run (page 137)

This is when the winners of a competition skate a lap around the rink after the awards are given.

Exhibition gala (page 146)

After a competition, the winning skaters and other special guests may sometimes perform in a kind of ice show called an exhibition gala. This gives them an opportunity to skate without having to worry about rules, so they often do things like use props or play music with lyrics. (Editor's Note: Originally, skaters were not allowed to perform to music with lyrics. In 2014, the International Skating Union announced that they would allow skaters to perform to music with lyrics during figure skating competitions.)

Banquet (page 148)

Banquets are often held for everyone involved after the opening or closing ceremonies of skating events.

Judges (page 151)

The judges are the people tasked with scoring skaters to determine their final placement in competitions.

Akiyuki Kido

Born on August 28th, 1975, Akiyuki Kido represented Japan in ice dancing at the 2006 Winter Olympics in Turin, Italy. He took fifteenth place, the highest Japan had ever placed in ice dancing at the time. Today, he works as a coach at the Shin-Yokohama Skate Center.

Knight of the Ice Skater Profile 1

1 Kokoro Kijinami

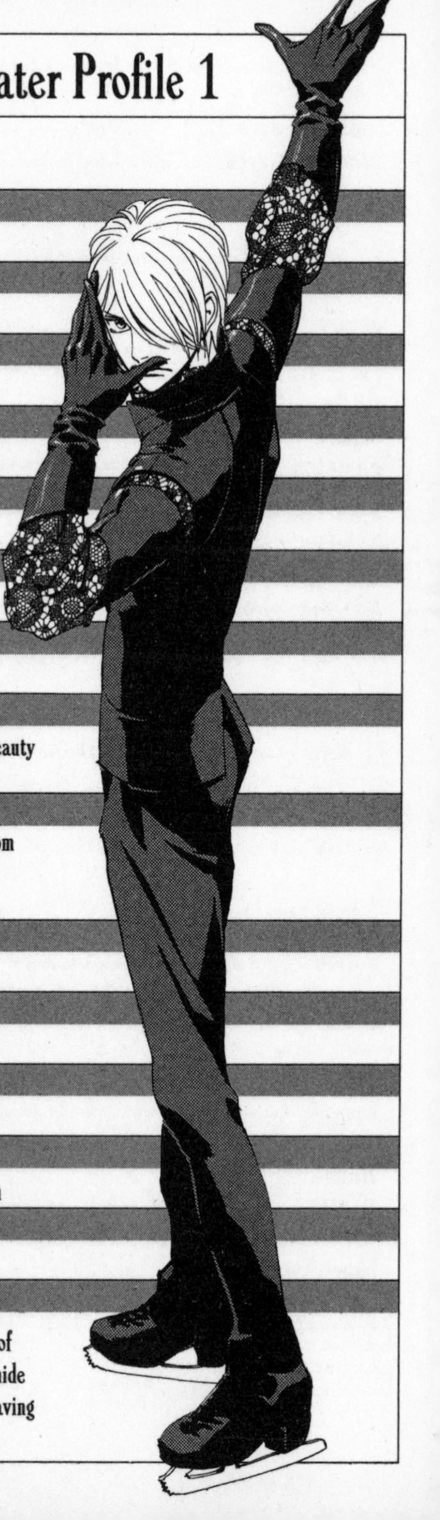

Height:

179 cm (approx. 5'9")

Blood type:

B

Birthday:

March 3rd

Birthplace:

Fukushima Prefecture

Strongest element:

Jumps

Strongest jump:

Lutz

Most difficult jump performed to date:

Quadruple toe loop

Strength:

The technical flawlessness of his jumps and the beauty his height lends to his quadruple jumps

Weakness:

His psychological fragility, which prevents him from competing effectively unless his childhood friend casts a spell

Hobby:

Watching anime (not public knowledge)

Talent:

Drawing (not public knowledge)

Family composition:

Two parents and his younger twin sisters

Favorite food:

Mamador cakes, his hometown's famous confection

Least favorite food:

Boiled whitebait (the eyes are too creepy)

Notes:

Heir of the Kijinami Group, which owns a number of boutique ryokan. A man of few words, possibly to hide his regional accent. Fluent in English, thanks to having been tutored in it since he was a child.

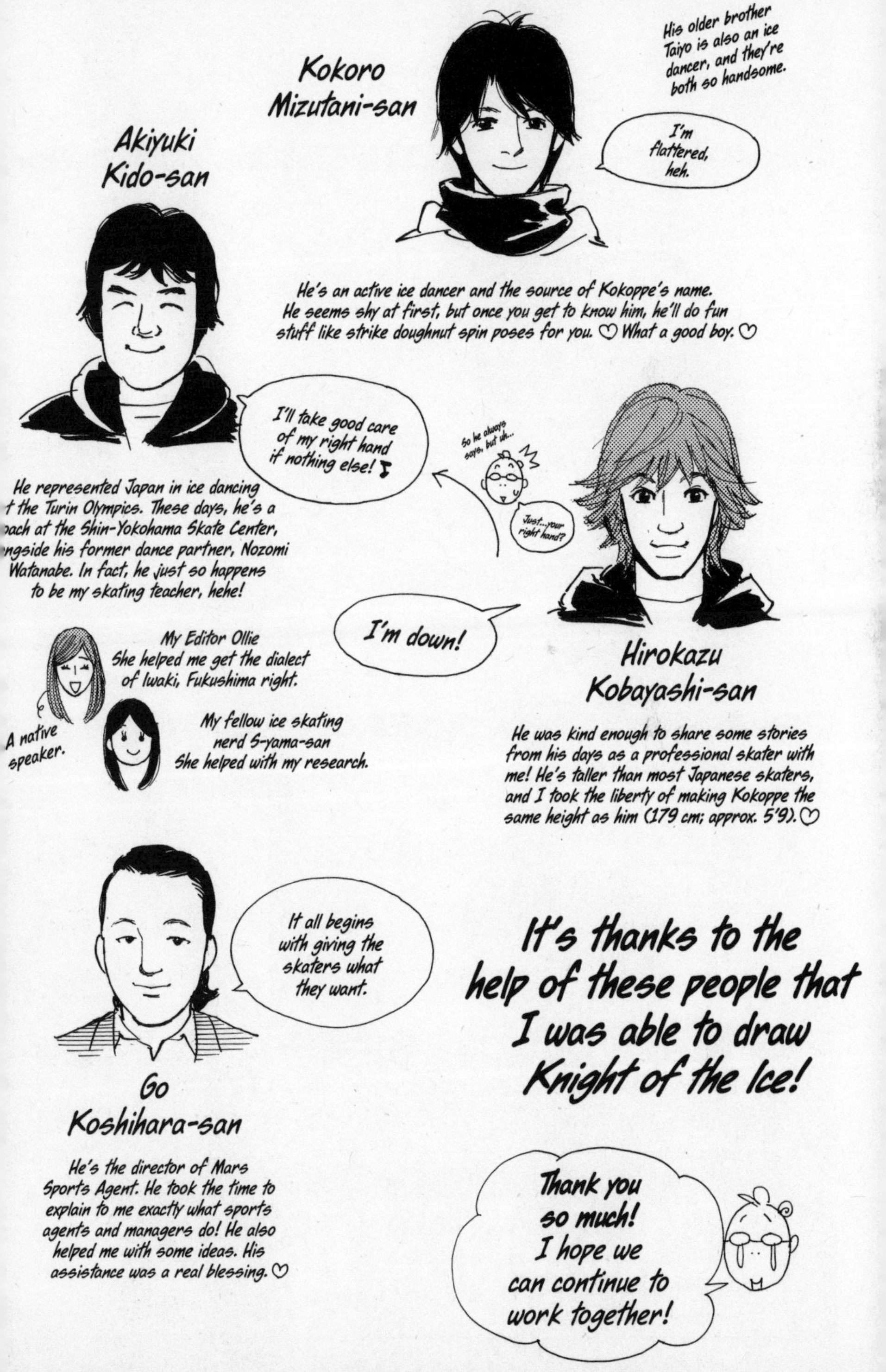
Kokoro Mizutani-san
His older brother Taiyo is also an ice dancer, and they're both so handsome.
I'm flattered, heh.
He's an active ice dancer and the source of Kokoppe's name. He seems shy at first, but once you get to know him, he'll do fun stuff like strike doughnut spin poses for you. ♡ What a good boy. ♡
Akiyuki Kido-san
I'll take good care of my right hand if nothing else! ♪
So he always says, but uh...
Just...your right hand?
He represented Japan in ice dancing t the Turin Olympics. These days, he's a pach at the Shin-Yokohama Skate Center, ngside his former dance partner, Nozomi Watanabe. In fact, he just so happens to be my skating teacher, hehe!
I'm down!
Hirokazu Kobayashi-san
He was kind enough to share some stories from his days as a professional skater with me! He's taller than most Japanese skaters, and I took the liberty of making Kokoppe the same height as him (179 cm; approx. 5'9). ♡
My Editor Ollie She helped me get the dialect of Iwaki, Fukushima right.
A native speaker.
My fellow ice skating nerd S-yama-san She helped with my research.
Go Koshihara-san
It all begins with giving the skaters what they want.
He's the director of Mars Sports Agent. He took the time to explain to me exactly what sports agents and managers do! He also helped me with some ideas. His assistance was a real blessing. ♡
It's thanks to the help of these people that I was able to draw Knight of the Ice!
Thank you so much! I hope we can continue to work together!

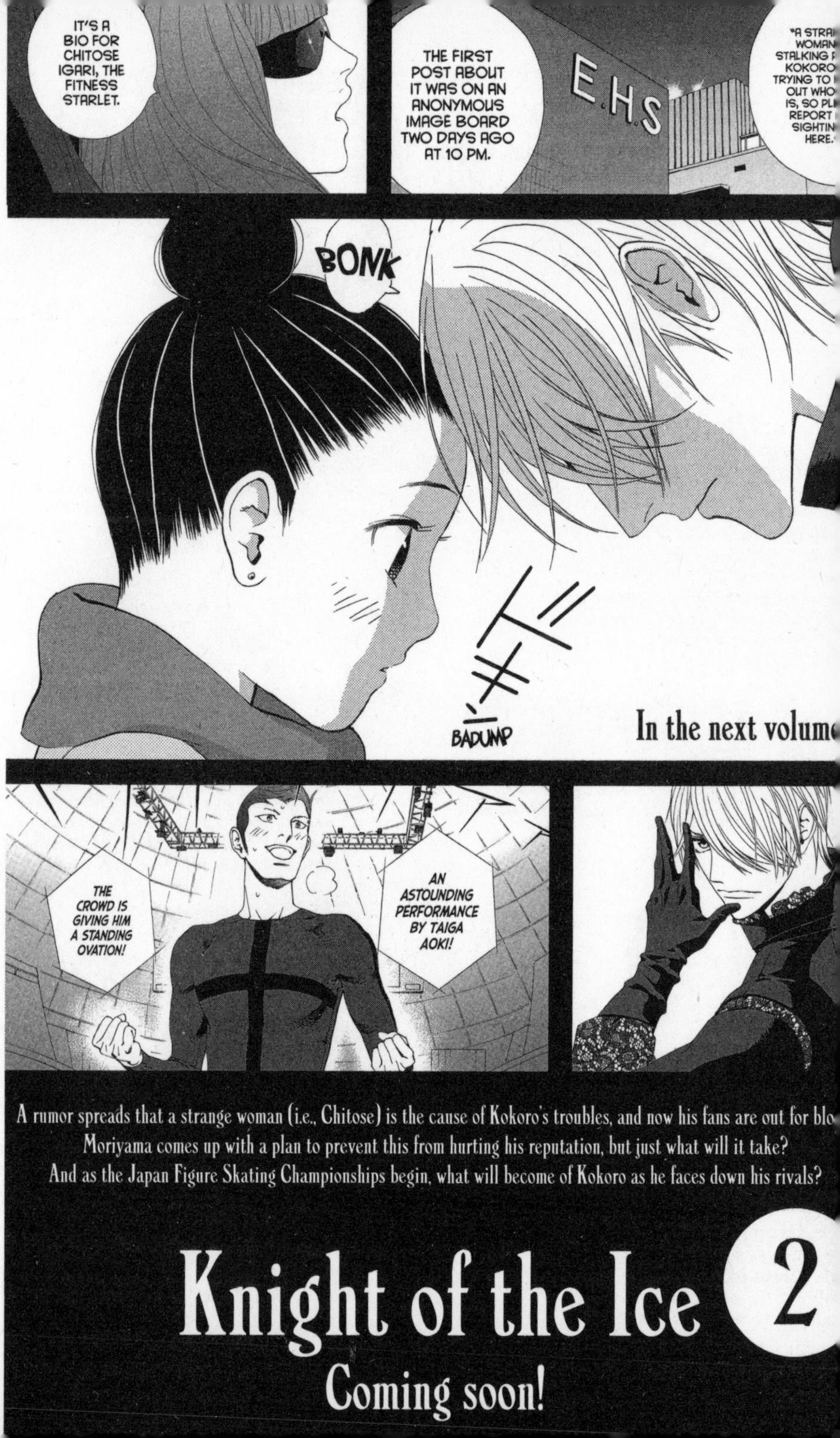
"A STRA
WOMAN
STALKING
KOKORO
TRYING TO
OUT WHO
IS, SO PL
REPORT
SIGHTIN
HERE.
THE FIRST POST ABOUT IT WAS ON AN ANONYMOUS IMAGE BOARD TWO DAYS AGO AT 10 PM.
IT'S A BIO FOR CHITOSE IGARI, THE FITNESS STARLET.
BONK
BADUMP
In the next volum
AN ASTOUNDING PERFORMANCE BY TAIGA AOKI!
THE CROWD IS GIVING HIM A STANDING OVATION!

A rumor spreads that a strange woman (i.e., Chitose) is the cause of Kokoro's troubles, and now his fans are out for blo
Moriyama comes up with a plan to prevent this from hurting his reputation, but just what will it take?
And as the Japan Figure Skating Championships begin, what will become of Kokoro as he faces down his rivals?

Knight of the Ice 2

Coming soon!

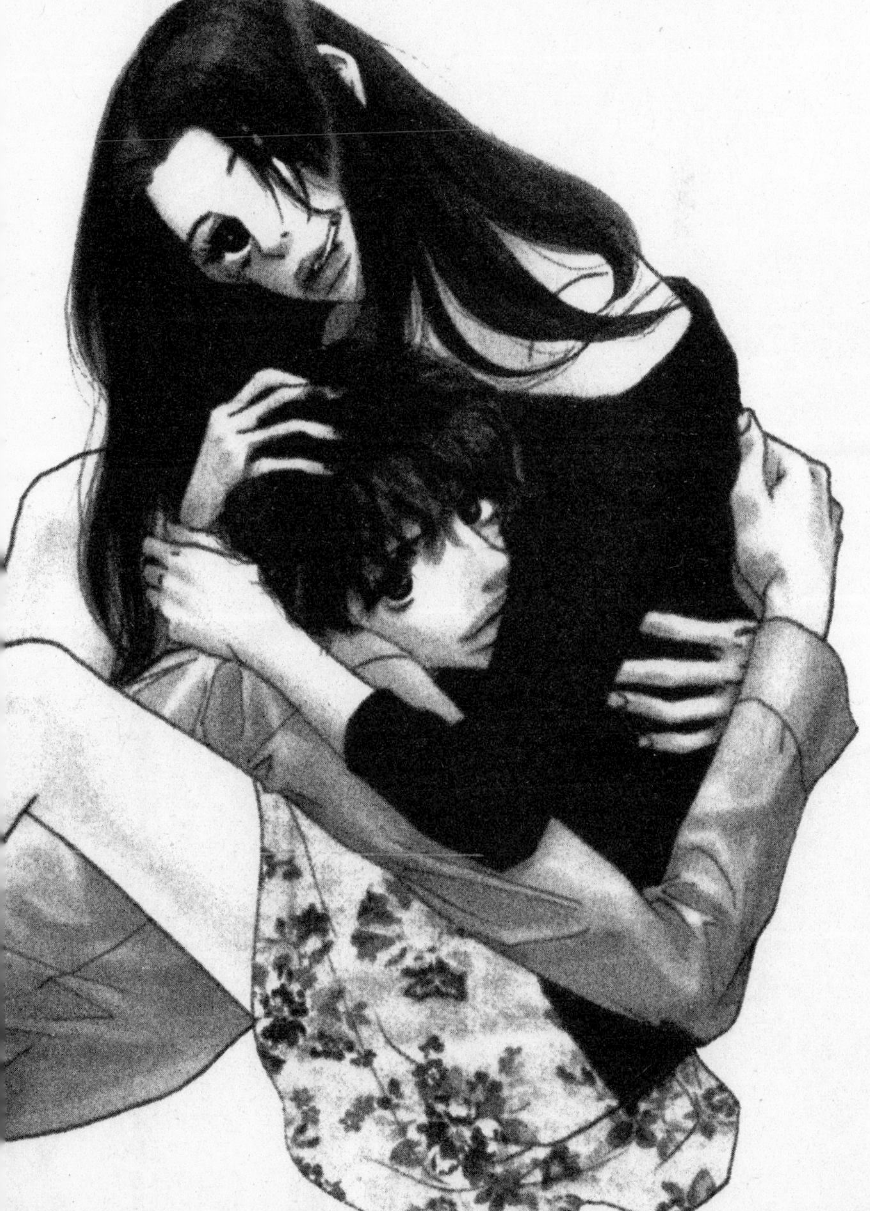

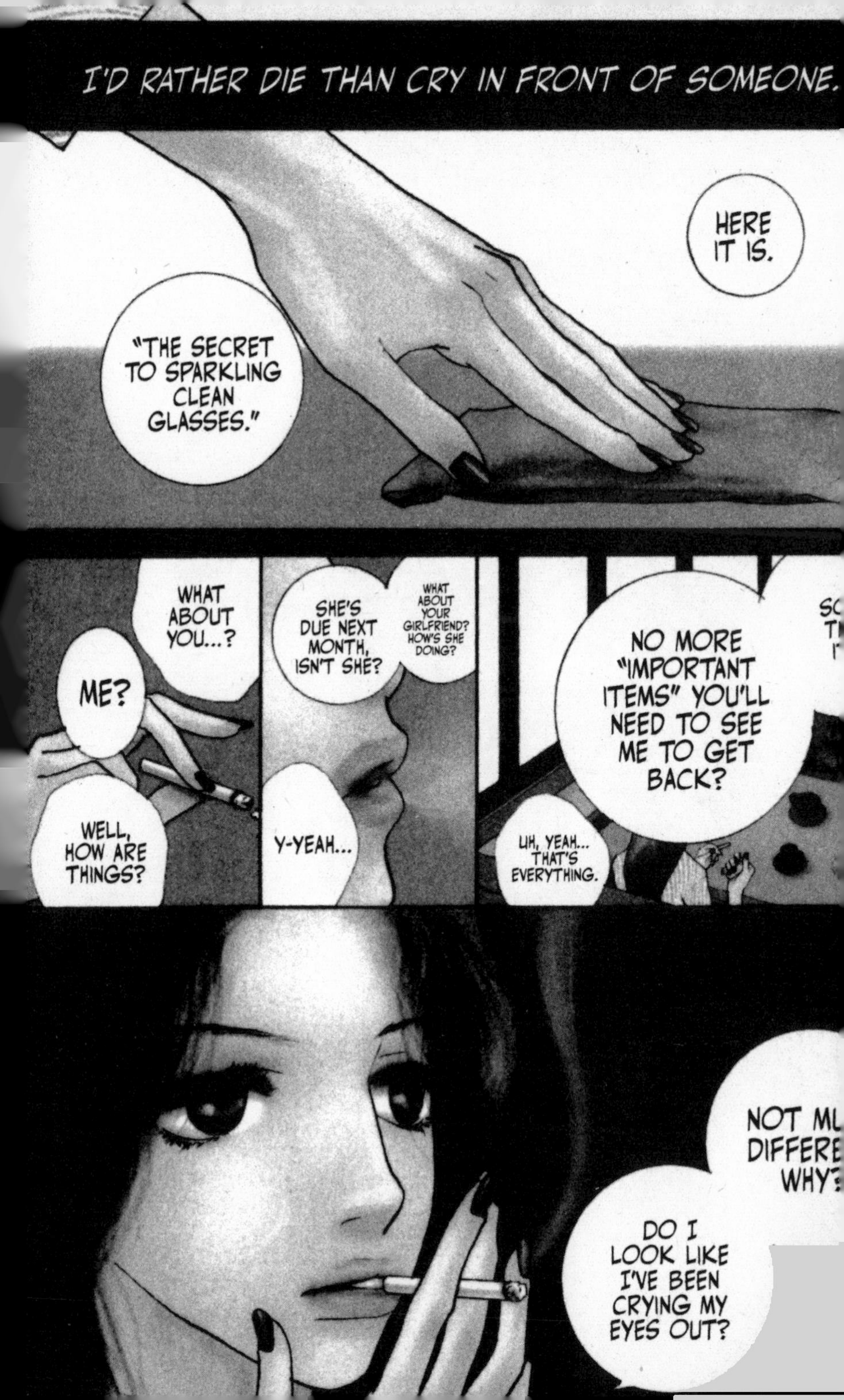
I'D RATHER DIE THAN CRY IN FRONT OF SOMEONE.
HERE IT IS.
"THE SECRET TO SPARKLING CLEAN GLASSES."
NO MORE "IMPORTANT ITEMS" YOU'LL NEED TO SEE ME TO GET BACK?
UH, YEAH... THAT'S EVERYTHING.
WHAT ABOUT YOUR GIRLFRIEND? HOW'S SHE DOING?
SHE'S DUE NEXT MONTH, ISN'T SHE?
Y-YEAH...
WHAT ABOUT YOU...?
ME?
WELL, HOW ARE THINGS?
DO I LOOK LIKE I'VE BEEN CRYING MY EYES OUT?

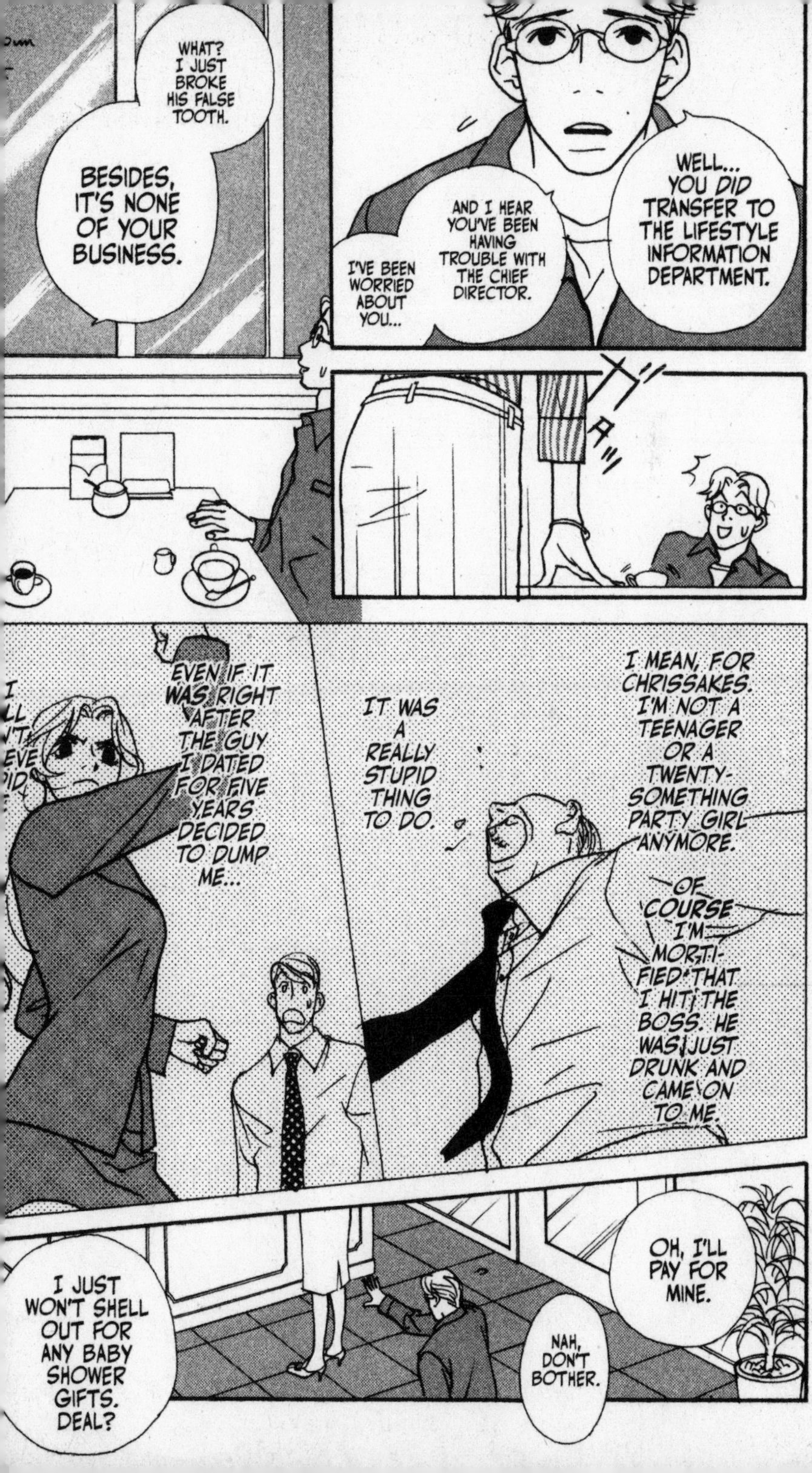
WELL... YOU *DID* TRANSFER TO THE LIFESTYLE INFORMATION DEPARTMENT.
AND I HEAR YOU'VE BEEN HAVING TROUBLE WITH THE CHIEF DIRECTOR.
I'VE BEEN WORRIED ABOUT YOU...
ガタッ
WHAT? I JUST BROKE HIS FALSE TOOTH.
BESIDES, IT'S NONE OF YOUR BUSINESS.
I MEAN, FOR CHRISSAKES. I'M NOT A TEENAGER OR A TWENTY-SOMETHING PARTY GIRL ANYMORE.
OF COURSE I'M MORTIFIED THAT I HIT THE BOSS. HE WAS JUST DRUNK AND CAME ON TO ME.
IT WAS A REALLY STUPID THING TO DO.
EVEN IF IT WAS RIGHT AFTER THE GUY I DATED FOR FIVE YEARS DECIDED TO DUMP ME...
OH, I'LL PAY FOR MINE.
NAH, DON'T BOTHER.
I JUST WON'T SHELL OUT FOR ANY BABY SHOWER GIFTS. DEAL?

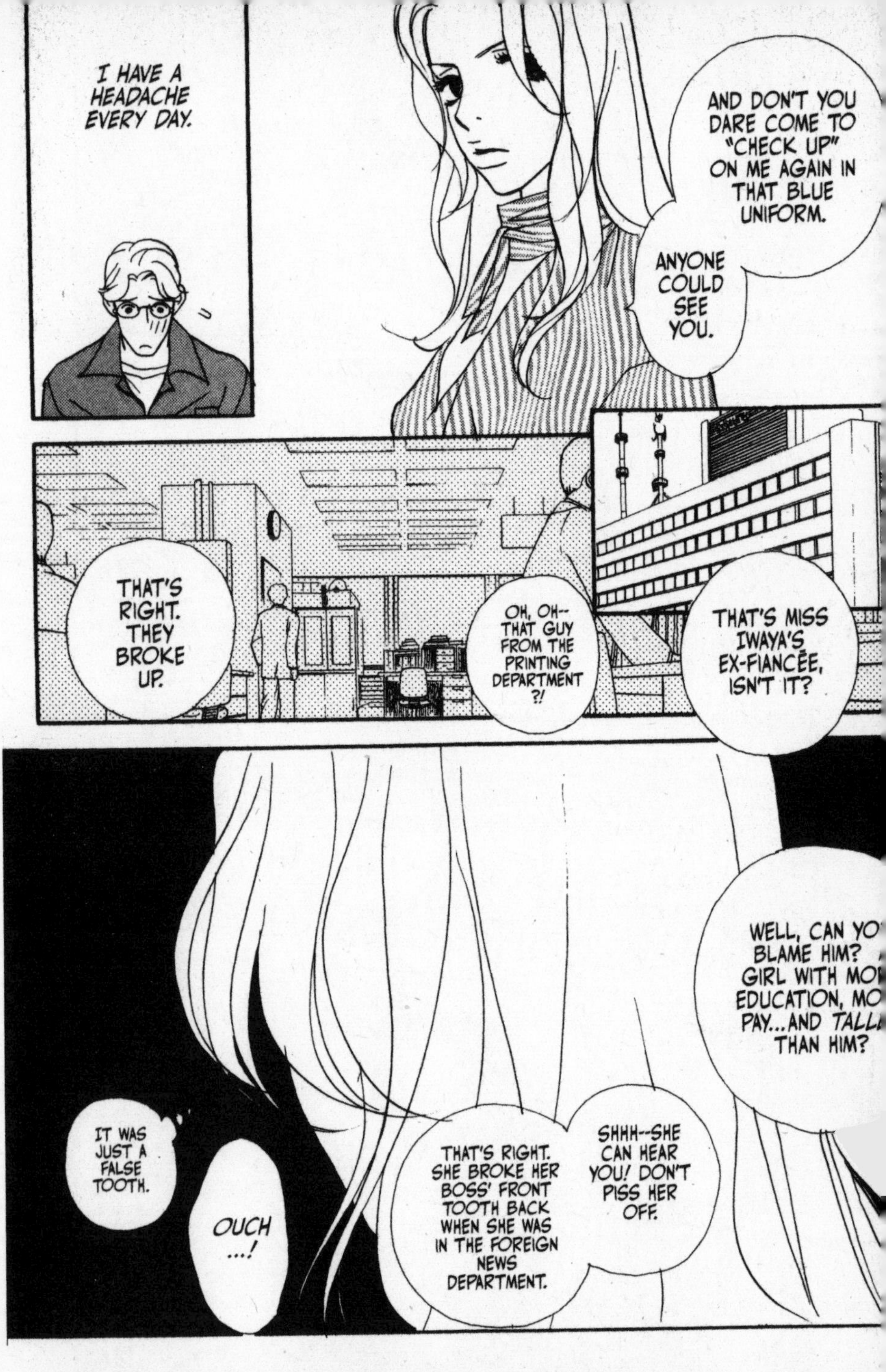
AND DON'T YOU DARE COME TO "CHECK UP" ON ME AGAIN IN THAT BLUE UNIFORM.
ANYONE COULD SEE YOU.
I HAVE A HEADACHE EVERY DAY.
THAT'S MISS IWAYA'S EX-FIANCÉE, ISN'T IT?
OH, OH-- THAT GUY FROM THE PRINTING DEPARTMENT ?!
THAT'S RIGHT. THEY BROKE UP.
WELL, CAN YO BLAME HIM? GIRL WITH MO EDUCATION, MO PAY...AND TALL THAN HIM?
SHHH--SHE CAN HEAR YOU! DON'T PISS HER OFF.
THAT'S RIGHT. SHE BROKE HER BOSS' FRONT TOOTH BACK WHEN SHE WAS IN THE FOREIGN NEWS DEPARTMENT.
OUCH ...!
IT WAS JUST A FALSE TOOTH.

THERE'S NO SUCH THING AS "EQUAL OPPORTUNITY" FOR WOM

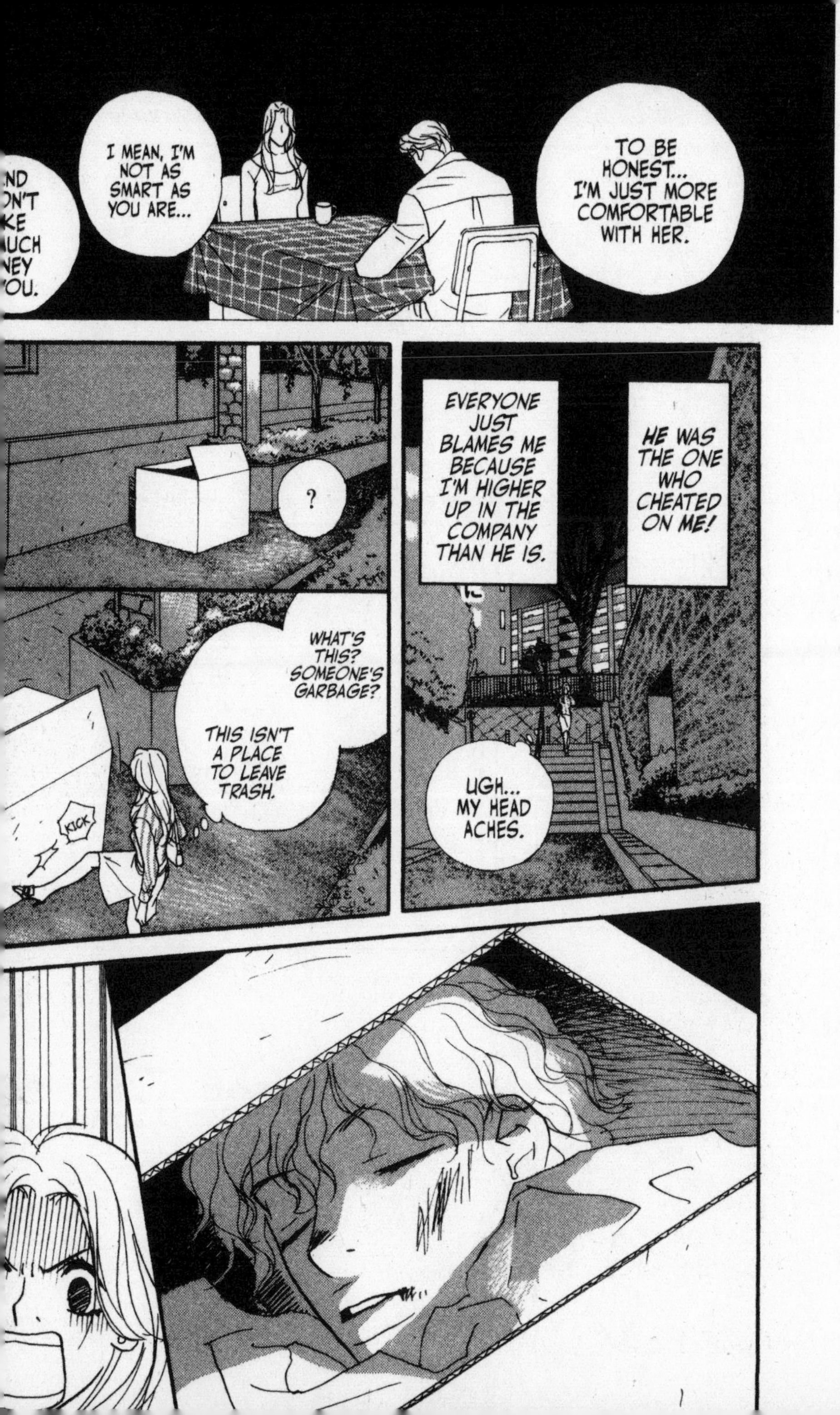
TO BE HONEST... I'M JUST MORE COMFORTABLE WITH HER.
I MEAN, I'M NOT AS SMART AS YOU ARE...
HE WAS THE ONE WHO CHEATED ON ME!
EVERYONE JUST BLAMES ME BECAUSE I'M HIGHER UP IN THE COMPANY THAN HE IS.
UGH... MY HEAD ACHES.
?
WHAT'S THIS? SOMEONE'S GARBAGE?
THIS ISN'T A PLACE TO LEAVE TRASH.
KICK

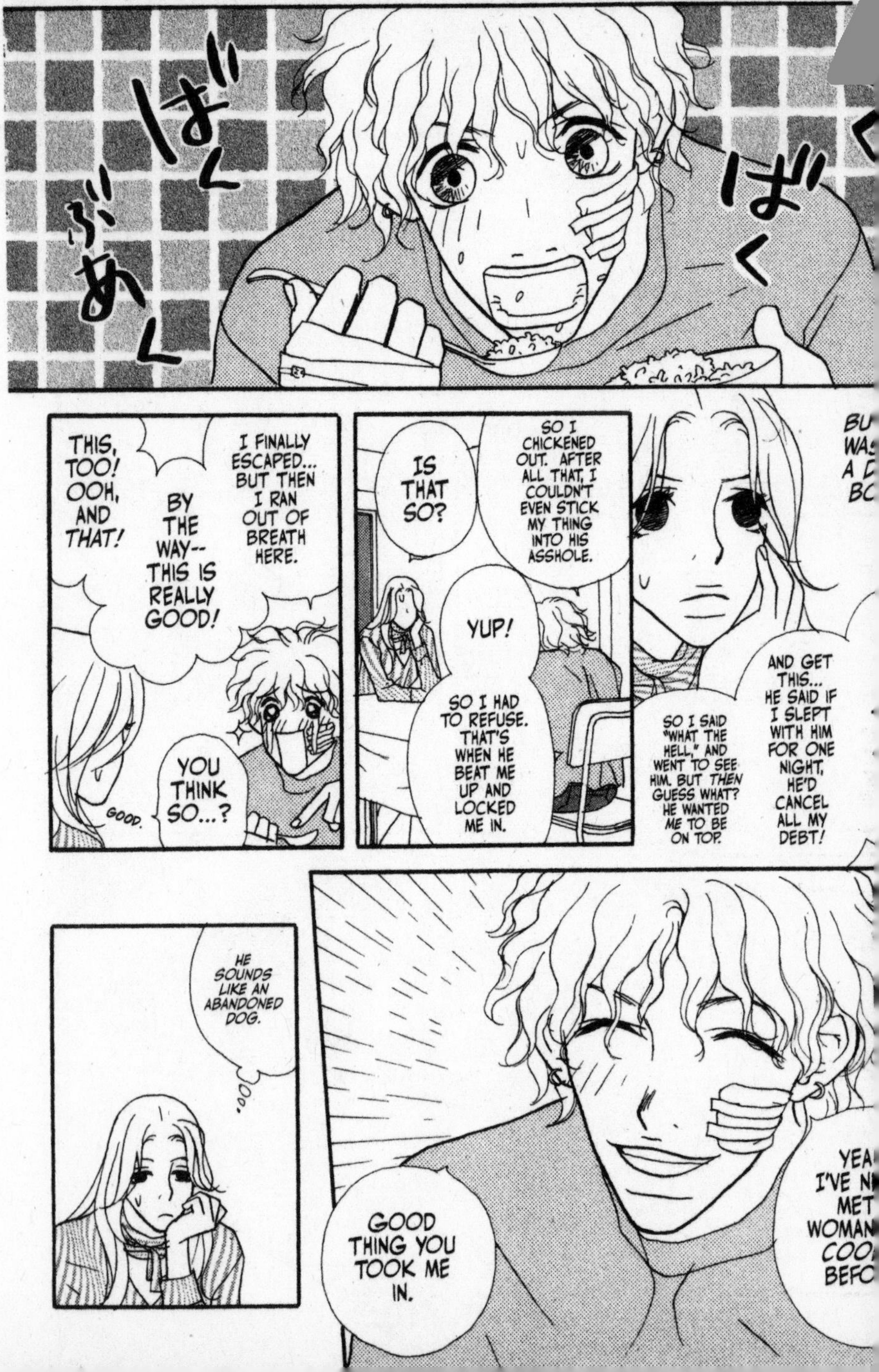
ぱく
ぱく
AND GET THIS... HE SAID IF I SLEPT WITH HIM FOR ONE NIGHT, HE'D CANCEL ALL MY DEBT!
SO I SAID "WHAT THE HELL," AND WENT TO SEE HIM. BUT THEN GUESS WHAT? HE WANTED ME TO BE ON TOP.
SO I CHICKENED OUT. AFTER ALL THAT, I COULDN'T EVEN STICK MY THING INTO HIS ASSHOLE.
IS THAT SO?
YUP!
SO I HAD TO REFUSE. THAT'S WHEN HE BEAT ME UP AND LOCKED ME IN.
I FINALLY ESCAPED... BUT THEN I RAN OUT OF BREATH HERE.
BY THE WAY-- THIS IS REALLY GOOD!
THIS, TOO! OOH, AND THAT!
YOU THINK SO...?
GOOD.
GOOD THING YOU TOOK ME IN.
HE SOUNDS LIKE AN ABANDONED DOG.

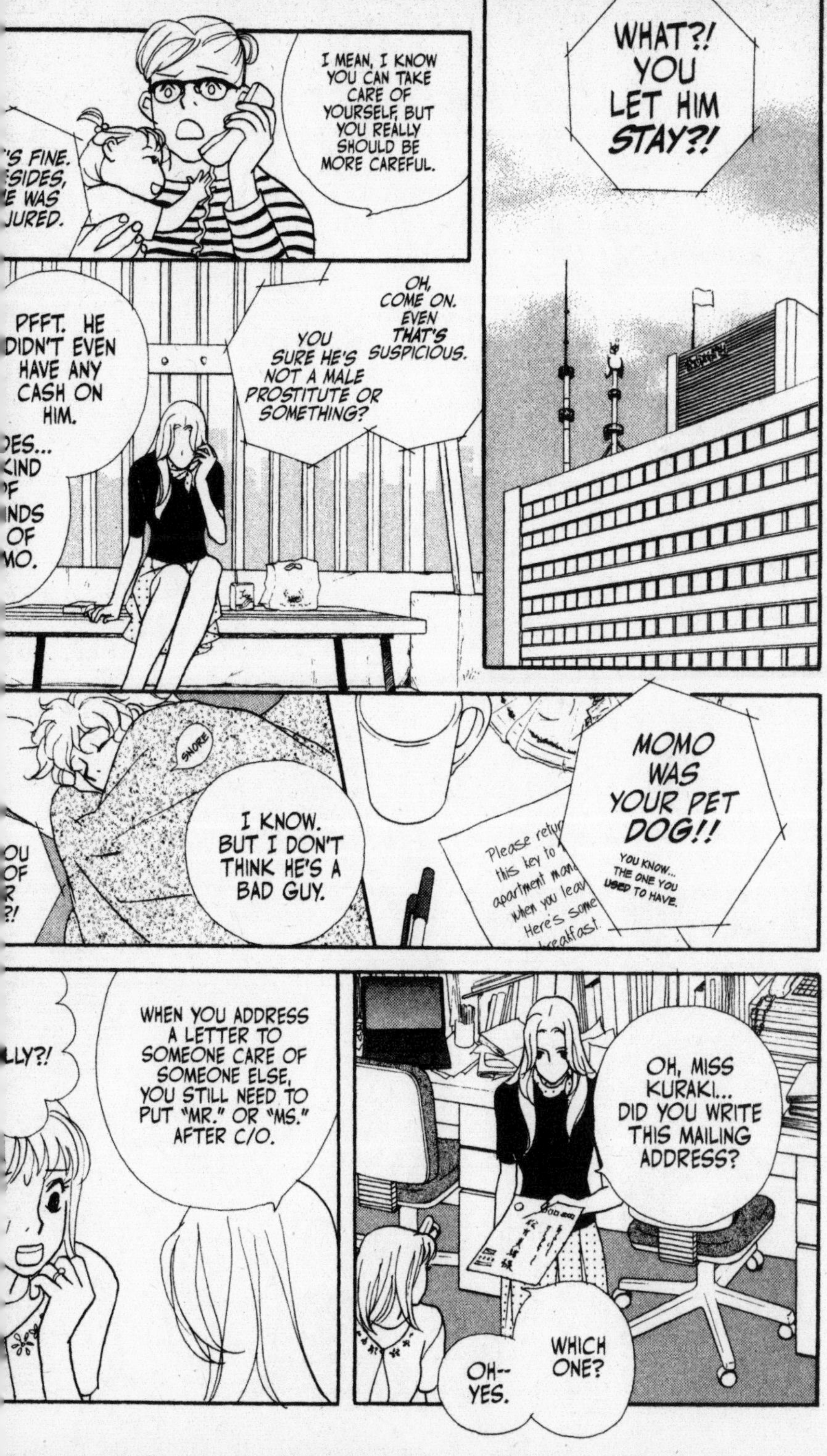
WHAT?! YOU LET HIM STAY?!
I MEAN, I KNOW YOU CAN TAKE CARE OF YOURSELF, BUT YOU REALLY SHOULD BE MORE CAREFUL.
'S FINE. ESIDES, E WAS JURED.
OH, COME ON. EVEN THAT'S SUSPICIOUS.
YOU SURE HE'S NOT A MALE PROSTITUTE OR SOMETHING?
PFFT. HE DIDN'T EVEN HAVE ANY CASH ON HIM.
ES... KIND F NDS OF MO.
MOMO WAS YOUR PET DOG!!
YOU KNOW... THE ONE YOU USED TO HAVE.
Please retu this key to apartment man when you leav Here's some breakfast.
I KNOW. BUT I DON'T THINK HE'S A BAD GUY.
SNORE
OU OF R ?!
OH, MISS KURAKI... DID YOU WRITE THIS MAILING ADDRESS?
WHICH ONE?
OH-- YES.
WHEN YOU ADDRESS A LETTER TO SOMEONE CARE OF SOMEONE ELSE, YOU STILL NEED TO PUT "MR." OR "MS." AFTER C/O.
LLY?!

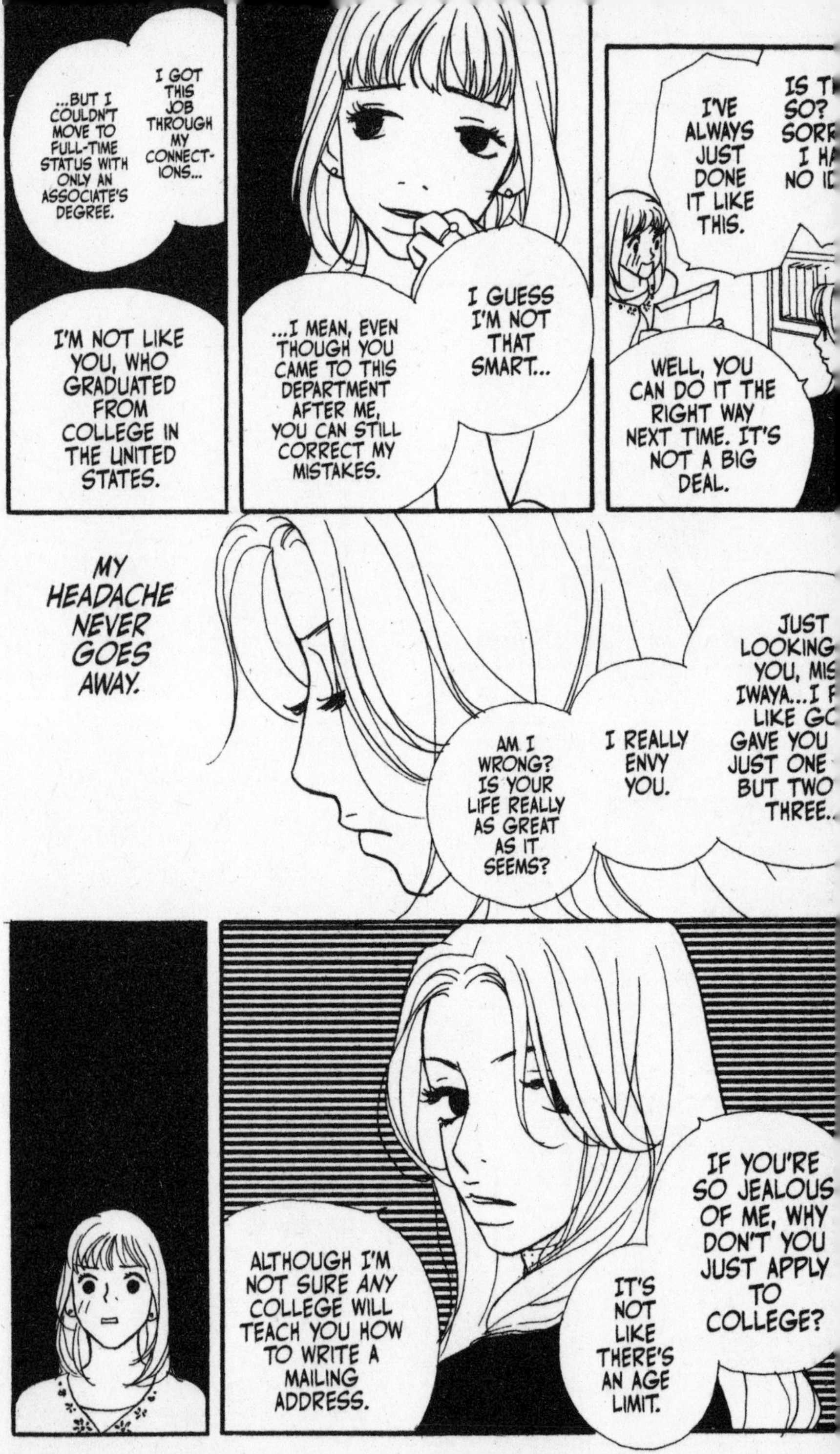
IS T SO? SORR I HA NO ID
I'VE ALWAYS JUST DONE IT LIKE THIS.
WELL, YOU CAN DO IT THE RIGHT WAY NEXT TIME. IT'S NOT A BIG DEAL.
I GUESS I'M NOT THAT SMART...
...I MEAN, EVEN THOUGH YOU CAME TO THIS DEPARTMENT AFTER ME, YOU CAN STILL CORRECT MY MISTAKES.
I GOT THIS JOB THROUGH MY CONNECTIONS...
...BUT I COULDN'T MOVE TO FULL-TIME STATUS WITH ONLY AN ASSOCIATE'S DEGREE.
I'M NOT LIKE YOU, WHO GRADUATED FROM COLLEGE IN THE UNITED STATES.
JUST LOOKING YOU, MIS IWAYA...I F LIKE GO GAVE YOU JUST ONE BUT TWO THREE...
I REALLY ENVY YOU.
AM I WRONG? IS YOUR LIFE REALLY AS GREAT AS IT SEEMS?
MY HEADACHE NEVER GOES AWAY.
IF YOU'RE SO JEALOUS OF ME, WHY DON'T YOU JUST APPLY TO COLLEGE?
IT'S NOT LIKE THERE'S AN AGE LIMIT.
ALTHOUGH I'M NOT SURE ANY COLLEGE WILL TEACH YOU HOW TO WRITE A MAILING ADDRESS.

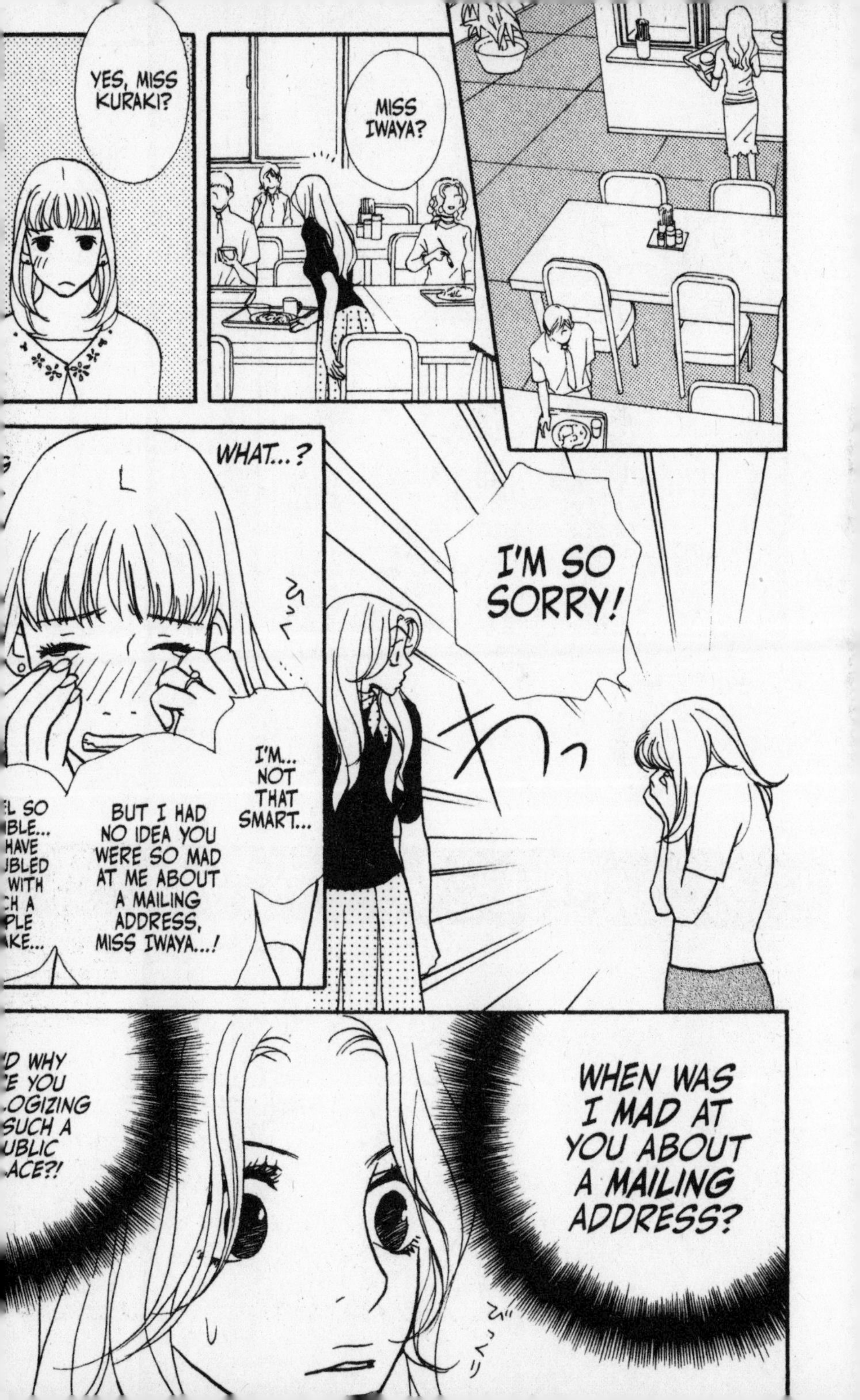
MISS IWAYA?
YES, MISS KURAKI?
I'M SO SORRY!
WHAT...?
I'M... NOT THAT SMART...
BUT I HAD NO IDEA YOU WERE SO MAD AT ME ABOUT A MAILING ADDRESS, MISS IWAYA...!
WHEN WAS I MAD AT YOU ABOUT A MAILING ADDRESS?

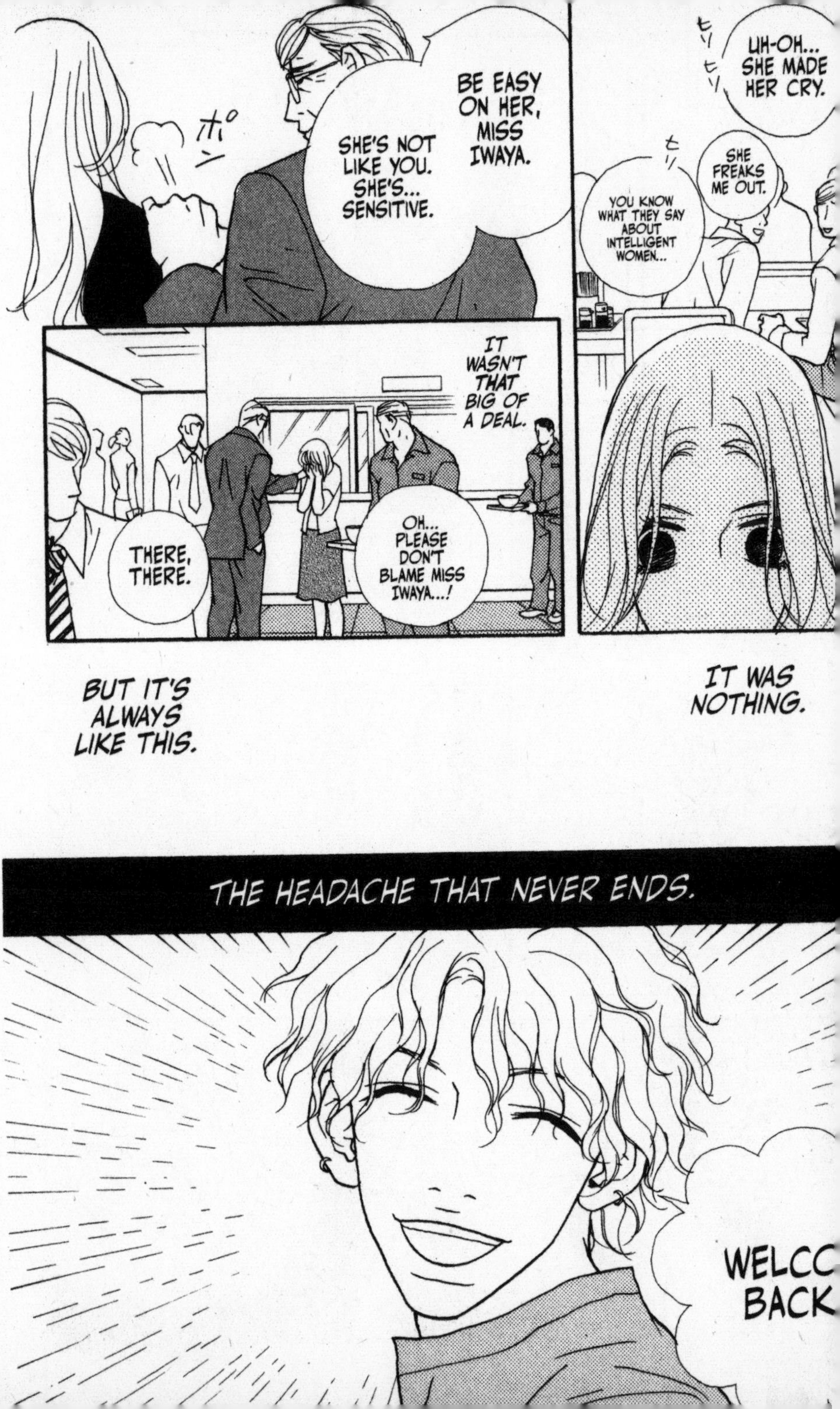
UH-OH... SHE MADE HER CRY.
SHE FREAKS ME OUT.
YOU KNOW WHAT THEY SAY ABOUT INTELLIGENT WOMEN...
BE EASY ON HER, MISS IWAYA.
SHE'S NOT LIKE YOU. SHE'S... SENSITIVE.
IT WASN'T THAT BIG OF A DEAL.
OH... PLEASE DON'T BLAME MISS IWAYA...!
THERE, THERE.
IT WAS NOTHING.
BUT IT'S ALWAYS LIKE THIS.
THE HEADACHE THAT NEVER ENDS.
WELC
BACK

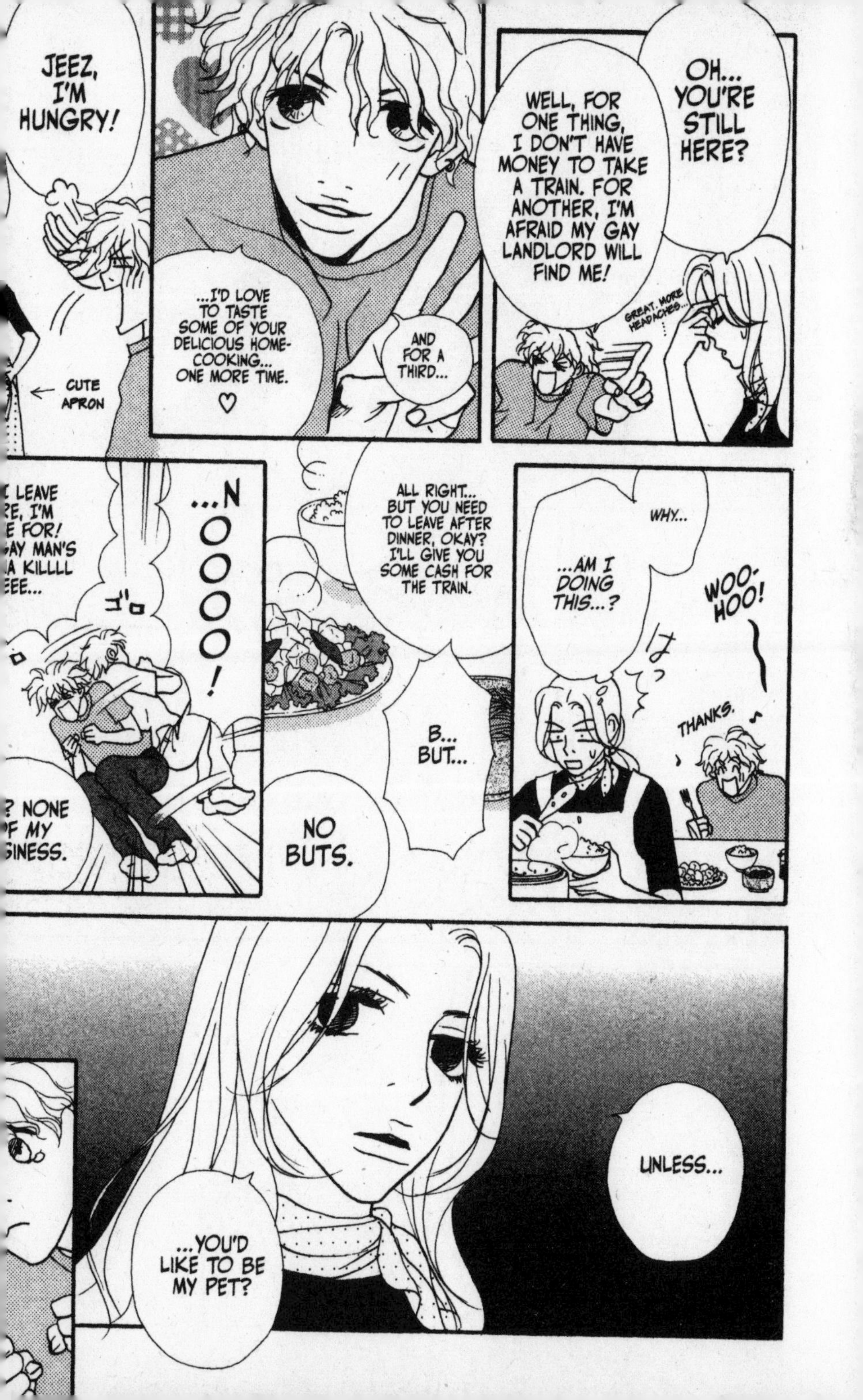
OH... YOU'RE STILL HERE?
WELL, FOR ONE THING, I DON'T HAVE MONEY TO TAKE A TRAIN. FOR ANOTHER, I'M AFRAID MY GAY LANDLORD WILL FIND ME!
GREAT. MORE HEADACHES...
AND FOR A THIRD...
...I'D LOVE TO TASTE SOME OF YOUR DELICIOUS HOME-COOKING... ONE MORE TIME. ♡
JEEZ, I'M HUNGRY!
CUTE APRON
WHY...
...AM I DOING THIS...?
はっ
WOO-HOO!
THANKS.
ALL RIGHT... BUT YOU NEED TO LEAVE AFTER DINNER, OKAY? I'LL GIVE YOU SOME CASH FOR THE TRAIN.
B... BUT...
NO BUTS.
...NOOOOO!
ゴロ
UNLESS...
...YOU'D LIKE TO BE MY PET?

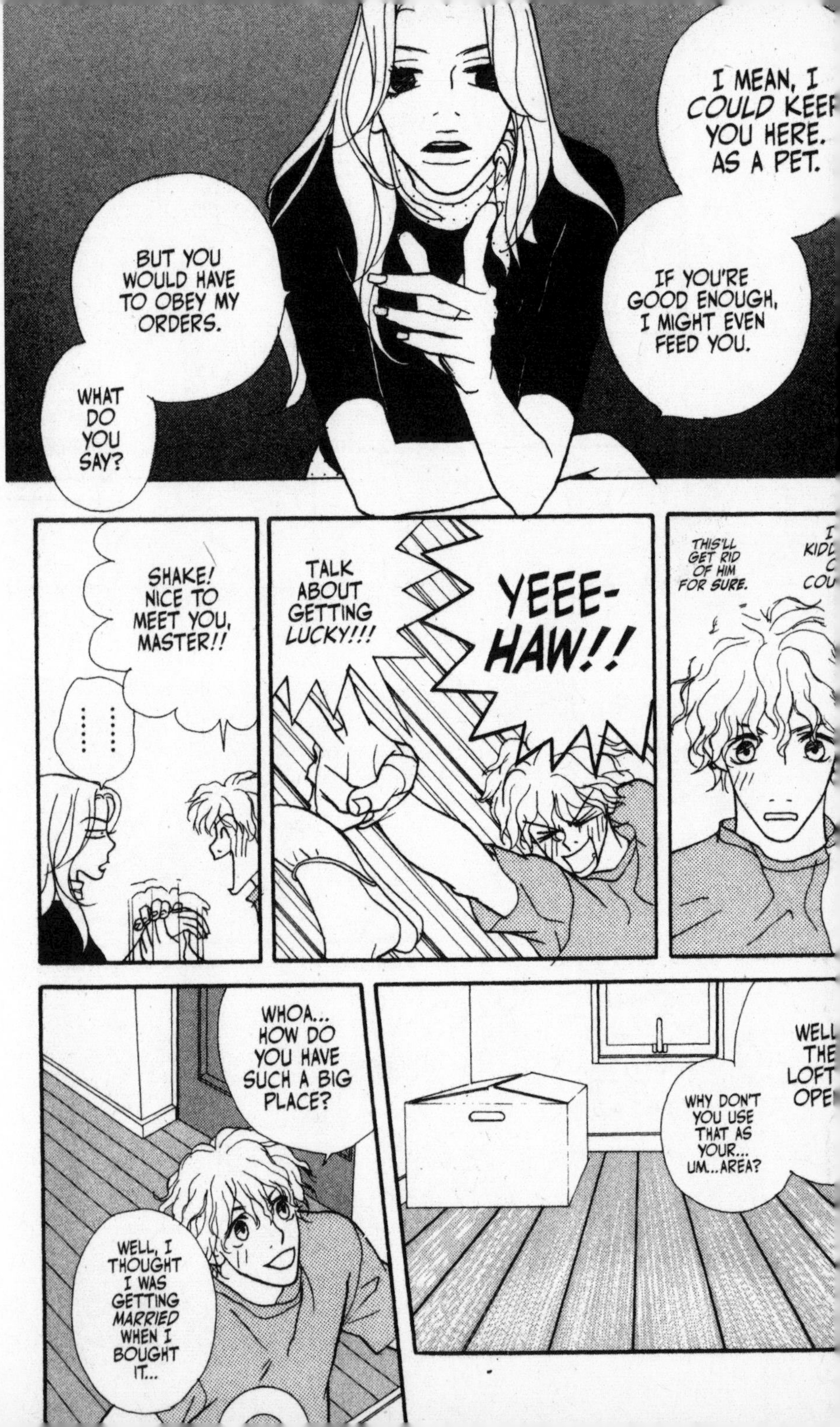
I MEAN, I COULD KEEP YOU HERE. AS A PET.
IF YOU'RE GOOD ENOUGH, I MIGHT EVEN FEED YOU.
BUT YOU WOULD HAVE TO OBEY MY ORDERS.
WHAT DO YOU SAY?
THIS'LL GET RID OF HIM FOR SURE.
YEEE-HAW!!
TALK ABOUT GETTING LUCKY!!!
SHAKE! NICE TO MEET YOU, MASTER!!
......
WELL THE LOFT OPE
WHY DON'T YOU USE THAT AS YOUR... UM...AREA?
WHOA... HOW DO YOU HAVE SUCH A BIG PLACE?
WELL, I THOUGHT I WAS GETTING MARRIED WHEN I BOUGHT IT...

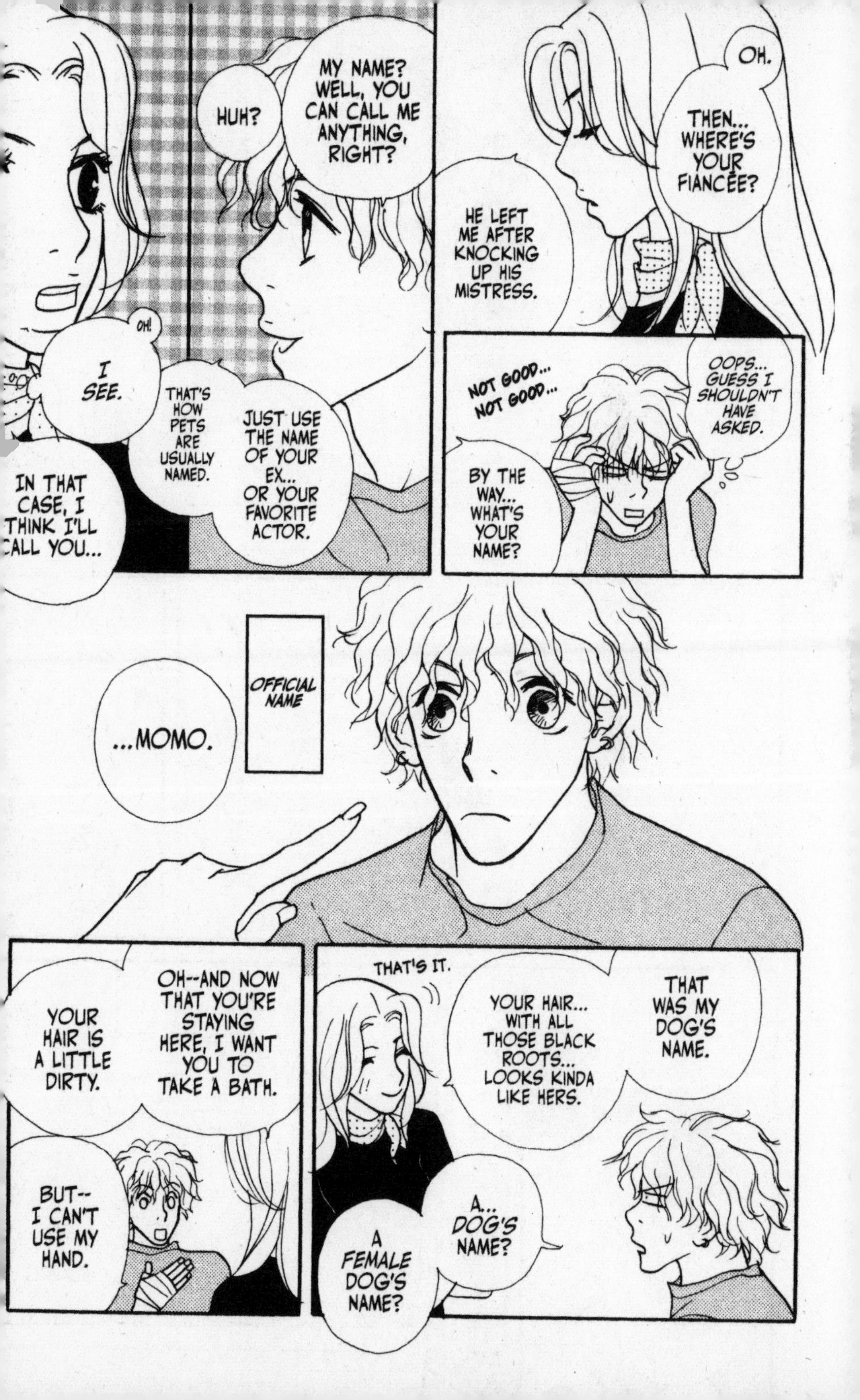
OH.
THEN... WHERE'S YOUR FIANCÉE?
HE LEFT ME AFTER KNOCKING UP HIS MISTRESS.
OOPS... GUESS I SHOULDN'T HAVE ASKED.
NOT GOOD... NOT GOOD...
BY THE WAY... WHAT'S YOUR NAME?
HUH?
MY NAME? WELL, YOU CAN CALL ME ANYTHING, RIGHT?
JUST USE THE NAME OF YOUR EX... OR YOUR FAVORITE ACTOR.
THAT'S HOW PETS ARE USUALLY NAMED.
OH!
I SEE.
IN THAT CASE, I THINK I'LL CALL YOU...
OFFICIAL NAME
...MOMO.
THAT WAS MY DOG'S NAME.
YOUR HAIR... WITH ALL THOSE BLACK ROOTS... LOOKS KINDA LIKE HERS.
THAT'S IT.
A... DOG'S NAME?
A FEMALE DOG'S NAME?
OH--AND NOW THAT YOU'RE STAYING HERE, I WANT YOU TO TAKE A BATH.
YOUR HAIR IS A LITTLE DIRTY.
BUT-- I CAN'T USE MY HAND.

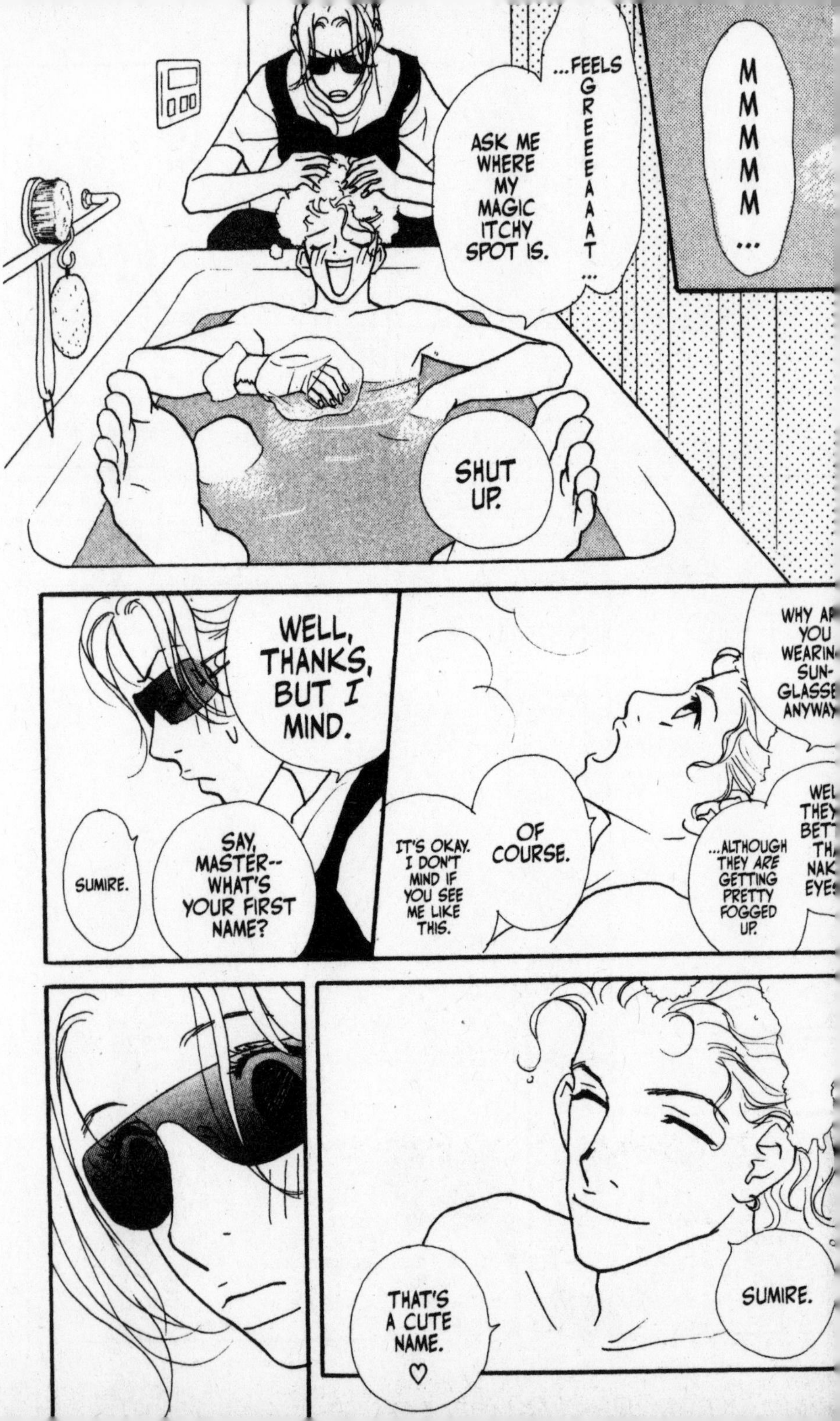
MMMMM...
...FEELS GREEEAAAT...
ASK ME WHERE MY MAGIC ITCHY SPOT IS.
SHUT UP.
WHY AR YOU WEARIN SUN-GLASSE ANYWAY
WEL THEY BET THA NAK EYE
...ALTHOUGH THEY ARE GETTING PRETTY FOGGED UP.
OF COURSE.
IT'S OKAY. I DON'T MIND IF YOU SEE ME LIKE THIS.
WELL, THANKS, BUT I MIND.
SAY, MASTER-- WHAT'S YOUR FIRST NAME?
SUMIRE.
SUMIRE.
THAT'S A CUTE NAME. ♡

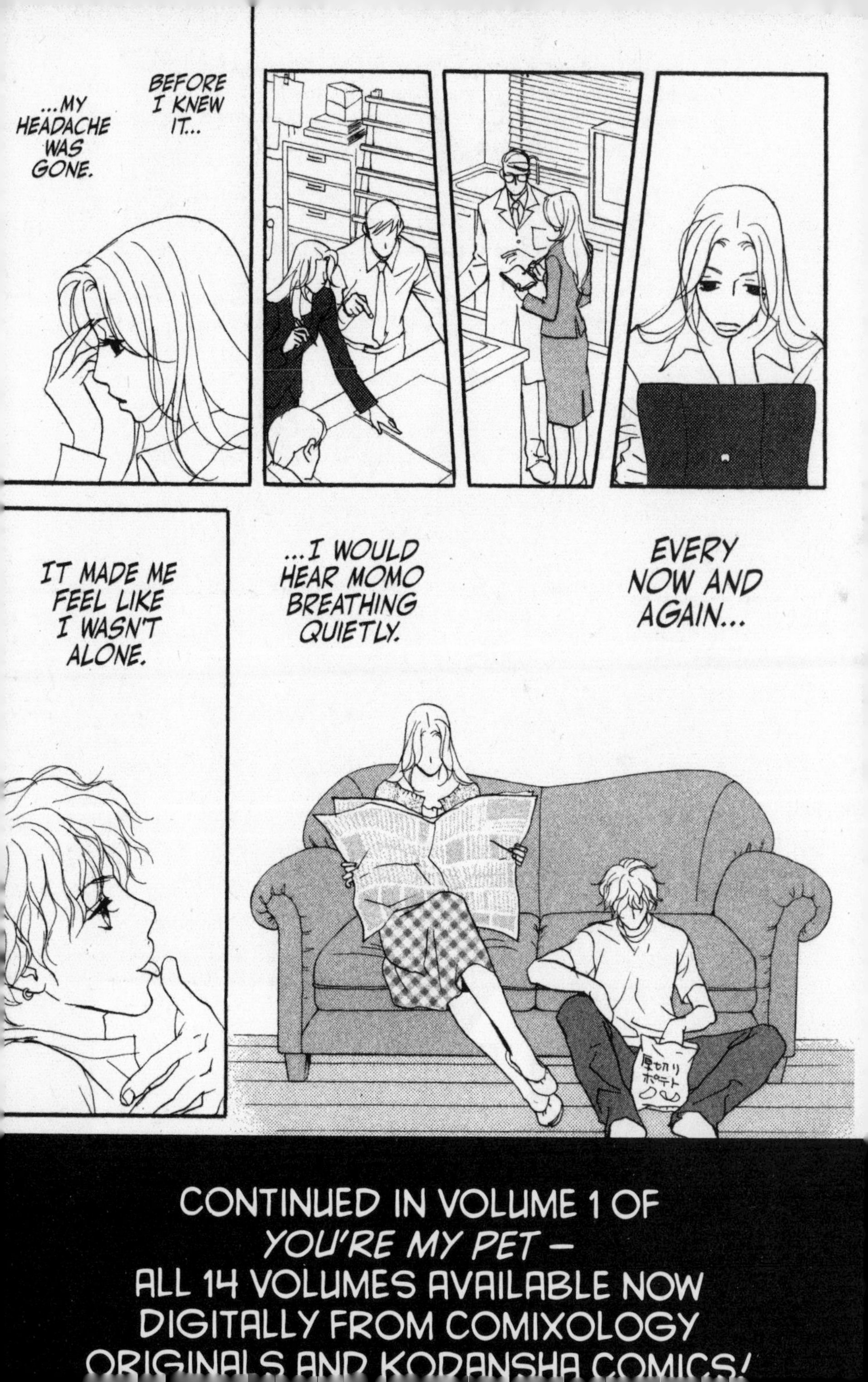
BEFORE I KNEW IT...
...MY HEADACHE WAS GONE.
EVERY NOW AND AGAIN...
...I WOULD HEAR MOMO BREATHING QUIETLY.
厚切り ポテト
IT MADE ME FEEL LIKE I WASN'T ALONE.

CONTINUED IN VOLUME 1 OF
YOU'RE MY PET –
ALL 14 VOLUMES AVAILABLE NOW
DIGITALLY FROM COMIXOLOGY
ORIGINALS AND KODANSHA COMICS!

A Kodansha Comics Trade Paperback Original
Knight of the Ice 1 copyright © 2013 Yayoi Ogawa
English translation copyright © 2020 Yayoi Ogawa

You're My Pet 1 copyright © 2000 Yayoi Ogawa
English translation copyright © 2019 Yayoi Ogawa

Published in the United States by Kodansha Comics, an imprint of Kodansha USA Publishing, LLC, New York.

Publication rights for this English edition arranged through Kodansha Ltd., Tokyo.

First published in Japan in 2013 by Kodansha Ltd., Tokyo as *Ginban Kishi*, volume 1.

ISBN 978-1-63236-810-2

Printed in the United States of America.

www.kodanshacomics.com

9 8 7 6 5 4 3 2 1
Translation: Rose Padgett
Lettering: Jennifer Skarupa
Editing: Tiff Ferentini
Kodansha Comics edition cover design by Phil Balsman

Publisher: Kiichiro Sugawara
Managing editor: Maya Rosewood
Vice president of marketing & publicity: Naho Yamada

Director of publishing services: Ben Applegate
Associate director of operations: Stephen Pakula
Publishing services managing editor: Noelle Webster
Assistant production manager: Emi Lotto